* Volumes with an asterisk following the title are a part of the NCRLL set: Approaches to Language and Literacy Research, edited by
   JoBeth Allen and Donna Alvermann.

(Continued)

Research on Composition

MULTIPLE PERSPECTIVES ON
TWO DECADES OF CHANGE

Edited by Peter Smagorinsky

Teachers College Press, Columbia University
New York and London

Published by Teachers College Press, 1234 Amsterdam Avenue, New York, NY 10027

Library of Congress Cataloging-in-Publication Data

Smagorinsky, Peter.
    Research on composition: multiple perspectives on two decades of change / Peter Smagorinsky.
        p.   cm. — (Language and literacy series)
    Includes bibliographical references and index.
    ISBN 0-8077-4637-1 (cloth : alk. paper)
    1. English language—Rhetoric—Study and teaching.   2. English language—Composition and exercises—Study and teaching.   3. Report writing—Study and teaching.   I. Title.
II. Language and literacy series (New York, N.Y.)

    PE1404.S596 2005
    808'.042'071—dc22

                                                                                    2005051418

ISBN 13: 978-0-8077-4637-0   ISBN 10: 0-8077-4637-1 (cloth)

Printed on acid-free paper
Manufactured in the United States of America

13 12 11 10 09 08 07 06   8 7 6 5 4 3 2 1

Contents

Research on Composition

CHAPTER 1

Overview

Peter Smagorinsky

In 1963 the National Council of Teachers of English (NCTE) published Braddock, Lloyd-Jones, and Schoer's *Research in Written Composition*, a review of writing research that covered writing studies from the early part of the 20th century through 1962. In 1986 the National Conference on Research in English (NCRE) and the Educational Resources Information Center (ERIC) copublished George Hillocks's *Research on Written Composition: New Directions for Teaching*, a volume that reviewed writing research from 1963 to 1983. The 2006 volume follows these two landmark reviews, covering the period between 1984 and 2003.

Taken together, the first two volumes and the current effort reveal the evolution of composition studies as they are situated within developments in the broader theoretical and philosophical environment of the social sciences and humanities. Braddock and colleagues, for instance, framed their analysis with the observation that research in writing "has not frequently been conducted with the knowledge and care that one associates with the physical sciences" (p. 5). They maintained that research on writing needed to be characterized by the qualities that distinguish investigations in the hard sciences: reliability, validity, and replicability. They viewed studies that did not meet these criteria as representing alchemy rather than science, "laced with dreams, prejudices, and makeshift operations" (p. 5).

This analogy of composition as emerging from the Dark Ages and into the age of Enlightenment, noted Lloyd-Jones (1986) in his introduction to Hillocks's review, was primarily the vision of Braddock. The field of composition at that time was struggling for credibility and stature within the academy. As Kinneavy (1971) noted about the persistent problem of composition's low status as a discipline:

> Composition is so clearly the stepchild of the English department that it is not a legitimate area of concern in graduate studies, it is not even recognized as a subdivision of the discipline of English in a recent manifesto put out by the major professional association (MLA) of college English teachers, . . . in some universities is not a valid area of scholarship for advancement in rank, and is generally the teaching province of graduate assistants or fringe members of the department. (p. 1)

One way of raising the standing of composition studies was to adopt a scientific method to guide scholarship, much as the field of literary criticism had done in its move to New Criticism in the 1940s (Marshall, Smagorinsky, & Smith, 1995). Renouncing the current state of composition studies as medieval and setting a more scientific agenda and method, then, was a way for Braddock and colleagues to formalize composition studies as a scholarly field with greater gravitas in the academy. Indeed, *Research in Written Composition* reads as much like a handbook about how to conduct scientific studies as it does as like a review of research findings: The authors' intent is clearly didactic, with a chapter on how to design research, a glossary of research terms, critiques of the flaws of many studies, a section on how to read research critically, and extended reviews of a small set of exemplary reports. The reader is presumed to be unacquainted with the precepts of scientific research methods and in need of that knowledge in order to read such research knowledgeably or produce it competently.

The new emphasis on composition as a scientific discipline suggested the need for scholarly journals in which to publish research on written composition; much of what Braddock and colleagues reviewed consisted of unpublished dissertations and articles in journals not specifically oriented to writing or English studies. Braddock soon became the founding editor of NCTE's *Research in the Teaching of English* (*RTE*), with the first issue appearing in 1967; *RTE* joined the venerable *College Composition and Communication* (*CCC*), launched in 1949, as one of two outlets designed for publishing scholarship on writing. Prior to the availability of *CCC* and particularly *RTE*, research on writing had appeared, along with practical ideas, curriculum theory, teacher education pieces, and much else, in *English Journal*. Braddock's vision of research largely informed what he published in *RTE*. As Lloyd-Jones (1999) wrote in retrospect:

> He intended merely to encourage teaching practices that were in accord with what people actually knew, but he found that the evidence from research was thin indeed. . . . He recognized that some theory was essential—Aristotle and Dewey were his guides—but he did not really recognize theoretical studies or even historical studies as research. *RTE* was narrowly empirical. (p. 41)

Continuing with his hortatory intent, Braddock introduced the first issue of *RTE* with two articles about the conduct of research, Budd's "Research Designs of Potential Value in Investigating Problems in English" and Gunderson's "Flaws in Research Design," saying in a brief preface that

> With its first two articles, *Research in the Teaching of English*, newly arrived itself, is serving readers relatively new to the field. Mr. Budd's contribution provides a context for the reading of research reports by defining "research" and its various categories. In her review of Smith's study of unsuccessful research proposals, Miss Gunderson offers many basic and practical suggestions for the improvement of research projects. (p. 1)

Braddock's educative intentions seem clear and suggest that *RTE*'s original mission was not only to publish exemplary studies but to instruct the next generation of researchers in how to conduct their investigations. Braddock, then, through his definitive contributions to *Research in Written Composition* and *Research in the Teaching of English* and his paternalistic stature, helped to establish composition research as a legitimate field of study. This field was marked by a reliance on scientific methods, with limited attention to how theory shapes method or frames problems, and primary attention to how to improve writing instruction in school.

Research in the Teaching of English was but one of many journals to be established following the publication of *Research in Written Composition*. In addition, the following journals were inaugurated, mostly during the period encompassed by Hillocks's 1963–1983 review: *The Journal of Basic Writing*, 1975; *WPA: Writing Program Administration*, 1977; *The Writing Center Journal*, 1980; *Pre/Text*, 1980; *The Journal of Advanced Composition*, 1980; *Texte*, 1981; *The Writing Instructor*, 1981; *The Journal of Teaching Writing*, 1981; *Rhetoric Review*, 1982; *Rhetorica*, 1983; *Computers and Composition*, 1983; *Written Communication*, 1984; *Reading & Writing Quarterly*, 1984; *Teaching English in the Two-Year College*, 1984; *Journal of Second Language Writing*, 1992; and *Assessing Writing*, 1993. If not everyone accepted Braddock and colleagues' scientific orientation to research, at the very least their review helped to create an imperative for the publication of scholarship in the discipline.

The field's orientation to instruction-oriented quantitative studies of writing persisted through much of the period covered by Hillocks's 1963–1983 review. Shortly before he died, Roy O'Donnell, who edited *RTE* from 1978 to 1982, told me of a letter he'd received from Alan Purves, who succeeded Braddock as *RTE* editor and served from 1973 to 1978. In his letter Purves strongly criticized O'Donnell for publishing a qualitative study in *RTE*. Purves was concerned that qualitative research was not sufficiently rigorous to appear in NCTE's archival research journal. Given Purves's high stature in the field and the likelihood that his view was shared by many, it seems reasonable to assume that a strong quantitative bias persisted through much of the era reviewed by Hillocks.

Toward the end of the 1970s, however, researchers were beginning to look to other disciplines for theories and methods of investigating writing. Janet Emig's (1971) *The Composing Processes of Twelfth Graders* showed the potential of case studies for understanding the process of writing, a new area of inquiry following the field's historical focus on written products and a major emphasis of Braddock and colleagues in setting the agenda for the next generation of writing research. Donald Graves (1979) argued soon thereafter that teachers were rejecting published research because they found it boring. Experimental research, he wrote, "wasn't readable and was of limited value. It couldn't help [teachers] in the classroom. They could not see their schools, classrooms, or children in the data" (1980, p. 914). In the late 1970s and early 1980s, Graves and colleagues began producing accessibly written case studies of elementary school writing that teachers found more engaging than the statistical reports found in scholarly journals. Their work helped open the door to other ways of thinking about how one could conduct and represent research about writing.

Qualitative researchers were, however, still struggling for credibility toward the end of Hillocks's 1983 cutoff date and were accorded lesser significance in his review. Hillocks used a meta-analysis of experimental research as the cornerstone of his claims about the most effective methods of writing instruction, locating his review within the quantitative tradition with which Braddock and colleagues affiliated theirs. As a reflection of the shift that had begun taking place within the field, some reviewers of Hillocks's volume took exception to his quantitative orientation (e.g., Durst, 1987; Newkirk, 1987) and argued for a more ecumenical vision of writing research. The research reviewed in the current volume reflects this more inclusive view of what composition is and how one might investigate and write about it.

RESEARCH ON COMPOSITION, 1984–2003

This volume, while concerned with findings about effective practice and research conducted according to traditions of the hard sciences, embodies the myriad of other interests and approaches that have developed since the publication of Hillocks's volume. Issues of equity, gender, cultural practice, social relationships, tacit hierarchies and power relationships, the social nature of textuality, and other concerns have emerged as a focus of research, both arising from and contributing to perspectives provided by scholars oriented to the various "post" positions—poststructural, postmodern, postcolonial, postfoundational, postrevolutionary, postemancipatory, and so forth—as well as feminism, critical theory, queer theory, multiculturalism, socioculturalism, and other ontologies and epistemologies that have influenced society and education in recent years. These theories have brought new research perspectives, questions, and methods to the study of composition, drawing on traditions from research in anthropology, communication, sociology, psychology, philosophy, and other disciplines that have been adopted since the publication of Hillocks's volume. While researchers still seek to identify effective instructional practices, many are working to contextualize practice to answer new questions, often a variation on the inquiry, Why is this happening here and now?

Indeed, Hillocks's 1983 cutoff date coincidentally marked an epochal change in composition studies. A remarkable number of events took place in and around 1983 that have changed dramatically the conduct of research on composition.

Teacher Research

Some form of action research, practitioner research, or teacher research has informed instructional practice for some time, going back at least to the 1950s. If any form of reflective practice is considered, teacher research has had an impact on instruction since teachers first took to the podium. Yet in 1983, teacher research was not included in Hillocks's review. Indeed, there were few outlets in scholarly journals where teacher research could be published and thus be located through the labor-intensive search instruments—that is trips to the library to track down references recorded on 3 × 5 index cards—available when Hillocks sought the sources for his 1963–1983 review.

Since then, various factors have helped establish teacher research as a serious source of knowledge both for practitioners and for a broader audience. Nancie Atwell's *In the Middle* (1987) was a significant publication, showing that a well-written reflection on one's own practice could describe and document effective pedagogy and become a bestseller. With a robust market established, publishers were more willing to contract work by teachers, who previously had been regarded as consumers rather than producers of knowledge. The publication of Atwell's book, which won NCTE's David H. Russell Award for Distinguished Research in the Teaching of English, helped to establish teacher research as a player in the field of composition studies, as a marketable commodity, and as a worthwhile and manageable pursuit for practicing teachers.

Efforts such as Atwell's were aided by university researchers interested in reflective practice. Cochran-Smith and Lytle's *Inside/Outside: Teacher Research and Knowledge* (1993) outlined a rationale and presented a typology for teacher research and presented a set of practitioner inquires that illustrated their vision. In 1993 Brenda

Power launched the journal *Teacher Research: The Journal of Classroom Inquiry*, whose credibility enabled the development of other practitioner research journals such as *Networks: An Online Journal for Teacher Research*. The expansion of the Internet provided outlets for teachers who wished to share their work through Web sites and other electronic archives. With both book markets and journals established as publication outlets, teacher research achieved a new visibility that gave it a profile within mainstream discussions of research. The American Educational Research Association, for instance, added Special Interest Groups in Action Research and Teacher as Researcher in the mid-1990s. These formal groups within the world's most distinguished educational research organization further contributed to the vitality of teacher research and greater visibility and recognition for its contributions.

The studies presented by Cochran-Smith and Lytle came from the work of the Philadelphia Writing Project and Project S.T.A.R.T., formal organizations that provided a network for teachers interested in reflective practice. Since 1983, such organizations have thrived with metro-area associations such as those in Philadelphia; nationally coordinated efforts such as those supported by the National Writing Project; cross-site organizations such as the M-CLASS researchers (see Freedman, Simons, Kalnin, Casareno, & the M-CLASS Teams, 1999); local, self-sustaining groups such as the Brookline Teacher Researcher Seminar (e.g., 2003) in Massachusetts; and university-based groups such as the Developing Inquiring Communities in Education Project at the Ontario Institute for Studies in Education from which the *Networks* online journal was launched.

More disparately scattered teacher researchers have formed virtual communities through Internet listserves such as XTAR, AELACTION, and others. Through such groups practitioner researchers have access to colleagues and information, such as funding opportunities provided by the Spencer Foundation and the NCTE Research Foundation or program space at conferences such as those sponsored by the NCTE Assembly for Research. These increased opportunities for teachers who conduct research have helped to fortify practitioner inquiry and provide the kind of organized support that can help sustain it and distribute its efforts.

Multimodal Conceptions of Composition

In 1983 Howard Gardner introduced his theory of multiple intelligences in *Frames of Mind*. Gardner criticized Western education's heavy emphasis on linguistic expression, arguing from both a cognitive and cultural perspective that people use seven (later eight) intelligences to negotiate the world. Limiting school learning to a narrow set of these intelligences, he argued, narrowed students' opportunities for thinking. Gardner did not position himself as a composition theorist, instead arguing for a greater role for the arts in education. His ideas, however, ultimately had implications for composition theorists who began to view writing as one tool in a modern literacy tool kit.

Almost simultaneous with Gardner's publication, Jerome Harste, Virginia Woodward, and Carolyn Burke published *Language Stories and Literacy Lessons* (1984) in which they included student drawings among their literacy efforts, and Charles Suhor (1984) proposed a semiotic curriculum that stressed multiple sign systems. The introduction of semiotics into composition studies began to alter scholarly thinking about what it meant to "write." If the children observed by Harste and colleagues and by Graves (1983) and his colleagues alternated between writing and drawing in the same effort to communicate, what distinguished writing as a distinct mode of expression? The field of semiotics, with its attention to sign systems, provided a conceptual vocabulary for conceiving of "composition" as including more than just writing; composing could include any process that produced a set of signs that could be "read": a musical score, a drawing, a performance, a sculpture, and so on.

Concurrent with these developments, cultural psychologists such as Wertsch (1985) were reaching broader audiences with their interpretations of Vygotsky (1978, 1934/1987), Bakhtin (1981), and others who viewed language as, in Lotman's words, "any communication system employing signs that are ordered in a particular manner" (cited in Holquist, 1981, p. 430). This formulation entered composition studies through Witte's (1992) notion of a "constructivist semiotic" of writing that was employed in later studies by Smagorinsky (1995), the New London Group (1996), and others. This new conception enabled researchers to include both traditional arts (dance, drawing) and emerging capabilities (computer graphics) to be considered along with writing as modalities or mediational means for developing and representing meaning.

Family and Community Literacy

Shirley Brice Heath's landmark ethnography of community literacy, *Ways with Words*, was published in 1983. In her study she documented the distinct literacy practices promoted in three neighboring yet culturally different communities in the American southeast. Heath's study was significant for a number of reasons. First of all, she drew on her background in anthropology to conduct a 10-year community ethnography. In doing so she created a new possibility for composition researchers, that of borrowing methods from outside the scientific tradition to investigate writing. Second, she revealed the relation between home and community literacy practices and school success. She found, for instance, that White Christian fundamentalist children became oriented to reading through family and church readings of the *Holy Bible*, a text that in their community presented an absolute truth that was not open to question. These same children, upon entering school, often struggled with reading assignments that required interpretation, questioning, and open-ended thinking. Their literal cultural orientation to the practice of reading made this transition quite difficult and affected their prospects for academic success.

Heath's study helped to awaken educational researchers to the importance of understanding home and community literacy practices in order to anticipate and address educational struggles and to rethink schooling to be more responsive to the range of literacy practices students bring from home. This recognition coincided with field-wide trends that stressed the situated nature of cognition, the local nature of cultural practice, and the ways in which particular cultures establish their norms as authoritative and natural (e.g., Newman, Griffin, & Cole, 1989; Rogoff & Lave, 1984). The 1980s and 1990s also saw the increasing influence of ontologies and epistemologies that deconstruct institutions and the ways in which they foster particular kinds of relationships, especially those that create exploitation, suppression, inequity, and other social hierarchies. Heath's study revealed the ways in which schools normalize the values of the White middle class, making other ways of being literate appear to be less efficacious in school and creating status differentials within the school culture. Studies of community literacy often have picked up on this stream, with increased attention to providing better educational opportunities for socially, economically, racially, and culturally marginalized groups in school.

Family and community literacy studies also have viewed home literacies independent from their impact on schooling. Increasingly, researchers are interested in understanding the ways in which community members engage in situated literacy practice, as a way of understanding broader social structures. To what authentic purposes do people put writing in their lives? How does writing position them socially and politically? How does writing work in conjunction with other "funds of knowledge" (Moll, 2000) to enable people to function in society? How are social relationships, including those that are inequitable, sustained by access to literacy practices? These questions and many others have been investigated as composition researchers have moved the scope of their work outside the school walls and into the lives of people who write as a means of social action.

Writing in the Workplace and Professions

In 1984 John Daly and Stephen P. Witte instituted the journal *Written Communication*. Among their goals was to provide a forum for research that departed from NCTE's emphasis on classroom writing instruction. Daly and Witte, with backgrounds in communication and rhetoric, wished to view writing beyond the bounds of the classroom and edited *Written Communication* with the intention of publishing research on writing regardless of site or pedagogical implications (S. Witte, personal communication). Within a year Odell and Goswami (1985) published an edited collection called *Writing in Nonacademic Settings*. These publications helped to establish the need to investigate the roles, processes, and purposes of writing produced in the course of daily professional activity. Research on writing instruction often had claimed implications for preparing students for "real-world" writing; researchers now were beginning to turn their attention to what that writing might entail.

Studies of workplace and professional writing took on importance because of their fit with the theories that were becoming central to composition researchers. Writing increasingly was seen as a means to authentic communication, which was often difficult to produce in school given the typical teacher-as-examiner relationship of the classroom. Workplace and professional writing offered a setting in which writing needed to be clear and purposeful and thus offered a site in which writing theories could be tested and revised.

Furthermore, the social nature of workplace and professional writing fit well with developing interests in intertextuality, writing genres, socially situated cognition, and other theoretical streams that have flowed through composition studies in the past 20 years. M. M. Bakhtin's *The Dialogic Imagination* was translated into English in 1981, introducing the key constructs of dialogism and heteroglossia to diverse fields of scholarship; Carolyn Miller's "Genre as Social Action" was published in 1984, bringing to the field of composition the Bakhtinian notion that writing genres are socially constructed. Roland Barthes's "Theory of the Text" appeared in 1981, and Julia Kristeva's *Revolution in Poetic Language* was translated in 1984, introducing the construct of intertextuality. During this time, translations of Jacques Derrida's *Of Grammatology* (1974), Vygotsky's *Mind in Society* (1978), and other key texts were gaining a wider audience and beginning to influence composition theory. The field's new thinking was realized in publications such as Martin Nystrand's *The Structure of Written Communication* (1986) in which writing was viewed as a sociocultural process conducted in relationship with socially situated others.

These developments helped to establish the importance of studying how people write at work, where specific genres such as the business memo distill the cultural values of the workplace, require knowledge of discourse, are intended to communicate high-stakes information, and otherwise bring into play extensive social networks of knowledge and relationships that are played out through the production of the memo. Significantly, the knowledge required to write the memo departs radically from the kinds of writing taught and valued in college, further contributing to writing theories that challenge the notion of generic properties of good writing and beliefs about best instructional practice.

In addition, workplace writing has been studied in conjunction with the physical spaces in which it is conducted, such as a journalism school's location of offices and access to resources (e.g., telephones) for graduate students that afford and constrain their ability to produce effective reportage (Chin, 1994). Research on workplace writing also has taken into account the ways in which writing is accompanied often by accoutrements that both suggest additional meaning and constrain what ought to be written for the occasion and purpose; for example, the flowers that might accompany certain kinds of writing in a business environment (Beaufort, 1999). By situating composition studies in the workplace, writing researchers have begun to provide a far more complex understanding of writing in relation to the social and artifactual context in which writing is produced.

Workplace writing also requires particular attention to the technologies that mediate writing. In 1983, personal computers were scarce, electronic mail was primitive, and the World Wide Web was a dozen or so years from widespread accessibility and usage. The exponential proliferation of computer-related technologies has changed dramatically the ways in which people read, write, and transmit texts to others. Increasingly, computer-based text combines written communication with other media: graphics, sound, and other images that the technology allows. The study of workplace writing, then, has further complicated composition studies that were limited to speech-based communication, given the myriad ways in which a text now can be produced and read.

THE CURRENT PROJECT

RESEARCH ON COMPOSITION reflects these significant developments in the field of composition studies. The volume has been substantially expanded beyond the scope of its two predecessors. Given the specialized knowledge required to understand each focus represented here, this volume was conceived as an edited book in which people of diverse expertise were asked to cover specific parts of the field. The categories for these chapters are not neatly bounded; historical studies are produced in the field of rhetoric, developmental studies may overlap stages of schooling, teacher research may be conducted at any level of schooling, and so on. The effort here is not to reify these categorical distinctions but to provide rough boundaries for authors as they cover their fields. In cases where a particular study might reasonably fit into more than one category, chapter authors consulted with one another and decided how to proceed.

In order to ensure a sense of coherence across the chapters, they adhere to the following guidelines:

- With the exception of teacher research, the reviews focus on published research. Previous volumes have included unpublished dissertations and conference presentations. The present volume focuses instead on research that has survived a rigorous review process. The purpose of this limitation is twofold: to help manage the amount of work covered in this expanded volume (Hillocks's bibliography of school-oriented research alone covered 102 pages) and to eliminate from consideration those studies too flawed to be published in a field that has seen a great proliferation of publication opportunities.
- Authors endeavor to include studies from abroad and studies written in languages other than English. Previous volumes have focused on English-language research, primarily conducted in the United States, which narrowed the scope of what kinds of questions could be answered. In the past 20 years, concern for multiculturalism, sociocultural perspectives on teaching and learning, equity for traditionally underrepresented groups, educational access for immigrant groups, and other factors suggest the need for this volume's scope to include international perspectives on literacy.
- In their reviews of composition, authors include not only writing but other mediating tools (e.g., drawing, performance, computers) that are used for composition. The previous two volumes focused solely on writing, with that focus specifically named in the books' titles. The past 20 years have seen broader conceptions of literacy outlined in composition research and they are reflected in this edition.
- Each chapter includes attention to a common set of concerns. Regardless of organizing principle, each author includes the following:

  1. Research published between 1984 and 2003. In order to provide historical perspective, some authors include work from before 1984, particularly in those chapters covering topics that were not included in the Braddock and colleagues. and Hillocks volumes.
  2. A review of the theories that have motivated research in this area, showing trends over time and situating these trends within broader philosophical, political, ontological, epistemological, and theoretical perspectives influencing both scholarship and society at large.
  3. A review of research methods that have been used in this area, looking for links between theoretical frameworks and investigative approaches.
  4. A review of research findings and conclusions.
  5. A review of implications for theory, practice, policy, and so on, argued by researchers and inferred by the chapter author.
  6. A complete bibliography of research covered during this period.

Readers of this volume will find that authors' voices and other characteristics of the discourse community vary greatly from chapter to chapter, suggesting the broadening of floor space for perspectives on composition research over the past 2 decades reflected in the diversity of genres available for scholarly presentations.

ORGANIZATION OF THE BOOK

Marilyn Chapman opens the survey with a review of school-based research conducted in the primary grades. With schools now varying greatly in the grade-level break between elementary and middle school, the coverage in this chapter is determined by what kind of school the research is situated in. Research that identifies the site as pre-K, kindergarten, preschool, elementary school, or primary school is included in this chapter. Typically, these sites have relatively few teachers, each of whom teaches a variety of subjects. While language arts lessons are often the focus of such studies, research may also investigate writing in subject areas (e.g., science) and include attention to other modalities (e.g., relations between drawing and writing).

George Hillocks, Jr., reviews research that takes place at sites identified as middle school, junior high school, secondary school, and high school. In these sites English emerges as a distinct discipline and core subject area, taught by a specialist with specific credentials for teaching the subject. Composing in other domains (e.g., history, science) and through other modalities (e.g., interpreting literature through art) also has been a focus of study at the secondary level and is included in this review.

Russel K. Durst reviews composing in postsecondary educational settings, including any formal site of education beyond high school: 2-year colleges, 4-year colleges and universities, graduate studies at universities, adult continuing education, and distance education. While sharing some concerns of writing at other levels of schooling, writing instruction in these sites analyzes problems that are unique in terms of schooling: transitions to higher education and attendant issues in first-year composition, socialization into disciplinary communities and practices, and so on.

Bob Fecho, JoBeth Allen, Claudia Mazaros, and Hellen Inyega review teacher research, which merits distinct treatment as a separate genre in this volume. One could argue that teacher research should be woven through the other chapters. Doing so, however, likely would confine the research included to studies that resemble those conducted by university researchers, given the affiliations of most journal editorial review board members. Teacher research often is conducted for reasons other than publication, appears in different forms, follows different conventions, answers different questions, and is otherwise different from university-based studies in a number of ways. It therefore deserves treatment as a distinct mode of inquiry in this volume.

Ilona Leki, Alister Cumming, and Tony Silva review research in second-language composition teaching and learning. Greater concern for educating people from diverse backgrounds has prompted an increased emphasis on issues of bilingualism and ESL instruction, and the position of the United States in global politics and commerce has necessitated research in foreign language and EFL studies. These issues are critical to understanding research in composition in the past 20 years, with potentially great implications for the allocation of funds in urban schools and other policy questions. Because second-language writing research often attends to different issues than does first-language writing research, it is accorded separate treatment in this volume.

Victor Villanueva, Jan Swearingen, and Susan McDowall review research in rhetoric. The two previous volumes focused on empirical research from a social science perspective. Yet much research is conducted in the humanities under the aegis of rhetoric. Rhetoric defines the rules that should govern prose composition or speech designed to influence the judgment or the feelings of people and is therefore concerned with invention, arrangement, style, memory, and delivery. Current rhetoricians often focus on the ways in which the study of rhetoric can reveal power relationships and how they are established and perpetuated through language. Rhetoricians, unlike empirical researchers in the social science tradition, typically study texts rather than people. Because text analysis emerges from different traditions and employs different methods, even while sharing some concerns, rhetoric merits distinct treatment in this volume.

Home and community composition is reviewed by Ellen Cushman, Stuart Barbier, Catherine Mazak, and Robert Petrone. Their review takes into account nonacademic composing that takes place outside the workplace, covering compositions undertaken to suit the personal, pragmatic, social, and political needs of citizens in the course of their daily pursuits.

Anne Beaufort reviews research on composing in the workplace and professions. These studies include attention to both the mundane writing (e.g., memos, e-mail) that sustains the functioning of the workplace and the longer, more formal writing that is more summative in effect: legal briefs, literary criticism, scientific reports, and so on.

David R. Russell reviews historical research in composition. Studies have been produced that have historicized the past in new ways and identified new topics for historical study. These studies have been important in a number of ways, at times taking new perspectives on old topics, at others presenting for the first time previously unrecognized literacy practices. Historical studies inevitably reveal how both writing and conceptions of writing have changed over time, particularly as situated within broader changes in values, economics, politics, and other factors.

CHANGING ORTHODOXIES

Taken together, these chapters provide an unprecedented depth and scope to reviewing the field of composition studies. The previous two reviews have proven to be milestone publications in composition studies. If Braddock and colleagues' review helped to move composition studies from medieval origins to a state of rational inquiry, then Hillocks's review could be said to cover the maturity of composition's age of reason. Yet during this period the authority of science as a way of knowing was called into question. This skepticism had origins in the early part of the 20th century, with Einstein's theory of relativity and Heisenberg's uncertainty principle introducing hedges into the belief in science's ability to reveal the true nature of the world, and Dewey (1929) questioning the humanities' quest for certainty. One might argue that this stream of thought dates at least to the age of Heraclitus, who 2,500 years ago advised his student, "You cannot step into the same river twice," to which his student replied, "Not even once, since there is no *same* river."

In the 1960s and 1970s, along with the general tendency to question established societal structures, academia was changed by the work of Berger and Luckman (1966), Derrida (1967/1974), Foucault (1961/1965), Latour and Woolgar (1979), and others who questioned the premises of objectivity involved in scientific thinking, deconstructed the social order to reveal its inequities, posited the indeterminacy of meaning, and argued for the inherent subjectivity of perspective. At roughly the same time, translations of Vygotsky (1962) and the publication of such works as Geertz's *The Interpretation of Cultures* (1973) and Hymes's *Foundations in Sociolinguistics: An Ethnographic Approach* (1974) helped turn composition theorists' and researchers' attention to the social and cultural bases of literacy.

These ideas began to infiltrate composition studies in the 1980s and became well established during the 20-year period covered by the current review. Indeed, one might argue that the scientific orthodoxy of composition research prior to the 1980s was joined, if not displaced, by a cultural and poststructural orthodoxy lasting through the beginning of the 21st century. Although the two often have coexisted contentiously, the field has benefited from the dynamic tension and the more creative environment that has ensued. While some (e.g., Stotsky, 1999) have argued that the inclusion of new perspectives has caused a decline in literacy research, others feel that the field has never been more robust, inclusive, or vibrant.

The emergence of the Enlightenment contributed to changes in the structure of European thought itself: systematic doubt, empirical and sensory verification, the abstraction of human knowledge into separate sciences, and the view that the world functions like a machine. One might say that the period from 1984 to 2003 similarly brought about changes in the structure of thinking about composition research. Guided by the general premise of the decentering of the subject and the idea that meaning cannot be fixed in language, many researchers have moved from the search for universals (e.g., best practices for teaching regardless of setting and participants) and generated new questions about the situated nature of teaching and learning as they are enacted amid competing political agendas, constructed subjectivities, social goals and structures, discourses, and value systems. At the same time, the enduring promise of Enlightenment rationalism has maintained the value of empiricism in its quest for revealing truths about social practices. The authors of the chapters in this book work in the thick of the productive tensions provided by these competing schools of thought to provide great insight into what composition research has explored during this 20-year period.

REFERENCES

Atwell, N. (1987). *In the middle: Writing, reading, and learning with adolescents.* Portsmouth, NH: Heinemann.

Bakhtin, M. M. (1981). *The dialogic imagination: Four essays by M. M. Bakhtin* (M. Holquist, Ed.; C. Emerson & M. Holquist, Trans.). Austin: University of Texas Press.

Barthes, R. (1981). Theory of the text. In R. Young (Ed.), *Untying the text* (pp. 31–47). Boston: Routledge & Kegan Paul.

Beaufort, A. (1999). *Writing in the real world: Making the transition from school to work.* New York: Teachers College Press.

Berger, P. L., & Luckman, T. (1966). *The social construction of reality.* New York: Doubleday.

Braddock, R., Lloyd-Jones, R., & Schoer, L. (1963).

Research in written composition. Champaign, IL: National Council of Teachers of English.

Brookline Teacher Researcher Seminar. (2003). *Regarding children's words: Teacher research on language and literacy*. New York: Teachers College Press.

Chin, E. (1994). Redefining "context" in research on writing. *Written Communication, 11*, 445–482.

Cochran-Smith, M., & Lytle, S. L. (1993). *Inside/outside: Teacher research and knowledge*. New York: Teachers College Press.

Derrida, J. (1974). *Of grammatology* (G. C. Spivak, Trans.). Baltimore: Johns Hopkins University Press. (Original work published 1967)

Dewey, J. (1929). *The quest for certainty*. New York: Minton Balch.

Durst, R. K. (1987). [Review of the book, *Research on written composition: New directions for teaching*]. *Quarterly of the National Writing Project, 8*(3), 23–25.

Emig, J. A. (1971). *The composing processes of twelfth graders*. Urbana, IL: National Council of Teachers of English.

Foucault, M. (1965). *Madness and civilization: A history of insanity in the age of reason* (R. Howard, Trans.). New York: Vintage Books. (Original work published 1961)

Freedman, S. W., Simons, E. R., Kalnin, J. S., Casareno, A., & the M-CLASS Teams. (1999). *Inside city schools: Investigating literacy in multicultural classrooms*. New York: Teachers College Press.

Gardner, H. (1983). *Frames of mind: The theory of multiple intelligences*. New York: Basic Books.

Geertz, C. (1973). *The interpretation of cultures*. New York: Basic Books.

Graves, D. H. (1979). Research doesn't have to be boring. *Language Arts, 56*, 76–80.

Graves, D. H. (1980). A new look at writing research. *Language Arts, 57*, 913–919.

Graves, D. H. (1983). *Writing: Teachers and children at work*. Portsmouth, NH: Heinemann.

Harste, J. C., Woodward, V. A., & Burke, C. L. (1984). *Language stories and literacy lessons*. Portsmouth, NH: Heinemann.

Heath, S. B. (1983). *Ways with words: Language, life, and work in communities and classrooms*. New York: Cambridge University Press.

Hillocks, G., Jr. (1986). *Research on written composition: New directions for teaching*. Urbana, IL: National Conference on Research in English/ERIC Clearinghouse on Reading and Communication Skills.

Holquist, M. (1981). Glossary. In M. Holquist (Ed.), *The dialogic imagination: Four essays by M. M. Bakhtin* (pp. 423–434). Austin: University of Texas Press.

Hymes, D. (1974). *Foundations in sociolinguistics: An ethnographic approach*. Philadelphia: University of Pennsylvania Press.

Kinneavy, J. L. (1971). *A theory of discourse*. Englewood Cliffs, NJ: Prentice-Hall.

Kristeva, J. (1984). *Revolution in poetic language* (M. Waller, Trans.). New York: Columbia University Press.

Latour, B., & Woolgar S. (1979). *Laboratory life: The social construction of scientific facts*. Thousand Oaks, CA: Sage.

Lloyd-Jones, R. (1986). Introduction. In G. Hillocks, *Research on written composition: New directions for teaching* (pp. xiii–xiv). Urbana, IL: Natural Conference on Research in English/ERIC Clearinghouse on Reading and Communication Skills.

Lloyd-Jones, R. (1999). Afterword to R. Braddock, The frequency and placement of topic sentences in expository prose. In L. Ede (Ed.), *On writing research: The Braddock essays 1975–1998* (pp. 41–42). Boston: Bedford/St. Martin's.

Marshall, J. D., Smagorinsky, P., & Smith, M. W. (1995). *The language of interpretation: Patterns of discourse in discussions of literature* (NCTE Research Report No. 27). Urbana, IL: National Council of Teachers of English.

Miller, C. R. (1984). Genre as social action. *Quarterly Journal of Speech, 70*, 151–167.

Moll, L. (2000). Inspired by Vygotsky: Ethnographic experiments in education. In C. D. Lee & P. Smagorinsky (Eds.), *Vygotskian perspectives on literacy research* (pp. 256–268). New York: Cambridge University Press.

The New London Group. (1996). A pedagogy of multiliteracies: Designing social futures. *Harvard Educational Review, 66*(1), 60–92.

Newkirk, T. (1987). [Review of the book *Research on written composition: New directions for teaching*.] *Teachers College Record, 81*, 155–157.

Newman, D., Griffin, P., & Cole, M. (1989). *The construction zone: Working for cognitive change in school*. New York: Cambridge University Press.

Nystrand, M. (1986). *The structure of written communication: Studies in reciprocity between writers and readers*. Orlando, FL: Academic Press.

Odell, L., & Goswami, D. (Eds.). (1985). *Writing in nonacademic settings*. New York: Guilford.

Rogoff, B., & Lave, J. (Eds.). (1984). *Everyday cognition: Its development in social context*. Cambridge, MA: Harvard University Press.

Smagorinsky, P. (1995). Constructing meaning in the disciplines: Reconceptualizing writing across the curriculum as composing across the curriculum. *American Journal of Education, 103,* 160–184.

Stotsky, S. (1999). *Losing our language: How multicultural classroom instruction is undermining our children's ability to read, write, and reason.* New York: The Free Press.

Suhor, C. (1984). Towards a semiotics-based curriculum. *Journal of Curriculum Studies, 16,* 247–257.

Vygotsky, L. S. (1962). *Thought and language.* Cambridge, MA: MIT Press.

Vygotsky, L. S. (1978). *Mind in society.* Cambridge, MA: Harvard University Press.

Vygotsky, L. S. (1987). Thinking and speech. In L. S. Vygotsky, *Collected works* (vol. 1, pp. 39–285) (R. Rieber & A. Carton, Eds; N. Minick, Trans.). New York: Plenum. (Original work published 1934)

Wertsch, J. V. (1985). *Vygotsky and the social formation of mind.* Cambridge, MA: Harvard University Press.

Witte, S. (1992). Context, text, intertext: Toward a constructivist semiotic of writing. *Written Communication, 9,* 237–308.

CHAPTER 2

Preschool Through Elementary Writing

Marilyn Chapman

ALTHOUGH ELEMENTARY schools typically end at sixth grade, some schools now vary greatly in the grade-level break between elementary and middle school. The determination of what to cover in this chapter is based primarily on the type of school being studied. Typically, elementary schools have relatively few teachers, each of whom teaches a variety of subjects. While the primary focus is on research from 1983 to 2003, select works prior to 1983 are discussed here, particularly in topics, such as emergent writing, that were not included in Braddock, Lloyd-Jones, and Schoer (1963) and Hillocks (1986). The definition of "composition" has expanded over the past decade; consequently, while focusing primarily on writing, this chapter also attends to other modalities (e.g., relations between drawing and writing) and includes not only writing but also other mediating tools (e.g., drawing, talking, computers) that are used in or for composition.

An overview of key theoretical ideas that have motivated the research in children's written composition opens the chapter. This overview situates theoretical issues within broader philosophical, political, and ontological perspectives influencing both scholarship and society at large. A key example is the "social turn" (Gee, 1999) that has occurred during the past decade, a movement away from a primarily cognitive or psychological orientation to a social perspective. Next is a review of the methods used in researching children's writing and the links between theoretical frameworks and investigative approaches employed. Research findings and conclusions are grouped into four major areas: (1) the emergence of writing, (2) cognitive and sociocognitive dimensions of children's composing, (3) social and cultural dimensions of children's writing, and (4) research on the teaching of writing. These four major areas of research are interrelated rather than separate. For example, an abundance of evidence highlights the interaction between cognitive and social aspects of children's composing processes. Similarly, because children and teachers share the social spaces we call classrooms, social and cultural dimensions of children's writing are intrinsically linked with contexts, tasks, and teachers' actions.

CHANGES IN THEORETICAL PERSPECTIVES
AND FRAMEWORKS SINCE THE 1986 EDITION

Four interrelated theoretical perspectives inform writing research in the preschool through elementary years since Hillocks (1986): constructivism, emergent literacy, the "social turn" (Gee, 1999), and "multiliteracies."

Constructivism

Constructivism focuses on the processes of knowing, based on the assumption that learning is a process of constructing knowledge. Children come to school with a range of prior knowledge, concepts, skills, attitudes, and beliefs that influence how they interpret and organize information, which in turn affects their abilities to reason, acquire new knowledge, and solve problems. Some studies of children's writing focus on individual writers and psychological aspects of writing, influenced to a great extent by the work of Piaget (1985). These studies argue that children construct meaning by integrating new information with what they already know (assimilation) or, when there is a dissonance between existing and new information, by changing the structure of their conceptions (schemata) through a process of accommodation. This cognitive constructivist perspective views language as secondary to, and a reflection of, thought. Following Piagetian notions of stages of development, researchers look for common developmental processes, stages, or patterns in children's writing. Piaget held the view that development preceded learning, and thus an important task for teachers of writing would be to determine a child's developmental stage in writing and teach accordingly.

In the mid-1980s a significant shift occurred as researchers of young children's writing began to heed the work of Vygotsky (1934/1962, 1978), who argued that once language begins (at about the age of 2), language and thought are inextricably related. (Cole [1996] has revised Vygotsky's view, arguing that this relation begins with the child's first human contact.) An essential difference from Piaget's theory is that learning precedes development as more knowledgeable others mediate children's learning through social interaction in *the zone of proximal development*, which Vygotsky (1978) describes as "the distance between the actual developmental level as determined by independent problem solving, and the level of potential development as determined through problem solving under adult guidance or in collaboration with more capable peers" (p. 86). From a *social constructivist*, Vygotskian perspective, child writers are seen as literacy apprentices who appropriate the functions and forms of written language from their social worlds and who use literacy artifacts (e.g., the alphabet, books, pencils, computers) and more capable literacy users as resources for learning to write. Children internalize what they experience through external activity in an active process of transformation: "Every function in the child's cultural development appears twice: first, on the social level, and later, on the individual level; first, *between* people (*interpsychological*) and then *inside* the child (*intrapsychological*)" (p. 57; emphasis in original).

For the most part, cognitive and social constructivist perspectives are now seen as complementary rather than competing explanations, contributing insights into different dimensions of writing development. A *sociocognitive constructivist perspective* is based on the premise that writing is both a personal and social activity. While writing is determined to a great extent by the experiences and intentions of the individual writer, rather than being a biological, adaptive reaction to the environment, writing is better thought of as a purposeful and culturally meaningful activity that varies according to context. Furthermore, as children engage in cognitive processes in composing meaning, such as problem solving and self-regulation, they draw on declarative, procedural, and genre knowledge learned in social contexts.

An Emergent Literacy Perspective

The youngest age discussed by Hillocks (1986) was first grade, regarded at that time as "the beginning" of writing. During the early 1980s a significant change occurred, as researchers began to rethink young children's preconventional literacy development: The beginnings of writing came to be seen as rooted in the early childhood years. This shift became known as an *emergent literacy perspective* (Teale & Sulzby, 1986). This new term signaled a theoretical shift from the "reading readiness" paradigm, which was based on the view that young children needed to be taught "readiness skills" as prerequisites to reading and that children must first learn to read conventionally before writing is introduced. In contrast, an emergent literacy perspective holds that children are constructors of meaning, that literacy development takes place in social settings as children interact with adults and peers, and that literacy develops most fully in contexts that promote meaning and purpose in writing and reading (Teale & Sulzby, 1986).

The construct of emergent literacy arose out of studies of children's writing in the 1970s, especially the work of Clay (1975) and Read (1975), that revealed the intentionality in children's earliest writing attempts and the thinking behind their unconventional scribbles. A substantial number of studies in the 1980s examined cognitive aspects of very young children's writing processes, especially the emergence of conventional written form. As the theoretical perspective of emergent literacy evolved, it increasingly has taken the social dimension into account, such as the influences of children's interactions with their social worlds. Vygotsky's (1978) theories about the role of symbolic play in development and "the prehistory of written language" (p. 113)—that writing develops out of gesturing and drawing—are particularly relevant to an emergent literacy perspective on research in young children's writing.

The Social Turn

While a cognitive view of writing dominated research up to and including the 1980s, the past 2 decades have seen a greater impact of the social, with an increasing interest in sociocognitive, sociolinguistic, sociocultural, and sociopolitical perspectives on literacy. Several traditions of research have contributed to and shaped the social turn that began in the mid-1980s. Of particular impact on the study of writing are Vygotskian activity theory (e.g., Russell, 1997; Wertsch, 1985), ethnographies of communication (e.g., Heath, 1983; Taylor, 1983), Bakhtin's (e.g., 1979/1986) dialogism, and the New Literacy Studies (e.g., Gee, 1996; New London Group, 1996).

Vygotskian activity theory. Vygotsky (1978) argued that language, writing, mathematics, and other sign systems significantly influence how people think and interact.

He believed that sign systems, which vary according to culture, are psychological tools that mediate thought. Vygotsky felt that writing was especially important for its effects on thinking and that the effects of writing vary depending on the nature of the symbol systems in different cultures and the uses of writing in particular social contexts. Activity theory, arising from Vygotsky's work, primarily through Leont'ev (1981), positions the mind in society rather than in isolation. Activities are not ends in themselves but serve larger purposes. Scribner and Cole (1981) documented how different writing systems and particular writing and reading activities lead to specific ways of thinking. The concept of *literacy practices* (introduced by Scribner and Cole), which emphasizes social context and the interrelations among skills, knowledge, and technologies, is also central to the notion of "multiliteracies," discussed later in this chapter.

Ethnographies of communication. Ethnographies of communication reflect the insights from anthropological and linguistic methods to the study of literacy. A key finding from this research, in particular Heath's (1983) ethnography of life in three communities in the Piedmont Carolinas, is that children from diverse backgrounds are socialized differently into ways of using oral and written language. This socialization leads to differential preparation for school literacy, which in turn results in greater success in school for some children than for others. Ethnographies of writing explore the ways in which children's social worlds within and out of school foster, enable, and constrain their writing (Dyson, 1989, 1993, 1997; MacGillivray, 1994; Rowe, 1994) and how children use writing as one of many symbolic systems to participate in communities of practice, negotiate their social worlds, construct identity, and deal with social relationships and issues of power (Dyson, 1997).

Bakhtin's dialogism. Bakhtin argued that all language is *dialogic* because understandings of words and how to use them are shaped by and developed through interactions with others. Even when people write to and for themselves, they use words in ways that they have learned from their communities and cultures. Key ideas central to Bakhtin's dialogism are *addressivity* (meaning that all utterances are directed to someone, either specific or indefinite), *text* (referring in the broadest sense to any coherent complex of signs), *intertextuality* (indicating the ways in which all texts reflect other texts and anticipate responses from future texts), *voice* (suggesting multiple, internalized perspectives that are polyphonic and ideological), *heteroglossia* (representing a plurality of voices reflected in the language/s of a culture), and *ventriloquation* (reflecting appropriation from one's culture).

An important contribution of Bakhtin's work is his discussion of *genres*, structures that are embedded in and develop out of the various spheres of human activity. Genres are flexible models, not merely generic forms that writers slot ideas into. "Each sphere of activity contains an entire repertoire of . . . [oral and written] genres that differentiate and grow as the particular sphere develops and becomes more complex" (Bakhtin, 1979/1986, p. 60). Genres provide a set of signals that enable a speaker/writer and listener/reader to interpret the particulars of a specific communicative interaction. Yet genres are sufficiently open-ended to allow for individual choice, creativity, and voice—writers make choices about what they write about and how they write it, and they express the uniqueness of their own personalities in their writing—so writing is very much an individual creative process as well as a social one.

Bakhtin's perspective helps to reveal genres as typified social actions rather than text types. Formal features are not ends in themselves, but are derived from and related to "the writer's social motive in responding to a recurrent social situation of a certain type" (Freedman & Medway, 1994, p. 3).

New Literacy Studies. New Literacy Studies (NLS), building on sociolinguistic and anthropological theories, investigate literacy in out-of-school contexts, such as local literacies, with a focus on distribution of and access to social power. Barton (1991), for example, demonstrated how "everyday literacies" are associated with domains of activity within particular cultures, and how they make use of various media and symbol systems. A key concept in NLS is *Discourse*, "ways of behaving, interacting, valuing, thinking, believing, speaking, and often reading and writing that are accepted instantiations of particular roles (or 'types of people') by *specific groups of people*. . . . [Discourses] are, thus, always and everywhere *social* and products of social histories (Gee, 1996, p. viii; emphasis in original). There are two major kinds of Discourse: the primary Discourse of the home and community, and the secondary Discourses of the public sphere—institutions such as public schools. Gee explains that Discourses are recognizable by others within particular "affinity groups" and thus are tied to affiliation, membership, and identity.

Multiliteracies

Another key idea in NLS is the notion of *multiliteracies*, a term introduced by the New London Group (1996) to connote multiple media, hybrid text forms, and new social relations. There are four key ideas related to *multiliteracies*: (1) a plurality of literacies (rather than a single, monolithic literacy), (2) the use of multiple sign systems, (3) the availability of hybrid text forms, and (4) the development of new social relations, with an emphasis on the sociopolitical. Rather than as a generic set of skills, a multiliteracies perspective sees writing as variable, arising from, embedded in, and mutually constituting social contexts. This plurality reflects an awareness of an increasing cultural and linguistic diversity. The multiliteracies perspective takes a sociopolitical stance, stressing the ways in which literacy practices are imbued with ideologies and power relations and thus are "infused with a critical literacy stance" (Pappas & Pettegrew, 1998, p. 42).

As in other sociocultural perspectives, notions of composing and text are conceived more broadly to include an array of symbol systems, linguistic and nonlinguistic composing processes, forms of representation, and means of communication. Because texts are used for particular purposes and situated within particular contexts, writers draw on various verbal and graphic forms to convey meaning, creating hybrid texts that may integrate verbal and graphic forms. In this electronic age, as writers use new technologies, new genres and forms of hybridity emerge, for example, in the creation of hypertext or Web pages.

RESEARCH METHODS

Changes in theoretical perspectives on writing since 1983 have been accompanied by shifts in research methods. Research in written composition in the preschool through elementary years has been conducted for the most part within an empirical tradition, using systematic observation and data reduction (Berkenkotter, 1991). Over the past 2 decades, however, there has been a general increase in qualitative or naturalistic methodologies with proportionately fewer experimental or quasi-experimental studies of writing. The movement toward a greater focus on processes than products, begun in the late 1970s, has continued, but has become more oriented toward, or has incorporated, social dimensions of writing. This new orientation includes a shift in focus away from individuals and toward groups of children, or toward "the individual as bearer of a social role" (Gunnarsson, 1997, p. 140) or multiple roles within particular cultural or social contexts. At the same time, "as attention to cultural aspects of teaching and learning has increased, the need to focus on text as well as on literacy and learning processes has reemerged after many years of de-emphasizing text form" (Daiute, 1998, p. 138).

Cognitive and social dimensions of writing are not discrete categories, and researchers from both traditions use triangulation, multiple measures, and realistic and communicative writing tasks and texts. Research into cognitive processes continues to use a number of methodologies introduced prior to 1983, such as think-alouds (e.g., Bereiter & Scardamalia, 1987), retrospective accounts, and interviews (e.g., Langer, 1986), with the resulting texts used as prompts for retrospections or to complement think-aloud data. Cognitive researchers who are concerned that thinking aloud may change the processes writers normally use (see Smagorinsky, 1998) ask children to write in dyads, and use the resulting dialogue as data. Researchers working from sociocognitive or sociocultural perspectives strive to study writers and writing in familiar situations, such as in specific contexts of activity within a classroom. These researchers use in-depth observations, for example, in ethnographies of children engaged in writing in the context of play, and examine texts arising from and embedded in activities. Researchers have become increasingly aware of the situatedness of writing and variability among young writers. Rather than generic "child writers," researchers attempt to include a wider ranger of children from diverse sociocultural, linguistic, and economic backgrounds and are increasingly sensitive to issues of generalizability or transferability of results.

Some researchers, especially those working from a social stance, investigate writing through oral or written discourse analysis. There are a number of different methods and foci, for example, *textual-level* discourse analysis, which attends to the lexico-grammatical features of the texts themselves; *discursive practice*, which includes how participants produce texts within a social context, and *social practice*, which focuses on the specific writing situation, school context, or wider social contexts, especially in terms of social power and ideologies (Titscher, Meyer, Wodak, & Vetter, 2000). Written text analyses continue to play a role in writing research at the preschool through elementary levels. A broadened notion of text, or multiliteracies, has prompted researchers to examine multiple media and sign systems in addition to alphabetic writing, for example, young children's composing through multimedia, in multiple sign systems, and in activities that engage children in talking, playing, drawing, and writing. Young children's preconventional representations are analyzed to provide insights into children's emerging knowledge and understandings of the functions and forms of writing and other symbol systems. Researchers also document children's writing development over time and in different situations or spheres of activity, analyzing both the written and multimedia texts children compose and the contexts in which they arose. Discursive practice analysis is used by researchers interested in intertextuality, for example, in describing and explaining how young writers draw on their experiences from their literary and social worlds (including instruction), and interdiscursivity, the ways in which children use genres and discourses for text production. Other researchers use social practice analyses in ethnographic studies, for example, to describe young writers as social actors and explain the ways in which they construct identity, voice, and social power as writers.

RESEARCH FINDINGS

Research findings may be grouped into three categories: the emergence of writing, cognitive and sociocognitive dimensions of children's writing processes, and social and cultural aspects. These categories recognize that literacy processes, even those that are considered to be cognitive, originate in social interaction and are acquired in contextualized activity (Vygotsky, 1978) and that writing is best thought of as a set of culturally based discursive practices rather than as merely a set of cognitive skills (Gover & Englert, 1998). Research also offers new findings on the teaching of writing.

The Emergence of Writing

When researchers and teachers use the terms *emergent literacy* or *emergent writing*, they usually are referring to children from infancy through kindergarten or first grade. Because children's earliest writing attempts integrate other sign systems such as drawing, emergent writing most often refers not only to written texts but also to other representational forms. The development of conventional orthography is an important component in the process of learning to write within this period. Studies related to the development of spelling and other conventions are discussed here if they are situated within the context of writing. Studies that treat those conventions as discrete skills are not included.

The nature of writing development. Luria (1929/1977–1978), a colleague of Vygotsky and the first person to study young children's understanding of the symbolic nature of writing, identified four developmental stages: (1) undifferentiated-noninstrumental scribbles, which are not used as signs of any kind and reflect no awareness of the functions of graphic marks; (2) undifferentiated ostensive sign use, in which marks are used to point to particular content but are not true signs in the symbolic sense; (3) undifferentiated to differentiated transformation of sign-stimulus to sign-symbol; and (4) pictographic use of sign. The earliest studies of preschool children's writing in English, by Legrun (1932) and Hildreth (1936), document stages of development beginning with random scribbles, progressing to scribbles with horizontal and vertical characteristics, to consistent linearity, to structures that approximate real letters, and finally to conventional alphabetic forms. Clay (1975) and Read (1975) sparked an explosion of research in very young children's writing that provided evidence to support Legrun's and Hildreth's findings (e.g., Bissex, 1980; DeFord, 1980; Sulzby, 1985).

Some of the most important insights into emergent writing have come from case studies such as those of Bissex (1980) and Baghban (1984), who documented their own children's writing development. The richest description of the development of a child writer to date remains Bissex's (1980) longitudinal case study of her son from ages 5 through 10. Bissex concluded that the development of writing must be seen as part of the development of the person rather than as merely the product of an instructional writing sequence. Baghban (1984), who studied the literacy development of her daughter from birth to age 3, argues that her child's writing began when she "could hold a writing instrument, with each activity she intended to write and considered herself to be writing" (p. 103), which occurs as early as 18 months.

Children's earliest writing is playful and interrelated with other forms of communication, especially talk and drawing (Dyson, 1986a, 1986b). Clay's (1975) research shows that while 2-year-olds apparently scribble-write for the enjoyment of movement and creation of a visible object, somewhere between the ages of 3 and 5, most children become aware that writing involves making marks purposefully. Harste, Woodward, and Burke (1983, 1984a, 1984b) demonstrate that young children growing up in cultures with writing systems other than English, such as Arabic and Hebrew, produce scribble-writing that resembles the written language of their cultures. Harste and colleagues (1984b) conclude that the data "support the notion that young children are written language users and learners long before they receive formal instruction and that they actively attend to written language" (p. 82).

One of the most important learning tasks for children is differentiating the unique aspects of written language (Sulzby, 1986). Differentiation between drawing and writing entails distinguishing two modes of representation: *iconic*, in which the representation relates to the form of an object (as in drawing), and *non-iconic*, in which the representation refers to something other than an object's form (as in writing) (Ferreiro, 1990). Dyson (1984) proposes that learning to write is like solving a puzzle and that children must solve the written language puzzle "by gradually differentiating its pieces and, at the same time, actively manipulating those pieces within the context of a meaningful whole" (p. 174). She suggests that becoming a writer involves learning about writing's perceptual features (i.e., what writing looks like), symbolic nature (that writing is a system of signs), structural characteristics (e.g., elements of stories), discursive procedures (e.g., encoding), sociocognitive nature (i.e., that writing must be able to be interpreted independently from the specific context in which it was written), and functions or purposes of writing. Children's awareness of spoken and written language is at first tacit; it then becomes explicit and finally reflective (Roberts, 1992).

Gradually, children develop an awareness of the relation between speech and symbol, first through the syllabic hypothesis, using one symbol to represent one syllable, with no phonetic relation (Ferreiro, 1990); then they develop an understanding of the alphabetic principle (that there is a relation between letters and speech sounds) (Chomsky, 1971; Gentry, 1982; Read, 1971, 1975) and progress through a series of developmental stages (e.g., invented spelling) toward standard spelling (Beers & Henderson, 1977; Gentry, 1982). Segmentation (into words and sentences) and punctuation develop in a similar way, moving through a series of approximations to conventional forms (Cazden, Cordeiro, & Giacobbe, 1985; Edelsky, 1983).

While earlier research sought to identify patterns or stages of development in writing, the concept of emergent literacy is not one of "ages and stages" in the Piagetian sense, since social context is paramount (Sulzby, 1986). Writing development is best thought of as a sociocognitive constructivist process. Rather than being an invariant sequence, there are individual differences among children who vary in their experiential backgrounds, learning styles, abilities, and rates of development. Furthermore, different purposes, tasks, and discourse forms influence children's writing processes.

The development of written genres. Learning genres is an emergent process that is similar to other aspects of writing development (Chapman, 1994a). The earliest research in children's written genre development focused on narrative, which traditionally has been seen as the most appropriate form for young children (Pappas, 1993). Applebee (1978) described how two basic processes, first centering and then chaining, produce increasingly mature narrative forms, from "heaps" to true narratives. Subsequent studies (e.g., Chapman, 1994a) demonstrate that centering and chaining can occur at the same time in development. Children's narrative writing exhibits increasing cohesion and coherence as they progress through elementary school (Spiegel & Fitzgerald, 1990).

Newkirk (1987) showed how centering and chaining apply in genres other than narrative. He demonstrated that children develop more complex nonnarrative forms from the label (a one-word or one-sentence identification of a picture) and the list (a series of names, dates, facts, etc., usually not in sentence form). Chapman (1995, 1996) demonstrated that narrative and nonnarrative development in a first-grade writing workshop are interrelated rather than discrete lines of development. Children's stories, for example, often emerge from labels or captions (nonnarrative forms) accompanying their drawings. Langer's (1986) study of 8- to 14-year-old writers found that new organizational structures arose from simpler patterns in limited contexts. With age and experience, students' repertoires of organizational patterns increase and students become more able to use them as central organizers for longer pieces of writing.

Kindergarten children can write informational texts and stories and are aware of how they are different, even before they can write with conventional spellings (Donovan, 2001). A subsequent study (Donovan & Smolkin, 2002) found that many kindergarten children could differentiate between narrative and expository genres and were able to produce texts classified at more advanced levels than labels and statements, and that by second grade almost all children could do so. Kamberelis (1999) and Kamberelis and Bovino (1999) showed that fewer children in grades K–2 were able to produce reports in comparison to stories. In a study of good and poor readers' narrative and expository writing in third and fifth grades, Cox, Shanahan, and Sulzby (1990) found that good readers tended to be good writers, and that their writing was more complex than that of poor readers, regardless of grade or genre.

In four case studies Read (2001) investigated the collaborative writing of pairs of first- and second-grade children writing informational books using source texts. These children were able to produce "information pieces that went beyond fact-based, encyclopedia-like rehearsals of surface knowledge" (p. 342). In an analysis of first-grade science writing in family message journals, notebooks in which children write to their families with a message about what they have learned in school, Wollman-Bonilla (2000) found that the children's writing reflected both conventional and nonconventional characteristics of science genres. She concluded that the dialogic nature of the journal encouraged children to recontextualize conventional features of science writing. A longitudinal case study of cross-curricular writing from grades K–3 (Chapman, 2002) documents one child's writing development in social studies, science, mathematics, and music, and the impact of classroom curriculum and mode of instruction on his writing repertoire.

Children construct their knowledge of written genres in response to texts embedded in their social worlds and actively appropriate genres from their literacy environments (Chapman, 1995). Anderson (1994) documented the emerging "workplace literacy" of his daughter, Terri, from ages 3 to 5 as she emulated adult uses of literacy in her play, for example, transacting "business," a type of workplace or community literacy. In Walker and Allen's (1997) study of a play "travel agency" in a preschool classroom studying transportation, the children made lists for their trips and wrote postcards, as well as completing a "travel form," which was the only genre formally introduced by their teachers.

Elementary children can use their genre knowledge playfully and creatively, transforming traditional genres into popular culture genres, such as raps (Sipe, 1993), or producing "anti-genres," that is, mocking, parodying, or exaggerating them, using their genre knowledge subversively as a form of resistance (Fox, Martin, & Evershed, 1984). They also can use a variety of "classroom workplace" or "classroom community" genres, such as reading logs, records of attendance, club memberships, reminder notes, agendas, and so on (Chapman, 1999). These "primary genres," in the Bakhtinian sense, are learned in the context of activities, without formal instruction. One of the major debates about genre learning is whether, and to what degree, children benefit from instruction in genres related to academic disciplines, which Bakhtin (1979/1986) argued are removed from immediate social contexts and thus more difficult to learn.

Cognitive and Sociocognitive Dimensions of Children's Composing

Early research on cognition and writing has established that composing begins before the physical process of putting words on a page. From a cognitive perspective, writing is a complex and recursive process that involves several subprocesses, for example, topic selection, planning, accessing prior knowledge, generating ideas, rehearsing, attending to spelling and handwriting, reading, organizing, editing, and revising. The most influential cognitive processing models over the past 2 decades were those developed by Hayes and Flower (1980) and Scardamalia and Bereiter (1986). Studies built on these two models have made important contributions to the knowledge on cognitive and self-regulatory aspects of composing.

In cognitive processing models, composing often is described as consisting of three phases—*planning, translating,* and *revision*—which operate in a recursive fashion. In the Hayes and Flower (1980) model, planning includes setting goals and generating and organizing ideas. The planning phase is very different for novice and experienced writers. Young writers tend to write what they retrieve from long-term memory, with little consideration for organization and goal setting (Graham & Harris, 2000). The second phase, sentence generation or idea translation, places enormous cognitive and physical demands on young writers. Fluency in translating is related partly to the degree to which writers can draw upon their background knowledge and experiences (Needels & Knapp, 1994). The third phase, revision, which includes reorganizing, deleting, adding, and evaluating text, also places great demands on young writers.

Throughout the 1980s and 1990s, researchers working from a psychological perspective continued to focus on developing cognitive models to describe children's writing processes. Bereiter and Scardamalia (1987), for example, describe two types of cognitive processes, *knowledge-telling* and *knowledge-transforming*. In knowledge-telling, writing flows from language acquired through everyday experience. Once writers have identified a topic and ideas related to the writing task, they proceed from one idea to the next using a "what next" strategy rather than developing an overall plan or having a sense of the composition as a purposeful whole. Bereiter and Scardamalia found that this knowledge-telling process was common in younger writers. In knowledge-transforming, on the other hand, which is more typical of experts, writers transform their ideas through "a two-way interaction between continuously developing knowledge and continuously developing text" (p. 13). Writers draw upon different types of knowledge as they compose for different purposes: knowledge about the goals or purposes of composing, knowledge about different discourse forms, and knowledge about the needs of different types of audiences (Stein, 1986).

Zimmerman and Riesemberg's (1997) model includes affect as an important factor in writing as a self-regulating process. Self-regulation strategies include goal setting, planning, information gathering, organizing, rehearsing, transforming, self-monitoring, self-evaluating, revising, and seeking assistance. Zimmerman and Riesemberg include three categories of processes that regulate writing: environmental, behavioral, and personal. Environmental processes regulate the physical or social context of writing, behavioral processes regulate overt motor processes, and personal processes regulate affective states and cognitive beliefs about writing. These processes interact as writers monitor, modify, abandon, or continue the strategies they are using. A greater awareness of the role of affect in writing also is reflected in the revision of the Hayes and Flower (1980) model. In the updated model (Hayes, 2000), cognitive processes and monitoring have been combined and renamed *the individual*, with four parts: motivation/affect, working memory, long-term memory, and cognitive processes.

Over the past 2 decades there has been greater recognition of the role of children's social worlds on cognition. Thus, current psychological perspectives on writing processes are described more aptly as sociocognitive. For example, self-regulation is seen as a result of internalized dialogue, or appropriation, from one's social world (Burns, 2001). Because writing is a communicative act, writers take into account the needs of a reader or audience. Analyses of specific textual features, *rhetorical moves*, provide evidence of audience awareness. Rhetorical moves include *naming moves* (addressing readers), *context moves* (providing information the audience needs and omitting what the reader is assumed to already know), *strategy moves* (appealing to the audience's interests, feelings, concerns, or sense of humor), and *response moves* (stating, explaining, or accommodating the audience's potential concerns) (Ryder, Vander Lei, & Roen, 1999; Wollman-Bonilla, 2001).

Children's conceptions of writing. Children's conceptions of writing change with age and experience. Bradley (2001) investigated first-grade children's conceptions of writing, concluding that their perceptions and actions are greatly influenced by what their teachers say about writing. Children defined "good writing" as making sense, demonstrating conventional correctness, and having an acceptable appearance. Likewise, the second-grade children interviewed by Kos and Maslowski (2001) focused on the conventions of writing as qualities of "good writing." McCarthey (2001) examined fifth-grade students' notions of good writing. These students focused on the use of imagination, expressiveness, and capacity for a variety of genres.

Nistler (1990) inquired into first, third, and fifth graders' perceptions of themselves as authors before, during, and after bookmaking activities. Fewer children considered themselves as authors at each succeeding grade level, with no fifth graders viewing themselves as authors. First graders' sense of self as an author was tied to the physical production of the text and a concern for correct mechanics, while third and fifth graders' conceptions were related to meaning making. At all grade levels, children identified authors as writers of books. Nistler also inquired into children's notions of control and ownership in authoring. The first-grade children saw control residing in others, especially their teachers, and particularly in an evaluative role. Third-grade children indicated a greater sense of control over decisions regarding their writing, with a focus on "the sense of text, its appeal to their audience, its form and its topic" (p. 365). Two thirds of the grade 5 students identified themselves as the decision maker, and they had both a greater awareness of options such as genre and style, and greater audience awareness.

A number of studies indicate gendered conceptions of writing (e.g., Fleming, 1995; Gray-Schlegel & Gray-Schlegel, 1995–1996; Kamler, 1993; McAuliffe, 1994; Trepanier-Street & Romatowksi, 1991). Peterson (2000) asked intermediate students (grades 4 and 6) to list preferred writing topics and identify markers they used to identify authors of stories written by students at their grade levels. Children of both genders identified topics related to family, friends, and home life as feminine and viewed girls as more competent and conscientious writers than boys. Students attributed the presence of violence to male writers. Girls positioned female characters in both powerful and powerless roles and included some male characters. Boys, on the other hand, positioned male characters in powerful roles and reflected limited roles for female characters.

Writing processes of young children: Preschool through primary.

Building on the work of Donald Graves in the 1970s and 1980s, researchers have paid considerable attention to young children's writing over the past 2 decades. Following Graves's (1981) observation that 6-year-olds' writing processes "resemble spontaneous play" (p. 7), a number of studies have explored the theme of writing-as-play. In recognition that writing development begins before children start formal schooling, children's use of writing within the context of play has been studied in the home (Anderson, 1994; Baghban, 1984; Bissex, 1980), in preschool (Neuman & Roskos, 1989, 1990; Schrader, 1989), and in kindergarten (Hipple, 1985; Sulzby, 1985; Vukelich, 1993). Studies such as these show that children understand much about the functions and forms of writing long before their writing becomes conventional. In a year-long study of first-grade writing, MacGillivray (1994) found that play serves as way of exploring ideas when children are writing.

Dyson (1986a) uses the metaphor of "symbol weaving" to describe the ways in which children draw on various symbol systems or media, particularly drawing and talking, in their writing. Talk is central to younger children's writing. Children talk their way through writing events: before writing, during writing (as though they are thinking aloud), and after writing (rereading aloud what they have written) (MacGillivray, 1994). They talk about the mechanics of writing (e.g., letter formation, spelling) as well as ideas (Chapman, 1994b; Cioffi, 1984). Cox (1994) argues that the first graders in her study used talk to control the text's content by checking meaning and figuring out what to write next. Bereiter and Scardamalia (1987) propose that talk helps young children monitor their writing processes because they write without planning, writing from one idea to the next with a "what's next" approach. As children gain experience with writing, "evidence of planning and rehearsal of ideas prior to actual writing begins to appear" (Dahl & Farnan, 1998, p. 25), and talk before and during composing diminishes (Cioffi, 1984). Younger writers show little goal-directed behavior during writing (Scardamalia & Bereiter, 1986), often writing by pattern (McCutchen, 1995). As they progress through the primary grades and beyond, children become less focused on mechanics and more on content.

In a rich, descriptive case study of a first grader's self-initiated and teacher-assigned writing, Sipe (1998) identified four factors that influenced shifts over time in the child's writing processes: the pull of conventional forms, the social nature of composing, the importance of topic choice, and the role of the teacher. The focal child's revisions, although consisting mostly of erasing during his attempts at encoding, included many instances of revising for meaning. Sipe argues that children do not necessarily find conventional forms inhibiting and that teachers should not dismiss children's concerns with conventions as a problem: "What we may consider to be merely surface features of writing may be extremely important for children" (p. 378).

Primary children revise less often than older writers. With teacher support, some first-grade children are able to make meaningful revisions to their texts (Fitzgerald & Stamm, 1992). By second grade they can use content and genre knowledge (Perez, 2001) and are able to revise for surface and semantic errors (Cameron, Edmunds, Wigmore, Hunt, & Linton, 1997), but their revisions tend to focus more on mechanics than on meaning, and meaning-based revisions tend to involve only small units of text (Fitzgerald, 1987). Vukelich (1986) found that three quarters of second graders inserted information into their texts in response to peers' questions, most frequently at the end of their texts. While there is evidence that young writers typically pay little attention to the reader (McCutchen, 1995), Vukelich's study provides evidence that young writers can take into account the needs of an audience when it is real and immediate. Audience awareness also has been demonstrated in first grade when children write to a known reader, such as in family message journals (Wollman-Bonilla, 2001). Third graders in Nistler's (1990) study revised mostly at the word, sentence, and paragraph levels, and were concerned with both correctness and the meaning of what they wrote. Their "awareness of revision . . . was guided by a sort of inner-reader, and reportedly reflected teachers' emphases on spelling and mechanics of writing" (p. 364).

Young children show high levels of self-regulation during composing in settings that encourage it (Cameron, Hunt, & Linton, 1996). Perry's (1998) study of self-regulation in writing in grades 2 and 3 found that children in high self-regulated learning (SRL) classrooms, in comparison to low SRL classrooms, commented more often on meaning-related aspects of writing and the intrinsic value of their writing. Low-achieving writers in high SRL classrooms were not discouraged, indicating that although writing was difficult for them, they were encouraged by improvements in their writing and believed that they were receiving support that would help them become successful writers. Low-achieving students in low SRL classrooms, however, made statements reflecting perceptions of low ability and discouragement.

Writing processes of children in the intermediate grades. While the past 2 decades have seen great interest in the writing of preschool and primary children, there have been comparatively fewer studies of writing in the intermediate grades. Calkins (1994) demonstrates that intermediate writers gradually gain awareness and control of their writing processes, drawing on multiple sources of information as they write, including their own experiences, repertoires of knowledge, and social worlds. Whereas younger children focus to a great degree on the written code, intermediate writers begin to focus more on meaning and making connections among ideas (Langer, 1986). They also use writing as a vehicle for personal exploration and growth (McGinley & Kamberelis, 1992).

As students progress through the intermediate grades, they become more strategic in generating ideas and planning, constructing meaning through linking ideas, monitoring the development of ideas in their writing, and reviewing and revising for meaning (Langer, 1986). In an analysis of prewriting planning notes of students in grades 4 and 6, Scardamalia and Bereiter (1986) found that in fourth and sixth grades, students' planning and drafting processes were similar. In fourth grade, students generated complete sentences that they then incorporated into their drafts. In sixth grade, however, students generated lists of ideas during prewriting, which they then worked into their texts. In the intermediate grades young writers become more aware of the strategies they use in composing and are more self-regulated writers (Langer, 1986). Their talk during writing shows awareness of both content (e.g., what to include) and surface features (Langer 1986). In an investigation of how students in fourth grade selected writing topics, Connell and DiStefano (1991) identified three interrelated strategies: reflecting on specific aspects of writing instruction (personal experience, desire to impress peers), reflecting on school influences from instruction (strategies and genres previously taught, content-specific themes), and reflecting on influences outside school. More proficient writers used a wider range of strategies.

Intermediate writers are more able to revise than primary students, but they find it more difficult to revise their own writing than texts written by others (Cameron et al., 1997). Fifth graders in Nistler's (1990) study displayed a broader sense of audience that first and third graders, showed balance in revising for mechanics and meaning, demonstrated less concern for the physical appearance of their work, and exhibited greater awareness of multiple stages in the composing process. Frank (1992) asked fifth-grade students to compose and revise original texts for different audiences. She found that these young writers could do both but were more successful in writing for a third-grade audience than for an adult audience. Beal (1993) argues that a key problem in the revision process is that writers need to change their stance toward texts. Instead of making assumptions and inferences in order to comprehend a text, reading to revise entails noticing gaps, inconsistencies, and potential sources of confusion. She notes the inability to do the latter is "the result of cognitive limitations that it make it hard for them [elementary children] to view the text with a detached eye and to recognize that it does not really represent their meaning fully or accurately" (p. 650). Beal provides evidence to show that once children are helped to identify a problem spot in a text, they are able to revise their texts effectively, especially with training.

Social and Cultural Dimensions of Children's Writing

Dyson has been particularly influential in infusing Bakhtin's (1979/1986) theories about the nature of language and learning into research with young children and re-envisioning children's writing as a sociocultural process. As Dyson (1992) explains, using a genre is more than producing a particular type of text: "It involves assuming a certain stance toward other people and toward the world" (p. 5). From a sociocultural perspective children are *social actors* who use writing to "engage in social dialogues with other people, using certain genres to enact certain relationships" (p. 41). Ideology and power are integral to writing, even for young children, and thus it is important to inquire into taken-for-granted ways of acting and interacting within particular communities, including classrooms, and examine the ways in which particular ideologies influence learning and teaching (Rowe, 2000). An important aspect of learning to write is constructing one's identity as a writer, not in a generic sense but as "a boy or girl, to a person of a particular ages, ethnicity, race, class, religion, and on and on" (Dyson, 1995, p. 12). Yet this embodiment of culture does not mean that child writers passively adopt social norms. As Dyson observes, children are "meaning negotiators, learning to participate in the social world, to adopt, to resist, or to stretch available words" (p. 18).

Writing in the classroom community. Social worlds—cultures and communities—provide resources that writers draw upon when they construct and communicate meaning. These resources include people and the things they create, such as ways of thinking, communicating, and representing ideas; sign systems (e.g., alphabetic writing); texts of different kinds (e.g., literature, popular media texts); and participation structures. The classroom is a particular community, communicative group, or culture that defines literacy (genres, values, and conventions for participation) and provides models and demonstrations of a diverse array of functions and forms of writing that shape children's writing processes (Rowe, 1994), genres (Chapman, 1995, 1996; Kamler, 1992), content (Rowe, 1994), and conceptions of gender roles (Kamler, 1992). Children appropriate from their social contexts both cognitive aspects of writing and social conventions for participation (McCarthey, 1994).

Studies of writing in preschool (Rowe, 1994), kindergarten (Phinney, 1998; Wiseman, 2003), and primary classrooms (Dyson, 1992, 1993) reveal that young children use writing as a vehicle for social engagement and are developing understandings about social purposes for writing. The children in MacGillivray's (1994) first-grade study, for example, used writing to resolve peer issues and collaborate with peers. In a case study of fourth graders, McGinley and Kamberelis (1992) described how children used writing to restructure social relationships, promote dialogue, address complex societal problems, and "explore new social identities, roles, and responsibilities" (p. 337). McCarthey's (2001) case study of a fifth-grade classroom found that students' identity construction was influenced by peers', parents', and teachers' perceptions; involvement in writing activities; and the classroom literacy curriculum.

Children experiment with writing and explore ways of using a variety of discourse forms for different social purposes regardless of the specific approach to instruction (McIntyre & Freppon, 1994). Nevertheless, teachers cultivate, establish, and maintain particular uses of and approaches to writing within the classroom. In a longitudinal study of writing from kindergarten through the middle of second grade, Kamler (1992) observed that "free choice" of topics in primary classrooms is not truly free. The children's written genres—personal story genres (related to personal experience), childhood literary genres (based on models of children's literature), and labeling genres (primary pictures with labels attached)—were a response to the teacher's implicit expectations about acceptable writing. Likewise, the children's genres in Chapman's (1995) study of a first-grade writing workshop were shaped by events within and surrounding writing time and the way in which the teacher structured writing tasks.

Literary, popular, and peer cultures. Children draw on their cultures' uses of literacy as resources for writing, including an array of literature, popular culture, and media texts. First-grade children in Dahl and Freppon's (1995) study derived topics, character ideas, and structures for writing from their reading experiences and sometimes copied from their favorite books. Dressel (1990) demonstrated that listening to and discussing high-quality literature (as determined by professional raters) helped students write higher quality stories than students who had few opportunities to do so. Eckoff (1983) found that in comparison to students who read simplified texts, students who read many literary forms were better able to use different literary genres in their own writing. Comstock (1992) studied a grade 5 classroom in which students read, discussed, wrote, and shared poetry. Participating in this "poetic community" (p. 263) led to an increased use of imagery in the children's writing.

Children also draw on popular culture as a resource for writing, appropriating media as "textual toys" (Dyson, 2001). Dyson's (1997, 1999, 2001) case studies document how children recontextualize aspects of popular culture texts such as songs, movies, cartoons, and sports media shows in composing their own multimedia texts. In an ethnographic study in a second-grade classroom, for example, Dyson (1997) vividly describes how the children appropriated "good guys," such as Power Rangers, Ninja Turtles, and X-Men, using them as characters in their own stories and ventriloquating their voices to enact social relationships with classmates. Dyson (2001) demonstrates how one first grader, Noah, interweaves storybook and media characters, producing hybrid texts that resulted from "straddling semiotic worlds" (p. 422).

Peer culture plays a significant role in children's development as writers, beginning in the preschool years (Rowe, 1994). While peers may play a positive, supportive role in writing (Labbo, 1996; Rowe, 1994; Troyer, 1991), social pressures from classmates sometimes limit children's voice and writing identity (Phinney, 1998). In a study of first-grade writing, Rowe (2000) examined issues of power and the ways in which children negotiated their literate identities within peer culture and the official classroom culture, noting that the children were able to move freely between these cultures, playing multiple roles, using multiple voices, and addressing multiple audiences, often within the same literacy event. She also observed that children took one of three stances toward the official classroom culture (including instruction): "buying in," challenging some aspects, or rejecting it. Children in the latter group, despite being able, tended to use resistance and avoidance strategies that prevented them from engaging in literacy activities that would have fostered more advanced writing strategies.

Wiseman's (2003) study of kindergarten writing and Chapman's (1994b) study of a multiage kindergarten–second grade classroom demonstrate how classmates initiate, reinforce, and delimit particular writing practices or genres; scaffold one anothers' writing experiences; and judge particular topics as acceptable or unacceptable. Power's (1991) description of how "pop ups" caught on as a popular convention within a first-grade classroom provides insights into the ways in which children appropriate writing practices through interaction with others within their social worlds. Likewise, "hot topics illustrate how children transform cultural symbols as they make sense of them" (Daiute, 1998, p. 144).

Social interaction and writing. A number of studies document the ways in which peer interactions support elementary students' writing. Swafford, Akrofi, Rogers, and Alexander (1999), for example, demonstrated how second- and third-grade children assisted one another in reading and writing informational texts. More-able students provided three kinds of support for peers: technical support (e.g., mechanics, sequencing), social support (e.g., listening to, encouraging, collaborative problem solving), and content support (e.g., negotiating textual meaning, verifying answers). Peer interactions in Kos and Maslowski's (2001) investigation of writing in second grade found that peer interactions were more helpful for generating ideas than for revision and that students developed greater audience awareness through sharing writing with classmates. Wollman-Bonilla and Werchadlo's (1999) examination of first-grade children's literature response journals also found that peer response led to stronger voice and sense of audience in children's writing. Dahl's (1988) case study supports the use of peer revision conferences. She found that fourth graders talked about revising for clarity and focus and changing titles and sequences of events or information, and that 46% of suggestions made in peer conferences resulted subsequently in revisions. Similarly, peer feedback in a sixth-grade study improved the degree and quality of revision and the quality of writing (Olson, 1990).

A few studies have shown the benefits of older and younger children writing collaboratively. In an experimental study of emergent writers paired with older children experiencing difficulties with writing, Nixon and Topping (2001) found greater improvements for emergent writers who experienced the paired writing than for those who did not. A study of interactions among children writing in a multiage K–2 classroom (Chapman, 1994b) found that the older (grade 2) children assisted the younger children with many aspects of writing, particularly spelling and letter formation. The second graders also acted as teachers, socializing the younger ones into classroom routines and "how to do writing" in their classroom.

RESEARCH ON THE TEACHING OF WRITING

Over the past 2 decades research on the teaching of writing has examined different approaches to teaching writing, especially those modeled on attributes that Hillocks (1986) identified as beneficial from his meta-analysis of writing research from 1963 to 1983. Researchers interested in cognitive aspects of writing have, for example, investigated ways of improving young writers' composing strategies, especially for struggling writers. Researchers interested in the social dimensions of writing have inquired into the ways in which teachers enact writing instruction in their classrooms and their impact on writing in the classroom. Research also has explored the impact of new technologies, particularly the computer, on writing.

Process Approaches to Writing

In the decade following Hillocks's (1986) publication, there was a surge of interest in using a more strategic, process-oriented approach to writing instruction in elementary school. Recall that Hillocks's meta-analysis revealed that the *presentational* mode, characterized by teacher-led discussions, lectures, and written feedback on the qualities of effective writing, was the least effective approach to writing. Earlier process approaches (during the mid- and late 1980s), such as those popularized by researchers like Graves and Calkins, emphasized free writing on self-selected topics, and peer and teacher feedback. This *natural process* mode emphasized indirect rather than explicit instruction and posited the role of the teacher as a facilitator who guides students' searches for meaning and expression. Hillocks's meta-analysis showed that the natural process mode was more effective than the presentational mode, but less effective than the *environmental* mode. Like the natural process mode, the environmental mode also used peer group activities, but ones characterized by "highly structured problem-solving tasks which involve students in specific strategies parallel to those they will encounter in their writing" (p. 194). During the 1990s and beyond, "writing process" or "process writing" approaches became more consistent with Hillocks's environmental mode.

Sadoski, Wilson, and Norton (1997) carried out a study in 16 classrooms in various school districts in Texas to investigate the impact of the features of instruction Hillocks (1986) referred to as the environmental mode. Recall that Hillocks's meta-analysis found positive effects for sentence combining, freewriting, inquiry, and revision, and negative effects for teaching grammar and mechanics. Positive feedback and feedback on clear objectives had a positive effect, while negative feedback was detrimental. Sadoski and his colleagues used factor analysis to examine the general dimensions of the environmental approach rather than individual variables. Student writing was assessed using Spandel and Stiggins's (1990) holistic scoring system that takes into account content, organization, voice, word choice, sentence fluency, and conventions. Sadoski and colleagues found that writing in the lower grades was enhanced when teachers allowed considerable time for writing; encouraged students to produce more text; exposed students to well-written literature; provided opportunities for prewriting, inquiry, and freewriting (rather than using models); allowed teacher and peer conferencing; and used criteria in instruction and assessment. The researchers concluded that "the positive effect of a combination of instructional practices interpretable as the environmental mode was supported" (p. 143).

In an examination of NAEP writing data on 7,000 grade 4 students, Goldstein and Carr (1996) found positive effects for process approaches to writing instruction. In comparison to students in classrooms in which process-oriented strategies were not encouraged, students in process writing classrooms tended to be better writers, and average writing ability was higher. Students who were consistently encouraged to use prewriting strategies (e.g., lists, outlines, and diagrams, but not unrelated notes or drawings or simply writing first drafts) tended to achieve higher scores.

A number of studies have examined teacher feedback on children's writing. Teacher feedback has a positive effect on children's confidence, strategy development, and performance (Skinner, Wellborn, & Connell, 1990). Specific and explicit feedback has been found to be important for young writers because it helps them progress from where they are to where they would like to be, and provides them with information to help them achieve their goals (Schutz, 1993). Children respond positively to specific suggestions to help them improve their writing because it enhances their feelings of control (Straub, 1996, 1997).

In a review of the literature on process writing, Flood and Lapp (2000) conclude that a process approach "is most appropriate for children from a wide variety of language backgrounds because it enables children to write frequently, continually revising the content as well as the form" (p. 234). Yet process-based writing instruction also can be problematic. Gutierrez (1994) conducted a 3–year ethnographic study of seven elementary classrooms from which she identified three different types of "scripts" (patterns of activity, social action, and discourse) that shaped writing process pedagogy: recitative, responsive, and responsive/collaborative. These scripts differentially influenced participation structures, social relationships and hierarchies, and the degree and type of access to writing. The recitation script limited students' opportunities for participation, decision making, interacting with peers, and receiving support from peers. In the recitation script classrooms, "teaching writing process became teaching the writing process" (p. 344). The responsive script, while more relaxed in terms of participation structures and activity boundaries, still was aimed at doing writing process activities in particular ways. The responsive/collaborative script, on the other hand, provided greater opportunities for students to engage with one another and to negotiate classroom discussion and activities. Gutierrez (1994) argues for a need to revise writing process pedagogy, drawing on insights from sociocultural perspectives on writing.

Lensmire (2000) notes that while writing workshop approaches popularized by Graves (1983) and Calkins (1986) have had mostly positive influences on writing in the classroom, he became increasingly aware of problems with power relationships that privileged some students and subordinated others in his third-grade writing workshop. Lensmire argues that *voice* needs to shift from the way it is used by Graves, Calkins, and others, that is, "voice as individual expression" (p. 57), to "voice as participation," as it is used in critical pedagogy. He urges teachers to examine critically issues of identity, power, and equality of access within their classrooms and to strive for a balance between complete teacher control and complete student autonomy so that all students' voices can be heard.

Scaffolding and Explicit Instruction

Building on Vygotsky's (1978) notion of the zone of proximal development, educators use the metaphor of a scaffold to describe the ways in which adults' interactions foster children's learning and development, enabling them to carry out tasks they are not able to do independently. Instructional scaffolding can take many forms, including modeling, demonstrating, prompting, questioning, and joint construction of text. Much of the research on scaffolding in writing has been conducted with younger children. Kamberelis and Bovino (1999) investigated the role of scaffolding in kindergartners' through second graders' learning of narrative and informational genres. They found that most children, especially the younger ones, produced more well-formed texts in the scaffolded condition than the nonscaffolded condition. Wollman-Bonilla and Werchaldo (1999) examined the impact of scaffolding and explicit instruction on children's writing in response to literature. Their data led them to conclude that "perhaps repeated modeling, with student participation in constructing the models, may be a powerful instructional tool; explicit instruction may not be as essential as other researchers suggest" (Wollman-Bonilla, 2000, p. 58).

A number of studies have investigated process approaches to writing in which students are explicitly taught strategies for planning, drafting, and revising. There is evidence that instruction in revising strategies enhances intermediate students' knowledge of revision and also increases their efforts at revising (Fitzgerald, 1987). Writing quality and efficacy are enhanced by writing strategy training (e.g., Graham & Harris, 1989, 1993), building efficacy for using strategies (Schunk & Zimmerman, 1997), and strategy instruction combined with goal setting (Graham, MacArthur, & Schwartz, 1995). Explicit strategy instruction has been found to be particularly helpful for struggling writers (Graham et al., 1995). Explicit instruction is also beneficial for students with learning disabilities, who tend to have problems with planning, evaluating, and writing, which often lead to negative attitudes toward writing (Graham, MacArthur, Schwartz, & Page-Voth, 1992). Englert, Raphael, Anderson, Anthony, and Stevens (1991) found positive effects for writing effectiveness and metacognition with an intervention, Cognitive Strategy Instruction in Writing, for students with and without learning disabilities.

Some studies have investigated the role of explicit teaching of particular genres. Fitzgerald and Teasley (1986) found that explicit instruction improved the organization and quality of children's written narratives. Donovan's (1996) study of first-grade writers looked at the use of models in narrative and expository writing. She found that using models was effective for both genres. Yet Purcell-Gates, Duke, Hall, and Tower (2003), in researching informational and procedural writing in second and third grades, found a statistically significant effect for explicit instruction combined with authentic texts and purposes on procedural writing in grade 2 only.

Writing Tasks

Writing is enhanced when tasks are motivating, interesting, and appropriately challenging. Even when chosen for instructional reasons, writing tasks often are not connected to larger communicative or social purposes that can create interest and a sense of relevance, thus becoming an "assignment" to be completed (Flower, Stein, Ackerman, Kantz, McCormick, & Peck, 1990). Children benefit from engaging in authentic writing tasks that involve them in the immediate uses of writing for enjoyment and communication, rather than as skills to be learned for some unspecified future use (Hiebert, 1994). One-size-fits-all writing tasks tend to focus solely on technique and ignore the communicative purpose of writing. Dahl and Farnan (1998) argue that writing tasks need to "help students learn technique in the context of authentic communication" (p. 33).

Purcell-Gates and colleagues (2003) conducted a large longitudinal study of writing integrated with hands-on science activities. Twenty-six grade 2 and 3 classes were assigned randomly to one of two conditions: (1) immersion in reading and writing of informational and procedural texts for authentic purposes, and (2) the same immersion plus explicit instruction. The researchers found that the degree of authenticity was a statistically significant predictor of student growth for informational writing and verbal features in grades 2 and 3; for informational writing, visual features, and procedural writing in grade 3; and, in interaction with degree of explicitness in grade 2, for procedural writing and visual and verbal features.

Children write more on self-selected topics than on assigned topics (Meichenbaum & Biemiller, 1992; Scardamalia & Bereiter, 1986) and have significantly more content knowledge about topics they want to write about than about assigned topics (Gradwohl & Schumacher, 1989). Children also sustain engagement longer in open-ended writing tasks than in closed tasks and are more persistent when they experience difficulties (Turner, 1993). Publishing writing to be read by a known audience—for example, a classroom newspaper, which would be read by peers and families—increases student engagement and motivates students to engage in revision needed to enhance the clarity of their writing (Alber, 1999). Students also are motivated by cooperative writing tasks that help them learn different strategies and styles from one another (McCutchen, 1988).

Engagement is an essential component in fostering a positive emotional environment. Csikszentmihalyi (1975) defined engagement, realized in a "flow" experience, as a balance between a challenging task and the ability to carry it out. It is better to engage students in challenging writing tasks and provide them with the scaffolding and support they need to be successful than to assign simple tasks they can do without effort. Students find complex learning activities more interesting and challenging (Miller & Meece, 1999), which leads to greater motivation. Appropriately challenging tasks create interest, allow for self-improvement, and afford children opportunities to control their own learning (Turner & Paris, 1995). Children need to believe, however, that the task can be accomplished with reasonable effort. Open-ended writing tasks are particularly important because they allow for learner variability to promote meaning making, engagement, and control, and to foster feelings of competence and efficacy. Children also benefit from having clear expectations for their writing tasks. Young writers who have clear expectations and criteria tend to be more effective at self-evaluating and revising (Dahl & Farnan, 1998). Criterion-based rating scales are also beneficial (Sadoski, Willson, & Norton, 1997; Spandel & Stiggins, 1990).

Classroom Contexts

Several studies have compared the effects of different types of classroom contexts on children's writing. Dahl and Freppon (1995), for example, contrasted writing in skills-based and whole language classrooms in kindergarten and first grade. While children in both types of classrooms were concerned about accuracy, children who experienced difficulty in skills-based classrooms tended to be passive, whereas children in whole language classrooms were more persistent. There were strong differences in children's conceptions of themselves as writers in the two types of classrooms. Dahl and Freppon also noted very different kinds of writing: Children in whole language classrooms wrote sentence-, paragraph-, and story-level texts, while the "writing" in the skills-based classrooms consisted mostly of workbook assignments, sentence completion, fill-in-the-blanks, copying activities, and a few stories.

In a comparative study of writing in "traditional" kindergarten classrooms and more "child-centered" classrooms, Blazer (1986) found that there was more talk accompanying the children's writing in the child-centered classrooms. Rasinski and DeFord (1986) used a questionnaire to assess third and fourth graders' attitudes toward writing and purposes for writing in informal and traditional classrooms. Students in the informal classrooms had generally more favorable attitudes toward writing and were more internally motivated to write than students in the traditional classrooms.

Technology and Writing

Writing with new technologies is both a cognitive and a social process. Writing with a computer often involves exploration and play, which can enhance cognitive and social purposes for writing. With increasing use of technology, children are immersed in symbol systems such as icons and other visual and multimedia images that go beyond oral language and print. Young children who have opportunities to work and play with classroom computers become aware that the computer is a communicative tool (Labbo, 1996; Labbo, Reinking, & McKenna, 1995). Labbo (1996) adopted the metaphor of "screenland" to describe children's stances toward the computer screen—a place to play, create artwork, or write in order to accomplish personal or social goals. Labbo and Kuhn (1998) use the term *electronic symbol making* to refer to the "conceptual processes, strategies, and knowledge young children have the opportunity to develop when they use computers equipped with . . . multimedia and word processing programs" (p. 79). The researchers note that *transformative symbolism*, using one symbol in place of another, was most evident when children used the screen as a place to play.

Two case studies with first-grade children (Butler & Cox, 1992; Phenix & Hannan, 1984) identified differences in children's writing processes when they wrote with computers. The children read and reread their writing on screen to clarify ideas and plan what to do next, which was not the case when they wrote by hand. When using pencil and paper the children focused on getting their ideas down. In the Butler and Cox study, children used drawing to support their written texts in both hand-written and computer-generated compositions. In Dickinson (1986) and Fisher's (1994) examination of collaborative writing with the computer, children talked more about planning, writing, and responding than when they wrote by hand. Other studies (Haas, 1989; Yau, 1991) found that children planned less with computer writing, although no differences were noted in the quality of the children's compositions.

Research findings regarding differences in length and quality of compositions generated by computer in comparison to writing with paper and pencil are mixed. Cochran-Smith (1991) and Nichols (1996) found that computer-generated compositions were slightly longer, whereas Snyder (1993) found no differences. Schrader (1990) and Owston and Wideman (1997) found word-processed compositions to be of higher quality, while Nichols (1996) found no differences in writing quality even though compositions were longer. Jones and Pellegrini (1996) noted that first graders' stories composed with word processors were more lexically dense and cohesive. Jones (1994) found that second graders' stories composed with word processors were longer and of better quality. Snyder's (1993) study suggests that genre—narrative, report, or argument—has a greater impact on composing processes than does the writing tool. Regardless of the writing tool, children planned most for argument, less for reports, and least for narrative. Snyder observed that writing with the computer improved the quality of argument and reports, but not of narratives.

Technology can assist children in a number of ways. Daiute (1986) found that word processing can assist in reducing the cognitive demands related to some of the basic tasks in writing, thus allowing students to focus on the higher level demands of revision. Some research has shown that word processing can remove some of the difficulties young children encounter when they write by hand (Chang & Osguthorpe,

1990; Hoot & Silvern, 1988). On the other hand, Nuvoli's (2000) research into the use of a word processor to improve primary children's writing and revising found that children had greater difficulty drafting their texts with computers than with handwriting.

Computer programs that provide prompts assist young writers in being more strategic (Cochran-Smith, 1991; Daiute, 1986; Jones, 1994). Holdich and Chung (2003) conducted an experimental study to examine the impact of a Web-based computer tutor, HARRY, on primary children's approaches to writing and writing performance on a story-writing task. The children who used HARRY wrote more effective stories and used more mature revision strategies than the children who did not have access to HARRY. Multimedia composing programs have been shown to help children who often have difficulty with writing. In a study of underachieving fourth-grade students using a multimedia composing program, Daiute and Morse (1993) found that the compositions were longer and more elaborated when the multimedia program was used. Vincent (2000) conducted a case study of intermediate writers who were identified as having a visual learning style. Writing with a computer with visually rich software, these children were encouraged to experiment and play with visual and animation features while writing narratives, and their writing became much longer and more linguistically complex.

Children's enthusiasm for writing with computers is a consistent finding (Daiute, 1986; Miyashita, 1994; Nicholson, Gelpi, Young, & Sulzby, 1998; Seawel, Smaldino, Steele, & Lewis, 1994). Lomangino, Nicholson, and Sulzby's (1999) study suggests that collaborative writing with computers has a positive impact on student motivation. McBee (1994), however, found that writing experience was a more important factor in motivation than the writing tool or task. Nicholson and colleagues (1998) observed gender differences in the attitudes of first-grade students toward writing with computers. Boys were more eager to write with computers than were girls. Girls in mixed-gender groups were particularly reluctant.

A study of children from Finland and Britain (Kumpulainen, 1994) found that children writing collaboratively with computers focused their discussion on the writing task, provided one another with information, and did not spend much time talking about the computer itself. Snyder (1993) noted more interaction, cooperation, and collaboration when classes were writing with computers in comparison to writing with pencil and paper. Jones and Pellegrini (1996) observed that metacognitive talk was much higher when first graders wrote with computers. Cochran-Smith, Paris, and Kahn's (1991) 3-year ethnographic study of writing with word processors in kindergarten through fourth-grade classrooms, and a combined ethnographic and quantitative study in Australia by Snyder (1993), examined aspects of the classroom writing culture, writing processes, developmental issues, and overall contributions of word processors. Both studies found that the teacher's training, theoretical perspective, and view of his or her role were critical factors. These findings were supported by Canadian studies by Miller and Olson (1994) and Yau (1991).

CONCLUSIONS, IMPLICATIONS, AND RECOMMENDATIONS

Research in written composition from 1984 to 2003 supports many findings from research discussed in Braddock and colleagues (1963) and Hillocks (1986) and has provided new insights into the complexities of children's writing processes, especially the relations between cognitive and social aspects of writing. Researchers also have described the development of writing before children enter school, the social and cultural nature of writing, and relations between writing and composing with other sign systems and media. We thus begin the 21st Century with deeper understandings of writing as situated practices that vary according to social context, sphere of activity, purpose, and tools. Together, these findings suggest ways in which practices in the preschool and elementary years might change to promote and enhance children's development as writers.

Implications for Policy and Practice

Research in composition from 1984 to 2003 provides evidence that children's writing in the preschool and elementary years is complex and multidimensional, and thus no single instructional approach is appropriate for all contexts or purposes. Yet there is a convergence of evidence that children's writing is enhanced through a number of activities.

Addressing cognitive and social dimensions of writing rather than emphasizing one or the other. Young writers need to develop effective writing processes and strategies that enable them to use writing for an array of personal and social processes. They also need opportunities to learn various functions and forms of writing long before they can write conventionally, beginning in the preschool years.

Creating language- and literacy-rich learning environments. To promote their overall language and literacy growth as well as their writing development, children need opportunities to engage with quality literature through listening, reading, discussing, and responding. Children also benefit from opportunities to use writing to construct knowledge about themselves and their physical and social worlds.

Providing supportive, encouraging, and positive learning environments. Young writers need freedom to venture beyond what they can do easily and to take risks in their learning without fear of reprisal when they make errors. Children benefit when educators and policy makers view errors as integral to learning and as signs of growth. Positive feedback, together with specific suggestions and support, foster children's growth toward writing with competence and confidence.

Establishing participation structures that encourage social interaction. Children need opportunities to share ideas, collaborate, and respond to one another's writing. They also learn to write through demonstrations, modeling, and scaffolding by adults and more-able peers. Children benefit most when educators and policy makers are sensitive to political and ideological aspects of learning and issues of participation, voice, identity, and equality of access for all children.

Allowing connections to children's lives within and beyond the classroom. Motivation for writing comes in part from opportunities to make connections with one's own interests, ideas, and feelings. Young writers benefit from opportunities to draw from their peer and popular cultures, which are integral to their emotional and social worlds.

It is important to engage children in writing that is personally meaningful and to value different functions and genres for what they contribute to children's lives.

Situating writing experiences within the larger context of the classroom. Writing is situated when it is an integral and purposeful part of the various spheres of activity in the classroom. Classrooms provide many opportunities for "community" or "workplace" writing, arising out of situations where it is necessary and relevant to accomplish particular ends, and is part of genuine communication.

Emphasizing the communicative purposes of writing within different situational contexts. Writing is not a generic process, but a way of communicating within specific contexts and spheres of activity. Each curriculum area provides children with contexts for learning discipline-based ways of thinking, representing, and communicating ideas. Genres are cognitive tools and social actions rather than merely text types. Young writers need opportunities to learn an array of genres with the realization that textual features are important not as ends in themselves but as vehicles to allow readers and writers to communicate effectively. Emphasizing the communicative nature of writing fosters children's audience awareness and self-regulation.

Providing writing tasks that are authentic and appropriately challenging. Writing is fostered through engagement in tasks that are used for a purpose other than simply learning to write and for an audience other than the teacher as evaluator. Appropriately challenging tasks—those that can be accomplished through reasonable effort—foster motivation, interest, desire for self-improvement, and feelings of control. Open-ended writing tasks are particularly important because they allow children of varying levels of ability to be successful and to develop competence and confidence in themselves as writers.

Enabling opportunities to play with and explore multiple ways of composing, new literacies, new technologies, and multimedia. Learning to write is part of a larger process of meaning making through multiple sign systems. All children need opportunities to explore and experiment with composing, using a variety of media and tools for writing as well as new and emerging literacy practices and genres.

Integrating instruction with the processes of writing. Young writers, especially those who struggle with writing, benefit from explicit strategy instruction integrated within a process approach to writing. Similarly, directing attention to textual features can help children develop "genre awareness." Process and product need to be seen as complementary dimensions of writing. Awareness of both process and product fosters children's development as self-regulated writers.

Teaching with flexibility and variability rather than "one-size-fits-all" instruction. Children and writing are complex and multidimensional, and thus generic or rigid prewrite–write–rewrite approaches to instruction are not warranted. Young writers benefit from opportunities to choose their writing topics and the forms their writing may take, at least some of the time. They also benefit from instruction that addresses the specific writing situation and task, builds on their individual strengths and interests, and meets their learning needs.

Recommendations for Future Research and Theory Building

While research over the past 2 decades has made important contributions to understanding writers and writing in the preschool and elementary years, there is still much to be learned. Although the past 20 years have provided many insights into young children's writing, intermediate-age writers have received relatively little attention. Researchers thus need to pay greater attention to children in this age group. There is also a need for more longitudinal studies that examine writing within particular contexts. Research is needed on writing in the content areas at the elementary level, especially to investigate writing in relation to instruction and curricular contexts of the classroom, and the influences of context, task, and genre on cognitive dimensions of children's writing processes.

Another area requiring attention is the social and cultural contexts of classrooms and how they influence children's writing. More research is needed on issues of gender and culture in relation to children's writing and their development as writers. Research in the preschool and elementary years has focused for the most part on school contexts. It is important also to investigate preschool and elementary children's writing in nonacademic settings and out-of-school contexts.

As we move further into the 21st century, researchers need to continue to explore new literacies, multiliteracies, new technologies, and new genres. It is important to learn more about the cognitive demands of new literacies and new technologies and how technology transforms cognitive and social dimensions of children's writing processes.

REFERENCES

Alber, S. (1999). "I don't like to write, but I love to get published": Using a classroom newspaper to motivate reluctant writers. *Reading & Writing Quarterly, 15*, 355–361.

Anderson, J. (1994). "Daddy, what's a picket?": One child's emerging knowledge of workplace literacy. *Early Child Development and Care, 98*, 7–20.

Applebee, A. (1978). *The child's concept of story: Ages two to seventeen.* Chicago: University of Chicago Press.

Baghban, M. (1984). *Our daughter learns to read and write.* Newark, DE: International Reading Association.

Bakhtin, M. M. (1986). *Speech genres and other late essays* (V. W. McGee, Trans.). Austin: University of Texas Press. (Original work published 1979)

Barton, D. (1991). The social nature of writing. In D. Barton & R. Ivanic (Eds.), *Writing in the community* (pp. 1–13). Newbury Park, CA: Sage.

Beal, C. (1993). Contributions of developmental psychology to understanding revision: Implications for consultation. *School Psychology Review, 22*, 643–656.

Beers, J., & Henderson, E. (1977). First grade children's developing orthographic concepts. *Research in the Teaching of English, 11*, 133–148.

Bereiter, C., & Scardamalia, M. (1987). *The psychology of written composition.* Hillsdale, NJ: Erlbaum.

Berkenkotter, C. (1991). Paradigm debates, turf wars, and the conduct of sociocognitive inquiry in composition. *College Composition and Communication, 42*, 151–169.

Bissex, G. L. (1980). *Gnys at wrk: A child learns to write and read.* Cambridge, MA: Harvard University Press.

Blazer, B. (1986). "I want to talk to you about writing": 5–year-old children speak. In B. Schieffelin & P. Gilmore (Eds.), *The acquisition of literacy: Ethnographic perspectives* (pp. 75–109). Norwood, NJ: Ablex.

Braddock, R., Lloyd-Jones, R., & Schoer, L. (1963). *Research in written composition.* Champaign, IL: National Council of Teachers of English.

Bradley, D. (2001). How beginning writers articulate and demonstrate their understanding of the act of writing. *Journal of the College Reading Association, 40,* 273–296.

Burns, T. (2001). Being "social": Expanding our view of social interaction in writing workshops. *Language Arts, 78,* 458–466.

Butler, S., & Cox, B. (1992). DISKcovery: Writing with a computer in grade one: A study in collaboration. *Language Arts, 69,* 633–640.

Calkins, L. (1986). *The art of teaching writing.* Portsmouth, NH: Heinemann.

Calkins, L. (1994). *The art of teaching writing* (Rev. ed.). Portsmouth, NH: Heinemann.

Cameron, C., Edmunds, G., Wigmore, B., Hunt, A., & Linton, M. (1997). Children's revision of textual flaws. *International Journal of Behavioral Development, 20,* 667–681.

Cameron, C., Hunt, A., & Linton, M. (1996). Written expression as reconceptualization: Children write in social time. *Educational Psychology Review, 8,* 125–150.

Cazden, C., Cordeiro, P., & Giacobbe, M. (1985). Spontaneous and scientific concepts: Young children's learning of punctuation. In G. Wells & J. Nicholls (Eds.), *Language and learning: An interactional perspective* (pp. 107–164). London: Falmer Press.

Chang, L., & Osguthorpe, R. (1990). The effects of computerized picture-word processing on kinergartners' language development. *Journal of Research in Childhood Education, 5,* 73–84.

Chapman, M. (1994a). The emergence of genres: Some findings from an examination of first grade writing. *Written Communication, 11,* 348–380.

Chapman, M. L. (1994b). Literacy learning in a primary multi-age classroom: Some findings from an investigation of peer writing events. In C. Kinzer & D. Leu (Eds.), *Multidimensional aspects of literacy research, theory, and practice: Forty-third yearbook of The National Reading Conference* (pp. 550–559). Chicago: National Reading Conference, Inc.

Chapman, M. L. (1995). The sociocognitive construction of written genres in first grade. *Research in the Teaching of English, 29,* 164–192.

Chapman, M. L. (1996). More than spelling: Widening the lens on emergent writing. *Reading Horizons, 36,* 317–339.

Chapman, M. L. (1999). Situated, social, active: Rewriting genre in the elementary classroom. *Written Communication, 16,* 469–490.

Chapman, M. (2002). A longitudinal case study of curriculum genres, K–3. *Canadian Journal of Education, 27,* 41–64.

Chomsky, C. (1971). Invented spelling in the open classroom. *Word, 27,* 499–518.

Cioffi, G. (1984). Observing composing behaviors of primary-aged children: The interaction of oral and written language. In R. Beach & L. Bridwell (Eds.), *New directions in composition research* (pp. 171–190). New York: Guildford Press.

Clay, M. M. (1975). *What did I write?* Auckland: Heinemann.

Cochran-Smith, M. (1991). Word processing and writing in elementary classrooms: A critical review of the literature. *Review of Educational Research, 61,* 107–155.

Cochran-Smith, M., Paris, C., & Kahn, J. (1991). *Learning to write differently: Beginning writers and word processing.* Norwood, NJ: Ablex.

Cole, M. (1996). *Cultural psychology: A once and future discipline.* Cambridge, MA: Harvard University Press.

Comstock, M. (1992). Poetry and process: The reading/writing connection. *Language Arts, 69,* 261–267.

Connell, E., & DiStefano, P. (1991). A community of learners selecting and developing writing topics. In J. Zutell & S. McCormick (Eds.), *Learner factors/teacher factors: Issues in literacy research and instruction: Fortieth yearbook of the National Reading Conference* (pp. 305–312). Chicago: National Reading Conference.

Cox, B. (1994). Young children's regulatory talk: Evidence of emerging metacognitive control over literacy products and processes. In R. Ruddell & H. Singer (Eds.), *Theoretical models and processes of reading* (4th ed.; pp. 733–756). Newark, DE: International Reading Association.

Cox, B., Shanahan, T., & Sulzby, E. (1990). Good and poor elementary readers' use of cohesion in writing. *Reading Research Quarterly, 25,* 47–65.

Csikszentmihalyi, M. (1975). *Beyond boredom and anxiety.* San Francisco: Jossey-Bass.

Dahl, K. (1988). Peer conferences as social contexts for learning about revision. In J. Readance & S. Baldwin (Eds.), *Dialogues in literacy research: Thirty-seventh yearbook of the National Reading Conference* (pp. 307–315). Chicago: National Reading Conference.

Dahl, K., & Farnan, N. (1998). *Children's writing: Perspectives from research.* Newark, DE/Chicago: International Reading Association/National Reading Conference.

Dahl, K., & Freppon, P. (1995). A comparison of innercity children's interpretations of reading and writing instruction in the early grades in skills-based and whole language classrooms. *Reading Research Quarterly, 30,* 50–74.

Daiute, C. (1986). Physical and cognitive factors in revising: Insights from studies with computers.

Research in the Teaching of English, 20, 141–159.

Daiute, C. (1998). Points of view in children's writing. *Language Arts, 75,* 138–149.

Daiute, C., & Morse, F. (1993). Access to knowledge and expression: Multimedia writing tools for children with diverse needs and strengths. *Journal of Special Education Technology, 12,* 1–35.

DeFord, D. (1980). Young children and their writing. *Theory Into Practice, 29,* 157–162.

Dickinson, D. (1986). Cooperation, collaboration, and a computer: Integrating a computer into a first-second grade writing program. *Research in the Teaching of English, 20,* 357–378.

Donovan, C. (1996). First graders' impressions of genre-specific elements in writing narrative and expository texts. In C. Kinzer, K. Hinchman, & D. Leu (Eds.), *Literacies for the 21st century: Research and practice: Forty-fifth yearbook of the National Reading Conference* (pp. 183–194). Chicago: National Reading Conference.

Donovan, C. (2001). Children's development and control of written story and informational genres: Insights from one elementary school. *Research in the Teaching of English, 35,* 394–447.

Donovan, C., & Smolkin, L. (2002). Children's genre knowledge: An examination of K–5 students' performance on multiple tasks providing differing levels of scaffolding. *Reading Research Quarterly, 37,* 428–465.

Dressel, J. (1990). The effects of listening to and discussing different qualities of children's literature on the narrative writing of fifth graders. *Research in the Teaching of English, 24,* 397–414.

Dyson, A. H. (1984). Reading, writing, and language: Young children solving the written language puzzle. In J. M. Jensen (Ed.), *Composing and comprehending* (pp. 165–175). Urbana, IL: ERIC Clearinghouse on Reading and Communication Skills and NCRE.

Dyson, A. H. (1986a). The imaginary worlds of childhood: A multimedia presentation. *Language Arts, 63,* 799–808.

Dyson, A. H. (1986b). Transitions and tensions: Interrelationships between the drawing, talking, and dictating of young children. *Research in the Teaching of English, 20,* 379–409.

Dyson, A. H. (1989). *Multiple worlds of child writers: Friends learning to write.* New York: Teachers College Press.

Dyson, A. H. (1992). The case of the singing scientist: A performance perspective on the "stages" of school literacy. *Written Communication, 9,* 3–47.

Dyson, A. H. (1993). *The social worlds of children learning to write in an urban primary school.* New York: Teachers College Press.

Dyson, A. H. (1995). Writing children: Reinventing the development of childhood literacy. *Written Communication, 12,* 4–46.

Dyson, A. H. (1997). *Writing superheroes: Contemporary childhood, popular culture, and classroom literacy.* New York: Teachers College Press.

Dyson, A. H. (1999). Coach Bombay's kids learn to write: Children's appropriation of media material for school literacy. *Research in the Teaching of English, 33,* 367–402.

Dyson, A. H. (2001). Donkey Kong in Little Bear country: A first grader's composing development in the media spotlight. *Elementary School Journal, 101,* 417–433.

Eckoff, B. (1983). How reading affects children's writing. *Language Arts, 60,* 607–616.

Edelsky, C. (1983). Segmentation and punctuation: Developmental data from young writers in a bilingual program. *Research in the Teaching of English, 17,* 135–156.

Englert, C., Raphael, T., Anderson, L., Anthony, H., & Stevens, D. (1991). Making strategies and self-talk visible: Writing instruction in regular and special education classrooms. *American Educational Research Journal, 28,* 337–372.

Ferreiro, E. (1990). Literacy development: Psychogenesis. In Y. Goodman (Ed.), *How children construct literacy: Piagetian perspectives* (pp. 12–25). Newark, DE: International Reading Association.

Fisher, E. (1994). Joint composition at the computer: Learning to talk about writing. *Computers and Composition, 11,* 251–262.

Fitzgerald, J. (1987). Research on revision in writing. *Review of Educational Research, 57,* 481–506.

Fitzgerald, J., & Stamm, C. (1992). Variation in writing conference influence on revision: Two case studies. *Journal of Reading Behavior, 24,* 21–50.

Fitzgerald, J., & Teasley, A. (1986). Effects of instruction in narrative structure on children's writing. *Journal of Educational Psychology, 78,* 424–432.

Fleming, S. (1995). Whose stories are validated? *Language Arts, 72,* 590–596.

Flood, J., & Lapp, D. (2000). Teaching writing in urban schools: Cognitive processes, curriculum resources, and the missing links—management and grouping. In R. Indrisano & J. Squire (Eds.), *Perspectives on writing: Research, theory, and practice* (pp. 233–250). Newark, DE: International Reading Association.

Flowes, L., Stein, V., Ackerman, J., Kantz, M. J., McCormick, K., & Peck, W. C. (1990). *Reading-to-write: Exploring a cognitive and social process.* New York: Oxford University Press.

Fox, C., Martin, W., & Evershed, J. (1984). Genres, anti-genres, and the art of subversion in children's stories and play. *English in Education, 28* (2), 15–22.

Frank, L. (1992). Writing to be read: Young writers' ability to demonstrate audience awareness when evaluated by their readers. *Research in the Teaching of English, 26,* 277–298.

Freedman, A., & Medway, P. (1994). Introduction: New views of genre and their implications for education. In A. Freedman & P. Medway (Eds.), *Learning and teaching genre* (pp. 1–22). Portsmouth, NH: Heinemann.

Gee, J. (1996). *Social linguistics and literacies: Ideology in discourses* (2nd ed.). London: Taylor & Francis.

Gee, J. (1999). The future of the social turn: Social minds and the new capitalism. *Research on Language and Social Interaction, 32,* 261–268.

Gentry, J. (1982). An analysis of developmental spelling in "GNYS AT WRK". *The Reading Teacher, 36,* 373–377.

Goldstein, A., & Carr, P. (1996). *Can students benefit from process writing?* (NAEP Facts No. 1). Washington, DC: Department of Education, National Center for Education Statistics.

Gover, M., & Englert, C. (1998). *Orchestrating the thought and learning of struggling writers* (Report No. 1-002). Ann Arbor, MI: Center for the Improvement of Early Reading Achievement.

Gradwohl, J., & Schumacher, G. (1989). The relationship between content knowledge and topic choice in writing. *Written Communication, 6,* 181–195.

Graham, S., & Harris, K. R. (1989). Components analysis of cognitive strategy instruction: Effects on learning disabled students' compositions and self-efficacy. *Journal of Educational Psychology, 81,* 353–361.

Graham, S., & Harris, K. (1993). Self-regulated strategy development: Helping students with learning problems develop as writers. *Elementary School Journal, 94,* 169–181.

Graham, S., & Harris, K. (2000). The role of self-regulation and transcription skills in writing and writing development. *Educational Psychologist, 35,* 3–12.

Graham, S., MacArthur, C., & Schwartz, S. (1995). The effects of goal setting and procedural facilitation on the revising behavior and writing performance of students with writing and learning

problems. *Journal of Educational Psychology, 87,* 230–240.

Graham, S., MacArthur, C., Schwartz, S., & Page-Voth, V. (1992). Improving the compositions of students with learning disabilities using a strategy involving product and process goal setting. *Exceptional Children, 58,* 322–334.

Graves, D. E. (1981). *A case study observing the development of primary children's composing, spelling, and motor behaviors during the writing process* (Final report, NIE Grant No. G-78-0174. ED 218-653). Durham: University of New Hampshire.

Graves, D. H. (1983). *Writing: Teachers and children at work.* Portsmouth, NH: Heinemann.

Gray-Schlegel, M., & Gray-Schlegel, T. (1995–1996). An investigation of gender stereotypes as revealed through children's creative writing. *Reading Research and Instruction, 35,* 160–170.

Gunnarsson, B. (1997). The writing process from a sociolinguistic viewpoint. *Written Communication, 14,* 139–188.

Gutierrez, K. (1994). How talk, context, and script shape contexts for learning: A cross-case comparison of journal sharing. *Linguistics and Education, 5,* 335–365.

Haas, C. (1989). How the writing medium shapes the writing process: Effects of word processing on planning. *Research in the Teaching of English, 23,* 181–206.

Harste, J., Burke, C., & Woodward, V. (1983). *The young child as writer-reader, and informant* (Final Report, NIE-G-80-0121). Bloomington: Indiana University.

Harste, J., Woodward, V., & Burke, C. (1984a). Examining our assumptions: A transactional view of literacy and learning. *Research in the Teaching of English, 18,* 84–108.

Harste, J., Woodward, V., & Burke, C. (1984b). *Language stories and literacy lessons.* Portsmouth, NH: Heinemann.

Hayes, J. (2000). A new framework for understanding cognition and affect in writing. In R. Indrisano & J. Squire (Eds.), *Perspectives on writing: Research, theory, and practice* (pp. 6–44). Newark, DE: International Reading Association.

Hayes, J. R., & Flower, L. (1980). Writing as problem solving. *Visible Language, 14,* 388–399.

Heath, S. B. (1983). *Ways with words: Language, life, and work in communities and classrooms.* New York: Cambridge University Press.

Hiebert, E. (1994). Becoming literate through authentic tasks: Evidence and adaptations. In R. Ruddell, M. Ruddell, & H. Singer (Eds.), *Theoretical models and processes of reading* (pp. 391–413). Newark, DE: International Reading Association.

Hildreth, G. (1936). Developmental sequences in name writing. *Child Development, 7*, 291–303.

Hillocks, G., Jr. (1986). *Research on written composition: New directions for teaching.* Urbana, IL: National Conference on Research in English/ERIC Clearinghouse on Reading and Communication Skills.

Hipple, M. (1985). Journal writing in kindergarten. *Language Arts, 62*, 255–260.

Holdich, C. E., & Chung, P. W. (2003). A "computer tutor" to assist children develop their narrative writing skills: Conferencing with HARRY. *International Journal of Human-Computer Studies, 59*, 631–669.

Hoot, J., & Silvern, S. (1988). *Writing with computers in the early grades.* New York: Teachers College Press.

Jones, I. (1994). The effects of a word processor on the written composition of second-grade pupils. *Computers in the Schools, 11*, 43–55.

Jones, I., & Pellegrini, A. (1996). The effects of social relationships, writing media, and microgenetic development of first-grade students' written narratives. *American Educational Research Journal, 33*, 691–718.

Kamberelis, G. (1999). Genre development and learning: Children writing stories, science reports, and poems. *Research in the Teaching of English, 33*, 403–460.

Kamberelis, G., & Bovino, T. (1999). Cultural artifacts as scaffolds for genre development. *Reading Research Quarterly, 34*, 138–170.

Kamler, B. (1992). The social construction of free topic choice in the process writing classroom. *Australian Journal of Language and Literacy, 15*, 105–122.

Kamler, B. (1993). Constructing gender in the process writing classroom. *Language Arts, 70*, 95–103.

Kos, R., & Maslowski, C. (2001). Second graders' perceptions of what is important in writing. *The Elementary School Journal, 101*, 567–584.

Kumpulainen, K. (1994). Collaborative writing with computers and children's talk: A cross-cultural study. *Computers and Composition, 11*, 262–273.

Labbo, L. D. (1996). A semiotic analysis of young children's symbol making in a classroom computer center. *Reading Research Quarterly, 31*, 356–385.

Labbo, L. D., & Kuhn, M. (1998). Electronic symbol making: Young children's computer-related emerging concepts about literacy. In D. Reinking,

M. C. McKenna, L. D. Labbo, & R. Kieffer (Eds.), *Handbook of literacy and technology: Transformations in a post-typographic world* (pp. 79–91). Mahwah, NJ: Erlbaum.

Labbo, L. D., Reinking, D., & Mckenna, M. C. (1995). Incorporating the computer into kindergarten: A case study. In K. Hinchman, D. Leu, & C. Kinzer (Eds.), *Perspectives on literacy research and practice: Forty-fourth yearbook of the National Reading Conference.* Chicago: National Reading Conference.

Langer, J. (1986). *Children reading and writing: Structures and strategies.* Norwood, NJ: Ablex.

Legrun, A. (1932). How and what kindergarten pupils "write." *Zeitschrift fuer Paedagogische Psychologie und Experimentelle Paedadogik, 33*, 322–331.

Lensmire, T. (2000). *Powerful writing: Responsible teaching.* New York: Teachers College Press.

Leont'ev, A. N. (1981). *Problems of the development of mind.* Moscow: Progress Publishers.

Lomangino, A., Nicholson, J., & Sulzby, E. (1999). *The nature of children's interactions* (Report No. 2–005). Ann Arbor, MI: Center for Improving Early Reading Achievement. Available at http://www.ciera.org/library/reports/inquiry-2/index.html.

Luria, A. R. (1929/1977–1978). The development of writing in the child. *Soviet Psychology, 16*, 65–113.

McGillivray, L. (1994). Tacit shared understandings of a first grade writing community. *Journal of Reading Behavior, 26*, 245–266.

McAuliffe, S. (1994). Toward understanding one another: Second graders' use of gendered language and story styles. *The Reading Teacher, 47*, 302–310.

McBee, D. (1994). *The effect of technology on emergent writing* (Report No. 143. ERIC ED 372390).

McCarthey, S. (1994). Authors, text, and talk: The internalization of dialogue from social interactions during writing. *Reading Research Quarterly, 29*, 200–231.

McCarthey, S. (2001). Identity construction in elementary readers and writers. *Reading Research Quarterly, 36*, 122–151.

McCutchen, D. (1988). Functional automaticity in children's writing: A problem of metacognitive control. *Written Communication, 5*, 306–324.

McCutchen, D. (1995). Cognitive processes in children's writing: Developmental and individual differences. *Issues in Education: Contributions from Educational Psychology, 1*, 123–160.

McGinley, W. J., & Kamberelis, G. (1992). Transformative functions of children's writing. *Language Arts, 69*, 330–338.

McIntyre, E., & Freppon, P. (1994). A comparison of children's development of alphabetic knowledge in a skills-based and a whole-language classroom. *Research in the Teaching of English, 28,* 391–418.

Meichenbaum, D., & Biemiller, A. (1992). In search of student expertise in the classroom: A metacognitive analysis. In M. Pressley, K. Harris, & J. Guthrie (Eds.), *Promoting academic competence and literacy in school* (pp. 3–56). San Diego, CA: Academic Press.

Miller, L., & Olson, J. (1994). Putting the computer in its place: A study of teaching with technology. *Journal of Curriculum Studies, 26,* 121–141.

Miller, S., & Meece, J. (1999). Third graders' motivational preferences for reading and writing tasks. *Elementary School Journal, 100,* 19–35.

Miyashita, K. (1994). Effects of computer use on attitudes among first- and second-grade children. *Journal of Computing in Childhood Education, 5,* 73–82.

Needels, M., & Knapp, M. (1994). Teaching writing to children who are underserved. *Journal of Educational Psychology, 86,* 339–349.

Neuman, S., & Roskos, K. (1989). Preschoolers' conceptions of literacy as reflected in their spontaneous play. In K. McCormick & J. Zutell (Eds.), *Cognitive and social perspectives for literacy research and instruction: Thirty-eighth yearbook of the National Reading Conference* (pp. 87–94). Chicago: National Reading Conference.

Neuman, S., & Roskos, K. (1990). The influence of literacy-enriched play settings on preschoolers' engagement with written language. In J. Zutell & S. McCormick (Eds.), *Literacy theory and research: Analyses from multiple paradigms. Thirty-ninth yearbook of the National Reading Conference* (pp. 179–187). Chicago: National Reading Conference.

The New London Group. (1996). A pedagogy of multiliteracies: Designing social futures. *Harvard Educational Review, 66*(1), 60–92.

Newkirk, T. (1987). The non-narrative writing of young children. *Research in the Teaching of English, 21,* 121–144.

Nichols, L. (1996). Pencil and paper vs. word-processing: A comprehensive study of creative writing in the elementary school. *Journal of Research on Computing in Education, 29,* 159–166.

Nicholson, J., Gelpi, A., Young, S., & Sulzby, E. (1998). Influences of gender and open-ended software on first graders' collaborative composing activities on computers. *Journal of Computing in Childhood Education, 9,* 3–42.

Nistler, R. (1990). A descriptive analysis of good readers' and writers' concepts of authorship at grades one, three and five. In J. Zutell & S. McCormick (Eds.), *Literacy theory and research: Analyses from multiple paradigms: Thirty-ninth yearbook of the National Reading Conference* (pp. 359–368). Chicago: National Reading Conference.

Nixon, J., & Topping, K. (2001). Emergent writing: The impact of structured peer interaction. *Educational Psychology Review, 21,* 41–59.

Nuvoli, G. (2000). Revision of texts with word-processing. *Psychological Reports, 78,* 1139–1146.

Olson, V. (1990). The revising processes of sixth-grade writers with and without peer feedback. *Journal of Educational Research, 84,* 84–106.

Owston, R., & Wideman, H. (1997). Word processors and children's writing in high-computer-access settings. *Journal of Research on Computing in Education, 30,* 202–221.

Pappas, C. (1993). Is narrative "primary"? Some insights from kindergarteners' pretend reading of stories and information books. *Journal of Reading Behavior, 25,* 97–129.

Pappas, C., & Pettegrew, B. (1998). The role of genre in the psycholinguistic guessing game of reading. *Language Arts, 75,* 36–44.

Perez, S. (2001). Revising during writing in a second grade classroom. *Educational Research Quarterly, 25,* 27–33.

Perry, N. (1998). Young children's self-regulated learning and contexts that support it. *Journal of Educational Psychology, 90,* 715–729.

Peterson, S. (2000). Fourth, sixth, and eighth graders' preferred writing topics and identification of gender markers in stories. *The Elementary School Journal, 101,* 79–100.

Phenix, J., & Hannan, E. (1984). Word processing in the grade one classroom. *Language Arts, 61,* 804–812.

Phinney, M. (1998). Children "writing themselves": A glimpse at the underbelly. *Language Arts, 75,* 19–27.

Piaget, J. (1985). *The equilibration of cognitive structures: The central problem of intellectual development* (T. Brown & K. Thampy, Trans.). Chicago: University of Chicago Press.

Power, B. P. (1991). Pop ups: The rise and fall of one convention in a first grade writing workshop. *Journal of Research in Childhood Education, 6,* 54–66.

Purcell-Gates, V., Duke, N., Hall, L., & Tower, C. (2003, December 3–6). *Explicit explanation of genre within authentic literacy activities in science: Does it facilitate development and achievement?* Paper presented at the 53rd annual meeting of the National Reading Conference, Scottsdale, AZ.

Rasinski, T., & DeFord, D. (1986). Students and their writing: Perceptions, motivations, and behaviors. In J. Niles & R. Lalik (Eds.), *Solving problems in literacy: Learners, teachers, and researchers: Thirty-fifth yearbook of the National Reading Conference* (pp. 294–299). Chicago: The National Reading Conference.

Read, C. (1971). Preschool children's knowledge of English phonology. *Harvard Educational Review, 41*, 1–34.

Read, C. (1975). *Children's categorizations of speech sounds in English*. Urbana, IL: National Council of Teachers of English.

Read, S. (2001). "Kid mice hunt for their selfs": First and second graders writing research. *Language Arts, 78*, 333–342.

Roberts, B. (1992). The evolution of the young child's concept of word as a unit of spoken and written language. *Reading Research Quarterly, 30*, 96–109.

Rowe, D. (1994). *Preschoolers as authors: Literacy learning in the social world of the preschool*. Cresskill, NH: Hampton Press.

Rowe, D. (2000, December 5–8). *Power, identity, and instructional stance in the writers' workshop: Sociocultural perspectives on the learning and teaching of writing in elementary classrooms*. Paper presented at the 51st annual meeting of the National Reading Conference, Scottsdale, AZ.

Russell, D. (1997). Rethinking genre in school and society. *Written Communication, 14*, 504–554.

Ryder, P., Vander Lei, E., & Roen, D. (1999). Audience considerations for evaluating writing. In C. Cooper & L. Odell (Eds.), *Evaluating writing* (pp. 93–113). Urbana, IL: National Council of Teachers of English.

Sadoski, M., Willson, V., & Norton, D. (1997). The relative contributions of research-based composition activities to writing improvement in the lower and middle grades. *Research in the Teaching of English, 31*, 120–150.

Scardamalia, M., & Bereiter, C. (1986). Research on written composition. In M. Wittrock (Ed.), *Handbook of research on teaching* (3rd ed.; pp. 778–803). New York: Macmillan.

Schrader, C. (1989). Written language use within the context of young children's symbolic play. *Early Childhood Research Quarterly, 4*, 225–244.

Schrader, C. (1990). *The word processor as a tool for developing young writers*. (ERIC Document Reproduction Service No. ED321276).

Schunk, D., & Zimmerman, B. (1997). Developing self-efficacious readers and writers: The role of social and self-regulatory processes. In J. Guthrie & A. Wigfield (Eds.), *Reading engagement: Motivating readers through integrated instruction* (pp. 34–50). Newark, DE: International Reading Association.

Schutz, R. (1997). Additional influences on response certitude and feedback requests. *Contemporary Educational Psychology, 18*, 427–441.

Scribner, S., & Cole, M. (1981). *The psychology of literacy*. Cambridge: Cambridge University Press.

Seawel, L., Smaldino, S., Steele, J., & Lewis, J. (1994). A descriptive study comparing computer-based word processing. *Journal of Computing in Childhood Education, 5*, 43–59.

Sipe, L. (1993). Using transformations of transitional stories: Making the reading-writing connection. *The Reading Teacher, 47*, 18–27.

Sipe, L. (1998). Transitions to the conventional: An examination of a first grader's composing process. *Journal of Literacy Research, 30*, 357–388.

Skinner, E. A., Wellborn, J. G., & Connell, J. P. (1990). What it takes to do well in school and whether I've got it: A process model of perceived control and children's engagement and achievement in school. *Journal of Educational Psychology, 82*, 22–32.

Smagorinsky, P. (1998). Thinking and speech and protocol analysis. *Mind, Culture & Activity, 5*, 157–178.

Snyder, I. (1993). Writing with word processors: A research review. *Educational Research, 35*, 49–68.

Spandel, V., & Stiggins, R. (1990). *Creating writers: Linking assessment and writing instruction*. New York: Longman.

Spiegel, D. L., & Fitzgerald, J. (1990). Textual cohesion and coherence in children's writing. *Research in the Teaching of English, 24*, 48–66.

Stein, N. (1986). Knowledge and process in the acquisition of writing skills. In E. Rothkopf (Ed.), *Review of research in education* (Vol. 13, pp. 225–258). Washington, DC: American Educational Research Association.

Straub, R. (1996). The concept of control in teacher response: Defining the varieties of "directive" and "facilitative" commentary. *College Composition and Communication, 47*, 223–251.

Straub, R. (1997). Students' reactions to teacher comments: An exploratory study. *Research in the Teaching of English, 31*, 91–119.

Sulzby, E. (1985). Kindergarteners as writers and readers. In M. Farr (Ed.), *Advances in writing research: Vol. 1. Children's early writing development* (pp. 127–199). Norwood, NJ: Ablex.

Sulzby, E. (1986). Writing and reading: Signs of oral and written language organization in the young child. In W. Teale & E. Sulzby (Eds.), *Emergent literacy: Writing and reading* (pp. 50–89). Norwood, NJ: Ablex.

Swafford, J., Akrofi, A., Rogers, J., & Alexander, C. (1999). Primary-grade students' interactions with one another as they read and write informational texts. In T. Shanahan & F. Rodriguez-Brown (Eds.), *48th yearbook of the National Reading Conference* (pp. 294–305). Chicago: National Reading Conference.

Taylor, D. (1983). *Family literacy.* Portsmouth, NH: Heinemann.

Teale, W., & Sulzby, E. (1986). Emergent literacy as a perspective for examining how young children become writers and readers. In W. Teale & E. Sulzby (Eds.), *Emergent literacy: Writing and reading* (pp. vii–xxv). Norwood, NJ: Ablex.

Titscher, S., Meyer, M., Wodak, R., & Vetter, E. (2000). *Methods of text and discourse analysis.* Thousand Oaks, CA: Sage.

Trepanier-Street, M., Romatowski, J. (1991). Achieving sex equity goals: Implications from creative writing research. *Educational Horizons, 70,* 34–40.

Troyer, C. (1991). From emergent literacy to emergent pedagogy: Learning from children learning together. In J. Zutell & K. McCormick (Eds.), *Learner factors/teacher factors: Issues in literacy research and instruction: Fortieth yearbook of the National Reading Conference* (pp. 119–126). Chicago: National Reading Conference.

Turner, J. (1993). Situated motivation in literacy instruction. *Reading Research Quarterly, 28,* 288–289.

Turner, J., & Paris, S. (1995). How literacy tasks influence children's motivation for literacy. *The Reading Teacher, 48,* 662–673.

Vincent, J. (2000). The role of visually rich technology in facilitating children's writing. *Journal of Computer Assisted Learning, 17,* 242–250.

Vukelich, C. (1986). The relationship between peer questions and seven-year-olds' text revisions. In J. Niles & R. Lalik (Eds.), *Solving problems in literacy: Learners, teachers, and researchers:*

Thirty-fifth yearbook of the National Reading Conference (pp. 300–305). Chicago: National Reading Conference.

Vukelich, C. (1993). Play: A context for exploring the functions, features, and meaning of writing with peers. *Language Arts, 70,* 386–392.

Vygotsky, L. (1962). *Thought and language.* Cambridge, MA: MIT Press. (Original work published in 1934)

Vygotsky, L. (1978). *Mind in society: The development of higher psychological processes* (M. Cole, V. John-Steiner, S. Scribner, & E. Souberman, Trans.). Cambridge, MA: Harvard University Press.

Walker, C., & Allen, D. (1997). Should we travel by plane, car, train, or bus? Teacher/child collaborating in developing a thematic literacy center. *The Reading Teacher, 50,* 524–529.

Wertsch, J. V. (Ed.). (1985). *Culture, communication and cognition.* Cambridge, UK: Cambridge University Press.

Wiseman, A. (2003). Collaboration, initiation, and rejection: The social construction of stories in a kindergarten class. *The Reading Teacher, 56,* 802–810.

Wollman-Bonilla, J. (2000). Teaching science writing to first graders: Genre learning and recontextualization. *Research in the Teaching of English, 35,* 35–65.

Wollman-Bonilla, J. (2001). Can first-grade writers demonstrate audience awareness? *Reading Research Quarterly, 36,* 184–201.

Wollman-Bonilla, J., & Werchadlo, B. (1999). Teacher and peer roles in scaffolding first graders' responses to literature. *The Reading Teacher, 52,* 598–611.

Yau, M. (1991). *Potential and actual effects of word processing on students' creative writing processes* (Report No. 198). Toronto: Toronto Board of Education.

Zimmerman, B., & Riesemberg, R. (1997). Becoming a self-regulated writer: A social cognitive perspective. *Contemporary Educational Psychology, 22,* 73–101.

CHAPTER 3

Middle and High School Composition

George Hillocks, Jr.

RESEARCH PRODUCED on writing in the secondary school from 1984 to 2003 has changed in many ways from that produced in the decades of 1963 to 1983. Between 1963 and 1983 many studies focused on the syntax of student writing, its changes across age levels and under varying conditions, its relation to quality of writing, and the impact of certain kinds of instruction (e.g., sentence combining) on the syntax of student writing. Many quasi-experimental studies focused on the impact of various foci and modes of instruction (see Hillocks, 1986) on student writing. Some of these were carefully designed, meeting fairly rigorous criteria for useful research, but many more were not. Many studies focused on the general processes of writing. Others focused on cognitive processes involved in planning, drafting, and revising.

The theoretical bases for these studies varied. Because of the many studies of syntax, the names of various linguists and applied linguistic researchers appeared, Chomsky being the most frequent. Other studies referred to the sources of an instructional idea being investigated and to Dewey and Piaget.

The quantity of research in writing appears to have reached a pinnacle by the early 1980s, if we judge by numbers of studies published in *Research in the Teaching of English* (*RTE*), but to have diminished thereafter. In 1984 *RTE* published 16 articles, 13 (81%) of which dealt with writing. In 1999, 15 years later, it published 13 articles, of which two (15%) focused on composition. Research interests also have shifted. Interest in the syntactic features of writing as a primary focus has all but disappeared. Langer's (1986) study of writing development uses measures of syntactic complexity as one of many measures that include the complexity of reasoning, the elaboration of responses, the degree of self-awareness, and so forth. Quasi-experimental studies have diminished sharply. Studies of cognitive processes are fewer, although notable publications are of important value, for example, Bereiter and Scardamalia (1987) and Hayes (2000). In place of such studies at the secondary level, studies look in detail at response to student writing, teacher–student writing conferences, peer group conferences, the idea of role in class discussion, how teachers acquire knowledge of writing, the education of writing teachers, the concept of composing across disciplines, and many other dimensions of teaching and learning that were not investigated earlier.

Further, many more studies in recent decades use qualitative or ethnographic methods that are able to provide levels of detail not possible in earlier research. Quantitative studies have not disappeared, but they no longer dominate studies of writing as they once did. The growth of qualitative research in writing appears to go hand in hand with researchers', if not teachers', perceptions of writing as socially situated and with the theorists they use to elucidate their ideas, primarily Vygotsky (1978) and Bakhtin (1981). Indeed, these two theorists seem to have had enormous impact on some of the most important studies of literacy, for example, Nystrand (1997), Langer (2001), Johnson, Smagorinsky, Thompson, and Fry (2003), and Lee and Smagorinsky (2000). The developmental theory of Piaget, which was so important 20 years before, has all but vanished from the pages of research. The disappearance indicates a profound shift in thinking about writing. In the 1960s and 1970s many researchers and theorists, adopting the theories of Piaget and others, assumed that "if a child's mental functions (intellectual operations) have not matured to the extent that he is capable of learning a particular subject, then no instruction will prove useful" (Vygotsky, 1978, p. 80). But Vygotsky makes a strong case that "learning results in mental development" and makes development possible (p. 90). He argues that learning takes place in the "zone of proximal development," defined as "the distance between the actual developmental level as determined by independent problem-solving and the level of potential development as determined through problem-solving under adult guidance or in collaboration with more capable peers" (p. 86). The trick, then, becomes not one of waiting for the learner to develop and for learning to appear naturally, but of finding ways to promote learning in the zone of what the student is capable of doing with help so that development may take place.

The review that follows is selective because of the difficulty of commenting thoughtfully on a great deal of research in the pages allotted. In an attempt to determine what major ideas the whole of research offers for teaching writing in secondary schools, this chapter examines research on assessment, teaching of writing in schools, approaches to teaching, and finally, education of teachers of writing.

WRITING ASSESSMENT

In the 2 decades from 1963 to 1983, researchers were dealing with the problem of how to judge writing fairly so that a writer's score would not be dependent on the reader. In some early studies, researchers found that most papers scored by a number of different raters received every possible rating. Because the raters had different backgrounds, they had different responses to student writing. Some seemed to care most about mechanics, some about organization, others about style or content (Diedrich, 1974). It quickly became very clear that if assessors of writing were to have agreement, they would have at least to share the same criteria for judging writing. By the late 1970s several different kinds of scales were adopted for assigning ratings to student writing.

Three kinds of scales have been used with high rater agreement. Some researchers see the drive for agreement as problematic in that it may obscure qualities that researchers and teachers need to attend to (Broad, 2000; Huot, 1990). One kind of scale is called *holistic* because it represents the quality of a piece of writing as whole. It usually is guided by a scoring rubric listing criteria for assigning scores for each level of quality. The National Assessment of Educational Progress (2002), for example, presents the following description of an excellent eighth-grade response to its narrative prompt: tells a clear story that is well developed and shaped with well-chosen details across the response; is well organized with strong transitions; sustains variety in sentence structure and exhibits good word choice; reduces errors in grammar, spelling, and punctuation so that they do not interfere with understanding. The description is quite general. It does not, for example, explain what counts as "well developed and shaped with well-chosen details." But ordinarily, the descriptions are accompanied by compositions that exemplify each level of competence.

White (1985) argues that holistic ratings have the virtue of representing the piece as a whole as opposed to analyzing the parts in a reductionist way, and that such scoring has "satisfied reasonable demands for both economy and reliability and ha[s] led the way to restoring the role of writing in testing" (p. 27) by allowing raters to avoid the reductionism of multiple choice tests. On the other hand, he points out that such scoring can only rank order the writing in a given test, relative to the test and the context in which it was administered. It provides little specific information about the characteristics of a particular piece of writing.

More-specific information can be provided by *primary trait* scales. White argues that holistic scales are closely allied to primary trait scales, the difference being that the primary trait scales define the criteria more explicitly in terms of whatever dimensions the assessor wishes to examine. In fact, White states that the two are "conceptually the same" (p. 142). However, a primary trait scale allows for the consideration of particular traits rather than an overall impression. For example, it might allow scoring of the use of specific imagery in narrative writing and exclude attention to mechanics, sentence structure, and spelling and other matters not relevant to specific imagery. For teachers, primary trait scales have the advantage of allowing concentration on certain aspects of writing while ignoring others. As White points out, writing is so complicated that many teachers concentrate on the specific features of writing, one at a time, for example, the use of evidence in making a case or argument.

Most scales in state assessments are holistic. Few use primary trait scales. Some use what are called *analytic* scales. These differ from holistic and primary trait scales in asking raters to judge several important traits individually, usually on subscales. Illinois uses an analytic scale with ratings for organization, elaboration, mechanics, and so forth. The paper score is the sum of ratings on the subscales. Such scales tend to be more difficult to use and more time-consuming and therefore more expensive.

National Assessment of Educational Progress: Writing

For several decades now the major source of data indicating how well American students write has been the National Assessment of Educational Progress (NAEP), which tests writing every few years. It is a nationally representative sample survey of achievement in writing as determined by the extent to which students in grades 4, 8, and 12 across the nation reach certain standards of achievement set by the "national Assessment Governing Board as part of its statutory responsibilities. The achievement levels are a collective judgment of what students should know and be able to do for each grade tested" (NAEP, 2002, p. xi). These tests purport to examine achievement in three kinds of writing: narrative, informative, and persuasive. Students receive writing tasks that are supposed to generate responses in each of these types. The tasks vary by grade level, with eighth-grade tasks frequently classroom-related and twelfth-grade tasks moving beyond classroom and school. Eighth- and twelfth-grade tasks for informative and persuasive writing in 2002 provide some sort of material to which students are supposed to respond in 25 or 50 minutes. NAEP uses as many as 20 writing prompts at each grade level, with participating students responding to two of the 25-minute prompts or one of the 50-minute prompts. These prompts are used to test thousands of students. The 2002 NAEP writing report card is based on testing of "approximately 276, 000 students in 11,000 schools" (p. xii). Results presented in the report card are for the 25-minute samples.

For both the 1998 and 2002 NAEP assessments, the writing produced by students was scored by trained raters using a six-point scale (unsatisfactory, insufficient, uneven, sufficient, skillful, and excellent), with the criteria for judgment differing by grade level. "Acknowledging developmental differences" among the grades tested, "the scoring guides reflect higher performance expectations for students in higher grades" (NAEP, 2002, p. 6). For example, for a score of 4 at grade 12 in persuasive writing, the rubric states that a paper "takes a clear position and supports it with some pertinent reasons and/or examples; there is some development" (NAEP, 2002, p. 94). For a score of 4 (or sufficient), an eighth-grade paper "takes a clear position and supports it with some reasons and/or examples" (p. 91). That is, apparently, in eighth grade the reasons need not be pertinent and there need be no development. But if that is the case, it is unclear how nonpertinent reasons can provide any of the required support. Neither the 1998 or 2002 writing report card explains what counts as support or development.

The Nation's Report Card: Writing 2002 explains that the 1988 NAEP legislation created a National Assessment Governing Board whose specific directive was to develop a set of standards, "appropriate student achievement levels" (p. 7), for each area tested by NAEP. The standards were set by a "cross section of educators and interested citizens" who were asked to "judge what students should know and be able to do relative to a body of content reflected in the NAEP assessment framework for writing. This achievement level setting process was reviewed by an array of individuals that included policymakers, representatives of professional organizations, teachers, parents and other members of the general public" (p. 8).

The three levels of achievement are basic, proficient, and advanced, and are introduced as what students should be able to do at each level. NAEP qualifies those expectations "with the constraints" of the NAEP testing in mind. The only constraint named is the 25-minute period for writing. But the topics provide important constraints, especially in light of the fact that student writers have no resources to help them examine the problem stipulated for writing, for example, whether one should bother registering to vote. Given a topic about which one has little or nothing to say, and given 25 minutes to write about it, what exactly should a proficient writer in twelfth grade be able to do? How does anyone know? Here is what the Governing Board decided:

> Twelfth-grade students performing at the Proficient level should be able to produce an effectively organized and fully developed response within the time allowed that uses analytical, evaluative, or creative thinking. Their writing should include details that support and develop the main idea of the piece, and it should show that these students are able to use precise language and variety in sentence structure to engage the audience they are expected to address. (NAEP, 2002, p. 11)

The standard attempts to define the characteristics of writing that are likely to be judged as proficient. And it is no more precise in its meaning than are the scoring criteria. It calls for support and elaboration but does not provide a hint of what counts as support or elaboration. One result is that students need not meet very high standards of writing to be rated proficient.

Even with the weaknesses in scoring, it is possible to compare scores from 1998 to 2002 (although not from earlier years) and across various groups, geographical areas, states, and types of community, and by students' eligibility for reduced or free lunch program, ethnic group, and gender. NAEP (2002) indicates that both eighth and twelfth grades show gains in the percentage of students scoring at the level of proficient or above from 1998 to 2002, with eighth graders moving from 27% to 31% and twelfth graders moving from 22% to 24%. At the same time the percentage of twelfth graders scoring at basic or above dropped from 78% to 74%, a significant change. (Comparisons among grade levels cannot be made because the samples are scored independently.) The problem is that even though American students need not meet high standards for support, elaboration, or precise language, only about a quarter of them score at the level of proficient. The vast majority are not proficient according to the expert definition, even though the standards are vague and not very stringent.

IEA Studies of Written Composition

In 1959, the International Association for the Evaluation of Educational Achievement (IEA) was established, with various member countries, for the purpose of examining educational practices and policies, including the teaching and learning of various subject matters, such as mathematics, science, literature, and writing, in the member countries. The two major volumes from the study of written composition are Gorman, Purves, and Degenhart (1988) and Purves (1992).

Researchers developed a variety of writing tasks based on a model of school writing built to take "a balanced account of the three major factors that influence writing: (a) aims of writing including purpose and audience, (b) level of cognitive processing involved in writing, and (c) the content (topic) of writing" (Purves, 1992, p. 11). Another influence in the selection of tasks was an analysis of school curricula for writing. That is, tasks were limited to those that appeared to resonate with school curricula. Researchers selected nine tasks to be used with three different populations, elementary (ages 10–12), secondary (ages 15–17) and pre-university (ages 17–19). One task was common for all students in each subpopulation; several were rotated through each subpopulation, and a few were optional for each group. The population included 50 intact classes of students in the elementary population, 100 in the secondary, and 50 in the pre-university. The team collected three writing samples, each based on a different task, from each student. This sampling resulted in a total of 43,563 students and 116,597 pieces of writing. The samples were drawn from Chile, England, Finland, Germany, Hungary, Indonesia, Italy, the Netherlands, New Zealand, Nigeria, Sweden, Thailand, and the United States.

Given that diversity, it was necessary to devise a scale that could be viewed as common for all participating countries and particular to each. Researchers examined curriculum documents and discerned four shared factors for rating: content, organization, style, and tone. To these they added a general factor of overall impression. Scales were constructed using benchmark papers to illustrate poor, average, and excellent writing in terms of overall impression, content, organization, style, and tone. Each national center for the study submitted 12 pieces of writing for each topic, selected to represent the three quality ratings. These compositions were translated into English to serve as a means of validating each country's scale by an international jury. These processes and the resulting scales are explained in detail in Gorman, Purves, and Degenhart (1988). Purves (1992) attributes variation in the scales and in their use to differences in cultural norms. In addition, he reports that while "each system's scoring had its own integrity" (p. 129), the scoring from center to center was organized differently enough that "we cannot assert that the scores mean precisely the same thing across all situations" (p. 129), thereby rendering direct comparisons of achievement across countries impossible.

However, in a different study, Connor and Lauer (1988) rescored a sample of 150 persuasive compositions from three English-speaking countries, including the United States. Their results indicate that American writers scored significantly lower than their counterparts in England and New Zealand. Indeed, the U.S. students fell over a full standard deviation below the English and over two-thirds of a standard deviation below the New Zealanders.

State Writing Assessments

In the 1980s, in the United States, certain states began the direct testing of writing, using samples of writing rather than objective tests. At present nearly all 50 states require such writing exams. As of mid-2005, Illinois has abolished its writing test program. While it is arguable that this nationwide testing has had a major impact on the teaching of writing across the country, little research has been conducted to examine its effect. A search of ERIC turned up several hundred citations for documents concerning writing assessment in secondary schools. However, nearly all were either state documents such as reports to state legislative assemblies, NAEP documents, or unpublished pieces describing some aspect of a state assessment.

Hillocks (2002) studied the impact of state assessments intensively in five states—Illinois, Kentucky, New York, Oregon, and Texas—through examination of state documents, curricular materials, teacher handouts, and published materials to aid in achieving better scores. In each state, he conducted interviews with more than 60 teachers and more than 20 administrators or supervisors in six school districts (urban, suburban, small town, and rural). He found that nearly all of the state assessments require that students write on demand in a limited time period. A few states require portfolios of writing, but only in Kentucky is the portfolio score a major component in the formula for assessment of the individual school. In Vermont, the portfolio has been dropped. In Oregon, while the English language arts teachers are supposed to keep "work" portfolios for each student, the state does not use them to evaluate writing achievement.

The NAEP tests of writing involve three kinds of writing at three levels of schooling. It should be no surprise that nearly all states do the same, with slight variations. Nearly all announce that students at various levels should be prepared to write narrative, expository, or persuasive prose. Some add descriptive prose. Most offer no or only very shallow rationales for the choices. Oregon offers no rationale, for example, while Illinois provides a general statement that the three types represent all three domains of writing (Illinois State Board of Education, 1994). New York does not present a theory of kinds of writing so much as a theory of language that includes speaking and listening. As a result, the Regents exams in eleventh grade include one section in which students listen to a passage that is read aloud and write a response. All the writing tested in the four parts of the exam probably would be classified by most people as expository, but involves some analysis and presentation of evidence in support of claims.

Both Texas and Kentucky present more elaborate theories of writing. Texas presents an analysis of writing based on a theory of discourse developed by Kinneavy (1971), which posits four purposes (informative, persuasive, literary, and expressive) and four modes of discourse (narrative, descriptive, classificatory, and evaluative). Theoretically these distinctions provide a four by four matrix with 16 types of writing possible, a far richer array than is available in most other states. Texas does not take advantage of the richness, however. Rather, the state focuses on four types for testing. The Texas Education Agency limits these even further. For example, fourth- and eighth-grade teachers refer to the informative narrative prompt as the "how-to," because it always asks students to write about how to do something, such as how to make a gift for a parent.

The Kentucky portfolio assessment is based on the theory of discourse advanced by Britton and his colleagues (1975). The result is that writing for the portfolio must include several types of writing, including literary (poems, stories, children's books, plays, etc.), personal (narratives, memoirs, etc.), and transactional (arguments, proposals, historical pieces, research-focused papers, and so forth). The eighth- and twelfth-grade portfolios contain five pieces. Two pieces must come from subject areas other than English, the idea being to encourage writing across the curriculum.

Testing conditions are similar in most states. When Hillocks (2002) began his study, Illinois assessed student writing at four grade levels: 3, 6, 8, and 10. In each grade students had 40 minutes to respond to a prompt that indicated an issue, such as extending the school year. The prompt typically gave a little background and suggested an audience to write to, and no more. Students were on their own. Most of the state writing assessments used very general prompts, chosen because the examiners assumed that students would have opinions that they could support on the basis of general knowledge. Directors of state assessments in Illinois, Oregon, and Texas said that they could not hold students responsible for content, that is, specific knowledge.

In contrast, the New York Regents exams, in three of the four essay prompts, provide material for students to draw upon in their writing. For the fourth, the exam asks students to write about a literary work they have read. The Oregon writing exam is spread over 3 days, suggesting the possibility for students to gather information. In Kentucky the problem is obviated by the nature of the assessment. Students are supposed to choose their own topics and they have plenty of time to collect adequate information.

Time available for writing varies from state to state, but in most assessments the time is limited to less than an hour. In Texas, however, writers have up to a full day to complete their responses. In Oregon students have three class periods on three consecutive days to complete the required writing. The New York Regents provide an hour and a half for students to read the material, answer a few multiple choice questions, and write the essay.

For all assessments, scoring of compositions is based on a rubric similar to those used for the NAEP. Hillocks (2002) argues that the benchmark papers used to illustrate the rubric reveal that very low levels of writing suffice to pass the exam, especially in states such as Illinois and Texas that ask students to produce a piece of writing in a restricted time period with no access to information. Yet the vast majority of teachers interviewed by Hillocks indicate that they used the models from the scoring guides to teach writing. It is obvious that students are receiving a diet of poor writing instruction that cannot provide appropriate nourishment for their growth as writers.

Hillocks (2002) concludes that the state assessments affect the standards for good writing adopted by teachers, the kind of instruction offered, and the writing curriculum available to students. Few teachers had advanced training in writing and largely accepted the standards set by the state. When asked how well they thought their state assessments supported a writing program that was desirable in their state, some teachers had no response. However, in each state a majority of teachers responding thought that their state assessment did support a desirable writing program. This belief was particularly prevalent in Illinois and Texas, which have the kind of assessment most likely to encourage formulaic writing. In Texas, for example, 61% of the teachers interviewed thought the assessment provided support for a desirable writing program; only 24% thought it did not. In New York, where so much of the Regents exam requires responding to literature, the major focus of teaching is writing about literature. In Kentucky, because the assessment requires a diversified portfolio of writing, the writing curriculum is far richer than in the other states studied.

Studies of Test Score Gaps

Researchers have identified test score gaps among various segments of the general population based on race and ethnicity, social class, and gender. Researchers from the right and left have agreed for decades that on standardized tests of ability and achievement, African American and other minority groups score significantly lower than their White counterparts (Herrnstein & Murray, 1994; Jencks & Phillips, 1998). These differences are substantial, on the order of a full standard deviation or more. According to Jencks and Phillips (1998b), "the typical American black . . . scores below 75% of American whites on most standardized tests. On some tests the typical American black scores below more than 85% of whites" (p. 1). In a footnote the authors state that similar results hold for Latino/as and Native Americans.

Scholars have attempted to investigate the variables responsible for the differences in test scores. According to Jencks and Phillips (1998b), these variables have included segregation, poverty, the mother's background (including her test scores and years of schooling), school resources (including teachers' test scores), various kinds of test bias, and many others. These attempts have been largely unsuccessful in explaining much of the variance. However, the character and quality of teaching have not been among the variables studied. Some studies have examined teacher attitudes and teacher scores on standardized tests, but not the character or quality of teaching. For many educators, these results imply that Blacks and Latino/as can be expected to do less well than Whites on all school tasks.

The test score gap holds for writing as well. The National Assessment of Educational Progress writing report card for 1998, for example, indicates that while only 10% of White eighth graders score at the lowest level of writing skill, 28% of Blacks and 31% of Latino/as do. Conversely, while 32% of White eighth graders score at the proficient level, only 8% of Black and 11% of Latino/a eighth graders do. Hedges and Nowell (1998) argue that while the test score gap has narrowed, it remains large. In examining the data from NAEP writing tests from 1984 to 1994, they found that the differences between Blacks and Whites in writing scores yielded standard deviations ranging from 0.67 to 0.86. According to Cohen's (1977) definitions, a standard deviation of less than 0.2 is trivial, one of 0.2 to 0.5 is small, one of 0.5 to 0.8 is medium, and one of 0.8 or more is large. By that criterion, the differences in writing scores are substantial. In the NAEP results for 2002, the gaps appear to have remained large. (For more information, see Table 3.3, p. 49 of NAEP, 2002.)

A second kind of gap appears in relation to variables that attempt to measure some aspect of socioeconomic status (SES). The NAEP uses three indices of SES: eligibility for free or reduced price lunch, participation in Title I schools, and student-reported highest level of parent education. In 2002, 31% of eighth graders tested and 19% of twelfth graders were eligible for free or reduced-price lunch, and 19% of eighth graders and 10% of twelfth graders attended Title I schools. In 2002, eighth and twelfth graders participating in the NAEP writing assessment were asked to indicate the highest level of education they thought their parents had attained. Four levels of education were reported: less than high school, graduation from high school, some college, and college graduation. As one might expect, all three indices appear strongly related to how well students performed on the writing assessment.

NAEP (2002) clearly indicates that writing performance is strongly related to SES, whether estimated by eligibility for free or reduced-price lunch, participation in Title I schools, or level of parent education. In both eighth and twelfth grades, students in the free or reduced-price lunch group or who participate in Title I schools fall substantially short of the levels of achievement in higher SES groups. Eighth graders and twelfth graders not classified in the lower SES groups score at proficient or above nearly two and a half times as frequently as students in the lower groups. Even so, it seems remarkable that only 43% of eighth graders and 32% of twelfth graders who say their parents graduated from college score at the level of proficient or above. If their reports are true, these students are likely to be in the highest income brackets, suggesting that a large proportion of the most advantaged students do not respond well to the writing assessment.

We have known about gaps in the mean test scores by racial group and by SES for a long time. Venezky, Kaestle, and Sum (1987) warned about the economic and political dangers of the literacy gap among young adults of different racial/ethnic groups. They argued that low literacy levels are associated with lower earnings, fewer job opportunities, and a large unskilled workforce. An information-driven economy, demands higher and higher standards of literacy for participation. There are political ramifications as well. Low levels of literacy are associated with low rates of voting, greater likelihood to remain uninformed about current events and public issues, and lower rates of participation in various kinds of community groups. Venezky, Kaestle, and Sum were concerned with reading, but they treated reading along with writing as essential literacy skills. Eighteen years later, the literacy gap is still a severe problem.

A third startling subgroup comparison is that between males and females. In the NAEP writing assessment for 2002, 21% of eighth-grade boys scored at or above proficient, while twice as many females, 42%, scored at the same level. Results for twelfth graders were similar, but the gap was greater: 14% of boys , scored at proficient or advanced, while 33% of girls did. Purves (1992), in reporting the IEA results, states that "there is a widespread gender bias favoring girls that cuts across languages, cultures, and stages of economic development" (p. 146).

Hedges and Nowell (1995) studied gender differences in mental test scores, their variability, and the numbers of high-scoring individuals. They "performed secondary analyses on six large data sets collected between 1960 and 1992," each of which "used a nationally stratified probability sample of adolescents" (p. 42). One of the data sets was from the NAEP for those years. Across the areas of reading, mathematics, science, and writing, they examined the difference between boys' and girls' scores as effect sizes (the difference divided by the standard deviation of the population). They comment, "Average sex differences were small [they cite the Cohen criterion described earlier] except for writing, in which females performed substantially better than males in every year. Although average sex differences in mathematics and science have narrowed over time, differences in reading and writing scores have not" (p. 44). They view this situation with more alarm than do most composition teachers of my acquaintance. "The large sex differences in writing ability suggested by the NAEP trend data are alarming. . . . The data imply that males are, on average, at a rather profound disadvantage in the performance of this basic skill" (p. 45). They believe that the larger number of males who perform near the bottom of the distribution in reading comprehension and writing has policy implications: "It seems likely that individuals with such poor literacy skills will have difficulty finding employment in an increasingly information-driven economy. Thus, some intervention may be required to enable them to participate constructively in the workplace" (p. 45).

As far as I know, no one has compared these data across all indices of race/ethnicity, SES, and gender, perhaps because the results would be overwhelming. My guess is that White female offspring of college graduates would have far and away the highest scores and that Black males from poor families would trail far behind. It is not possible to exaggerate the danger of this disparity.

THE TEACHING OF WRITING IN SECONDARY SCHOOLS

Applebee (1981, 1984) studied writing in American secondary schools across subject matter areas. The study consisted of three parts: observations of 209 class sessions in two midwestern high schools, a national questionnaire of a stratified random sample of ninth- and eleventh-grade teachers, and case studies of students in the schools observed. The observations were conducted in one highly selective private school and one urban public school. The questionnaire involved 196 schools and 754 teachers, all of whom had been recommended by the school principal as good teachers, representing six subject matter areas—English, social science, math, science, foreign language, and business education. The questionnaire asked about the teaching of writing in one class during the spring semester of the academic year. In addition, teachers in the national sample were asked to submit two compositions from a recent assignment. Various case studies followed a sample of students in the classes observed for a period of time as they wrote. Some met with researchers to discuss their writing.

Although writing was a major presence in all subjects, taking up "an average of 44% of the observed lesson time" (Applebee, 1981, p. 30), researchers found that students were spending only about 3% of their school time—in class or for home-work—on writing of paragraph length or longer. On the other hand, students were engaged in a variety of related activities that involved writing but not composing: fill-in-the-blank exercises, worksheets requiring only short responses, and the like. Even in those contexts where students were asked to write at some length, the writing often served merely as a vehicle to test knowledge of specific content, with the teacher functioning primarily as an examiner (Applebee, 1984, p. 2).

Applebee (1981) and the research team classified the kinds of extended writing in which students engaged as informational, personal, imaginative, and other. Informational writing was further categorized hierarchically: the simplest note taking to record (ongoing experience), report (recounting experience observed), summary, analysis, and theory. Persuasive writing was added as another category in which "the attempt to convince overrides other functions" (p. 29).

The criteria for what counts as analysis allow the marshaling of known facts to establish known conditions and events. For the most part, as Applebee (1984) explains, "even when students were asked to write an essay, the essays were treated as tests of previous learning. The task for the student was one of repeating information that had already been organized by the teacher or textbook, rather than of extending or integrating new learning for themselves" (p. 3). Applebee points out that the topics assigned are a good indication of this approach to writing. "In many cases students were asked to write on topics that were in a real sense impossible" (p. 3). He provides an example from social science that asks students to "describe the political, economic, social and cultural changes that Europe was going through at the time of the Reformation." Applebee comments, "Books could be written in response to such a question. It becomes a possible topic for school writing only because it serves to index bodies of previously presented information" (p. 4).

Analysis was the most frequent kind of school writing both in teacher reports and in samples submitted. In the national survey, 41.7% of English teachers, 42.9% of science teachers, and 49.5% of social science teachers reported using analysis frequently. The reported frequent use of theory dropped to 20.3% for English and 16.8% for social science teachers, while remaining a fairly high 41.7% for science teachers. On the other hand, only 3% of the writing samples submitted were categorized as theorizing.

The teaching of writing in most cases studied by Applebee (1981) appeared to be little more than the making of assignments. "In the observational studies, the amount of time devoted to prewriting activities amounted to just over three minutes. That included everything from the time the teacher started introducing the topic until the first student began to write" (p. 74). The "most popular technique of helping students get started was to have them begin their writing in class, so that they could ask questions about what was expected if they found themselves in difficulties" (p. 78). Model pieces of writing were reportedly used in 29% of the classes as a means of "introducing new forms of writing" (p. 78). "Finally," according to Applebee, "brainstorming . . . was reported in use by some 37% of English teachers, and by no more than 14% in any of the other subject areas" (p. 80).

Applebee (1981) indicates that activities designed to help students during writing were "almost nonexistent" (p. 90). One of the most popular, although not widespread, was having the students write in class so that the teacher could help. However, one of the most frequent contexts for in-class writing was the "essay exam, during which the technique loses its effectiveness as an instructional procedure and becomes one of monitoring behavior" (p. 89). Just under 33% of teachers asked for more than a single draft. Applebee suggests that may be because so much of the writing functioned as tests of subject matter knowledge rather than explorations of new material. Applebee concludes that "the major vehicle for writing instruction, in all subject matter areas, was the teacher's comments [on] and corrections of completed work. Errors in writing mechanics were the most common focus of these responses; comments concerned with the ideas the student was expressing were the least frequently reported" (pp. 90–91).

Even the textbooks appear to support these findings. Applebee (1984) examined three of the most popular textbooks in each of the subject areas studied. He found that the "writing experiences provided in high school textbooks are narrow and limiting, whether one examines the role of the activity within the learning process or the kind of writing task the student is being asked to undertake" (p. 35). The types of activities suggested were also limited.

> Textbooks in all subjects seemed to be constructed around a base of exercises that required only minimal writing: fill-in-the-blank exercises, short answer responses, and the like. Some subjects—literature and the social sciences in particular—supplemented this base of restricted activity with more extensive writing tasks. (p. 35)

However, even these more extensive writing tasks are no more than assignments. One cited by Applebee asks students to write their own blues song, presumably after they have read some in the literature text. Another suggests that students write a modern version of a story in which a character sells his soul to the devil.

In short, a quarter of a century ago, when Applebee conducted the study, writing was widely treated in very superficial ways. Teachers appeared to assume that very general knowledge of writing would suffice for most purposes. The tasks of learning were simple and uncomplicated.

Two and a half decades after Applebee conducted this study, is the teaching of writing in secondary school any different? It is difficult to tell. There has been no comparable study. But there are some indications that the teaching of writing has changed in some ways and remained the same in others.

The goal of Hillocks (2002) was to determine the impact of state writing assessments on the teaching of writing. He did not observe classes as Applebee did, but he did interview more than 300 teachers and more than 130 administrators and supervisors. Most teachers and supervisors described practice in considerable detail, and it appears that they were quite honest and straightforward about their practices.

In the approximately 20 years or so between the time of the Applebee (1981, 1984) study and the Hillocks (2002) study, there was significant change. First, while Applebee indicates that only 3% of the time spent on writing was devoted to work on pieces of a paragraph or more, nearly all teachers interviewed by Hillocks talked only about the writing of multiparagraph compositions, even at the elementary level. In many districts, the focus was on writing five-paragraph themes (FPT), thus imposing a limit of sorts. But it is very clear that, as a result of the state assessments, students in the states studied by Hillocks, and probably in all states that collect writing samples as part of their assessments, are writing far more than they did 20 years ago.

Second, the detail provided by teachers in the Hillocks study indicates that they spend far more time in preparation for writing than the 3 minutes for the teachers in the Applebee study. Indeed, most teachers describe strings of activities that precede writing. Some teachers describe reading and studying several models of writing, analyzing their characteristics in class, brainstorming for ideas, and organizing those ideas, all before writing. Many interviews make it evident that such activities may take several class sessions.

Third, there is greater attention to audience, or at least greater seeming attention to audience. Most of the state assessments use topics that allude to some audience (your principal, your senator, the mayor of your town, other students), and teachers use these in their assignments. But exactly what students make of such audiences named in their assignments is less than clear.

Fourth, teachers appear to be preparing students more for writing than Applebee found. Across the five states Hillocks examined, an average of 78% of the language arts teachers interviewed used model pieces of writing or more abstract descriptions of the kinds of writing students were to do, nearly two and a half times the number Applebee found. Further, in the national survey, Applebee asked about instructional procedures that teachers felt were important. Only slightly over 37% of English teachers mentioned brainstorming. Hillocks found that over five states an average of slightly over 71% mentioned using such activities as brainstorming as a prewriting activity. Applebee indicates that 26.4% of English teachers reported using class time for students to read one another's writing. In Hillocks's study, 65.8% reported using peer response regularly.

On the other hand, while Applebee found that 59.3% of English teachers thought that writing more than one draft was important in teaching, Hillocks found that an average of 60.4% mentioned revising as an important instructional technique, suggesting no real change at all. However, the percentages differ widely by state. In Kentucky, which has a portfolio assessment, the percentage of teachers emphasizing revision was 81%; in Oregon, with a 3-day, 3-class-period time for the assessment, 84% emphasized revision. In the three other states, with assessments calling for students to write in a single time period, the average percentage of teachers emphasizing revision was only 45.7%, an indication of the impact of state assessments.

Despite these apparent advances, there is an underlying similarity in the way writing was taught during the two periods. In both periods, teachers and curriculum makers assumed that the knowledge necessary for effective writing is general knowledge of a few principles that are applicable to all or most writing.

In this regard, it is interesting to note three case studies. The first was conducted by Anagnostopoulos (2003) in 1996–1999, about 20 years after Applebee conducted his study. She observed classes in a Chicago school that had been placed on probation as a result of low test scores. In order to hold teachers and principals accountable for student outcomes, Chicago had instituted its own Chicago Academic Standards Examination (CASE). The test was accompanied by criteria for scoring, a rubric that, according to Anagnostopoulos, "constructs readers as not only uncritical, but minimally skilled as well." She comments on the criteria: "According to these criteria, 'good readers' can cite details from a text. They do not, however, use these details to identify key ideas or 'significant concepts.' In fact, the details that students include in their essays could be 'irrelevant' to the simplistic interpretations that students develop" (p. 191).

In order to prepare students for the test, the teachers she observed consistently conducted recitations about a few chapters of the novel (cut short because of time pressures) and showed the film version to ensure that students would know the major events of the story. Anagnostopolous analyzed the questions asked and found that nearly all were literal, with some leading to simple inferences, but no complex inferences about characters or events, the thematic content, or the structure of the book. Teachers would predict possible exam questions, pose a thesis statement, and use recitation to draw students into supplying the evidence to support it. She describes how one of the teachers suggested that the question on the exam might ask about the title of the novel or who the mockingbirds in the novel might be. In one classroom segment examined in detail, the class considered Boo Radley as a possible mockingbird, a person who does nothing but good for others. The teacher, Mr. Jones, asked for examples of the good things that Boo Radley does, and students provided several examples. Anagnostopoulos calls their responses "text reproduction." She comments, "The students fulfilled their role in text reproduction by recalling details that fit into Mr. Jones' framing of the novel. After they offered a series of plot details, Mr. Jones congratulated the students on 'gettin it all,' and stated that if the question appeared on the CASE, the students would do well because they [understood] it" (p. 198). Sometimes, after such recitations, he explained how to put it all into an FPT. Anagnostopolous interprets this teaching behavior as an effect of the high-pressure testing. However, it is highly reminiscent of what Applebee observed 20 years earlier.

A second case study indicates that standardized tests alone are not responsible for such teaching. Kahn (2000) studied the materials for evaluation of students used by a cohort of grade 10 English teachers in a suburban high school that had been recognized as a Center of Excellence by the National Council of Teachers of English. The school had a population of mostly White (78%) and Asian (13%) students, 71% of whom planned to attend either a 2- or 4-year college. Kahn states that "the school's average scores for reading and writing in the state testing program tended to be significantly higher than the state and national averages" (p. 277).

Kahn studied the teachers' quizzes, unit tests, final exams, and composition assignments. Teachers used a point system, with each test item worth a particular number of points and each test worth the total of the points per item. She found that over 65% of the points available for the semester were based on multiple choice, matching, or true/false items. Most of these involved highly literal information that had been presented in the textbook or by the teachers in class. For example, the literature text provided a "good theme statement" for one story. This theme statement appeared verbatim as a possible response on a multiple choice question that asked what a good theme statement for that story would be. "Teachers indicated that they were especially irritated when students missed a question like that when, as they explained, it is in the book and they had told them on the review day that they should know that information for the test" (p. 282). Likewise, questions that might have called for interpretation actually expected students to recall the interpretations presented in class. For example, in one question for the novel *A Separate Peace*, "students were asked to label 12 objects, situations, places, and characters as (a) a symbol of peace or (b) a symbol of war. . . . Students did not have to judge whether something was a symbol, explain why something is a symbol, or analyze the effect or meaning of the symbol" (p. 284). Obviously, these answers had been determined and represented substantial knowledge that students were supposed to have acquired. In short, these students appeared to be doing less processing of content for writing than even those studied by Applebee 20 years previously.

Further, there was one unit on writing during the semester, lasting 2 weeks and focusing on the FPT. The final exam questions that dealt with writing were multiple choice, asking students to recall the rules of the FPT. For example, one question read as follows: "In the last paragraph, the thesis statement is always the _____ sentence." The choices are "a. first, b. second, c. last, d. doesn't matter" (p. 282). The correct answer, by the way, is a. It appears that the teaching of writing in at least some schools has deteriorated to well below the levels of instruction that Applebee found.

Finally, a detailed case study of a teacher's learning to teach the FPT, by Johnson and colleagues (2003), helps to explain the deterioration. The study details how a neophyte teacher learns to teach the FPT. Johnson and colleagues provide an excellent summary of the origins and possible reasons for the endurance of the form, including enculturation to the traditions of schooling, the limitations of teacher education programs, the shortcomings of teachers, poor working conditions, institutional pressures, and claims by writers such as Dean (2000) that "students benefit from learning forms that, when appropriated, allow them to generate and express ideas" (cited in Johnson et al., 2003, p. 142). Claims such as Dean's conveniently ignore the research finding that the study of forms (or models) is second only to traditional school grammar in having the least impact on student writing (Hillocks, 1986). In fact, careful examination of student writing that follows the FPT format indicates that the formula is conducive not to ideas but to cliches, commonplaces, and blather (see Hillocks, 2002, pp. 108–120, for an analysis of the FPT in Illinois).

Johnson and colleagues had access to interviews with and observations of the neophyte (Leigh) from student teaching through the first full year of teaching, and communication after a few years of teaching. The authors contend that four of the six possible reasons for the persistence of the FPT are implicated in Leigh's learning to teach it and accept it. They see her as an outstanding teaching candidate and present evidence of her doing a better job of teaching the FPT than many other teachers appear to do, helping students to generate content, to revise, and so on. They see her working conditions as good. But they contend that the other four reasons come to bear. Her own deeper belief system, developed during her apprenticeship of observation, predisposed her to favor the FPT. Her teacher education program did not help her develop a "strong conceptual framework for critiquing the five-paragraph theme or developing a rationale for teaching writing in other ways" (p. 167). Instead, she was left to "develop her conception of writing through apprenticeships with mentors and colleagues she found in the field" (p. 168), and they focused on highly specified and rigid forms of writing, not on learning strategies for examining the content, which might dictate form. In addition, the pressures experienced from the school, community, and state for students to do well on the exam led to a belief that the FPT is necessary and, in some eyes, the epitome of strong writing.

RESEARCH ON TEACHING WRITING

Writing to Learn

Langer and Applebee (1987) in a study entitled *How Writing Shapes Thinking* examined, in considerable detail, the question of how writing affects learning. They based the study on the assumption that "to improve the teaching of school writing, particularly in the context of academic tasks, is also to improve the quality of thinking of schoolchildren" (p. 3). To determine how writing affected the thinking of schoolchildren, they studied 18 science and social studies teachers recommended for their interest in including writing in their programs. However, "the teachers felt they had little time or inclination to include many writing activities in their classrooms. . . . When the teachers did use writing, the content often became a vehicle for teaching conceptual skills rather than facts to be mastered by students." For example, in writing about the great depression, "the primary objective was the practice of broader conceptual skills that could be transferred to other social studies tasks. Students were considered successful if they had learned a set amount of information about the Depression, but could argue or write convincingly about it. Such uses of writing were rare, however, even in this highly select sample of teachers" (p. 21).

The study was conducted through a combination of observations, interviews with students and teachers, and think-aloud protocols, and data from planning sessions in which teachers discussed how they might use writing in their classrooms. Nearly all of the teachers came to use writing in new ways in their classrooms. The researchers believe that "subject-area writing can be used in three primary ways: (1) to gain relevant knowledge and experience in preparing for new activities; (2) to review and consolidate what is known or has been learned; and (3) to reformulate and extend ideas and experiences." The researchers continue, "Our analyses of students' papers and their self-reports indicate that writing used to reformulate and extend knowledge led to more complex reasoning than did other types of writing: review writing led to the least" (p. 136).

With a small sample of six students, Langer and Applebee conducted studies to determine the kinds of thinking involved in writing about text material when writing involved answering specific questions about the text, taking notes about the text, and writing essays about it. Analysis of think-alouds indicated that writing essays involved the most complex thinking, with students making more hypotheses. Another set of studies with a sample of 208 students in 6 ninth- and 6 eleventh-grade classes attempted to determine the impact of the different kinds of writing tasks on learning about text material. At each grade level students were assigned randomly by the packet received to one of four study conditions: answering comprehension questions, note taking, essay writing, and normal studying. On the first day of the study, students took a passage-specific knowledge test (comparable to that used by Langer, 1984), read the relevant passage from a social studies text, completed the study task, and were administered the passage-specific knowledge test again. Four weeks later, three different instruments were used to assess student learning: a passage-specific knowledge measure, an essay, and a multiple choice test of content.

The researchers found that "there were no differences among the four study tasks in their effects on the multiple choice comprehension task" (p. 109). On the passage-specific knowledge test, the "essay writing group scored consistently lower than groups in the other conditions, and the normal studying group did consistently better at both the immediate and four week post-test" (p. 110). On the posttest essay, "the essay writing and comprehension-question conditions were consistently superior to the normal studying and the assigned note-taking groups" (p. 110).

However, in a third and similar study, using somewhat different study tasks (read and study, comprehension questions, summarizing, and analytic writing) and different measures, the results were somewhat different. One of the measures focused on the specific items of content that writers "manipulated" in their writing. In a posttest 1 week after the initial study tasks were completed, these specific items were recalled at quite different rates depending on the study task; "manipulation involved in the analytic writing led to the best retention (43 percent), summary writing next (32 percent), and comprehension questions least (24 percent)" (p. 127). These findings suggest that more-complex writing probably involves selective attention to the texts in order to support the writing effort, but that those items of content selected for processing are retained more deeply than items that do not receive such focus.

Taken together, these results suggest that analytic writing "leads to a more thoughtful focus on a smaller amount of information. While fewer ideas are considered, they are dealt with in more complex ways; ideas are linked and understanding is reconstrued. Although less information is likely to be remembered, over time this information is longer lived" (p. 135).

Learning to Write

Assuming that the goal of teachers of writing is to improve the quality of student writing, we are confronted with three questions. First, what constitutes quality in writing? Second, what is involved in producing various kinds of writing? Third, what is the relative effectiveness of various methods of teaching writing in the secondary school?

General ideas about the quality of writing, discussed in the section on assessment above, have a long history in rhetoric, if not so long in secondary schools. During the late 1970s, researchers began seeking indices of writing quality that underlie our general ideas about writing quality. The NAEP scales, for example, call for variety of sentence structure and transitions that help unify writing. The possibility exists that these features can be identified and counted. A number of researchers have sought countable indices of quality and used primary trait scales to help understand the quality of writing. In addition, they have explored various conditions that might have an impact on the quality of writing produced.

For example, Langer (1984) examined the effects of knowledge available to students on the quality of their writing in a study of 99 tenth graders (in two classes under each of two teachers) responding to two writing prompts in American history. Each teacher assigned two pieces of writing appropriate to the instructional units they taught at intervals during the semester. Before distributing the writing assignments, the teachers presented three words that indicated three major concepts the teachers "considered critical for student learning." These concepts were the "basis for a free-association measure of topic-specific knowledge" (p. 29) for which "students were asked to write everything that came to mind about these words" (p. 32). Student responses were analyzed using three measures: a count of responses to the free-association words, which "measures topic-specific fluency" (p. 32); a scale for judging organization, including three levels (diffusely, partially, or highly organized, the latter including superordinate ideas, the linking of ideas, precise definitions, and analogies); and a measure that combined the first two.

One assignment for each teacher presented a thesis for the students to support. The other required a comparison/contrast for which students had to compose their own thesis. The researcher used five measures of writing: quality rating, coherence, syntactic complexity, audience, and function. Correlations among the free-association scores and the holistic scores were all significant, with the combined knowledge score the highest at .30, p < .001. Within topic results varied. For compare/contrast topics, organization of knowledge and the combined knowledge scores were correlated significantly to the holistic scores, .39 (p < .001) and .42 (p < .001) for one topic and .68 (p < .001) and .31 for the other. Langer points out that these "findings imply that different assignments, given for different purposes, tap different aspects of a writer's knowledge of a topic" (p. 40).

Langer concludes that the data clearly suggest a strong and consistent relationship between topic-specific background knowledge and the quality of student writing. More interesting is the evidence that different kinds of knowledge predict success in different writing tasks. When the assignment calls for a simple reiteration of facts, or elaborations of a given idea, a large amount of unintegrated (or loosely linked) information will suffice. However, when the student is required to present a thesis, analyze it, and defend it, the degree of organization of knowledge, as opposed to simple fluency, determines success.

Chesky and Hiebert (1987), basing their study on approaches comparable to those used by Langer (1984), chose two topics, one that they believed would be a high prior-knowledge topic ("the problems with teachers") and one a low prior-knowledge topic ("tobacco price supports") for eleventh graders. In addition, on the basis of previous research and opinion, they hypothesized that the audience for whom students wrote would be a factor in the quality of writing produced. They assigned half of each group to write to an audience of peers and half to an audience of teachers. They found that the writing of 40 students assigned to write about the problems with teachers produced qualitatively better essays (p < .001) and longer essays (p < .001). Differences between the high and low prior-knowledge groups in *t*-unit length, cohesion, and number of errors were not significant. The difference in assigned audience had no significant impact on quality.

Several researchers examined the effect of coherence or cohesion on the quality of writing. Bamberg (1984) developed a four-point scale of coherence ranging from highly coherent (4) to incoherent (1) in order to examine coherence in the 1969 and 1974 NAEP writing samples. She describes a fully coherent paper as "one that clearly identifies the topic, . . . does not shift topics or digress, . . . orients the reader by creating a context or situation, . . . organizes details according to a discernible plan that is sustained throughout the essay, . . . [skillfully] uses cohesive ties such as lexical cohesion, conjunction, reference, etc. to link sentences and/or paragraphs together, . . . often concludes with a statement that gives the reader a definite sense of closure, [and] . . . flows smoothly—few or no grammatical and/or mechanical errors interrupt the reading process" (pp. 317–318). Scoring a sample of 2,698 compositions written by 13- and 17-year-olds, she found significant correlations of her coherence scores with the NAEP holistic ratings: .64 for 13-year-olds and .65 for 17-year-olds. Such relatively high correlations should not be surprising given the similarity of the NAEP rubric and Bamberg's coherence scale. Three of the four NAEP criteria are echoed in at least five of Bamberg's seven criteria for coherence.

Crowhurst (1987) examined cohesion in argument and narration at three grade levels. Coherence, as defined by Bamberg (1984), includes "macro-structures" or organizational plans, while cohesion, as defined by the work of Halliday and Hasan

(1976), is concerned with the linguistic features of discourse that keep language together within and across sentences or utterances, such as "pronominal-reference ties, demonstratives and definite articles, . . . same lexical items, synonyms, [and] collocational items" (Crowhurst, 1997, p. 199).

Crowhurst examined over 600 compositions from students in grades 6, 10, and 12, counted the number of cohesive ties per 100 words, and concluded that "there was no overall tendency for the frequency of cohesive ties to increase with grade level. Some types of cohesion increased with grade level, namely, collocation and the use of synonyms. . . . Greater use of synonyms and collocation by higher grades seems to reflect vocabulary development and a greater tendency to elaborate" (p. 189).

McCulley (1985) also examined cohesion and coherence in a random sample of 493 persuasive compositions drawn from NAEP. He used three measures of the papers to examine the relationship of quality to cohesion and coherence. These included the NAEP scale for judging the quality of persuasive writing (which McCulley calls a primary trait scale), the NAEP primary trait scale for coherence, and counts of the Halliday and Hasan (1976) features of cohesion. He found that certain of the Halliday and Hasan features were fairly highly correlated with the quality score for persuasive writing: demonstrative reference, .26 ($p < .05$); noun substitution and ellipsis, .22 ($p < .05$); and lexical synonyms, hyponyms, and collocations, .39 ($p < .01$). While each of these was significant, even the largest accounts for only 15% of the variance. It is interesting to note, however, that all of these cohesive ties were involved in the elaboration of content.

Connor (1990) analyzed a sample of 150 persuasive essays written for the IEA international study of writing by English-speaking students from England, New Zealand, and the United States. She made the analysis in terms of six different variables—syntactic features, coherence as related to topic development, and four variables related to persuasiveness: (1) frequency of four different argument slots; (2) a scale measuring Toulmin's categories of claim, data, and warrant; (3) a scale measuring three appeals, rational, affective, and credibility; and (4) a scale measuring audience adaptiveness. Connor and Lauer (1988) indicate that the Toulmin scale rates claim, data, and warrant on a three-point scale. For a claim to receive three points it must present "a specific, explicitly stated problem with consistent point of view accompanied by several well-developed subclaims explicitly tied to the major claim," all of which are "highly relevant to the task" and offer a "solution" that is "feasible, original, and consistent with the major claim" (p. 145). The scales for data and warrant are similarly developed.

Connor reports that the highest correlations with the holistic score were for word count (.69), the Toulmin score (.70), the credibility appeal (.48), and a syntax factor indicating a more formal style (.31). A stepwise analysis of regression indicated that the variable with the greatest explanatory power was the result of the Toulmin scale, which accounted for 48% of the variance in the holistic scores. Word count added another 7%, credibility appeal added another 3%, and the more formal style added another 1%, for a total of 59%. The remaining variables add only 2% more. In explaining the high correlation between word count and the Toulmin variable of claim, data, and warrant (.74), Connor argues that "in order to develop adequate *claim*, *warrant*, and *data*, the students simply had to write more" (p. 80; emphasis in original).

Effective Teaching

Writing assignments. Applebee (1981, 1984) indicates that when he conducted his survey, the writing assignment virtually stood alone. Since then, there has been considerable research and writing about assignments and the best ways to frame them for student learning and assessment. Ruth and Murphy (1987) present a very thorough analysis of assignments for assessment and the research about them. The specific topics or writing prompts exemplified in the book are quite comparable to topics in the various volumes published by NCTE for use by teachers. The book discusses the problems with topics for writing, especially as they stand alone for assessment. Before use, they need to be pretested for such problems as ambiguity, level of information required to write about them, and the impact of the level of rhetorical specification. The book also reviews research related to such issues.

Responding to student writing. Applebee (1981) called response to writing "the major vehicle for writing instruction, in all subject matter areas" (p. 90; cf. Anson, 1989). Freedman's (1987) study of response to writing is one of the most important in terms of both breadth and depth. Freedman set out to examine the nature of response teachers make and the impact that response has on student writing. She did this by conducting a survey of 560 teachers nominated as successful teachers of writing by National Writing Project site directors, a survey of selected students of those teachers, and ethnographies of two skilled teachers of ninth-grade academic writing. She redefined response to writing to include teacher and peer written and oral response not only to final products but also to drafts in progress and, most important, to the thinking that students do as they participate in discussion and generation of ideas in preparation for writing. The latter usually is not thought of as response to writing, but it may be the most important kind. The surveys and ethnographies illustrated and supported three conditions for successful response to student writing: "Successful teachers . . . resist taking over the writing of their students"; they "communicate high expectations for all students"; and they provide plentiful help and support for students during the writing process (p. 160).

Sperling and Freedman (1987), in a case study of a student culled from Freedman (1987), examined the question of why even the most promising students misunderstand and/or misconstrue the comments that teachers write on their papers even when the comments are accompanied by conferences, peer group response, and whole-class discussion of responses. They studied the responses of a high-achieving, ninth-grade girl to her teacher's comments on segments of text (what they call "response rounds") of a character study developed over several drafts. They categorized the teacher comments as either reflecting information made explicit by the teacher in class or not. In all of the student's drafts, many of the teacher's comments had no in-class referents. In every such case the student's attempts at revision failed in some way. Of the teacher's comments with in-class referents, about half were positive reinforcements and half indicated a need for revision. Sperling and Freedman report that the student had no problems processing the former. When the teacher complimented word choice or the use of detail, the student noted it and tried to produce more in the next piece of writing. The student's attempts to revise for comments indicating a need for change, however, even when they had in-class referents, often were complicated by differences between the teacher's and student's values and knowledge, suggesting that when responding to written drafts is the major vehicle for composition instruction, it is probably not very effective.

Sperling (1990) provides an analysis of one teacher's conferences with students about their writing. She says that "participating in the explicit dialogue of teacher–student conversation, students collaborate in the often implicit act of acquiring and developing written language" (p. 282). She indicates that the conferences she examined had a range of purposes: "to plan future text, . . . to clarify the teacher's written comments . . . , to give feedback on texts on which there were no written comments," and "to cover concerns tangential . . . to those above" (p. 289). Sperling presents an analysis of the number of units of discourse initiated by the focal students or teacher and completed by the students or teacher, to show that the conferences are collaborations and represent a "context for dialogic learning to blossom" (p. 318). While it is easy to imagine that the concerns might be matters of form, every conference quoted in the study had a substantive focus. That is, it developed the potential content of the writing.

Specificity of knowledge. In 1992 Smagorinsky and Smith examined the question of what kinds of knowledge were being taught and studied in the name of knowledge of composition and literary understanding, particularly in regard to specificity. They relate the question to a long-standing controversy in educational psychology concerning the kinds of knowledge likely to transfer. This controversy is particularly concerned with the questions, "To what extent is knowledge specific to particular situations? To what extent can learners transfer knowledge from one context to another? Can people learn general skills that help them solve problems in a variety of fields?" (p. 280).

Smagorinsky and Smith observe that three positions have emerged among theorists and researchers in composition and literary understanding in relation to transfer of knowledge. The first is that of general knowledge, the advocates of which believe that a few general strategies suffice for any sort of writing. Smagorinsky and Smith cite, for example, Warriner and Griffith's (1977) comment, "No matter what you are writing about the basic steps involved in writing are almost always the same." The steps outlined in the book "include selecting and limiting a topic, assembling materials, organizing and outlining ideas, writing a draft that follows a particular form (usually including five paragraphs), revising, and preparing a final draft" (p. 282).

Smagorinsky and Smith point out that "faith in the sufficiency of general knowledge of text structure is rare among the professoriate and has been replaced by a belief in general procedural knowledge that has begun to transform teaching and textbooks" (p. 283). They point to the development of heuristics as one departure from the more traditional Warriner approach. Even that has been "supplanted in popularity by general procedures for producing texts that rely on nonlinear thinking such as brainstorming, clustering, and free writing" (p. 283). According to Smagorinsky and Smith, the idea of "nonlinear thinking" has been advanced as general knowledge of the writing process most earnestly by Murray (1980, 1987) and Elbow (1973, 1981). They cite Murray (1987) as referring to the process approach to writing "as consisting of five steps: collecting, focusing, ordering, developing, and clarifying. Writers can apply this general process to any composing problem and couple the five steps with general strategies such as free writing, brainstorming, and mapping" (p. 283).

Smagorinsky and Smith cite Elbow as perhaps "the most passionate advocate of general procedures" (p. 284). They indicate that he advocates two different writing processes. The first is for use when the writer does not want to do much new thinking, as in memos, reports, somewhat difficult letters, and even essays. He calls this the direct writing process and advocates simply dividing the available time in half, using the first half for writing without worrying about organization, language, correctness, or precision. The second half is for revision. The second process, used for more difficult tasks, is described in similar terms but with the metaphor of a voyage out and a voyage in. Smagorinsky and Smith explain, "He gives several quite disparate examples of possible applications of the loop process: a comparison/contrast of Freud and Jung, an analysis of the causes of the French Revolution, a report on levels of pollution of various chemicals in Puget Sound, an analysis of government expenditures for various kinds of armaments and defense, and a paper on abortion" (p. 284). They comment that "the assumption behind this conception of composing knowledge is that writing consists of a very few simple procedures that one develops and uses effectively through practice"(p. 284).

The second position is that knowledge for writing is task specific and argues that different writing tasks require knowledge not only of different forms of writing but of task-specific procedures or strategies for dealing with both content and form necessary to produce the desired product. Smagorinsky and Smith cite research on teaching students to write extended definitions of abstract concepts (e.g., Smagorinsky, 1991). They outline the following enabling strategies for developing the content: "1) to circumscribe the concept generally, 2) to compare examples in order to generate criteria which discriminate between the target concept and related but essentially different concepts, and 3) to generate examples which clarify the distinctions" (p. 286). Smagorinsky and Smith present a list of works presenting a comparable approach to teaching writing.

The third position they identify is one that argues that advanced or professional writing is not only task specific but contextualized in highly specific communities and that the communities have conventions and standards that are specific to the communities but that may not be shared by others. That is, those who wish to become literary critics in the academy must learn the standards and priorities of that community or they will not be able to achieve recognition in that community of scholars. Those who wish to become effective lawyers and judges must have the knowledge and ability to find the precedents that will provide for the backing of the warrants by which they show that their data actually provide evidence in support of their claims. See, for example, Stratman's (1990) discussion of legal thinking and writing.

Smagorinsky and Smith suggest that these distinctions indicate a "curricular path" (p. 299). They summarize: "The general knowledge position is most widely substantiated at the elementary level, the task-specific position is best supported at the secondary and collegiate levels, and community-specific position is most typically investigated at the upper levels of schooling and in the professions" (pp. 298–299). The curricular path is apparent. Beginning writers need to know and learn to use the writing process. But as students become older, at some point they need additional, task-specific knowledge to successfully meet the demands for the writing they encounter. Even if students learn task-specific critical thinking skills in high school and college, they have to learn how to adapt them to the specific professional communities they enter.

In the roughly 2 decades preceding the Applebee (1981, 1984) studies, some teachers and researchers were concerned with the effects of various kinds of teaching prior to writing as ways not only of preparing students to write but of improving their writing. Results of these studies were reported in Hillocks (1986), a meta-analysis that found great variation in the impact of the different approaches to teaching. Classifying studies along several dimensions, Hillocks found that the dimensions of mode and focus of instruction displayed significant differences among the studies included. Under mode of instruction, Hillocks found that teaching approaches that had clear objectives and emphasized strong interaction among students and the teacher about the focus of instruction were most effective by far. Under focus of instruction, he found that approaches focusing on task-specific procedural knowledge (namely, learning a rubric and how to revise to achieve its demands; learning how to manipulate parts of sentences through sentence combining; and inquiry, learning strategies for producing the content of specific writing tasks) were most effective by far.

The mean effect sizes under focus of instruction were, for grammar, $-.29$, well below the impact of any other focus of teaching; for the study of models, $.22$; for free writing, $.16$; for sentence combining, $.35$; for scales, $.36$; and for inquiry, $.56$. All mean effect sizes are homogeneous, indicating that the studies in each group are evaluating comparable effects.

Several studies have turned attention to the analysis of specific knowledge involved in particular writing tasks. For example, Durst (1987) sets out to examine "writers' ways of thinking through content in forming, refining, and elaborating ideas . . . the critical thinking about subject matter that many educators view as so important" (p. 349). To do this he studied think-aloud protocols and the written products of 20 high school boys and girls who wrote both summaries and analytic pieces. He divided transcripts of the 40 protocols into communication units, more or less comparable to t-units. These were categorized for cognitive operations (lower and higher level of both questioning and planning, restating content, constructing meaning, and evaluating), text level (global, intermediate, and local), and focus (process or product). In addition, he analyzed the essays using holistic scales focused on level of abstraction, with generalized summary as the most concrete and focused interpretation as the most abstract. T-units in the essays were coded for hierarchical structuring of the units. Finally, he categorized cohesive conjunctions as additive, temporal, causal, and adversative. The differences for analysis of cognitive operations were highly significant, indicating that "students writing analytically employed a more varied and complex set of cognitive operations than when writing summaries" (p. 356). Results for text-level comments differed significantly by task. While the overwhelming number of text level comments focused on local issues, analytic writing tasks involved more intermediate and global comments than did summary tasks. The analysis of focus indicated that "analytic writing required students to attend more to their own thinking than did summary" (p. 363).

Analysis of the level of abstractness indicates that all the summaries were coded at the lower levels of abstraction, indicating that students were writing narrative or chronological summaries. For the analytic essays, five average-ability students wrote summaries, ignoring the analytic task. The remainder wrote more-abstract essays dealing with an interpretation of the texts read. Further, "analytic and summary essays differed significantly in top level organization. . . . Analytic essays were primarily organized around evaluative thesis statements suggesting a point of view, while summaries mainly used . . . an introductory statement synthesizing the reading passage" (p. 368). Durst comments that "when students *are thinking analytically*, they may not be writing very analytically; their texts may not reflect the critical reasoning they have engaged in" (p. 374; emphasis in original). Harking back to Applebee's (1981, 1984) findings, he points out that what appears to be critical thinking about issues in writing in school really is often simply a summary of someone else's thinking, namely, that of the teacher. In part, he thinks this accounts for the relatively weak performance of students on NAEP writing tasks. He concludes, "If, as educators, we truly wish to foster in students the use of higher level thinking processes, then we need to encourage writing tasks in which students do their own analyzing, rather than finding a ready interpretation to summarize" (p. 375).

McCann (1989) uses the Toulmin model of argument to examine student knowledge of argument at three grade levels: 6, 9, and 12. He uses the model to devise criteria for assessing written arguments and for examining constructed passages that he asked students and a group of adults to judge as arguments. He finds that sixth graders' arguments included only some features of arguments. Ninth and twelfth graders included more. Students at all grade levels included propositions concerning the policy issue—whether students could leave school for lunch. Claims are statements related to the proposition and amount to reasons for support of the proposition. Ninth graders used more claims than sixth and twelfth graders. At all grade levels students had difficulty incorporating data or evidence into their texts, but differences were not significant. Students seldom used warrants, but ninth and twelfth graders used them more often than sixth graders did. In responding to the constructed passages, which ranged from carefully developed passages with all parts of an argument to a passage with only a narrative, students at all grades rank ordered the three most complete arguments as did the expert adults, indicating that they are able to recognize arguments. McCann suggests, given this knowledge fund, that instruction in argument may be feasible at earlier grade levels than is the case now, with nearly all major textbook series holding it off until eleventh grade or later.

Smagorinsky (1991) studied the task-specific composing processes of 18 students in writing extended definition, six selected randomly from each of three different instructional treatments lasting for 12 days each: study of model compositions; use of general procedures such as freewriting and brainstorming in addition to the study of models; and study of task-specific procedures in addition to the study of some models. Task-specific procedures focused on procedures of devising criteria to identify the membership or nonmembership in the concept defined. For example, one problem examined by students in small groups in the task-specific sections involved reading a set of problematic examples related to freedom of speech, constructing criteria for inclusion or exclusion, and devising examples and contrasting examples to support the criteria developed. Smagorinsky collected think-aloud protocols for the 18 students who wrote on either leadership or friendship for the pretest and the other topic for the posttest. He used a system of categorizing each sentence unit of the protocols and the written essays to determine changes in purposeful composing and critical thinking. Purposeful composing had to do with the changes in the percent of generalizations constructed that were supported by examples or contrasting examples. He also calculated a critical thinking score by examining differences in the numbers of attempted criteria as opposed to actual criteria. Mean improvement scores for the three treatment groups (models, general procedures, and task-specific procedures) on purposeful composing in the written essays are 3.5, 5.5, and 9.33, respectively; for critical thinking in the written essays, 0, 5.667, and 7.167, respectively. Smagorinsky concludes, "Students in the models treatment entered the study with a poor ability to discriminate and gave evidence on the post-test of a still-poor but improved ability; students in the General Procedures entered with a good ability and did not improve it; students from the Task-Specific Procedures treatment entered with a poor ability and gave evidence of improvement towards a relatively good ability" (p. 358).

Yeh (1998) studied the teaching of task-specific procedures for writing argument to minority middle school students in two experimental groups and two comparison groups with a total of 110 students. All groups worked on writing argument and shared a book that involved issues (e.g., "throw[ing] toxic wastes into the ocean") and related information for debate. All students read the materials and were engaged in debate teams to make presentations to their classmates, after which they each wrote an essay on the issue, writing eight essays in the course of 10 weeks. All groups also pursued the writing process from prewriting to revision and final draft. The difference between the groups was in the kind of prewriting that students were taught. In the experimental groups students were taught explicitly how to use a "heuristic" for developing an argument based on Toulmin's model of argument. The comparison groups were encouraged to develop their ideas through the use of a web "(Concept map), with the opinion (main claim) in the middle and branches for an introduction, three supporting reasons and a conclusion" (p. 62), which sounds suspiciously like an FPT. The experimental groups outperformed the comparison groups from pre- to posttests by a margin comparable to those in the inquiry group of the Hillocks (1986) meta-analysis, an effect size of .74.

Teachers who beat the odds. Some of the most valuable research about teaching writing in secondary schools is that of Langer (2001), examining three groups of teachers in urban schools with diverse populations, some of which consistently beat the odds by helping students to higher achievement in English than socioeconomic data would predict. She finds six major distinctions between teachers who beat the odds and those who do not.

First, she finds that high-performing teachers use a combination of approaches to teaching skills. They separate them for specific attention, for example, explaining with examples and exercises how to use certain punctuation marks. They use what Langer calls "simulated instruction" in which students are asked to produce short units of text for the purpose of applying the skills. Finally, they integrate the skills taught with ongoing larger curricular goals, tasks in which students are asked to apply the skills in question. Typically performing teachers, however, very often use only the method of separating the skill to be taught, without integrating it into the ongoing curriculum.

Second, in like manner, she found that high-performing teachers integrate preparation for district- or statewide tests into the ongoing curriculum, while typically performing teachers separate it.

Third, Langer finds that at least 88% of high-performing teachers "overtly pointed out connections . . . among concepts and experiences within lessons; connections across lessons, classes, and even grades; and connections between in-school and out-of-school knowledge and experiences, classes, and grades, and across in-school and out-of-school applications." In contrast, "the more typical teachers tended to make no connections at all" (p. 864). They treat knowledge and skills as discrete entities.

Fourth, Langer finds that "all of the more successful teachers overtly taught their students strategies for organizing their thoughts and completing their tasks, whereas only 17% of the more typical teachers did so. The other 83% of the more typical teachers left such strategies implicit." For example, "Most teachers in the higher performing schools share and discuss with students rubrics for evaluating performance; they also incorporate them into their ongoing instructional activities as a way to help their students develop an understanding of the components that contribute to a higher score" (p. 868). In short, in the higher performing schools there was a clear emphasis on teaching procedures, a development of metacognitive knowledge. In contrast, "in more typical schools, instruction focused on the content or the skill, but not necessarily on providing students with procedural or meta-cognitive strategies" (p. 869).

Fifth, Langer finds that all the high-performing teachers adopted a generative approach to student learning, going beyond students' acquisition of the skills or knowledge to engage them in deeper understandings. In comparison, all of the more typical teachers tended to move on to other goals and activities once they had evidence that the target skills or knowledge had been learned (p. 870).

Sixth, Langer finds that high-performing teachers create social contexts for learning. In schools that beat the odds, she says,

> English learning and high literacy (the content as well as the skills) were treated as social activity, with depth and complexity of understanding and proficiency with conventions growing out of the shared cognition that emerges from interaction with present and imagined others.

In contrast, the more typical classrooms

> emphasized individual activity and individual thinking, with students tending to work alone or to interact primarily with the teacher. Even when group work occurred in such classrooms, the activity usually involved answering questions rather than engaging in substantive discussion from multiple perspectives. (p. 872)

Langer (2000) also studies the professional lives of the teachers and finds that those who outperform the more typical teachers work in environments that promote both student achievement and teacher professional development. The teachers have opportunities to share their teaching ideas and to work on new ideas together. Their environment includes structured improvement activities and encourages teacher caring, commitment, and respect for lifelong learning.

Sperling and Woodlief (1997) also studied expert writing teachers who taught in the ways the National Writing Project recommends and displayed characteristics that Langer finds in her successful teachers. They gave their students many opportunities to write about literature, current events, and firsthand experience, while at the same time devoting plenty of time to preparatory activities; feedback, including whole-class interaction; and teacher conferences. One class was located in a suburban White, middle-class suburb, and the other in an inner-city school serving a racially diverse population.

During the 6 weeks of observation, the former class was working on a research project that involved their collecting data through interviews and print sources, while the latter was working on writing about an event that had been pivotal in their lives. It is clear that these teachers make clear the connections across the days of instruction, taking time to help students develop the skills required to develop their target projects in related activities and discussions. Through interviews and classroom transcripts, the researchers show how each teacher, using comparable approaches, develops a strong community of writers who talk to each other about their ideas and writing, share drafts, and become a cohesive group in the process. The transcripts and descriptions of events strongly suggest that the teachers and their classrooms share the characteristics of Langer's successful teachers and of Hillocks's (1986) inquiry focus and environmental mode, as does the teacher in Sperling (1995).

EDUCATION OF TEACHERS OF WRITING

Researchers and many teachers know quite a bit about what constitutes effective teaching of writing. We have evidence that teachers are paying more attention to writing than they did 25 years ago. Yet the evidence indicates that teachers are either unaware of the research evidence for task-specific knowledge, or they do not put it into practice. While Langer (2001), Sperling and Woodlief (1997), Sperling (1995), and Hillocks (1999) show exemplary teachers, most teachers appear to know little about the teaching of writing beyond the most general knowledge.

Smagorinsky and Whiting (1995) surveyed English education programs in 81 universities, which returned syllabi for methods classes. The methods courses designated as surveys appear to treat composition in a few sessions because they are structured to address a host of topics, from censorship to computers. Most programs appear to present only the most general knowledge about writing, focusing instead on literature. Even courses devoted to writing tended to be workshops for students to work on their own writing rather than courses in the teaching of writing.

Kennedy (1998) examines a variety of teacher education programs, including some secondary preservice and inservice programs. She classifies them as traditional or reform, with traditional focusing on the mechanics of presenting lessons but largely ignoring the subject matter of writing, and reform programs focusing on the subject matter. Kennedy's goal is to determine whether teacher education makes a difference. She presents two descriptions of classrooms, one traditional and one reform. The traditional focuses exclusively on lesson design, which is formulaic, and the reform professor lectures about the ineffectiveness of teaching grammar and usage but says nothing about how to teach. Kennedy finds that the programs do make a difference in the students, but her evidence has to do with little more than teachers' attitudes toward mechanics. One can conclude, however, that in the programs she studied, students learn only the most general knowledge about writing and its teaching. One might conclude that colleges and universities simply do not prepare teachers for the teaching of writing, and therein lies the problem with writing in schools.

This review suggests that we have considerable knowledge about approaches to teaching writing and that we have gleaned it in the decades following Applebee's studies of writing in secondary schools. We find more attention to the specific processes for particular writing tasks and more attention to the need for and effects of focusing on strategies that help students learn to work with the content of their writing. Nearly all studies reviewed make a contribution to this knowledge. But all of that knowledge apparently is not an important part of what beginning English teachers have learned. We are starting to have the knowledge necessary to decide what pedagogical content knowledge teachers of writing should have. The failure to convey the pedagogical content knowledge for teachers of writing is in no small part responsible for the poor showing of American students on various writing assessments.

REFERENCES

Anagnostopoulos, D. (2003). Testing and student engagement in urban classrooms: A multi-layered approach. *Research in the Teaching of English, 38*(2), 177–212.

Anson, C. (Ed.). (1989). *Writing and response: Theory, practice, research*. Urbana, IL: National Council of Teachers of English.

Applebee, A. N. (1981). *Writing in the secondary school: English in the content areas* (NCTE Research Report No. 21). Urbana, IL: National Council of Teachers of English.

Applebee, A. N. (1984). *Contexts for learning to write*. Norwood, NJ: Ablex.

Bakhtin, M. M. (1981). *The dialogic imagination: Four essays by M. M. Bakhtin* (M. Holquist, Ed.); C. Emerson & M. Holquist, Trans.). Austin: University of Texas Press.

Bamberg, B. (1984). Assessing coherence: A reanalysis of essays written for the National Assessment of Educational Progress, 1969–1979. *Research in the Teaching of English, 18*, 305–319.

Bereiter, C., & Scardamalia, M. (1987). *The psychology of written composition*. Hillsdale, NJ: Erlbaum.

Britton, J. N., Burgess, T., Martin, N., McLeod, A., & Rosen, H. (1975). *The development of writing abilities* (pp. 11–18). London: Macmillan.

Broad, B. (2000). Pulling your hair out: Crises of standardization in communal writing assessment. *Research in the Teaching of English, 35*, 213–260.

Chesky, J., & Hiebert, E. H. (1987). The effects of prior knowledge and audience on high school students' writing. *Journal of Educational Research, 80*, 304–313.

Cohen, J. (1977). *Statistical power analysis for the behavioral sciences*. New York: Academic Press.

Connor, U. (1990). Linguistic/rhetorical measures for international persuasive student writing. *Research in the Teaching of English, 24*, 67–87.

Connor, U., & Lauer, J. (1988). Cross cultural variation in persuasive student writing. In A. C. Purves (Ed.), *Writing across languages and cultures: Issues in contrastive rhetoric* (pp. 138–159). Newbury Park, CA: Sage.

Crowhurst, M. (1987). Cohesion in argument and narration at three grade levels. *Research in the Teaching of English, 21*, 185–201.

Dean, M. D. (2000). Muddying boundaries: Mixing genre with five paragraphs. *English Journal, 90*(1), 53–56.

Diedrich, P. B. (1974). *Measuring growth in English*. Urbana, IL: National Council of Teachers of English.

Durst, R. K. (1987). Cognitive and linguistic demands of analytic writing. *Research in the Teaching of English, 21*, 341–376.

Elbow, P. (1973). *Writing without teachers*. New York: Oxford University Press.

Elbow, P. (1981). *Writing with power: Techniques for mastering the writing process*. New York: Oxford University Press.

Freedman, S. W. (1987). *Response to student writing* (NCTE Research Report No. 23). Urbana, IL: National Council of Teachers of English.

Gorman, T. P., Purves, A. C., & Degenhart, R. E. (Eds.). (1988). *The international writing tasks and scoring scales: The international study of achievement in writing*. Oxford, UK: Pergamon Press.

Halliday, M. A. K., & Hasan, R. (1976). *Cohesion in English*. London: Longman.

Hayes, J. R. (2000). A new framework for understanding cognition and affect in writing. In J. R. Squire & R. Indrisano (Eds.), *Perspectives on writing: Research, theory, and practice* (pp. 6–44). Newark, DE: International Reading Association.

Hedges, L. V., & Nowell, A. (1995). Sex differences in mental test scores, variability, and numbers of high-scoring individuals. *Science, 269*, pp. 41–45.

Hedges, L. V., & Nowell, A. (1998). Black–white test score convergence since 1965. In C. Jencks & M. Phillips (Eds.), *The black–white test score gap* (pp. 149–181). Washington, DC: Brookings Institution Press.

Herrnstein, R., & Murray, C. (1994). *The bell curve: Class structure and intelligence in American life*. New York: Free Press.

Hillocks, G., Jr. (1986). *Research on written composition: New directions for teaching.* Urbana, IL: National Conference on Research in English/ERIC Clearinghouse on Reading and Communications Skills.

Hillocks, G., Jr. (1999). *Ways of thinking, ways of teaching.* New York: Teachers College Press.

Hillocks, G., Jr. (2002). *The testing trap: How state assessments of writing control learning.* New York: Teachers College Press.

Huot, B. (1990). The literature of direct writing assessment: Major concerns and prevailing trends. *Review of Educational Research, 60,* 237–263.

Illinois State Board of Education. (1994). *Write on, Illinois!* Springfield, IL: Author.

Jencks, C., & Phillips, M. (Eds.). (1998). *The black–white test score gap.* Washington, DC: Brookings Institution Press.

Johnson, T. S., Smagorinsky, P., Thompson, L., & Fry, P. (2003). Learning to teach the five-paragraph theme. *Research in the Teaching of English, 38*(2), 136–176.

Kahn, E. A. (2000). A case study of assessment in a grade 10 English course. *Journal of Educational Research, 93*(5), 276–286.

Kennedy, M. M. (1998). *Learning to teach writing: Does teacher education make a difference?* New York: Teachers College Press.

Kinneavy, J. L. (1971). *A theory of discourse.* Englewood Cliffs, NJ: Prentice-Hall.

Langer, J. A. (1984). The effects of available information on responses to school writing tasks. *Research in the Teaching of English, 18*(1), 27–44.

Langer, J. A. (1986). *Children reading and writing.* Norwood, NJ: Ablex.

Langer, J. A. (2000). Excellence in English in middle and high school: How teachers' professional lives support student achievement. *American Educational Research Journal, 37,* 397–439.

Langer, J. A. (2001). Beating the odds: Teaching middle and high school students to read and write well. *American Educational Research Journal, 38,* 837–880.

Langer, J. & Applebee, A. (1987). *How writing shapes thinking.* Urbana, IL: National Council of Teachers of English.

Lee, C. D., & Smagorinsky, P. (Eds). (2000). *Vygotskian perspectives on literacy research: Constructing meaning through collaborative inquiry.* New York: Cambridge University Press.

McCann, T. M. (1989). Student argumentative writing and ability knowledge at three grade levels. *Research in the Teaching of English, 23,* 62–76.

McCulley, G. A. (1985). Writing quality, coherence, and cohesion. *Research in the Teaching of English, 19*(3), 269–282.

Murray, D. (1980). Writing as process. In T. R. Donovan & V. W. McClelland (Eds.), *Eight approaches to teaching composition* (pp. 3–20). Urbana, IL: National Council of Teachers of English.

Murray, D. (1987). *Write to learn.* New York: Holt, Rinehart, & Winston.

National Assessment of Educational Progress. (1998). *The NAEP 1998 writing report card for the nation and the states.* Washington, DC: National Center for Education Statistics.

National Assessment of Educational Progress. (2002). *The nation's report card: Writing 2002.* Washington, DC: National Center for Education Statistics.

Nystrand, M., with Gamoran, A., Kachur, R., & Prendergast, C. (1997) *Opening dialogue: Understanding the dynamics of language and learning in the English classroom.* New York: Teachers College Press.

Purves, A. C. (Ed.). (1992). *The IEA study of written composition: Education and performance in fourteen countries.* Oxford, UK: Pergamon Press.

Ruth, L., & Murphy, S. (1987). *Designing writing tasks for the assessment of writing.* Norwood, NJ: Ablex.

Smagorinsky, P. (1991). The writer's knowledge and the writing process: A protocol analysis. *Research in the Teaching of English, 25,* 339–364.

Smagorinsky, P., & Smith, M. W. (1992). The nature of knowledge in composition and literary understanding: The question of specificity. *Review of Educational Research, 62,* 279–305.

Smagorinsky, P., & Whiting, M. E. (1995). *How English teachers get taught: Methods of teaching the methods class.* Urbana, IL: National Council of Teachers of English.

Sperling, M. (1990). I want to talk to each of you: Collaboration and the teacher–student writing conference. *Research in the Teaching of English, 24,* 279–321.

Sperling, M. (1995). Uncovering the role of role in writing and learning to write: One day in an inner-city classroom. *Written Communication, 12,* 93–133.

Sperling, M., & Freedman, S. W. (1987). A good girl writes like a good girl: Written responses to student writing. *Written Communication, 9,* 343–369.

Sperling, M., & Woodlief, L. (1997). Two classrooms, two writing communities: Urban and suburban tenth-graders learning to write. *Research in the Teaching of English*, 31, 205–239.

Stratman, J. F. (1989). The emergence of legal composition as a field of inquiry: Evaluating the prospects. *Review of Educational Research*, 60, 153–235.

Venezky, R. L., Kaestle, C. F., & Sum, A. M. (Eds.). (1987). *The subtle danger: Reflections on the literacy abilities of America's young adults*. Princeton, NJ: Educational Testing Service.

Vygotsky, L. S. (1978). *Mind in society: The development of higher psychological processes* (M. Cole et al., Eds.). Cambridge, MA: Harvard University Press.

Warriner, J. E., & Griffith, F. (1977). *English grammar and composition: Complete course*. New York: Harcourt Brace Jovanovich.

White, E. M. (1985). *Teaching and assessing writing*. San Francisco: Jossey-Bass.

Yeh, S. S. (1998). Empowering education: Teaching argumentative writing to cultural minority middle-school students. *Research in the Teaching of English*, 33(1), 49–83.

CHAPTER 4

Writing at the Postsecondary Level

Russel K. Durst

WHEN I started teaching at the University of Cincinnati in 1987, the library's composition and rhetoric holdings took up only a couple of shelves and included mainly classroom textbooks, many of them relics of what Berlin (1982) calls *current-traditional* teaching—that is, within the positivist perspective—from the 1950s and 1960s. Today the composition and rhetoric holdings require almost a full row of prime library real estate. The holdings now contain a much smaller proportion of textbooks and consist primarily of scholarly and theoretical texts. These texts often, but by no means always, focus in one way or another on the teaching and learning of written composition at the college level, as the field of writing research has gone far beyond a narrow focus on pedagogical concerns to address questions of literacy from rhetorical, philosophical, sociocultural, political, gender studies, and historical perspectives, sometimes all in the same study. Even more research on literacy, mainly dealing with primary and secondary educational contexts, can be found in the library's education holdings, in addition to studies of organizational literacy in the business section. In the years since the mid-1980s, the number of book series and journals has grown dramatically, new presses focusing on many different aspects of literacy have appeared, and leading publishers have significantly expanded their lists.

The present chapter will review the prodigious output of postsecondary studies from 1984 through 2003. Because one salient development in this period has been a sharp decline in empirical studies of writing at the postsecondary level, in favor of more humanisticially grounded theoretical and critical work, I also will include such nonempirical studies in my review when they make an important contribution to the field. In addition, I will include pedagogical and programmatic works that draw substantively upon composition research. The chapter will examine the particular ways in which postsecondary composition inquiry has developed over the past 20 years, investigating the topics, issues, and controversies that have dominated scholars' attention; the disparate theoretical and methodological frameworks writing specialists have employed in their investigations; and the ideas, events, and historical developments that have influenced work in this growing field. A discussion of 20 years of research on writing could be organized several different ways: by methodology, by the theory governing the inquiry, by the topic of the study, or by chronological order, to name just a few. I have chosen to arrange the chapter according to how scholars working in the field over the years have constructed, and also problematized, the following key aspects of postsecondary writing: the student writer, the instructor, and the contexts for writing.

THE STUDENT WRITER

Little published work thus far has looked in a systematic way at the development of composition studies as an academic field, as opposed to the history of composition teaching, which has its own rich literature. With foundational texts, such as those of Britton (1970), Corbett (1965), Elbow (1973), Emig (1971), Kinneavy (1971), Murray (1968), and Shaughnessy (1977), appearing mainly in the late 1960s and 1970s, the field of composition studies simply is not yet old and venerable enough to have inspired a well-developed interest in its history. However, some historically oriented discussions have appeared (e.g., Harris, 1997; Lindemann & Tate, 1991; Tobin & Newkirk, 1994), usually by way of introducing a particular study or a new line of inquiry, or in publications introducing the field to newcomers. These discussions tend to describe the field of composition studies since the early 1980s as moving its focus from a cognitive examination of process to a more social, ethnographic, and political examination of context. This way of discussing "the social turn," as the move to examine context generally is known in composition studies, is, in my view, an oversimplification. Even in the headiest days of writing process pedagogy and research, many authors, including some process adherents, took a wider interest in the scenes of writing and showed a marked concern for the politics of writing instruction. And in the current climate of composition studies, which is dominated by political and social concerns, often to the exclusion of all aspects of pedagogy, an examination of individual writers and their processes is sometimes still a part of composition inquiry. Yet it is undeniable that, over time, social, political, and economic considerations have become more and more central in all areas of composition studies, and scholars increasingly have tended to define student writers in light of such considerations.

In her study of composition authors' representations of student writers, Helmers (1994) argues that composition specialists mainly define students in terms of their shortcomings. A reading of published work in composition in the decade following this book suggests that the rather negative ways of depicting students continue, yet with a certain difference. Before the social turn began to influence composition scholarship in the late 1980s, the shortcomings highlighted by authors had to do mainly with writing and thinking skills, a certain lack of discipline and intellectual tenacity, and a tendency to conform and to avoid risk. With the social turn and the increasing emphasis on political awareness and action, students' weaknesses often are portrayed as more ideological than academic, linguistic, or literary.

Writing Processes

Most of the classic, early writing process studies appeared before 1984 and are discussed amply by Hillocks's (1986) comprehensive review of writing research. Yet until at least the late 1980s, writing process studies continued to appear with declining regularity in composition publications. The most visible writing process researchers,

Flower and Hayes, sometimes with co-collaborators who were generally graduate students working under them at Carnegie-Mellon University, produced a set of studies that for a time dominated college composition (e.g., Flower & Hayes, 1977, 1980, 1981). These studies mainly contrasted beginning college students with more experienced, published writers. Their work drew upon approaches from cognitive science (Hayes is a distinguished professor of psychology) developed by Nobel Prize winner Herbert Simon's studies of experts' and novices' problem-solving strategies (Newell & Simon, 1972).

Using audiotaped think-aloud protocols adapted from their Carnegie-Mellon colleagues Ericsson and Simon (1993), Flower and Hayes had their participants describe what they were thinking and doing, and why, as they wrote, yielding transcripts rich in psychological detail. Participants typically were asked to compose aloud while responding to a prompt such as, "Describe yourself for the readership of *Seventeen Magazine*," the idea being to create a prompt with a very specific audience and purpose so that the researchers could examine how the writers approached those aspects of the task. From their analysis of these transcripts, and by contrasting expert and novice responses to the researchers' writing prompts, Flower and Hayes developed a model of the writing process that was cognitive in nature, focusing on the writing task, audience, purpose, and prior knowledge, and requiring the writer to choose among a range of composing strategies, all while monitoring the developing piece and one's own practices. The model included a small area termed "the task environment," but Flower and Hayes defined this element in narrow terms, rather than in a broader cultural or political sense, and rarely discussed this aspect of the model in any significant detail.

The writer that emerged from these studies was a more or less universal or generic student, with no discussion of potential cultural or gender differences, and a mainly rational writer, responding to the demands of the task in an effort to produce a successful piece of writing for the audience in question that achieved the writer's understanding of the purpose motivating the writing task. The first-year college student novice writers typically differed from more experienced writers in having a more confused sense of the purpose for writing, little awareness of audience, and a weak or nonexistent overall monitor in charge of determining how and when to deploy particular composing strategies. Several studies focused specifically on revision, finding, rather predictably, that novice writers made fewer substantive revisions and tended to concentrate on low-level surface changes (e.g., Flower, Hayes, Carey, Shriver, & Stratman, 1986).

As this work appeared, opponents from within the field of composition, steeped in humanistic scholarly traditions, increasingly challenged its social science methodology, mechanistic view of the writer, and lack of attention to cultural factors (Bizzell, 1992). By the end of the 1980s, writing process studies largely had dried up. Leading process scholars such as Perl and Wilson (1986) and Sommers (1992) had moved into new areas of inquiry—profiles of master teachers and reflective autobiographical essays, respectively—that were more acceptable to the increasingly anti-cognitive/social science perspective in composition studies. Flower began highlighting and filling in the previously vague social dimension of her composing process model (1994), now described as a social cognitive model based on negotiated meaning, as opposed to a process involving solely the individual author, and her own research shifted to community literacy (2002). In addition, it could be said that composing process studies had gone as far as they could go in yielding useful, illuminating pictures of writers' general approaches. Having been inundated with process studies for close to a decade, composition scholars had achieved a solid understanding of the general process and were eager to explore other aspects of writing.

Academic Discourse

Responding to such concerns, starting in the mid- to late 1980s, researchers began examining college students' initiation into academic discourses and ways of thinking. These studies built upon the foundation laid by process research to examine the demands of the specific writing tasks and situations students encountered in the university, and how they understood and coped with college writing generally. Some of the most important and lasting work in this area was influenced by the writing across the curriculum/writing in the disciplines movement, moving beyond a concern with first-year English composition to investigate students' experiences in other disciplines and provide a fuller picture of the college student as writer. With the exception of some survey studies that attempted to determine the type and extent of writing required in different disciplines (e.g., Bridgeman & Carlson, 1984), this work for the most part eschewed experimental methods in which student participants respond under controlled conditions to a prompt supplied by the researcher.

Instead, researchers typically adopted a more "naturalistic" approach influenced by qualitative and ethnographic methods just beginning to appear in literacy studies. For example, McCarthy (1987) documented the vastly differing writing assignments and expectations a first-year student in a small private college encountered in English, biology, and history classes. Zooming in on one discipline and focusing more on students' approaches rather than possible shortcomings of instruction, North (1986) used a hermeneutic methodology to examine the journal writing of three students in a philosophy course, finding that students' preconceived notions and willingness to engage the subject matter greatly affected their ability to apply course concepts. Herrington (1985), using case study methodology, focused on the demands of writing in chemical engineering courses, again finding that instructors expected students to approach their writing very differently than they were taught to write essays in English, but often without giving students a clear sense of these differing expectations. Similarly, Chiseri-Strater (1991) contrasted two advanced undergraduate students' writing for an upper-level composition course with writing in the students' own majors, art history and political science, respectively, where students were expected to conform to narrow structural requirements and were often discouraged from drawing upon their own prior knowledge or interests in approaching writing tasks. The picture that emerges from these studies is one of some perplexity, as expectations are not clearly explained and the ground rules underlying teachers' evaluations are largely implicit.

Another set of studies attempts to understand how students approach the demands of particular kinds of writing activities across the college curriculum, what types of learning writing can promote, and how instructors best can structure such activities. Walvoord (1986; Walvoord & McCarthy, 1990; Walvoord, Hunt, Dowling, & McCarthy, 1997) examined classes in a variety of academic disciplines in which she had worked with faculty on incorporating writing activities. Findings show that students work more effectively when task demands and expectations are explicit, assignments are broken up as much as possible into discrete steps, and peer work and groupwork are incorporated. Greene studied students in a college history course (1993), a first-year writing class (1995), and a history of science course (2001) to show the active meaning-making strategies students employed in learning course subject matter and the ways in which writing activities substantially aided student learning. Mathison (1996) investigated writing of critiques in a sociology course, finding that students did better when basing their responses on disciplinary knowledge and close reading rather than on personal opinion.

Penrose and Sitko (1993) published an edited book of studies in the Flower and Hayes cognitivist tradition but rooted more in the analysis of actual classroom contexts and with a strong emphasis on pedagogical concerns. The chapters in this book depict college student writers as complex problem solvers and focus on such areas of cognitive analysis as the rhetoric of reading, writing, and learning, using secondary sources in writing, research processes, collaborative writing, audience awareness, and student–teacher conferences. Of particular note is Nelson's (1993) investigation of research writing (see also Nelson, 1990), in which she examined ways in which students, desiring a compact and efficient writing process, subverted activities intended to require complex critical thinking by finessing the more difficult steps.

While literacy researchers such as Fishman and McCarthy, Walvoord, and Greene continue to investigate the teaching and learning of writing across disciplines, the great bulk of research on college students and their writing is located in the field of English, and most still centers on the first-year composition course. A number of composition scholars have examined ways in which writing in general and the composition class in particular can serve as a vehicle for students' personal and intellectual development, self-understanding, and creative expression. For example, a series of studies by Newkirk (1984, 1995, 1997) explores the uses of what could be called a student-centered pedagogy, in which students come up with their own topics for writing, meet frequently with the teacher and with fellow peers to develop and hone their texts, and are encouraged to write about what is most important to them. In his work from the mid-1980s, Newkirk shows that students evaluate student writing very differently than do their composition instructors, and he argues that teachers need to be very explicit about their expectations if they wish to have students provide peer feedback. Newkirk (1997) employs Goffman's (1959) notion of the various "masks" that people employ to display themselves in public, to examine how students approach personal writing tasks, arguing that students do their best thinking and writing on personally meaningful material. Tobin (1991, 2003) examines a very similar pedagogical approach but from a more psychoanalytic perspective, arguing that the teacher–student relationship is fraught with conflict, sexual tension, and competition.

Writing Development

Several other scholars examine student writers using a developmental model. These authors compiled years of data on students' writing that they examined systematically and with clear theoretical frameworks. Each seems eager to put as positive a spin on students' writing and intellectual development as possible, in part to counter negative representations of student writers from both inside and outside the field. Haswell (1991) takes a mainly academic and linguistic approach, investigating mainstream, middle-class, mainly White students' mastery of writing conventions and sentence-level features. His longitudinal study does show, however, that even after students master a difficult construction and move on to try something new or wrestle with complicated points, they are likely to revert to earlier mistakes, at least temporarily.

Sternglass (1997), longtime writing director at City College of New York, has a political purpose that she explicitly acknowledges and defends in her book, a detailed study of open admissions students' writing and learning at City College. Working in part to counter the accusations of widespread failure of students of color at City College (e.g., Traub's [1994] critique of remedial instruction in which he recommends that such instruction be eliminated from the college), and the very real pressure from city officials to disband her program, Sternglass provides a much more positive depiction of student efforts. She shows, focusing closely on one particular student, that even those from underprivileged backgrounds, with little previous success in school, and with demanding out-of-school situations, can make enormous strides in their writing and learning. Even if often their writing still lacks certain features of polished academic prose, such as perfect sentence-level correctness, Sternglass argues that such is often the case with middle-class students who began the journey with far less distance to cover.

Herrington and Curtis (2000; Curtis & Herrington, 2003) focus mainly on personal development and its interrelationship with college writing in their long-term study of four students' varied experiences in college. The authors examine a gay male with a background of abuse, a woman whose father was an alcoholic, a Vietnamese immigrant, and a fiercely independent African American from a working-class, Spanish-speaking, immigrant background. Herrington and Curtis do a thorough job of examining how students' backgrounds, personalities, interests, emotions, and relationships affected their college writing, as well as how the writing helped students develop a sustaining personal identity.

Politics, Culture, and Student Writers

The social turn in composition might be said to begin with Bartholomae's (1985) close reading of entering college students' placement essays. Bartholomae argues that students writing a placement essay must recreate, or invent, the university as an academic discourse community, not so much in terms of sentence-level conventions as through the types of arguments they make and the attitude of budding expertise they convey. He shows how the strongest student writers put forward commonplaces that they go on to problematize, arguing that this way of dealing with complexity characterizes intellectual work in the academy. Bartholomae's work represents a social view of students as beginners attempting to enter an unfamiliar and in some ways unwelcoming discourse community; he argues that students typically put forward Herculean efforts to write the way they think college instructors wish them to.

Soon after the appearance of Bartholomae's (1985) essay, a more politically oriented brand of inquiry began to appear in composition studies. This work was influenced by work in the larger field of English studies drawing upon Marxist criticism (including Paolo Freire's 1970 pioneering discussion of the teaching of critical consciousness to Brazilian peasants), as well as British socialist Raymond Williams's (1958) analysis of socialism, class, and capitalist society, cultural studies' radical critiques of the educational system (e.g., Giroux, 1983, 1988), and poststructuralist theory (e.g., Berlin, 1988; Brodkey, 1987; Brooke, 1987; Chase, 1988; Paine, 1989).

These studies position the student in a first-year writing course not as disadvantaged, but rather as a somewhat privileged middle-class person in need of greater awareness about social inequities and improved ways of critiquing dominant discourse for the purpose of uncovering such inequities and helping to effect change. Typically abstract and theoretical in their presentations, these authors occasionally cite examples from their own classrooms, but they almost entirely avoid systematic empirical analysis of the politicized classroom approaches they advocate. While the authors, to varying degrees, take pains to argue that they wish to develop students' critical faculties, not to indoctrinate them to a particular ideology, the authors clearly are eager to, in the words of one writer, "influence (perhaps manipulate is the more accurate word) students' values through charisma or power" and "inculcate into our students the conviction that the dominant order is repressive" (Paine, 1989, p. 564).

A plethora of articles and books appeared at the beginning of the 1990s exploring the radical composition class and the student's role in it, a movement in composition studies that continues to the present day. Several edited collections early in the decade examine the intersections of writing and politics and declare the need to expose students to progressive views, even, in some cases, to try to move students away from conservative, consumerist attitudes. Hurlbert and Blitz's (1991) collection contains essays by leading scholars, along with transcripts of their discussions on literacy and politics from a day-long workshop devoted to radical pedagogy at the Conference on College Composition and Communication (CCCC). Chapters discuss various possible approaches to introducing students to oppositional thinking, critical discourse, and questioning of the status quo within the context of the composition classroom.

The contributors to Berlin and Vivion's (1992) edited collection consider ways of using cultural studies theories imported from Britain's Birmingham School (e.g., Hall & Jefferson, 1976) to help bring students to consciousness. Bullock and Trimbur's (1991) edited book envisions the kinds of activities and approaches that a progressive composition course could embody. Individual chapters consider such aspects of composition as grading, curriculum development, program administration, the academic job market, writing across the curriculum, women's struggles as both students and teachers, and basic writing issues. Bizzell (1992) speaks for a number of radical or critical pedagogy advocates when she describes her primary purpose in teaching her students at an expensive Catholic college: "to interest them in a social justice project for which they may not presently see any compelling reason" (p. 30). Harkin and Schilb's (1991) edited collection applies postmodern and feminist theory to the writing classroom in order to argue for a more politically focused pedagogy.

Throughout the 1990s up to the present, following these early, groundbreaking works, a great many journal articles, edited collections, and single-authored books have focused on the explicitly political composition class. Many of these studies consider students' receptivity to such pedagogy and argue for addressing more directly students' reactionary tendencies. The specific view of politics advocated rarely is spelled out in elaborate detail but generally involves an acknowledgment of middle-class privilege; a critique of consumerism; an awareness of class, race, and gender discrimination; a willingness to question injustice; and a desire to try to correct inequities (Berlin, 1996; Brodkey, 1996; Fitts & France, 1995; Knoblauch & Brannon, 1993; Shor, 1992, 1996; Sullivan & Qualley, 1994). Other salient politically oriented publications from the 1990s include Mortenson and Kirsch's (1993) examination of authority in writing; Fishman and McCarthy's (1996) presentation of a progressive pedagogy based on Dewey's educational philosophy but applied to critical thinking and learning in college; and Cushman's (1996) discussion of the rhetorician as an agent of social change and the implications of this view for literacy instruction at all levels.

In more recent years, this emphasis on the classroom as a political space and on students as in need of exposure to progressive views has continued. Prominent studies include Bizzell's (1997) article on a first-year English curriculum using documents discussing cross-cultural contact, conflict, and resolution throughout American history to teach progressive forms of persuasive discourse; Anderson (1997) on composition teaching as confrontation between progressive teacher and conservative student; Adler-Kassner (1998) and Spiegelman (1998) redefining the notion of students' "ownership" of their writing in a more political context; Welsh (2001) on resistance theory and composition teaching; Trainor (2002) on helping middle-class composition students deal with their "whiteness"; Herndl and Bauer (2003) on using liberation theology in composition instruction to show how marginal groups, such as oppressed minorities, can change society; and Roberts-Miller (2003) on the philosophy of communitarianism as a composition pedagogy. All of these publications represent students as comfortable, advantaged, and in need of a serious wake-up call to recognize their own privilege and to work to make society more fair and equitable.

Another set of studies has questioned the value of such confrontational pedagogy. Durst (1999) looked empirically at first-year students in a politically oriented English class and found students extremely resistant to the views advocated by the instructor and the course reader, entitled *Rereading America* (Colombo, Cullen, & Lisle, 1989). Students sought and found ways of choosing topics that allowed them to avoid the political subject matter at the center of the course. Durst advocates a pedagogical theory known as *reflective instrumentalism*, in which the instructor accepts students' desire to gain practical skills and certification, but then works to add a critical dimension to students' pragmatic views. Smith (1997) and Durst (2003) also critique confrontational pedagogies as ineffective and alienating, and offer alternative approaches.

Gender Issues

Scholarship on gender concerns in the composition class began to appear in the late 1980s. Most of this work deals with women students and is rooted in feminist approaches. Flynn (1988) draws upon the work of Gilligan (1982) and Belenky, Clinchy, Goldberger, and Tarule (1986) to explore the possibility that women students write differently than do male students. In examining narratives by only four students, two male and two female, Flynn finds evidence that the males focused more on achieving individual goals while the women focused on collaboration and connections among individuals, yet the author is careful not to make any large claims based on such a tiny sample.

Over the next decade, a number of studies discussed issues of gender in the composition classroom and in the academy more generally. Thirty-six of these essays appear in Kirsch, Maor, Massey, Nickoson-Massey, and Sheridan-Rabideau's (2003) collection, which includes work published between 1971 and 2000. The book contains chapters on early feminist voices and visions; feminist theories and research;

gender and forms of writing; gender, teaching, and equity; and feminism and the politics of the profession (see also Jarratt & Worsham, 1998; Phelps & Emig, 1995). Other salient pieces not included in these collections are Lamb's (1991) discussion of feminism and argumentation and Kirsch's (1993) monograph on women academics as writers. More recently, McCrary (2001) has discussed using womanist theology in the writing class, and Rhodes (2002) has examined the communities women college students form in on-line writing. Ritchie and Boardman (1999) review all published work on feminism and composition, focusing mainly on issues concerning professional conditions for women teaching in the field, but to a lesser extent on the situation of women students in college composition.

Race and Ethnicity

A growing body of work in composition focuses on the concerns of students of color, particularly African American students, in the college writing class. Two salient autobiographical books showing the plight of working-class students of color and the difficulties they face adjusting to the predominantly White culture of the academy are Gilyard (1991) and Villanueva (1993). The 1980s saw the publication of little scholarship specifically discussing students of color in college composition. Since the early 1990s, though, work in this area has appeared with increasing frequency. One set of studies considers the specific kinds of problems African American students tended to have in composition, traceable to teachers' inability to accept or deal with students' nonstandard dialects (Ball & Lardner, 1997; Coleman, 1997; Howard, 1996); to the hostile or neglectful environment students often meet in the academy (Gill, 1992; Gilyard, 1999a, 1999b; Gonsalves, 2003; Mutnick, 1995; Prendergast, 1998); and to the literacy, educational, and social backgrounds of African American college students (Harris, Kamhi, & Pollock, 2001). Barron (2003) examines the difficulties Latino/a American college students from different ethnic groups face due to the ways they see—and are seen by—the mainstream culture. Lyons (2000) and Powell (2002) discuss Native American students' approaches to writing and ways of engaging such students in college composition.

Other studies have examined the effectiveness of various approaches for teaching composition to students of color. Canagarajah (1997) found that a combination of "contact zone" and "safe house" classroom discourse situations helped students gain confidence and write more effectively. Focusing on African American women college students, Richardson (2002) argues that expertise in mother tongue literacy is an important key to the language education of students of color. Soliday (1996), in an analysis of one student's progress in writing, argues for mainstreaming writers deemed "underprepared" in writing placement tests. Horner and Lu (1999) articulate a pedagogy for marginalized students that focuses on questioning received truths and openly addressing political issues and questions of justice in the classroom. Wallace and Bell (1999) address the specific complications for urban African American male students attending a university that is overwhelmingly White and rural. Balester (1993), in an ethnographic study of eight successful African American student writers, found that code switching between Black and standard English was an effective strategy for composition students. Royster and Williams (1996) and Gilyard (1999a, 1999b) review studies of students of color and faculty in detailing the many contributions African Americans have made to the advancement of the field of composition studies. Villanueva (1993) considers the residues of racism in composition, evidenced in acts of exclusion and rejection.

Socioeconomic Class

A related and relatively recent area of inquiry concerns social economic class and composition, mostly consisting of studies of working-class students, who are more likely to feel out of place and do poorly in college composition. Rose (1989) traces his development as a first-generation college student from a working-class background and uses this background to consider programs and pedagogies designed to assist such students. Rose argues that marginalized students often know much more than they seem to but will respond best to approaches that welcome them to the academy, concentrate on students' strengths, and avoid focusing inordinately on surface mistakes (see also Rose, 1985; Hull & Rose, 1989, 1990; Hull, Rose, Fraser, & Castellano, 1991). Shor (1992, 1996) examines the inner workings of a critical pedagogy for working-class students in which students help to choose the course subject matter, requirements, and goals for assessment. Lindquist (1999) investigates discourse patterns in a working-class bar where she worked as a bartender and, in light of her own work experiences and working-class background, discusses class issues in composition. Durst (1999), drawing upon Sheeran and Barnes (1991), focuses on the difficulties working-class students may experience in figuring out the implicit ground rules governing classroom success.

Another strand of the literature on working-class student writers focuses on students in open admission community colleges. Tinberg (1997) provides a comprehensive introduction to this area of inquiry. In addition, Lewiecki-Wilson and Sommers's 1999 essay reviews the history of composition scholars' attitudes and approaches toward open admission students from the time of Mina Shaughnessy in the mid-1970s. The journals *Teaching English in the Two Year College* and the *Journal of Basic Writing* both regularly publish discussions of issues surrounding literacy teaching and learning and working-class and first-generation college students.

Sexual Orientation

The most recent student population to be studied by writing researchers has to do with sexual orientation, mainly involving gay and lesbian students, with some authors broadening their lens to include bisexual and transgender students as well. The majority of work in the emerging area of composition and sexual orientation thus far has focused either on queer theory and gay and lesbian studies as subject matter for or a way of conceptualizing the classroom (e.g., Haggerty & Zimmerman, 1995; Smith, 1997; Spurlin, 2000) or on issues concerning the gay and lesbian instructor (e.g., Gibson, Marinara, & Meem, 2000; Parmeter & Reti, 1988; Wallace, 2002). Fewer studies have focused on gay and lesbian students. Malinowitz (1995) offers a detailed analysis of composition classes with gay and lesbian subject matter at two universities in New York, one public and open admission, the other private, selective, and expensive. She contrasts the freedom students feel in her classes to express themselves freely and to discuss issues of sexual orientation, with the pressures they generally feel in most other classes not to broach the topic or provide information about themselves. Alexander (1997, 2002) also discusses issues affecting gay and lesbian students in composition and lays out curricula that examine issues of sexuality and sexual orientation. Several other essays (Bleich, 1989; Miller, 2000; Rothgery, 1993) discuss ways of approaching and countering homophobia in the classroom and in student writing.

Service Learning and Community Writing

Composition scholars increasingly have turned their attention to community service. The purposes of such work are to help students grow academically while helping others (many course projects are discipline specific), become more aware of social inequities, and develop the expertise and motivation to work toward change. Parks and Goldblatt (2000) lay out and examine a structure in which English departments could expand their scope well beyond the campus to take on community-based literacy projects. Deans (2000) provides a comprehensive vision of the student's role in community writing projects as part of a composition curriculum. Adler-Kassner, Crooks, and Watters's (1997) edited collection presents a range of discussions of individual service learning initiatives in college composition as well as an extensive bibliography. Flower (2002) investigates a community forum for youth of color administered by English composition and rhetoric specialists emphasizing reasoned discussion of controversial issues by all parties affected. Such initiatives attempt to apply the disciplinary expertise of composition studies to public service in new and interesting ways.

THE TEACHER

Research on postsecondary writing instruction over the past 20 years shows the teacher of composition moving, at times uneasily, between a focus on theory and one on praxis, between the conflicting roles of gatekeeper and liberator, indoctrinator of institutional values and iconoclastic social critic, supportive writing coach and confrontational advocate of an opposing world view. Theories of pedagogy emphasizing political awareness and action, a quest for social justice, and an emphasis on equality for the less privileged have dominated the field since their introduction in the late 1980s. Rather than focusing primarily on developing writing abilities, the curriculum increasingly calls upon instructors to develop in students—through reading, writing, critical thinking, and discussion—a certain sensibility, a way of looking at the world or disposition of mind in which the student writer is taught a commitment to community service, an awareness of inequities, a critical stance toward authority, and a questioning nature regarding established ways of thinking. This political emphasis in the teaching of writing has changed over the past decade and a half with the evolution of the social turn in composition studies. Teachers also wrestle with marginal status in current studies of composition, as adjuncts or graduate students lacking institutional power or security, or in terms of their ethnicity, gender, or sexual orientation.

College Writing Teachers in the Mid-1980s

The picture emerging from Hillocks (1986) and other published work of the era, in the mid- to late 1980s, shows the college composition specialist focused on teaching his or her students to write effectively but also struggling to determine exactly how to define effective writing, with considerable disagreement among writing specialists given their varying pedagogical approaches or schools of composition teaching. Developing these approaches, such as expressivist (Elbow, 1973; Murray, 1968; Newkirk, 1997), process (Emig, 1971; Flower & Hayes, 1977; Perl, 1978; Sommers, 1980), neoclassical (Corbett, 1965; Fulkerson, 1996), and social epistemic (Bartholomae, 1985; Berlin, 1987; Berthoff, 1981), was a major if not the primary activity for composition specialists at this time. The dominant approach by the late 1980s, at least in terms of what the majority of composition specialists wrote in journals and books in the field, was the social epistemic, which emphasized language as a key tool for the construction of meaning, a heuristic device, rather than merely a means of recording pre-existing meaning. Thus, the composition instructor's position took on greater significance, as it involved fundamental issues of thinking, learning, understanding, and even shaping the world, not simply learning formulas, rules, and conventions for essay construction.

By the mid- to late 1980s, a small number of scholars were beginning to question what they viewed as a narrow emphasis on effective writing as acontextual, a mere skill or approach to be learned, when divorced from the social, political, and economic climate in which readers and writers existed. Myers (1986) draws upon Marxist theory to argue for the "social and economic basis of education" (p. 162) and to suggest that composition scholars aim "not for a new kind of assignment, but for more skepticism about what assignments do to reproduce the structures of our society" (p. 170). Myers lays the groundwork here for a critical reconsideration of the relation between writing instruction and the larger social context.

Brodkey (1987) and Lu (1986) attempt to reconceptualize the act of writing away from its traditional understanding in composition studies as an academic, intellectual, and/or creative exercise and an attempt to communicate personally significant meaning. Brodkey describes literacy research and pedagogy as "a social, historical, and political construction of the participants whose individual and collective activities inside and outside the classroom determine whether writing is set aside as a school subject or is integrated into their lives" (p. 414). Lu draws upon her own experiences growing up in China during the cultural revolution, in which acts of language constantly were questioned and challenged, to argue for a politicized view of writing as struggle, conflict, and negotiation among differing groups. At about this same time, other composition scholars were advising instructors to take into consideration, when designing instructional approaches, students' feelings of alienation, their oppositional attitudes toward the "official" pedagogy of the composition class, and their occasional desire to subvert or work around the goals of the teacher (Brooke, 1987; Chase, 1988; Giroux, 1983, 1988).

Harris (1989) won a Braddock Award for his analysis of the applicability of the term "community" to the writing classroom, arguing that instructors should seek discussion of differing positions on social and political issues rather than emphasizing consensus. His 1997 book, *A Teaching Subject: Composition Since 1966*, examines not only the concept of community as a key term in composition but also other influential terms—process, growth, error, and voice—and their scholarly and pedagogical uses in the development of composition as a unique academic field emphasizing both published inquiry and a commitment to working intensively with first-year college students. Dean (1989) describes the increase in diversity in the college composition student body, with immigrants and international students from all over the world entering U.S. colleges, and argues that the curriculum must become more focused on cultural and political issues. These authors are taking the more individualist anti-authority politics of such expressionist figures as Elbow and Murray into larger political arenas.

Politics and Writing Instructors

Berlin (1988) expanded upon his concept of *epistemic rhetoric* in his effort to reveal the political realities of writing instruction. He had originally viewed this rhetorical approach as a way of looking at writing and the teaching of writing as not simply about recording reality but about using language to create that reality and to make sense of the world. In this essay, "epistemic" has become "social epistemic" and now refers to a rhetoric and to a writing classroom that "offers an explicit critique of economic, political, and social arrangements" (p. 490). More explicitly political than his previous discussions of the teaching of writing, Berlin argues here for a course whose subject matter is social inequities and students' implication in an unjust system.

Since then, numerous pedagogical studies have constructed the classroom as a political space in which the teacher has as a primary responsibility the task of introducing students to larger social issues. In the Afterword of Bizzell's (1992) collected essays, she asks the question, "What is to be done?" She answers that "students can be encouraged to see themselves as moral agents," and adds, "I want to range over the values my students are exploring and try to find those that could be used persuasively to turn students to my egalitarian values" (p. 292). Bizzell's pedagogy here comprises a reading and writing curriculum involving analysis of materials in U.S. history that document situations in which different groups came into contact and conflict and "there was a plurality of contending voices" (p. 293), to show that "Americans have very often been concerned about social justice, that if we do not often achieve it, neither can we forget about it" (p. 294). While allowing students to attempt to persuade her with their own "discriminatory views," she argues that the composition teacher must be willing to "prophecy for social justice" (p. 295).

Thus, in these early years of the social turn in composition studies, scholars were struggling to figure out how best to develop a "social justice" curriculum that would enhance students' literacy. Several authors consider feminist approaches, such as Lamb's (1991) discussion of less confrontational methods of argumentation and Jarratt's (1991) opposing argument that students who resist feminist approaches should be confronted about their views by teacher and fellow students. Other gender-oriented work includes Bauer (1990) on feminist notions of classroom authority, in which she argues that "political commitment—especially feminist commitment—is a legitimate classroom strategy and rhetorical imperative," as "the feminist agenda offers a goal toward our students' conversions to emancipatory critical action" (p. 389). Additional feminist-oriented publications from the early 1990s include Hollis (1992) on feminist pedagogy in the writing workshop, and a Braddock Award winning piece on the nature of authority in writing (Mortensen & Kirsch, 1993) that advocates teaching a more inclusive, less oppositional notion of authority. Fitts and France's (1995) collection includes several chapters discussing feminist approaches, including Rosenthal (1995) on feminist approaches to collaborative writing.

Cultural Studies

Many in composition, beginning in the early 1990s, championed a pedagogy of cultural studies in the writing class. George and Trimbur (2001) review the scholarship on cultural studies and the teaching of composition. This pedagogy is influenced by Frankfurt School theoreticians Adorno, Benjamin, and Horkheimer (see Arato & Gebhardt, 1978), British scholars such as Williams (1958), and their American counterparts Grossberg (1989), Johnson (1987), and Ross (1988). As an academic movement, cultural studies sought to redefine culture away from its elite and exclusive sense or as a high/low binary, while taking seriously the cultural pursuits of everyday people and showing the relation of those pursuits to people's social class consciousness. Primary advocates of cultural studies in composition include Trimbur (1989), who was the first to link these two fields by focusing on the history of working-class access to higher education and attitudes of the elite toward this access. Berlin (1991; Berlin & Vivion, 1992) used cultural studies theory to interrogate the discipline of English, which historically has privileged literature while keeping rhetoric subordinate. And rhetoric, Berlin argues, properly used, can help empower students to become aware of social inequities through a cultural studies approach and then question and fight the status quo. Several other composition specialists examine cultural studies through the lens of postmodernist theory (Faigley, 1992; Harkin & Schilb, 1991; Schilb, 1996), with its critique of modernist epistemology.

Collaboration

From the mid-1980s, a substantial number of studies have examined collaborative writing in the composition class and the teacher's role in shaping and engaging in the collaborative process. This subarea began with Bruffee's (1984) use of epistemic rhetorical theory to argue for the importance of talk and interaction, the social dimension of language use, in developing written meaning. This early work mainly stressed the benefits of paired and group discussion in helping writers figure out what they wanted to say and how best to say it, through forms of written and oral feedback and interaction that stressed peer review and reciprocal feedback (Forman, 1992; Gere, 1987; LeFevre, 1987). In addition, a fairly large body of work discussed the nature and benefits of collaborative writing, as a way of helping students learn to work constructively with peers and consolidate different perspectives in a piece of writing (Ede & Lunsford, 1990).

But fairly early on, as part of the incipient social turn in composition studies, some began to look critically at what they viewed as an undertheorized and overly positive assessment of collaboration. Trimbur (1989) was the first to argue that current approaches to collaboration too strongly emphasized consensus and unanimity of view, suggesting that for collaboration to be most beneficial, opportunities for disagreement and expression of divergent ideas need to be built in. The critical tradition he established was followed by Harris's (1989) rejection of the term "community" in favor of the less consensus-driven idea of the city, and his view of the classroom as a site where dissensus is not only tolerated but encouraged and explored.

Spiegelman (1998) examines the concept of ownership in the context of peer review groups, arguing that, depending in part on specific economic and social conditions, student writers tend to vacillate between an individual and a communal perspective on authorship, leading to ambivalence about the very idea of working in peer groups. Yancey and Spooner (1998) consider the disconnect between composition studies' celebration of student collaborative work and the institutional structures of academia that often discourage or forbid it. Howard (1999) investigates evolving notions of plagiarism, considering both teachers' and students' attitudes and approaches toward incorporating other voices in the their writing. In addition, a review essay by Howard (2001) surveys developments in collaborative pedagogy. On the whole, work in this area is a microcosm of the larger field, illustrating the move from a focus on using collaboration to help students get stronger feedback and improve their writing to an emphasis on the politics of collaboration, the benefits of disagreement and dispute, and the dangers of consensus.

Critical Pedagogy

The most common depiction of the college composition instructor in published work over the past 15 years is as a critical teacher, shaping students' literacy, intellectual, and cultural development through pedagogies of social justice and political analysis. Much influenced by Dewey's (1916) pedagogy of progressive education and Freire's (1970) Marxist approach to helping Brazilian peasant farmers learn basic literacy, critical pedagogy as applied in the United States takes as its instructional goal the raising of students' consciousness of their social and political situatedness. In one popular approach, Shor (1992, 1996) and other proponents (e.g., Bizzell, 1992; hooks, 1994; Knoblauch & Brannon, 1993; McLaren, 1989) advocate organizing a nontraditional classroom in which students work with the teacher to develop curriculum and set class rules and procedures. The idea is to empower students to take responsibility for their own learning, and while doing so, to teach not only reading, writing, and thinking, but also a more critical, sophisticated political analysis and a higher level of engagement in action for social change.

The Marginalized Instructor

Along with studies of students not always fully accepted within the academy is a literature that focuses on composition teachers who sometimes experience a marginal status of their own, such as racial and ethnic minorities and nontenure track faculty. Three 1999 articles, by Gilyard, Royster and Williams, and Smitherman, in *College Composition and Communication* (CCC) examine the many contributions to the field by African American composition teachers and scholars, as well as the difficulties facing such instructors, with Smitherman focusing on the role of African American compositionists, including, prominently, herself, in the development of the CCCC policy statement on Students' Right to Their Own Language, in the mid-1970s. Gilyard's 1999 edited collection not only discusses African American faculty concerns but also includes chapters by and about Native American and Asian American instructors. Smitherman and Villanueva's 2003 collection investigates issues inherent in linguistically diverse classes and considers teachers' options in working with students whose first language or dialect is not standard English. Villanueva (1993) offers an autobiographical analysis of his own experiences as a Puerto Rican native speaker of Spanish who becomes a distinguished scholar of composition, but not without suffering discrimination and misunderstanding along the way.

In 1986, composition specialists at a summer conference passed what came to be known as the Wyoming Resolution, protesting the exploitation of many writing teachers, particularly adjunct instructors (Robertson, Crowley, & Lentriccia, 1987). The resolution was endorsed unanimously at the following year's CCCC, and in 1989, the organization's Executive Committee put forward an official statement on professional standards urging fair compensation and decent working conditions for all college writing teachers. This statement was published in February of that year in *CCC*. Since the initial Wyoming Resolution, a number of publications, some by adjuncts or former adjuncts themselves, have examined the conditions of adjunct composition faculty and the effects of their exploitation not only on the instructors themselves but on the entire field. Eileen Schell's 1998 book, *Gypsy Academics and Mother-Teachers: Gender, Contingent Labor, and Writing Instruction*, centers on the predominance of women among the ranks of adjunct faculty. Several essays propose reforms such as the creation of a more humane, better compensated faculty position, with job security, benefits, and opportunities for professional development (e.g., Harris, 2000; Murphy, 2000; Trainor & Godley, 1998). Bosquet (2003) critiques the de facto two-tiered system such an approach creates, with large groups of composition faculty still occupying a position inferior to that of tenure track professors.

CONTEXTS

Research on contextual factors affecting postsecondary writing focuses on three areas of study: assessment, technology, and the academy itself as an institutional and cultural setting for college writing.

Assessment

Evaluating the quality of student writing, whether as a placement strategy, during a course, or at the exit point, has been and remains a major part of writing instructors' activity and researchers' inquiry. A core group of specialists publish regularly in this area, and important advances, such as the multiple uses of portfolios and development of new approaches to teacher response, have taken place in the past 20 years. Yet composition scholars, particularly those who focus on pedagogy, often show considerable discomfort with the emphasis on assessment. Negative associations with the act of grading are common, such as Belanoff's (1991) reference to grading as "the dirty thing we do in the dark of our offices" (p. 61). Indeed, one often-stated benefit of portfolio assessment is that grading can be deferred until late in a course and students ostensibly can focus instead on developing as writers and thinkers, without being distracted by worrying about the dreaded grade. Other scholars have countered that students' concerns about assessment are never far below the surface, no matter how much instructors seek to de-emphasize grading, and that evaluation anxiety may be most intense in courses that offer the least feedback on student performance (e.g., Tobin, 1991). Two major reviews of published work in writing assessment have appeared in recent years (Huot, 2002; Yancey, 1999). Salient developments in the field of writing assessment in the past 2 decades, in addition to studies of portfolios and teacher response, include recent attempts to place assessment in wider social, political, and pedagogical contexts; critical examination of the role and meaning of reliability and validity in assessment; continued analysis of techniques for holistic scoring; and increasing discussion of reflection as a learning and self-assessment strategy.

Portfolios first began to be discussed in college composition in the late 1980s and early 1990s, primarily as a form of assessment consistent with process pedagogy, which emphasized revision, multiple drafts, and multiple sources of feedback, and de-emphasized the grading of individual essays (Elbow & Belanoff, 1986). Authors also justified portfolios as a preferred alternative to timed writing assessments, such as the holistic scoring approach that many college composition programs used, and many still employ, to determine placement into or passage out of a program (Roemer, Schultz, & Durst, 1991; Yancey, 1992). Numerous college writing programs adopted portfolios in the early 1990s for a variety of purposes: placement at Miami University of Ohio (Daiker, Sommers, & Stygall, 1996); a large-scale, mid-program review at the University of Cincinnati (Durst, Roemer, & Schultz, 1994; Schultz, Durst, & Roemer, 1997) and many other schools; ongoing composition assessment at the University of Michigan (Condon & Hamp-Lyons, 1991); assessment of fiction writing (Romano, 1994); and evaluation of English teachers (Weiser, 1994; Yancey, 1994).

Earlier forms of writing assessment improved upon their predecessors, in the eyes of composition instructors, as with holistic scoring of timed student essays in many cases taking the place of multiple choice objective tests as measures of student writing quality. Yet portfolio assessment came on the scene to even more fanfare because a great many writing specialists viewed it as the best possible fit with current approaches to instruction. Berlin (1994) argued that the approach "represents one of the most progressive developments in composition studies since the process model of composing" (p. 56).

Despite all this optimism, Elbow (1994) worried that teachers and administrators might be led to adopt a reductive holistic score, undermining the complexity of a diverse portfolio, and also that a portfolio approach could overemphasize assessment, thus undermining risk, discovery, and play, key aspects of writing for Elbow and many others in composition. Hamp-Lyons and Condon (1993; Condon & Hamp-Lyons, 1994) show ways in which the authors' assumptions, upon developing the portfolio system, were not necessarily borne out in practice. For example, they found that teachers reading portfolios often made their judgments early, before having read the majority of texts. They conclude that program administrators need to work proactively and closely examine the work of the various stakeholders to ensure that the assessment is doing what they think it should be doing. Roemer, Schultz, and Durst (1991) demonstrate the importance of bottom-up planning and "buy-in" by writing instructors who will be conducting the assessment, if it is to be implemented successfully. Revisionist work on portfolios by Broad (2003) takes what he terms a hermeneutic as opposed to psychometric approach. Broad argues that portfolios are most useful in bringing teachers together to discuss criteria and raise pedagogical, evaluative, and theoretical issues in writing instruction, and that programs should not try to establish system-wide standards or develop rubrics. The portfolio has emerged as the form of writing assessment most preferable to composition specialists for its heuristic as well as its evaluative power.

The politics of assessment also has figured prominently in the research literature of the past decade and a half. Beginning with Bullock and Trimbur (1991), composition specialists undertook a rethinking of the nature and purpose of assessment, wishing to enhance its formative qualities and move away from the exclusivist notion of assessment as a weeding out process. In this volume, Schwegler (1991) argues against universal standards and for a different paradigm in which the teacher is viewed as a fellow reader and a writing coach rather than an authoritarian and prescriptive reader. Citing Althusser's (1971) view that education helps reproduce the dominant relations of production in a society, Schwegler acknowledges that teachers will always retain power but believes that they can undermine that power and make the class more egalitarian by responding to student work as readers and collaborators and by foregrounding rather than suppressing questions of value and ideology.

In later works, Ball (1997) and Gleason (2000) look at the interaction of culture and assessment as it impacts low-income students of color, while Holdstein (1996) attempts to conceptualize a system of writing assessment more congruent with feminist notions of self-reflectivity and inclusiveness. Huot's (2002) comprehensive analysis of research on writing assessment, including almost 2 decades of his own work, ends with a detailed discussion of theoretical principles that should underlie a programmatic assessment of students' written work at any level of education, emphasizing the local, context-dependent nature of such activity. All of these efforts to reshape writing assessment—while not yet serving to eliminate traditional forms of social and academic hierarchy—have succeeded at least in sensitizing writing instructors and program directors to problems with conventional assessment and in persuading many to reduce such problems as much as is possible within the constraints of higher education.

The concepts of reliability and validity have functioned as opposing poles in the history of writing assessment, as composition specialists have struggled to develop effective forms of assessment (Yancey, 1999). Reliability refers to the idea that different raters should assess as consistently with one another as possible. Validity traditionally is defined as making sure a test measures what it is supposed to measure. In recent years, composition professionals have focused more on validity in favoring portfolios, and less on reliability, which is easier to achieve with a more controlled, holistically scored essay test.

Holistic scoring of timed, impromptu essays is still common in college composition, particularly for placement of new students (Huot, 2002). While the procedures for holistic scoring initially were developed by the Educational Testing Service (ETS) (Diederich, 1974) for use in large-scale national testing, this approach was picked up and adapted by composition program directors as more valid than previously used tests of grammar and punctuation skills, or short answer and multiple choice questions about how best to construct an essay. ETS showed that strong interrater reliability could be achieved in holistic scoring, mainly to determine whether a student should be placed in a remedial writing course rather than directly into the standard first-year program, or, in some cases, into an accelerated writing course for a student rating very well on the placement essay. White (1990, 1993, 1994, 1995) has been the main force behind use of holistically scored timed essays in college composition, for placement and as a final exam. White (1995) argues that the advantages of timed essays and holistic scoring strongly outweigh the disadvantages, but only if the writing assessment is well designed, scored, and used. In recent years, this approach has come under increasing criticism. An alternative for ensuring that students enroll in the appropriate level of college composition, known as directed self-placement (DSP), has been proposed by Royer and Gilles (1998, 2003). Under this approach, composition administrators speak to large groups of incoming students, explaining the options open to them and recommending the appropriate course for students based on their perceived sense of writing ability. Self-placement saves the cost of a large-scale essay assessment and gives more autonomy to students, and Royer and Gilles say it has worked relatively well at their institution. However, some writing assessment specialists who have investigated the approach argue that students do not have sufficient information and lack perspective upon which to base their placement decisions, and that there is not yet enough empirical evidence that directed self-placement works effectively (Schendel & O'Neill, 1999). Huot (2002) suggests that program administrators might use DSP along with other measures, such as grades and standardized test scores, or even portfolios in certain cases.

Technology

Research in this area has focused mainly on the increasingly diverse uses of—and larger issues surrounding—computer technology in composition. Over the past 20 years, a steady stream of technological developments has thrust computers into an ever more prominent role in the teaching, learning, and uses of literacy. The journal *Computers and Composition* has been presenting this work since 1983. The new technology—from ever more efficient forms of word processing to computerized classrooms, e-mail, chatrooms, MOOs, listservs, bulletin boards, distance learning systems, digitalized archives, on-line databases, and the myriad Web applications—has created major transformations in the environments in which people read, write, and learn. At the same time, the growing importance of computer-based applications has had implications not just for practice but also for the dominant theories of literacy, and technological development has raised numerous social, political, and pedagogical questions for literacy scholars to investigate. An overview of this scholarship by Selfe and Selfe (2002) outlines the major theories and key studies on technology-related topics, and this section of the current chapter draws heavily upon the authors' synthesis. A historical analysis of computers and the teaching of writing in American higher education from the mid-1990s also provides a valuable frame of reference with which to understand technological developments and their impact on literacy pedagogy (Hawisher, LeBlanc, Moran, & Selfe, 1996).

Critical analysis of practical applications for computer technology, both inside and outside the classroom, constitutes a large and important strand of inquiry, as writers and readers are using forms of this technology in more and more contexts. Pedagogical possibilities in computerized college classrooms and labs are the focus of numerous studies (Bruce, Peyton, & Batson, 1993; Castner, 1997; Faigley, 1992). Other works examine the intersection of technology and the writing center, including the development of on-line centers for students who cannot or choose not to be physically present for a tutorial (Coogan, 1999; Inman & Sewell, 2000; Selfe, 1995). Another body of work investigates distance learning environments (Reisman, Flores, & Edge, 2003; Stacy, Goodman, & Stubbs, 1996). Web-based writing and reading activities are an increasingly critical area of inquiry (Gresham, 1999; Gruber, 2000). Many studies center specifically on the nature and role of e-mail, listservs, and MOOs in literacy teaching, learning, and/or use (Blair, 1996; Moran, 1994; Porter, 1998).

Another large set of studies examines social and political issues surrounding the relation among literacy, technology, and pedagogy. Many of these works focus on questions of access to technology and explore the issue of the "digital divide" in which low-income people, including a disproportionate number of people of color, and, to

a certain extent, women, face barriers to their use of the more sophisticated technical applications. The literature on gender, literacy, and technology includes a rapidly growing body of work, much of which looks not at access but at the distinctive
uses many girls and women are making of new technical capabilities (Balsamo, 1996;
Hawisher & Sullivan, 1998; Sullivan, 1997). Other studies focus on racial and socioeconomic class issues in technology and literacy (Moran & Selfe, 1999; Taylor,
1997). A related body of research investigates the intersection of sexual orientation,
technology, and literacy, looking at the distinctive on-line communicative forms,
discussion venues, and means of self-disclosure gay and lesbian students have developed (Alexander, 1997, 2002; Banks, 2003; DeWitt, 1997; Spurlin, 2000).

Institutional Contexts

Researchers have made significant strides in examining the nature of the academic
and cultural settings in which college writing and writing instruction take place. This
burgeoning body of work includes studies of the role of writing in the formation and
functioning of academic disciplines, as well as research on writing programs and
program administration, and investigations of the often-troubled relation between
writing and literature instruction in college English departments.

Disciplinarity has become an important concept in the cultural analysis of writing in the academy. Prior (1998) explores the enculturation processes that helped create
academic disciplines, focusing specifically on graduate education. His findings move
beyond standard notions of writing as transcription to a richer social understanding
of genres and the dialogic, multifaceted nature of authorship, and contest the idea
that an academic discipline functions as a unified discourse community. Other important studies of writing and academic disciplinarity include Bazerman (1988, 1994);
Berkenkotter and Huckin (1995); Berkenkotter, Huckin, and Ackerman (1988, 1991);
Chiseri-Strater (1991); Geisler (1994); Horner (2000); Messer-Davidow, Shumway,
and Sylvan (1993); Prior (1998); and Swales (1990).

College writing programs are a more and more varied group, but such programs
mainly emphasize the teaching of first-year composition. Yet an increasing number
now offer, and more than a few even require, intermediate and upper-level composition or writing-intensive courses (McLeod, Miraglia, Soven, & Thaiss, 2001;
Walvoord, Hunt, Dowling, & McCarthy, 1997). Many colleges also offer programs
in business and technical writing, creative writing, and journalism.

By the mid-1980s, composition studies was asserting itself as a lively and growing
academic field whose teaching and research missions were central to the academy. It
made little sense for such programs to be under the thumb of English departments
far more committed to their literature faculty and programs. In 1987, the journal
WPA: Writing Program Administration, the official organ of the WPA organization,
was born, and the inner workings of the college composition program began to be
an acceptable topic of scholarly inquiry and discussion. Since then, the journal has
published a steady stream of articles about aspects of program development such as
designing curriculum, developing new faculty, competing for and procuring resources
in a scarce institutional environment, flourishing administratively within an English
department or wherever the program was situated, and assessing the effectiveness of
both instructors and the program itself. A number of important books about writing
program administration have appeared since the field became a legitimate area of

inquiry (George, 1999; Rose & Weiser, 1999, 2002; White, 1994). While primarily programmatic in nature, these works critically examine the nature of administrative work in writing and thus contribute to the field's overall knowledge base.

Several works have looked at the marginal position of composition programs in the academy, examining their reliance on contingent labor, poor funding, and lack of institutional status. Crowley (1998) and Petragia (1995) take the "abolitionist" position, arguing that composition specialists should examine critically the nearly universal first-year writing requirement, in favor of either an optional or an upper-level course. Abolitionists see the requirement as coercive, emphasizing a focus on superficial aspects of writing and rhetoric, leading to exploitation of badly supported instructors, and destructive to the field in its emphasis on teaching first-year students as opposed to other academic disciplines, in which faculty work primarily with more advanced students and focus more on scholarship than on teaching students new to the academy. Roemer, Schultz, and Durst (1999) counter with a defense of the first-year requirement, pointing to their own and others' research that indicates the value to students of the course and the high-level focus of many programs' curricula.

CONCLUSION

Looking back over the past 20 years of composition scholarship, I would argue that the field presently finds itself in something of a rut. With a broad consensus on the most effective teaching methods, few composition specialists seriously challenge the approaches put forward by writing process adherents in the 1970s and 1980s, continuing to emphasize prewriting, revision, collaboration, conferencing, and critical reading. The perennial debates over such matters as the use of literature and the value of personal writing in the composition class still spark occasional discussion in professional journals, but the debate has lingered too long to be called a controversy. Similarly, to judge from published work, composition specialists largely have accepted the social turn in the field, regularly organizing courses around (and publishing works on) topics of political and cultural import and linking their courses with service and community work. In addition, many compositionists protest developments outside the field that affect what those in the field do, such as the increasing reliance on standardized testing in American education; the growth of nontenure track faculty positions in the academy; and attacks on minority access to higher education at City College of New York and elsewhere. Yet presently, the field lacks a defining feature or powerful orthodoxy *within* composition studies to work against, such as current-traditional teaching or the cognitive emphasis. And in the past, it has been the idea of working against an oppressive status quo that most strongly motivated composition scholars to develop exciting new interpretations and approaches.

However, despite the lack of major shifts in the landscape, some smaller fissures are evident. One promising area connects composition and the interdisciplinary field of disability studies. Recent publications focus on student writers with a variety of disabilities and examine ways in which the academy and the larger society construct and stigmatize disability. Many, although not all, scholars working in disability either have a disability themselves or have a family member with a disability, and much of the most powerful and compelling work in disability includes a reflective, autobiographical component that moves toward interpretation and theory. Two such scholars stand out. A leading literary researcher as well as a disability theorist, Lennard Davis, the hearing son of deaf parents, has published a memoir (2000) and an edited collection of essays on theories of disability (1997). A composition researcher working in the area of deafness, and a hearing-impaired person herself, Brenda Brueggemann, has published a study exploring writing pedagogy and disability (2001) and an essay arguing that increased awareness of disability in composition studies can productively disrupt conventional notions of writing while challenging normal/not normal binaries (Brueggemann, White, Dunn, Heifferon, & Cheu, 2001). Other studies examine visible physical disability (Mossman, 2002), learning disability (White, 2002), and embodiment theory and disability (Wilson & Lewiecki-Wilson, 2001). Given the increasing awareness of disability, work in this promising area seems to be only scratching the surface.

Another noteworthy trend is the growing internationalization of composition studies, as scholars seek to place theory and practice of American college writing in a larger global context. While Muchiri, Mulamba, Myers, and Ndoloi examined the teaching and learning of academic writing in African universities in a Braddock Award winning 1995 *CCC* article, more recently a host of other publications on postsecondary writing throughout the world have appeared. I simply will mention two noteworthy books originating on different sides of the Atlantic. David Foster and David Russell's 2002 edited collection discusses college writing curricula, preparation, and expectations in Europe, Asia, and Africa, and by doing so sheds light on U.S. composition contexts. Three British scholars, Carys Jones, Joan Turner, and Brian Street, edited a 1999 book that contrasts European and American perspectives on academic writing. Members of the writing special interest group of the European Association of Research on Learning and Instruction have published a book series on writing studies since 1996, with Amsterdam University Press and Kluwer Academic Press. While European critical theories have long held significant influence in U.S. literary and literacy studies, it is time for scholars working in this country to increase their awareness of the growing body of research on writing in international contexts.

REFERENCES

Adler-Kassner, L. (1998). Ownership revisited: An exploration in progressive era and expressivist composition scholarship. *College Composition and Communication, 49*, 208–233.

Adler-Kassner, L., Crooks, R., & Watters, A. (Eds.). (1997). *Writing the community: Concepts and models for service-learning in composition.* Washington, DC: American Association for Higher Education.

Alexander, J. (1997). Out of the closet and into the network: Sexual orientation and the computerized classroom. *Computers and Composition, 14*, 207–216.

Alexander, J. (2002). Homo-pages and queer sites: Studying the construction and representation of queer identities on the world wide web. *The International Journal of Sexuality and Gender Studies, 7*, 85–106.

Althusser, L. (1971). *Lenin and philosophy and other essays* (B. Brewster, Trans.). London: New Left Books.

Anderson, V. (1997). Confrontational teaching and rhetorical practice. *College Composition and Communication, 48*, 197–214.

Arato, A., & Gebhardt, E. (1978). *The essential Frankfurt School reader.* Oxford, UK: Basil Blackwell.

Balester, V. (1993). *Cultural divide: A study of African-American college level writers.* Portsmouth, NH: Boynton/Cook.

Ball, A. (1997). Expanding the dialogue on culture as a critical component when assessing writing. *Assessing Writing, 4*, 169–203.

Ball, A., & Lardner, T. (1997). Dispositions toward language: Teacher constructs of knowledge and the Ann Arbor Black English case. *College Composition and Communication, 48*, 469–485.

Balsamo, A. (1996). *Technologies of the gendered body: Reading cyborg women.* Durham: Duke University Press.

Banks, W. (2003). Written through the body: Disruptions and "personal" writing. *College English, 66*, 21–40.

Barron, D. (2003). Dear Saints, Dear Stella: Letters examining the messy lines of expectations, stereotypes, and identity in higher education. *College Composition and Communication, 55*, 11–37.

Bartholomae, D. (1985). Inventing the university. In M. Rose (Ed.), *When a writer writes: Studies of writer's block and other composing process problems* (pp. 134–165). New York: Guilford Press.

Bauer, D. (1990). The other "F" word: The feminist in the classroom. *College English, 52*, 385–396.

Bazerman, C. (1988). *Shaping written knowledge: The genre and activity of the experimental article in science.* Madison: University of Wisconsin Press.

Bazerman, C. (1994). *Constructing experience.* Carbondale: Southern Illinois University Press.

Belanoff, P. (1991). The myths of assessment. *Journal of Basic Writing, 10*, 54–66.

Belenky, M. F., Clinchy, B. M., Goldberger, N. R., & Tarule, J. M. (1986). *Women's ways of knowing: The development of self, voice, and mind.* New York: Basic Books.

Berkenkotter, C., & Huckin, T. (1995). *Genre knowledge in disciplinary communication: Cognition/culture/power.* Mahwah, NJ: Erlbaum.

Berkenkotter, C., Huckin, T., & Ackerman, J. (1988). Conventions, conversations, and the writer: Case study of a student in a rhetoric Ph.D. program. *Research in the Teaching of English, 22*, 9–44.

Berlin, J. (1982). Contemporary composition: The major pedagogical theories. *College English, 44*, 765–777.

Berlin, J. (1987). *Rhetoric and reality: Writing instruction in American colleges, 1900–1985.* Carbondale: Southern Illinois University Press.

Berlin, J. (1988). Rhetoric and ideology in the writing class. *College English, 50*, 477–494.

Berlin, J. (1991). Composition and cultural studies. In M. Hurlbert & M. Blitz (Eds.), *Composition and resistance* (pp. 47–55). Portsmouth, NH: Boynton/Cook.

Berlin, J. (1994). The subversions of the portfolio. In L. Black, D. A. Daiker, J. Sommers, &

G. Stygall (Eds.), *New directions in portfolio assessment: Reflective practice, critical theory, and large-scale scoring* (pp. 56–68). Portsmouth, NH: Boynton/Cook.

Berlin, J. (1996). *Rhetoric, poetics, and cultures: Refiguring college English studies.* Urbana, IL: National Council of Teachers of English.

Berlin, J., & Vivion, M. (Eds.). (1992). *Cultural studies in the English classroom.* Portsmouth, NH: Boynton/Cook Heinemann.

Berthoff, A. (1981). *The making of meaning: Metaphors, models, and maxims for writing teachers.* Montclair, NJ: Boynton/Cook.

Bizzell, P. (1992). *Academic discourse and critical consciousness.* Pittsburgh, PA: University of Pittsburgh Press.

Bizzell, P. (1997). The Fourth of July and the 22nd of December: The function of cultural archives in persuasion as shown by Frederick Douglass and William Apess. *College Composition and Communication, 48*, 44–60.

Blair, K. (1996). Microethnographies of electronic discourse communities: Establishing exigency for e-mail in the professional writing classroom. *Computers and Composition, 13*, 85–91.

Bleich, D. (1989). Homophobia and sexism as popular values. *Feminist Teacher, 4*, 21–27.

Bosquet, M. (2003). The rhetoric of "job market" and the reality of the academic labor system. *College English, 66*, 207–228.

Bridgeman, B., & Carlson, S. (1984). Survey of academic writing tasks. *Written Communication, 1*, 247–280.

Britton, J. (1970). *Language and learning.* London: Penguin.

Britton, J., Burgess, T., Martin, N., McLeod, A., & Rosen, H. (1975). *The development of writing abilities (11–18).* London: Macmillan.

Broad, R. (2003). *What we really value: Beyond rubrics in teaching and assessing writing.* Logan: Utah State University Press.

Brodkey, L. (1987). Modernism and the scene(s) of writing. *College English, 49*, 396–418.

Brodkey, L. (1996). *Writing permitted in designated areas only.* Minneapolis: University of Minnesota Press.

Brooke, R. (1987). Underlife and writing instruction. *College Composition and Communication, 38*, 141–153.

Bruce, B., Peyton, J. K., & Batson, T. (Eds.). (1993). *Network-based classrooms: Promises and realities.* New York: Cambridge University Press.

Brueggemann, B. J. (2001). An enabling pedagogy: Meditations on writing and disability. *JAC, 21*, 791–820.

Brueggemann, B. J., White, L. F., Dunn, P. A., Heifferon, B. A., & Cheu, J. (2001). Becoming visible: Lessons in disability. *College Composition and Communication*, 52, 368–398.

Bruffee, K. (1984). Collaborative learning and the conversation of mankind. *College English*, 46, 65–82.

Bullock, R., & Trimbur, J. (Eds.). (1991). *The politics of writing instruction: Postsecondary*. Portsmouth, NH: Boynton/Cook.

Canagarajah, A. (1997). Safe houses in the contact zone: Coping strategies of African American students in the academy. *College Composition and Communication*, 48, 173–196.

Castner, J. (1997). The clash of social categories: Egalitarianism in networked writing classrooms. *Computers and Composition*, 14, 257–268.

Chase, G. (1988). Accommodation, resistance, and the politics of student writing. *College Composition and Communication*, 39, 13–22.

Chiseri-Strater, E. (1991). *Academic literacies: The public and private discourse of university students*. Portsmouth, NH: Boynton/Cook.

Coleman, C. F. (1997). Our students write with accents: Oral paradigms for ESD students. *College Composition and Communication*, 48, 486–500.

Colombo, G., Cullen, R., & Lisle, B. (1989). *Rereading America: Cultural contexts for critical thinking and learning*. Boston: St. Martins.

Condon, W., & Hamp-Lyons, E. (1991). Introducing a portfolio-based writing assessment: Progress through problems. In P. Belanoff & M. Dickson (Eds.), *Portfolios: Process and product*. Portsmouth, NH: Boynton/Cook.

Condon W., & Hamp-Lyons, L. (1994). Maintaining a portfolio-based writing assessment: Research that informs program development. In L. Black, D. A. Daiker, J. Sommers, & G. Stygall (Eds.), *New directions in portfolio assessment: Reflective practice, critical theory, and large-scale scoring* (pp. 56–68). Portsmouth, NH: Boynton/Cook.

Coogan, D. (1999). *Electronic writing centers: Computing the field of composition*. Stamford, CT: Ablex.

Corbett, E. (1965). *Classical rhetoric for the modern student*. New York: Oxford University Press.

Crowley, S. (1998). *Composition in the university: Historical and polemical essays*. Pittsburgh, PA: University of Pittsburgh Press.

Curtis, M., & Herrington, A. (2003). Writing development in the college years: By whose definition? *College Composition and Communication*, 55, 69–90.

Cushman, E. (1996). The rhetorician as agent of social change. *College Composition and Communication*, 47, 7–28.

Daiker, D., Sommers, J., & Stygall, G. (1996). The pedagogical implications of a college placement portfolio. In E. White, W. D. Lutz, & S. Kamusikri (Eds.), *Assessment of writing: Politics, policies, practices* (pp. 257–270). New York: Modern Language Association.

Davis, L. J. (Ed.). (1997). *The disability studies reader*. New York: Routledge.

Davis, L. J. (2000). *My sense of silence: Memoir of a childhood with deafness*. Urbana: University of Illinois Press.

Dean, T. (1989). Multicultural classrooms, monocultural teachers. *College Composition and Communication*, 40, 23–37.

Deans, T. (2000). *Writing partnerships: Service learning in composition*. Urbana, IL: National Council of Teachers of English.

Dewey, J. (1916). *Democracy and education*. New York: Macmillan.

DeWitt, S. (1997). Out there on the Web: Pedagogy and identity in the face of opposition. *Computers and Composition*, 14, 229–244.

Diederich, P. (1974). *Measuring growth in English*. Urbana, IL: National Council of Teachers of English.

Durst, R. K. (1999). *Collision course: Conflict, negotiation, and the teaching of composition*. Urbana, IL: National Council of Teachers of English.

Durst, R. K. (Ed.). (2003). *You are here: Readings on higher education for college writers*. Upper Saddle River, NJ: Prentice-Hall.

Durst, R. K., Roemer, M., & Schultz, L. M. (1994). Portfolio negotiations: Acts in speech. In L. Black, D. A. Daiker, J. Sommers, & G. Stygall (Eds.), *New directions in portfolio assessment: Reflective practice, critical theory, and large-scale scoring* (pp. 286–302). Portsmouth, NH: Boynton/Cook.

Ede, L., & Lunsford, A. (1990). *Singular texts/plural authors*. Carbondale: Southern Illinois University Press.

Elbow, P. (1973). *Writing without teachers*. New York: Oxford University Press.

Elbow, P. (1994). Will the virtues of portfolios blind us to their potential dangers? In L. Black, D. A. Daiker, J. Sommers, & G. Stygall (Eds.), *New directions in portfolio assessment: Reflective practice, critical theory, and large-scale scoring* (pp. 40–55). Portsmouth, NH: Boynton/Cook.

Elbow, P., & Belanoff, P. (1986). State University of New York: Portfolio-based evaluation programs. In P. Connolly & T. Vilardi (Eds.), *New methods in college writing programs: Theory into practice* (pp. 95–105). New York: Modern Language Association.

Emig, J. (1971). *The composing processes of twelfth graders.* Urbana, IL: National Council of Teachers of English.

Ericsson, K. A., & Simon, H. A. (1993). *Protocol analysis: Verbal reports as data* (2nd ed.). Cambridge, MA: MIT Press.

Faigley, L. (1992). *Fragments of rationality: Postmodernity and the subject of composition*: Pittsburgh, PA: University of Pittsburgh Press.

Fishman, S. M., & McCarthy, L. (1996). Teaching for student change: A Deweyan alternative to radical pedagogy. *College Composition and Communication, 47,* 342–366.

Fitts, K., & France, A. (1995). *Left margins: Cultural studies and composition pedagogy.* Albany: State University of New York Press.

Flower, L. (1994). *The construction of negotiated meaning: A social-cognitive theory of writing.* Carbondale: Southern Illinois University Press.

Flower, L. (2002). Intercultural inquiry and the transformation of service. *College English, 65,* 181–201.

Flower, L., & Hayes, J. R. (1977). Problem solving strategies and the writing process. *College English, 39,* 449–461.

Flower, L., & Hayes, J. R. (1980). The cognition of discovery: Defining rhetorical problems. *College Composition and Communication, 31,* 21–32.

Flower, L., & Hayes, J. R. (1981). The pregnant pause: An inquiry into the nature of planning. *Research in the Teaching of English, 15,* 229–243.

Flower, L., Hayes, J. R., Carey, L., Shriver, K., & Stratman, J. (1986). Detection, diagnosis, and the strategies of revision. *College Composition and Communication, 37,* 16–55.

Flynn, E. (1988). Composing as a woman. *College Composition and Communication, 39,* 423–435.

Forman, J. (Ed.). (1992). *New visions of collaborative writing.* Portsmouth, NH: Boynton/Cook.

Foster, D., & Russell, D. (Eds.). (2002). *Writing and learning in cross-national perspective: Transitions from secondary to higher education.* Mahwah, NJ: Erlbaum.

Freire, P. (1970). Pedagogy of the oppressed (M. B. Ramos, Trans.). New York: Herder and Herder.

Fulkerson, R. (1996). *Teaching the argument in writing.* Urbana, IL: National Council of Teachers of English.

Geisler, C. (1994). *Academic literacy and the nature of expertise: Reading, writing, and knowing in academic philosophy.* Mahwah, NJ: Erlbaum.

George, D. (1999). *Kitchen cooks, plate twirlers, and troubadours: Writing program administrators tell their stories.* Portsmouth, NH: Heinemann.

George, D., & Trimbur, J. (2001). Cultural studies and composition. In G. Tate, A. Rupiper, & K. Schick (Eds.), *A guide to composition pedagogies* (pp. 71–91). New York: Oxford University Press.

Gere, A. R. (1987). *Writing groups: History, theory, and implications.* Carbondale: Southern Illinois University Press.

Gibson, M., Marinara, M., & Meem, D. (2000). Bi, butch, and bar dyke: Pedagogical performances of class, gender, and sexuality. *College Composition and Communication, 52,* 69–95.

Gill, G. E. (1992). The African-American student: At risk. *College Composition and Communication, 43,* 225–230.

Gilligan, C. (1982). *In a different voice: Psychological theory and women's development.* Cambridge, MA: Harvard University Press.

Gilyard, K. (1991). *Voices of the self: A study of language competence.* Detroit: Wayne State University.

Gilyard, K. (1999a). African American contributions to composition studies. *College Composition and Communication, 50,* 626–644.

Gilyard, K. (Ed.). (1999b). *Race, rhetoric, and composition.* Portsmouth, NH: Boynton/Cook.

Giroux, H. (1983). *Theory and resistance in education: A pedagogy for the opposition.* Westport, CT: Bergin-Garvey.

Giroux, H. (1988). *Schooling and the struggle for public life: Critical pedagogy in the modern age.* Minneapolis: University of Minnesota Press.

Gleason, B. (2000). Evaluating writing programs in real time: The politics of remediation. *College Composition and Communication, 51,* 560–588.

Goffman, E. (1959). *The presentation of self in everyday life.* New York: Anchor Books.

Gonsalves, L. M. (2003). Making connections: Addressing the pitfalls of white faculty/black male student communication. *College Composition and Communication, 53,* 435–465.

Greene, S. (1993). The role of task in the development of academic thinking through reading and writing in a college history course. *Research in the Teaching of English, 27,* 46–75.

Greene, S. (1995). "Making sense of my own ideas": Problems of authorship in a beginning writing classroom. *Written Communication, 12,* 186–218.

Greene, S. (2001). The question of authenticity in a first year college history of science class. *Research in the Teaching of English, 35,* 525–569.

Gresham, M. (1999). The new frontier: Conquering the world wide web by mule. *Computers and Composition, 16*, 395–408.

Grossberg, L. (1989). The formation of cultural studies: An American in Birmingham. *Strategies, 2*, 114–149.

Gruber, S. (Ed.). (2000). *Weaving a virtual Web: Practical approaches to new information technologies*. Urbana, IL: National Council of Teachers of English.

Haggerty, G. C., & Zimmerman, B. (1995). *Professions of desire: Lesbian and gay studies in literature*. New York: Modern Language Association.

Hall, S., & Jefferson, T. (Eds.). (1976). *Resistance through rituals: Youth sub-cultures in postwar Britain*. London: Hutchinson.

Hamp-Lyons, L., & Condon, W. (1993). Questioning assumptions about portfolio-based assessment. *College Composition and Communication, 44*, 176–190.

Harkin, P., & Schilb, J. (Eds.). (1991). *Contending with words: Composition and rhetoric in a postmodern age*. New York: Modern Language Association.

Harris, J. (1989). The idea of community in the teaching of writing. *College Composition and Communication, 40*, 11–22.

Harris, J. (1997). *A teaching subject: Composition since 1966*. Upper Saddle River, NJ: Prentice-Hall.

Harris, J. (2000). Meet the new boss, same as the old boss: Class consciousness in composition. *College Composition and Communication, 52*, 43–68.

Harris, J. L., Kamhi, A. G., & Pollock, K. E. (2001). *Literacy in African American communities*. Mahwah, NJ: Erlbaum.

Haswell, R. H. (1991). *Gaining ground in college writing: Tales of development and interpretation*. Dallas: Southern Methodist University Press.

Hawisher, G. E., LeBlanc, P., Moran, C., & Selfe C. L. (1996). *Computers and the teaching of writing in American higher education, 1979–1994*. Norwood, NJ: Ablex.

Hawisher, G. E., & Sullivan, P. (1998). Women on the networks: Searching for e-space of their own. In S. C. Jarratt & L. Worsham (Eds.), *Feminism and composition studies* (pp. 172–197). New York: Modern Language Association.

Helmers, M. (1994). *Writing students: Composition testimonials and representations of students*. Albany: State University of New York Press.

Herndl, C. G., & Bauer, D. A. (2003). Speaking matters: Liberation theology, rhetorical performance, and social action. *College Composition and Communication, 54*, 558–585.

Herrington, A. (1985). Writing in academic settings: A study of the contexts for writing in two college chemical engineering courses. *Research in the Teaching of English, 19*, 331–359.

Herrington, A., & Curtis, M. (2000). *Persons in process: Four stories of writing and personal development in college*. Urbana, IL: National Council of Teachers of English.

Hillocks, G., Jr. (1986). *Research on written composition: New directions for teaching*. Urbana, IL: National Conference on Research in English/ERIC Clearinghouse on Reading and Communication Skills.

Holdstein, D. (1996). Gender, feminism, and institution-wide assessment programs. In E. White, W. D. Lutz, & S. Kamusikiri (Eds.), *Assessment of writing: Politics, policies, practices* (pp. 204–226). New York: Modern Language Association.

Hollis, E. (1992). Feminism in writing workshops: A new pedagogy. *College Composition and Communication, 43*, 340–348.

hooks, b. (1994). *Teaching to transgress: Education as the practice of freedom*. New York: Routledge.

Horner, B. (2000). Traditions and professionalization: Reconceiving work in composition. *College Composition and Communication, 51*, 366–398.

Horner, B., & Lu, M. Z. (1999). *Representing the "other": Basic writers and the teaching of basic writing*. Urbana, IL: National Council of Teachers of English.

Howard, R. (1996). The great wall of African American Vernacular English in the American college classroom. *Journal of Advanced Composition, 16*, 265–283.

Howard, R. (1999). *Standing in the shadows of giants: Plagiarists, authors, collaborators*. Norwood, NJ: Ablex.

Howard, R. (2001). Collaborative pedagogy. In G. Tate, A. Rupiper, & K. Schick (Eds.), *A guide to composition pedagogies* (pp. 54–70). New York: Oxford University Press.

Hull, G., & Rose, M. (1989). Rethinking remediation: Toward a social-cognitive understanding of problematic reading and writing. *Written Communication, 6*, 139–154.

Hull, G., & Rose, M. (1990). This wooden shack place: The logic of an unconventional reading. *College Composition and Communication, 41*, 287–298.

Hull, G., Rose, M., Fraser, K. L., & Castellano, M. (1991). Remediation as social construct: Perspectives from an analysis of classroom discourse.

College Composition and Communication, 42, 299–329.

Huot, B. (2002). *(Re)Articulating writing assessment for teaching and learning.* Logan: Utah State University Press.

Hurlbert, M., & Blitz, M. (Eds.). (1991). *Composition and resistance.* Portsmouth, NH: Boynton/Cook.

Inman, J. A., & Sewell, D. N. (2000). *Taking flight with OWLs: Examining electronic writing center work.* Mahwah, NJ: Erlbaum.

Jarratt, S. C. (1991). Feminism and composition: The case for conflict. In P. Harkin & J. Schilb (Eds.), *Contending with words: Composition and rhetoric in a postmodern age* (pp. 105–123). New York: Modern Language Association.

Jarratt, S. C., & Worsham, L. (Eds.). (1998). *Feminism and composition studies: In other words.* New York: Modern Language Association.

Johnson, R. (1986–1987). What is cultural studies anyway? *Social Text, 16,* 38–80.

Jones, C., Turner, J., & Street, B. (Eds.). (1999). *Students writing in the university.* Amsterdam: John Benjamins.

Kinneavy, J. (1971). *A theory of discourse.* Englewood Cliffs, NJ: Prentice-Hall.

Kirsch, G. (1993). *Women writing the academy: Audience, authority, and transformation.* Urbana, IL: National Council of Teachers of English.

Kirsch, G., Maor, F., Massey, L., Nickoson-Massey, L., & Sheridan-Rabideau, M. (Eds.). (2003). *Feminism and composition: A critical sourcebook.* Urbana and Boston: National Council of Teachers of English and Bedford.

Knoblauch, C., & Brannon, L. (1993). *Critical teaching and the idea of literacy.* Portsmouth, NH: Boynton/Cook.

Lamb, C. E. (1991). Beyond argument in feminist composition. *College Composition and Communication, 42,* 11–24.

LeFevre, K. (1987). *Invention as a social act.* Carbondale: Southern Illinois University Press.

Lewiecki-Wilson, C., & Sommers, J. (1999). Professing at the fault lines: Composition at open admissions institutions. *College Composition and Communication, 50,* 438–462.

Lindemann, E., & Tate, G. (Eds.). (1991). *An introduction to composition studies.* New York: Oxford University Press.

Lindquist, J. (1999). Class ethos and the politics of inquiry. *College Composition and Communication, 51,* 225–247.

Lu, M. Z. (1986). From silence to words: Writing as struggle. *College English, 49,* 437–448.

Lyons, S. R. (2000). Rhetorical sovereignty: What do American Indians want from writing. *College Composition and Communication, 51,* 447–468.

Malinowitz, H. (1995). *Textual orientations: Lesbian and gay students and the making of discourse communities.* Portsmouth, NH: Heinemann.

Mathison, M. A. (1996). Writing the critique, a text about a text. *Written Communication, 13,* 314–354.

McCarthy, L. (1987). A stranger in strange lands: A college student writing across the curriculum. *Research in the Teaching of English, 21,* 233–265.

McCrary, D. (2001). Womanist theology and its efficacy for the writing classroom. *College Composition and Communication, 52,* 521–552.

McLaren, P. (1989). *Life in schools: An introduction to critical pedagogy in the foundations of education.* New York: Longman.

McLeod, S. H., Miraglia, E., Soven, M., & Thaiss, C. (Eds.). (2001). *WAC for the new millennium: Strategies for continuing writing across the curriculum programs.* Urbana, IL: National Council of Teachers of English.

Messer-Davidow, E., Shumway, D., & Sylvan, D. (Eds.). (1993). *Knowledges: Historical and critical studies in disciplinarity.* Charlottesville: University of Virginia Press.

Miller, R. (2000). Fault lines in the contact zone: Assessing homophobic student writing. In W. Spurlin (Ed.), *Lesbian and gay studies and the teaching of English* (pp. 234–25). Urbana, IL: National Council of Teachers of English.

Moran, C. (1994). Notes toward a rhetoric of e-mail. *Computers and Composition, 12,* 15–21.

Moran, C., & Selfe, C. (1999). Teaching English across the technology/wealth gap. *English Journal, 88,* 48–55.

Mortenson, P., & Kirsch, G. (1993). On authority in the study of writing. *College Composition and Communication, 44,* 556–572.

Mossman, M. (2002). Visible disability in the college classroom. *College English, 64,* 645–659.

Muchiri, M. N., Mulamba, N. G., Myers, G., & Ndoloi, D. B. (1995). Importing composition: Teaching and researching academic writing beyond North America. *College Composition and Communication, 46,* 175–198.

Murphy, M. (2000). New faculty for a new university: Toward a full-time teaching intensive track in composition. *College Composition and Communication, 52,* 14–42.

Murray, D. (1968). *A writer teaches writing.* Boston: Houghton Mifflin.

Mutnick, D. (1995). *Writing in an alien world: Basic*

writing and the struggle for equality in higher education. Portsmouth, NH: Heinemann.

Myers, G. (1986). Reality, consensus, and reform in the rhetoric of composition. *College English, 48,* 154–174.

Nelson, J. (1990). This was an easy assignment: Examining how students interpret academic writing tasks. *Research in the Teaching of English, 24,* 362–396.

Nelson, J. (1993). The library revisited: Exploring students' research processes. In A. M. Penrose & B. M. Sitko (Eds.), *Hearing ourselves think: Cognitive research in the college writing classroom* (102–124). New York: Oxford University Press.

Newell, A., & Simon, H. (1972). *Human problem solving.* Englewood Cliffs, NJ: Prentice-Hall.

Newkirk, T. (1984). Direction and misdirection in peer response. *College Composition and Communication, 35,* 300–311.

Newkirk, T. (1995). The writing conference as performance. *Research in the Teaching of English, 29,* 193–215.

Newkirk, T. (1997). *The performance of self in student writing.* Portsmouth, NH: Heinemann.

North, S. (1986). Writing in a philosophy class: Three case studies. *Research in the Teaching of English, 20,* 225–262.

Paine, C. (1989). Relativism, radical pedagogy, and the ideology of paralysis. *College English, 51,* 557–570.

Parks, S., & Goldblatt, E. (2000). Writing beyond the curriculum: Fostering new collaborations in literacy. *College English, 62,* 584–606.

Parmeter, S., & Reti, I. (Eds.). (1988). *The lesbian in front of the classroom: Writings by lesbian teachers.* Santa Cruz, CA: HerBooks.

Penrose, A. M., & Sitko, B. M. (Eds.). (1993). *Hearing ourselves think: Cognitive research in the college writing classroom.* New York: Oxford University Press.

Perl, S. (1978). The composing processes of unskilled college writers. *Research in the Teaching of English, 13,* 317–336.

Perl, S., & Wilson, N. (1986). *Through teachers' eyes: Portraits of writing teachers at work.* Portsmouth, NH: Heinemann.

Petraglia, J. (Ed.). (1995). *Reconceiving writing, rethinking writing instruction.* Mahwah, NJ: Erlbaum.

Phelps, L. W., & Emig, J. (Eds.). (1995). *Feminine principles and women's experience in American composition and rhetoric.* Pittsburgh, PA: University of Pittsburgh Press.

Porter, J. E. (1998). *Rhetorical ethics and internetworked writing.* Greenwich, CT: Ablex.

Powell, M. (2002). Rhetorics of survivance: How American Indians use writing. *College Composition and Communication, 53,* 396–434.

Prendergast, C. (1998). Race: The absent present in composition studies. *College Composition and Communication, 50,* 36–53.

Prior, P. (1998). *Writing/disciplinarity: A sociohistoric account of literate activity in the academy.* Mahwah, NJ: Erlbaum.

Reisman, S., Flores, J. G., & Edge, D. (2003). *Electronic learning communities: Current issues and best practices.* Greenwich, CT: Information Age Publishing.

Richardson, E. (2002). "To protect and serve": African American female literacies. *College Composition and Communication, 53,* 675–704.

Ritchie, J., & Boardman, K. (1999). Feminism in composition: Inclusion, metonymy, and disruption. *College Composition and Communication, 50,* 585–606.

Rhodes, J. (2002). "Substantive and feminist girlie action": Women online. *College Composition and Communication, 54,* 116–142.

Roberts-Miller, T. (2003). Discursive conflict in communities and classrooms. *College Composition and Communication, 54,* 536–557.

Robertson, L. R., Crowley, S., & Lentriccia, F. (1987). The Wyoming Conference Resolution opposing unfair salaries and working conditions for post-secondary teachers of writing. *College English, 49,* 274–280.

Roemer, M., Schultz, L. M., & Durst, R. K. (1991). Portfolios and the process of change. *College Composition and Communication, 42,* 455–469.

Roemer, M., Schultz, L. M., & Durst, R. K. (1999). Reframing the great debate on first-year writing. *College Composition and Communication, 50,* 377–392.

Romano, T. (1994). Removing the blindfold: Portfolios in fiction writing classes. In L. Black, D. A. Daiker, J. Sommers, & G. Stygall (Eds.), *New directions in portfolio assessment: Reflective practice, critical theory, and large-scale scoring* (pp. 73–82). Portsmouth, NH: Boynton/Cook.

Rose, M. (1985). The language of exclusion: Writing instruction at the university. *College English, 47,* 341–359.

Rose, M. (1989). *Lives on the boundary.* New York: Penguin.

Rose, S. K., & Weiser, I. (Eds.). (1999). *The writing program administrator as researcher.* Portsmouth, NH: Boynton/Cook.

Rose, S. K., & Weiser, I. (Eds.). (2002). *The writing program administrator as theorist.* Portsmouth, NH: Boynton/Cook Heinemann.

Rosenthal, R. (1995). Feminists in action: How to practice what we teach. In K. Fitts (Ed.), *Left margins: Cultural production and composition pedagogy* (139–156). Albany: State University of New York Press.

Ross, A. (Ed.). (1988). *Universal abandon: The politics of postmodernism*. Minneapolis: University of Minnesota Press.

Rothgery, D. (1993). "So what do we do now?": Necessary directionality as the writing teacher's response to racist, sexist, homophobic papers. *College Composition and Communication, 44,* 241–247.

Royer, D. J., & Gilles, R. (1998). Directed self-placement: An attitude of orientation. *College Composition and Communication, 50,* 54–70.

Royer, D. J., & Gilles, R. (Eds.). (2003). *Directed self-placement: Principles and practices.* Cresskill, NJ: Hampton Press.

Royster, J. J., & Williams, J. C. (1996). History in the spaces left: African American presence and narratives in composition studies. *College Composition and Communication, 50,* 563–584.

Schell, E. (1998). *Gypsy academics and mother-teachers: Gender, contingent labor, and writing instruction.* Portsmouth, NH: Boynton/Cook.

Schendel, E., & O'Neill, P. (1999). Exploring the theories and consequences of self-assessment through ethical inquiry. *Assessing Writing, 6,* 199–227.

Schilb, J. (1996). *Between the lines: Relating composition theory and literary theory.* Portsmouth, NH: Boynton/Cook.

Schultz, L. M., Durst, R. K., & Roemer, M. (1997). Stories of reading: Inside and outside the texts of portfolios. *Assessing Writing, 4,* 121–132.

Schwegler, R. A. (1991). The politics of reading student papers. In R. Bullock & J. Trimbur (Eds.), *The politics of writing instruction: Postsecondary* (203–226). Portsmouth, NH: Boynton/Cook.

Selfe, C., & Selfe, D. J. (2002). The intellectual work of computers and composition studies. In G. Olson (Ed.), *Rhetoric and composition as intellectual work* (pp. 203–220). Carbondale: Southern Illinois University Press.

Selfe, R. J. (1995). Surfing the tsunami: Electronic environments in the writing center. *Computers and Composition, 12,* 311–322.

Shaughnessy, M. P. (1977). *Errors and expectations: A guide for the teacher of basic writing.* New York: Oxford University Press.

Sheeran, Y., & Barnes, D. (1991). *School writing: Discovering the ground rules.* Milton Keynes, UK: Open University Press.

Shor, I. (1992). *Empowering education: Critical teaching for social change.* Chicago: University of Chicago Press.

Shor, I. (1996). *When students have power: Negotiating authority in a critical pedagogy.* Chicago: University of Chicago Press.

Smith, J. (1997). Students' goals, gatekeeping, and some questions of ethics. *College Composition and Communication, 48,* 299–320.

Smitherman, G. (1999). CCC's role in the struggle for language rights. *College Composition and Communication, 50,* 349–376.

Smitherman, G., & Villanueva, V. (Eds). (2003). *Language diversity in the classroom: From intention to practice.* Carbondale: Southern Illinois University Press.

Soliday, M. (1996). From the margins to the mainstream: Reconceiving remediation. *College Composition and Communication, 47,* 85–100.

Sommers, N. (1981). Revision strategies of student writers and adult experienced writers. *College Composition and Communication, 31,* 378–388.

Sommers, N. (1992). I stand here writing. *College English, 55,* 420–428.

Spiegelman, C. (1998). Habits of mind: Historical configurations of textual ownership in peer writing groups. *College Composition and Communication, 49,* 234–255.

Spurlin, W. (Ed.). (2000). *Lesbian and gay studies and the teaching of English.* Urbana, IL: National Council of Teachers of English.

Stacy, D., Goodman, S., & Stubbs, T. D. (1996). The new distance learning: Students, teachers, and texts in cross-cultural electronic communities. *Computers and Composition, 13,* 293–302.

Sternglass, M. S. (1997). *Time to know them: A longitudinal study of writing and learning at the college level.* Mahwah, NJ: Erlbaum.

Sullivan, L. L. (1997). Cyberbabes: (Self-) Representation of women and the virtual male gaze. *Composition and Computers, 14,* 25–54.

Sullivan, P., & Qualley, D. (Eds.). (1994). *Pedagogy in the age of politics.* Urbana, IL: National Council of Teachers of English.

Swales, J. (1990). *Genre analysis: English in academic and research settings.* Cambridge: Cambridge University Press.

Taylor, T. (1997). The persistence of difference in networked classrooms: Non-negotiable difference and the African American student body. *Computers and Composition, 14,* 169–178.

Tinberg, H. B. (1997). *Border talk: Writing and knowing in the two year college.* Urbana, IL: National Council of Teachers of English.

Tobin, L. (1991). *Writing relationships: What really*

happens in the composition class. Portsmouth, NH: Boynton/Cook Heinemann.

Tobin, L. (2003). *Reading student writing: Confessions, meditations, and rants*. Portsmouth, NH: Boynton/Cook/Heinemann.

Tobin, L., & Newkirk, T. (Eds). (1994). *Taking stock: The writing process movement in the 1990's*. Portsmouth, NH: Boynton/Cook.

Trainor, J. S. (2002). Critical pedagogy's "other": Constructions of whiteness in education for social change. *College Composition and Communication, 53*, 631–650.

Trainor, J. S., & Godley, A. (1998). After Wyoming. *College Composition and Communication, 50*, 153–181.

Traub, J. (1994). *City on a hill: Testing the American dream at City College*. Reading, PA: Addison-Wesley.

Trimbur, J. (1988). Consensus and difference in collaborative learning. *College English, 51*, 601–616.

Trimbur, J. (1989). Cultural studies and the teaching of writing. *Focuses, 1*, 5–18.

Villanueva, V. (1993). *Bootstraps: From an American academic of color*. Urbana, IL: National Council of Teachers of English.

Wallace, D. (2002). Out in the academy: Heterosexism, invisibility, and double consciousness. *College English, 65*, 53–66.

Wallace, D., & Bell, A. (1999). Being black at a predominantly white university. *College English, 61*, 307–327.

Walvoord, B. E. (1986). *Helping students write well: A guide for teachers in all disciplines* (2nd ed.). New York: Modern Language Association.

Walvoord, B. E., Hunt, L., Dowling, H., & McCarthy, L. (1997). *In the long run: A study of faculty in three Writing Across the Curriculum programs*. Urbana, IL: National Council of Teachers of English.

Walvoord, B. E., & McCarthy, L. P. (1990). *Thinking and writing in college: A naturalistic study of students in four disciplines*. Urbana, IL: National Council of Teachers of English.

Weiser, I. (1994). Portfolios and the new teacher of writing. In L. Black, D. A. Daiker, J. Sommers, & G. Stygall (Eds.), *New directions in portfolio assessment: Reflective practice, critical theory, and large-scale testing* (pp. 219–230). Portsmouth, NH: Boynton/Cook.

Welsh, S. (2001). "And now that I know them": Composing mutuality in a service learning course. *College Composition and Communication, 54*, 243–263.

White, E. (1990). Language and reality in writing assessment. *College Composition and Communication, 40*, 187–200.

White, E. (1993). Holistic scoring: Past triumphs, future challenges. In M. Williamson & B. Huot (Eds.), *Validating holistic scoring for writing assessment* (pp. 79–108). Cresskill, NJ: Hampton Press.

White, E. (1994). *Teaching and assessing writing* (2nd ed.). San Francisco: Jossey-Bass.

White, E. (1995). Apologia for the timed impromptu essay test. *College Composition and Communication, 46*, 30–45.

White, L. F. (2002). Learning disability, pedagogies, and public discourse. *College Composition and Communication, 53*, 705–738.

Williams, R. (1958). *Culture and society, 1780–1950*. London: Chatto & Windus.

Wilson, J. C., & Lewiecki-Wilson, C. (Eds.). (2001). *Embodied rhetorics: Disability in language and culture*. Carbondale: Southern Illinois University Press.

Yancey, K. (1992). *Portfolios in the writing classroom: An introduction*. Urbana, IL: National Council of Teachers of English.

Yancey, K. (1994). Make haste slowly: Graduate teaching assistants and portfolios. In L. Black, D. A. Daiker, J. Sommers, & G. Stygall (Eds.), *New directions in portfolio assessment: Reflective practice, critical theory, and large-scale testing* (pp. 210–218). Portsmouth, NH: Boynton/Cook.

Yancey, K. (1999). Looking back as we look forward: Historicizing writing assessment. *College Composition and Communication, 50*, 483–503.

Yancey, K., & Spooner, M. (1998). A single good mind: Collaboration, cooperation, and the writing self. *College Composition and Communication, 49*, 45–62.

CHAPTER 5

Teacher Research in Writing Classrooms

Bob Fecho, JoBeth Allen, Claudia Mazaros, and Hellen Inyega

PENNY STARR (1993), a teacher at the Pennsylvania School for the Deaf, noted that her students who were fluent in American Sign Language (ASL) struggled to learn standard edited English (SEE), which seemed to them "motionless and inert compared with the fire and intensity of signing" (p. 185). With ASL and English often conflicting in the lives of her students, Starr wondered how these complex transactions across language systems played out in her students' writing. Fascinated by Michael—a 10-year-old who, deaf from birth, was a strict user of ASL—she observed that as he composed in SEE, he would sign to himself both as he considered what to write and after writing as a means of checking for meaning. In effect, he was holding an interior dialogue. Starr began to wonder what ways Michael and other deaf students used ASL as a means for helping them become more fluent in SEE, and where dissonance might occur.

Through analysis of transcripts of the teacher–student writing conferences that Jodi Nickel (2001) conducted with her upper-grade elementary students, her multiple roles—now the helpful facilitator hovering next to writers, and now the authority passing critical judgment on the writer's work—became evident, but the students' roles did not. Worried by the indifference her students showed toward the outcomes of these conferences, Nickel wondered what her students had to say about such conferences and how she might use their insights to construct conferences in ways that would better support her students.

In an intermediate-grade classroom, Karolynne Gee (1990) suspected that she was shortchanging her students by not emphasizing the visual arts, particularly as a support for them as writers. Having taught younger students, she remembered how those students often had combined drawing with writing; she and her older students segregated art. Moreover, she often noticed some of her upper-grades students doodling when prewriting and how those doodles often connected directly and indirectly to what they wrote. What, she wondered, would happen if she encouraged students to use art to facilitate their writing?

In northern California, students in Alleyne Johnson's (1995) combined seventh- and eighth-grade "special" class were all too accustomed to seeing death and violence in their lives. Her Cluster Academy was "a classroom for bad students who were labeled 'at risk,' 'learning disabled,' 'violent,' 'disruptive,' and other debilitating terms, even by their own schoolmates" (p. 220). Seeking a way to "find power for ourselves in disempowering circumstances," Johnson wrote an open letter to the class expressing her desire to create an active communal learning environment where all voices mattered. She invited her students to work with her and together plan an end-of-semester project involving authentic writing.

In each instance a teacher was transfixed by some concern about the role of writing in the lives of her students and in those sociocultural playgrounds we call classrooms. Starr developed a systematic and intentional (Cochran-Smith & Lytle, 1993) means for observing Michael as he composed across language boundaries. Nickel listened to her students and refined the way she used conferences in her classroom. By inserting art into her writing instruction to help students visualize their work and by documenting that shift in instruction, Gee (1990) developed more complex and useful understandings of what such activity meant for her students. Finally, Johnson (1995), by engaging students in writing a class newspaper, helped them use writing to make meaning of the violence so prevalent in their lives.

These vignettes suggest that teacher research grows out of complex classroom contexts, complexities that cannot be addressed by large-scale studies. It is often the very particular complexities of teacher/students, student/student, or student/text transaction within dynamic sociocultural contexts of classroom, school, home, and community that prompt teacher research questions. Consequently, our review of composition research by K–12 teachers is organized around four key questions or strands of inquiry: (1) How do students develop as writers? (2) How do teachers use writing to learn about students and to become better teachers of writing? (3) How do teachers teach writing and what happens when they do? (4) How do teachers help students make meaning of their worlds and act upon them through writing? Along with highlighting a body of work that may be less familiar to some in the academic community, we argue that teacher research makes a significant and unique contribution to the field of composition, one in which the macro, or the larger issues associated with literacy education, frequently is found in the micro, the very human and day-to-day transactions in writing classrooms.

THE INEVITABILITY AND NECESSITY OF TEACHER RESEARCH

Various historical inquiries point to Comenius, Rousseau, Montessori, Dewey, Freire, Piaget, and Vygotsky as planting the methodological and theoretical seeds that have flowered in teachers' observing, reflecting, and writing about their classrooms. In looking at diverse influences rather than a linear unfolding, Ruth Hubbard and Brenda Power (1999) identified, among others, the interpretive tradition (Erickson, 1986), anthropology, the National Writing Project, and the shift toward process-centered classrooms.

Teacher research often springs from the necessity of improving practice. For example, teachers in Japan in the 1920s developed a writing curriculum emphasizing descriptive narratives, finding it to be most effective for their children living in poverty (Kitagawa, 1982). In 1916, a time in the United States when progressive education was championed by Dewey, his colleague Lucy Sprague Mitchell founded a teacher research group, the Bureau of Education Experiments, which in 1930 became the Bank Street School (Hubbard & Power, 1999).

There was a resurgence, or perhaps reincarnation, of teacher research that immediately preceded the period of our review (e.g., Ashton-Warner, 1967; Calkins, 1978; Martin, 1973, 1975). In England in 1967, Lawrence Stenhouse began his consortium for school inquiry, widely believed to be the impetus for the international teacher research movement (Hubbard & Power, 1999). Also in 1967, teachers and writers in New York City founded the Teachers & Writers Collaborative to foster the teaching of writing and provide an outlet for teachers' writing about writing.

Teacher research is inevitable because teachers are professionals who know more about their practice than anyone else, who ask the most critical questions in the education of their students, and who have the highest investment—after the students themselves—in learning from research. Teacher research is necessary because the questions teachers ask, the children on whose behalf they ask them, and the insights that result in improved educational practices are the embodiment of *engaged pedagogy* (hooks, 1994).

OUR PROCESSES AND PERSPECTIVES

We include work that, due to its accessibility and content, has influenced the larger educational community, as well as works that may be less well known. We searched literacy publishing houses (e.g., Heinemann, International Reading Association, National Council of Teachers of English, Teachers College Press) and reviewed each issue of *English Journal, Harvard Educational Review, Journal of Adolescent and Adult Literacy* and its predecessor *Journal of Reading, Language Arts, National Reading Conference Yearbooks, Primary Voices, Quarterly of the National Writing Project, Research in the Teaching of English, Teacher Researcher, The Reading Teacher*, and *Voices in the Middle*. Finally, we considered works by teacher research networks such as the Bread Loaf Teacher Network and the National Writing Project.

Each study we included (1) was about composition; (2) concerned pre-K–12 classrooms and was conducted solely by pre-K–12, school-based practitioners in their classrooms or in conjunction with students; (3) included a recognizable and specific data set, and provided discussion and purposeful analysis of those data; (4) used classroom data to make meaning; (5) communicated a sense of significance; (6) theorized and contextualized stories or teaching activities through reflection over time; (7) discussed writing in depth even if it was not the main focus of the study; and (8) was of sufficient length to generate thoughtful analysis. Further, by highlighting research that had influenced or held potential for influencing educational practice, we looked at the impact of teacher research—the "action" in action research—as a primary criterion.

As a result of questioning and acting upon their questions, teacher researchers engage in educational praxis—a continuing transaction between thought and action in the classroom. From their reports of praxis, we distilled the four lines of inquiry with which we organized this chapter, knowing full well how they overlap and might be contested on a number of grounds. We invite readers to engage with them, and with the teacher researchers we survey.

HOW DO STUDENTS DEVELOP AS WRITERS?

What distinguished these studies is an emphasis on how students developed as writers rather than the activities and pedagogical choices occurring in the classroom, although one cannot be viewed without the others. Teachers in these studies documented what occurred in their classrooms because they wondered how students were developing as writers.

Developing as Writers in a Writing Community

Classrooms being the sociocultural playgrounds they are, some teachers documented how their classrooms operated as spaces of collaboration and what that meant for developing writers (e.g., Crouse & Davey, 1989; Hauser, 1982; Kimbrell-Lee & Wood, 1995). Sylvia Read (2001) conducted four case studies to examine how her first and second graders worked together using source texts, how they interacted around those texts, what the content of their interactions was, and what they wrote. Read posited that distance from the source texts combined with immersion in the content led to better writing. She saw writing growth when students engaged in discussion of the content, made evaluative comments about their writing, and played with text in imaginative ways. For example, John and Cameron read from a variety of source texts, role played, and wrote simultaneously; writing was a rehearsal of what they learned rather than a rewrite of the books. Their writing showed a clear understanding of the subject in most cases, except when they tried to paraphrase too closely from the original. Read concluded that she needed to incorporate more reading and writing of information for students to make their own meaning, rather than letting the "story" dominate the curriculum.

Tom Newkirk and Nancie Atwell's 1982 and 1988 volumes included several teachers examining ways in which primary-grade writers develop within a community of writers, especially important because many teachers believed that young children didn't "really write" until they had learned letters, words, and sentences, an assumption questioned throughout Newkirk and Atwell's volumes. Judith Hilliker's 1988 analysis of four kindergartners revealed that they not only wrote, but also established writing styles, often using repetition in drawing to explore a theme. Ellen Blackburn Karalitz (1988b) studied first-grade writer Danny and found a year characterized by "surges and retreat" (p. 46) rather than a smooth progression, necessitating close observation in order to teach. This questioning of conventional wisdom often marks research conducted by teachers, particularly in terms of understanding how children develop as writers.

Writing clubs were a focus for some studies. Ruth Freedman (1995) watched as students in her second/third-grade classroom formed an eight-member writing club during writing workshop. Their collaborations resulted in giving social meaning to school literacy activities through the infusion of their own social concerns. Premlata Mansukhani (2002) started what he called an Explorers Club that nudged his third- and fourth-grade ESL students to bring their questions and their culture into classroom writing. By accessing the ESL curriculum through their interests, mini-lessons that were a natural offshoot from the language process, and context-based changes in their use of English, the children reveled in the process and maintained enthusiasm for writing.

Showing that writing communities can proliferate among early writers, Mary Racicot (2002) created a strong home and school connection. Through a survey to learn about her kindergartners' cultural backgrounds, she identified not only cultural differences among the parents, but also a heartfelt interest in their children's education, despite the daily struggles in their economically depressed neighborhood. Racicot introduced home journals that guided parents on motivating children's writing. While the children developed confidence, parents learned to assist their children at home, extending the classroom writing community.

Writers with Special Needs

Curricular reforms often begin with "regular" classrooms and students and then move to students with special needs (e.g., English-language learners, students with disabilities, and students in high-poverty communities). Although the work in this section focuses on students who for a variety of reasons struggled as learners, the teachers built on strengths, resulting in pedagogy that enhanced writing development for all students, regardless of labels. Like much teacher research, the investigations described here were primarily case studies in which teachers closely observed the struggles and achievements of students whose concerns challenged them.

The writing revolution fomented by Graves (1983), Calkins (1986), Atwell (1987), and others enlisted an advocate for "special" students in Susan Stires (1991c). In a volume with a dozen chapters by teacher researchers, Stires—a primary-grade teacher at the time—gathered teachers' accounts of students with special needs who became literate in resource, remedial, ESL, and mainstream classrooms. A strong example is Sylvie, one of many students for whom Esther Sokolov Fine (1991) "unlocked the silences" through drama. Prone to violent outbursts, Sylvie was drawn into the process of writing a play where her firsthand knowledge of the court system became useful. Joan Throne's (1991) case study of sixth-grade Nazar, a recent immigrant, documented the use of dialogue journals to establish a trusting relationship where he could take risks with his writing, as well as full inclusion in a writing workshop—initially using his native language of Urdu—to establish him as a valued member of the classroom community.

Stires (1991a, 1991b) contributed two case study chapters, the first a portrait of 2 first-grade students with language difficulties and the second a 2-year study of an intermediate-level student with learning disabilities. In the first, her discussion of content conferences, revision, and process conferences was supported by multiple writing samples. Her second study, of children who might have been removed from a regular classroom had she not insisted on their inclusion, was similarly well documented and emphasized literature and writing connections and growth that "was not straightforward or spectacular, but . . . was constant and real" (p. 90). She concluded about her students, as she might have for the entire book, that "they did learn, without being labeled and sent out of the classroom for long periods of time each day" (p. 112).

Inspired by Stires, Atwell (1991a) documented how Laura, long labeled as "language disabled," blossomed within writing workshop and came to use writing to overcome her shyness, cope with emotionally charged situations, and master skills that previously had been identified through testing as deficiencies. Somewhat similarly, Colleen Hartry (1990) searched for ways that her students with learning disabilities might engage in discussions, ways that would enhance their memory and processing skills. When her fifth-grade students found out that Hartry's volunteer film review column for parents was about to be syndicated, she seized on their interest and invited them to review movies. Hartry looked closely at three students: Rosi, a Mexican American fluent in English who struggled with literacy; Junio, more recently from Mexico, who had visual motor difficulties; and Carle, an African American who tested at gifted levels but who was diagnosed with attention deficit disorder. These case studies indicated that as students began to view themselves as writers, their writing progressed from short, co-constructed reviews to multiparagraph works written with increasing independence.

This theme of inclusion resonates in the work of both Carol Avery (1987) and Diane Parker (1997), who chronicled the ways they expected and supported students with physical and cognitive challenges to be full participating members of their writing classrooms. Traci was a "warm and loving . . . perceptive, sensitive" child (Avery, 1987, p. 72); academically she was characterized as having weak vision, impaired speech, immature language patterns, poor physical coordination, and weak cognitive processing. Avery documented how over 2 years Traci went from being unaware of the function of letters to reading at a 2.8 level, and how she took greater control of writing. Parker taught Jamie, a child with spinal muscular atrophy, from kindergarten through second grade. In a collaborative setting, Jamie shared her love of literature and writing with other children, who in turn accepted and supported her. Parker shared Jamie's writing during a 2-month stay in intensive care when she could no longer talk. "Stay here please," she wrote, and "I want my Dad." When Jamie died, her family and classmates wrote to celebrate her life and to make sense of their loss. Parker reflected not only on how literate classroom communities form and include all members, but also on the critical question, What is literacy for?

For Valerie Aubry (1995), Mary Krogness (1995), and Carol Weir (1998), concerns centered around children who struggled with school literacy. Like Fine (1991), Krogness incorporated drama, poetry, storytelling, and folklore into her classes of underachieving seventh- and eighth-grade students. In sharing specific engagements, negative as well as positive student responses and writing, and on-the-spot as well as well-planned teaching, Krogness showed both the complexities and potential of reaching students with histories of failure. Aubry and Weir, both working with adolescents, helped students see how writing is a tool for communicating and synthesizing ideas, with Aubry advocating that students needed to see one another as part of the audience and Weir arguing that the writing of metacognitive questions enabled students to be better interpreters of text.

English-Language Learners

In Caryl Crowell's (1991) case study of a bilingual third-grade classroom in Arizona, biliteracy was the goal. She examined Maria and Victor's Spanish and English writing samples for a variety of syntactical, mechanical, and cultural features, as well as their sociocultural choices of when to write and read in English or Spanish. Crowell concluded that these ongoing evaluation processes not only supported her instructional decisions but also provided evidence that the children "use what they know about literacy in their native language to support their experiments with English" (p. 110).

Jean Gunkel (1991) and Ann Lew (1999) also focused on ways students negotiated cultures and languages. Gunkel involved Keisuke, a fourth grader who knew little English, in authentic uses for writing based on his request to "please teach America." She provided examples of his progress, including his final book with observable growth in story structure, syntax, mechanics, dialogue, and plot development. Importantly, Gunkel explained a decision, despite her respect for his ownership, to rewrite second versions of his stories. For example, where he had written, "I'm sleep on the blanket," she added, "I'm sleeping in the blanket" (pp. 304–305). Scaffolding of Keisuke's English syntax seemed to support and encourage him. This kind of teacher decision making, respecting a child's self-selected needs, illustrates a hallmark of teacher research: questioning pedagogical orthodoxies in order to reach individual learners.

Lew (1999) focused on Linda, a Chinese American from Hong Kong, whom Lew had taught as a freshman and again as a senior. Lew asked Linda to take a piece she had written in ninth grade and create a new paper as a senior. The second composition was more sophisticated, showing greater length in sentence and theme structure, more complexity in sentence structure, and fewer agreement concerns. Through interviews, Lew discovered that Linda was more purposeful about her writing and had internalized admonitions such as "show-not-tell." Lew stressed that a rich immersion in literate practices and consistent feedback from caring teachers about variances from the standard were critical to supporting the writing of nonnative learners.

Focusing on classroom transactions, two National Writing Project teachers used peer conferencing and writing workshops to encourage voice, risk taking, and self-expression to a larger audience. Myron Berkman (1995) noted that during written exchanges between Quoc Tin, a Vietnamese boy, and Sona Diwa, an Indian girl, the writers became "more engaged with language as they struggle[d] to communicate their ideas . . . [and] . . . with almost every exchange they [were] becoming demonstrably more proficient writers" (p. 11). Howard Banford (1996) showed similar development in his case study of Maricar. In another multicultural classroom, Iona Whitshaw (1994) encouraged nonnative-language speakers to write poetry in their native language and then paired them with an English speaker to translate the poem. These collaborations accessed poetry conventions of the homeland and encouraged problem solving.

Connecting Reading and Writing

Teachers inquiring into their own classrooms have been especially curious about the ways reading and writing transact. A collection of teacher research (Hanson, Newkirk, & Graves, 1985) on reading–writing connections launched the publishing careers of some of the most influential teacher researchers. In an era where readiness exercises and handwriting dittos comprised the writing curriculum in many primary grades, Avery, Ellen Blackburn (later Karalitz), and others showed through case studies and careful documentation of teaching and learning how young children connect reading and writing as they become literate. Working with older writers, Atwell, Cora Lee Five, Jack Wilde, Susan Benedict, and Linda Rief explored reading–writing connections in themed studies and learning across the curriculum.

Several other reports of elementary students explored these connections. Marilyn Boutwell (1983) studied third-grade Marta, who became a re-reader of her own writing in order to revise. Similarly, Cynthia Merrill (2000) illustrated how a struggling third-grade reader, with extensive support from her teacher, used her own writing to become a reader. June McConaghy (1985) observed children engaged in "after story talk" in her first-grade classroom, showing how they responded to it on three levels: literal, role playing, and meaning making.

Genre studies also fostered reading–writing connections. Peter Lancia (1997) wondered how and with what frequency his second-grade students borrowed literary craft when they composed. He found that saturation in a literary genre provided important models for successful writing. Christine Duthie (1994) noted that a similar immersion in nonfiction helped her first-grade students exhibit familiarity and confidence when writing and reading in that genre.

Older students also benefited from connected reading and writing. Jan Powell (1990) documented how fluent readers, but struggling writers, could become more fluent composers if given more opportunity to write. Tammy Van Wyhe (2000) and Ann Phillips (1997) investigated the ways their students transacted with poetry as readers and writers. Van Wyhe's rural Alaskan high school classes embraced poetry as a part of their adolescent experience, engaging in poetic e-mail exchanges with students in Lucille Rossbach's class in Colorado. Discussions of poetry began to show up in hall talk; poems, like pictures of teen idols, got taped to lockers; and players on the hockey team delayed travel to a game to meet the visiting poet who had been their "e-mentor." In more longitudinal work, Phillips (1997) tracked Evania from fifth to eighth grade to understand better why some children expressed themselves so fully and listened so carefully through poetry. Through Evania, Phillips developed new ways to think about who children are, what they need to say, and what they need to be taught. She discussed the possibilities of poetry for gaining access to children's deepest capacities for language.

Because teacher researchers work so closely over time with students, they are uniquely situated to study how students develop as readers and writers. Consequently, we see in the studies reflected here detailed and rich description of students and teachers struggling with and working through composition processes in ways that frame this work as complex, but ultimately doable. As seems typical of much teacher research, the studies discussed in this section frequently call attention to either possible misconceptions about learning or the needs of students who don't fit overgeneralized conceptions of mainstream learners. As such, they perhaps do more for ensuring that no children get left behind than do any battery of standardized tests or binders full of standardized curricula.

HOW DO TEACHERS USE WRITING TO LEARN ABOUT STUDENTS AND BECOME BETTER TEACHERS OF WRITING?

Many teachers see writing not only as a skill to be learned but as a lens for understanding the children they teach. This section showcases investigations by teacher researchers who investigated the needs, concerns, and cultures of students to teach them.

Looking Closely at One Student

"Devin's Daybook" is indicative of how teachers look closely at students. Devin, a student in a democratic alternative school, co-authored the piece with his third-grade teacher, Linda Winston (Winston & Low, 1990). The story of how and why Devin kept a daybook is instructive because Winston broke many of the "rules" of process-oriented instruction at the time. Devin did not write at all for the first few weeks, rarely shared, and did not develop longer pieces from his daybook entries. Both authors concluded it was important for Devin to learn at his pace, to write primarily for himself, and to learn to write principally from reading.

Sometimes, the smallest moment inspires the reflective teacher to look closely. Such was the case with Judy Buchanan (1993) as a simple question about the abbreviation for *page* caused her to notice Anwar. Familiar with the inquiry processes of Vermont's Prospect School (Himley with Carini, 2000), Buchanan examined writing done by Anwar in the first 3rd of the year with other elementary teachers. Buchanan saw much progress in Anwar's work, particularly in his ability to structure his writing and to imbue it with his voice. Buchanan's work argued for teachers examining student writing together to assess student progress, influencing what, how, and why they teach. Ross Burkhardt (1984), intrigued by Becky's composing processes, asked her to "compose aloud" on several occasions. Burkhardt observed Becky frequently re-reading her work and searching for the "perfect" word, once spending half an hour writing a piece of prose that she later used to create a poem in under 8 minutes. Burkhardt learned to allow students to develop their own processes.

Students who catch the attention of teacher researchers frequently challenge existing assumptions. First grader Douglas preferred to draw than to write, an activity Jean Ann Clyde (1994) felt was more like play. A class newspaper project allowed Douglas to flourish as a sportswriter, a job for which he used pictures to write about basketball and skating. Art provided a more compatible format for Douglas's ideas, stabilizing and giving shape to his thought while freeing him from the demands of language. Douglas challenged Clyde to broaden her previous verbocentric curricular assumptions and experiences.

Anne Sumida (2000) used a postmodern lens to analyze one piece of writing, focusing her attention on complex layers of gender issues, social tensions, and economic social forces. In 7-year-old Ka'iulani's story, the main character, a new father in a family, fought a mermaid. The women in her story were passive, acquiescent, and conventional. There seemed to be a wide-ranging cultural identification of a man as adventurer/hero, controller of capital, ruler of kingdom, and oppositional power to conquer. The mermaid was a Caucasian with shiny blonde hair and "skin as white as cream," raising issues of race and even beauty. Treating a child's writing as a social/literary text gave Sumida insight into the many controversial issues, contradictions, and tensions manifested in the writing of even young children.

Looking Closely at Particular Writing Activities

Some teachers focused on the dynamics of writing, others on how their students developed as writers, and still others on understanding what their students already did as writers and how that knowledge might inform their teaching. For instance, Don Aker (1992), a high school English teacher, described how work with his students challenged his belief that texts contain a single meaning. The turning point was a response by Ronnie to the significance of paint in Sinclair Ross's "The Painted Door." Ronnie, who had recently broken up with his girlfriend, connected with one of the characters in a way that was real to both him and the rest of the class. Seeking to tap into other student experience, Aker had students write literary letters and dialogue journals, sometimes yielding engagement and sometimes shutting down that engagement. Ultimately, like Buchanan, Aker learned that in order to help his students engage more with literacy, he had to pay more systematic attention to what they did as writers and readers.

Also interested in exploring how her students' reading influenced their writing, Dina DeCristofaro (2001) analyzed her students' writing, finding that in a literature-rich classroom students appropriated topics, particular words, and author's style, although most were not cognizant of such intertextuality. When students have strong literary models, the authors of the books they read become additional writing teachers for them.

Carol Stumbo (1992) was interested in the ways talk, either informal or in conferences, transacted with student writing. A high school teacher in economically struggling eastern Kentucky, she engaged three student co-researchers to investigate what happened when students edited the interviews they had collected from members of the community, particularly as those editing decisions connected to the learner's sense of self. By looking closely at the editing work of the three student editors, Stumbo realized that these students focused on their attempts to make meaning of the texts. In editing long transcripts into shorter articles for their oral history magazine, students dealt with a range of language issues that helped them to see the power of words, punctuation, usage, and the full range of writing conventions.

How teachers respond to student journals (Werderich, 2002), how dialogue journals might influence student writing (Wells, 1990), and how writing in a teacher journal fostered reflection on practice (Crepps, 1993) were three ways that teacher researchers learned about themselves and their students. In a year-long study, Fracereta and Phillips (2000) examined how students valued writers' notebooks, a kind of journaling, as a learning tool. Roughly one quarter of their students saw little value, half saw some value, and the remaining quarter highly valued the writers' notebooks. Case studies revealed different uses. Josh, who struggled with mechanics, used his notebook to express his concerns about his father's illness. For Linda, whose mood swings and related medication made her an erratic participant in class, the notebook became a place to express her enjoyment of literature through words and richly detailed graphics.

Looking Closely at Writing Classrooms

In a remarkable precursor to the mid-1980s explosion of scholarship on writing in elementary classrooms, Anne Martin (1981) examined the work of her fourth-grade writers over several years and described how she formed relationships with children through their writing processes and talk. Martin learned that writing needs to be a "constant every-day activity," and to be "taken seriously and consistently shared," and that teachers can't "impose preconceived standards of form and language" (p. 2), although she did teach standard forms in conference. Further, observant teachers can tap into children's themes rather than assigning topics. She espoused this developmental view of writing, saying, "We run the almost inevitable risk of losing the thread of a child's development as an expressive person" (p. 60) when considering only 1 year's writing.

Two studies highlight the focus of this section: teachers learning about students through student work, talk, and writing. Nancy Nicolescu (1985) encouraged talk in her classroom "as a means to become more aware of the children's needs, knowledge, feelings, and points of view" (p. 500). She noticed that dialogue journaling and other forms of "talk" created spaces for learning. Observing and interviewing kindergartners, Diane Borgman (1986) noticed that when process rather than product was emphasized, children preferred to write their own stories, could read their own invented spelling more readily than their teacher's writing, developed a very strong sense of authorship even at an early age, responded positively to a sense of trust and respect for their writing, and wrote more freely and less self-consciously. Both studies indicate that children blossom as writers and learners when given support and venues for self-expression.

Researchers from the Brookline Teacher Research Seminar, with its emphasis on listening closely to and learning from the interaction of children, often wrote about the way language and culture figured into the learning life of the classroom. Jim Swaim's (1998) third-grade student Pamela created an inclusive community in writing and sharing her re-vision of the world, teaching Swaim to listen to his students with an open mind. Cynthia Ballenger (1996) questioned how language figured into the ways learning occurred across cultural borders in a Haitian preschool in Boston. From studying the children's interactions in a writing center, she contrasted her intended curriculum— the functions of print in our language system—with the children's "shadow" curriculum, "using letters to represent and interpret their relationships" (p. 321). She had to understand student purposes for print in order to teach. Karen Gallas (1994) studied teacher–learner interactions for 5 years in her first/second-grade classroom, analyzing the ways children talked, wrote, danced, drew, and sang their understanding of the world. These modes of expression not only allowed children to interrogate, interpret, and share their worlds, but also provided windows to their divergent world views and knowledge constructions. In writing about Imani, an immigrant child with no discernable literacy background who eventually became "a figure of importance and authority in the classroom" (p. 48), and Alex, Michael, and Charles whose oral and literate actions as "bad boys" disrupted the classroom, but provided disturbing insights about gender and power, Gallas reveals the narrative lives of children.

Also concerned about violence in the writing lives of young boys, Michael Anderson (2003) investigated how the boys in his class experienced and appropriated media and literacy. He found parallels between Jason's writing and popular culture, where both employed themes such as good versus evil, heroes as underdogs, kid heroes, actions/excitement/danger, and magical powers. Jason's writing, although violent, was not pathological and provided him with an important medium for connecting with popular culture and with his classmates.

Addressing issues within writing workshops, Jo Anne Deshon (1997) and Karen Evans (1995) examined and adjusted their instructional practices. An urban first-grade teacher, Deshon became uncomfortable with the instruction she was providing her Chapter I students. Through close analysis of these mostly African American students during writing workshop, she realized the negative impact of her scheduling decisions. Since they came back from their Chapter I class during writing workshop, students wrote in relative isolation and missed sharing with a large audience. Similarly discontent, Evans (1995) felt that writing workshop in her fifth-grade classroom was "a disaster," but reflecting on its failure led her to get to know and understand her students' worlds. Most were African American, Hispanic, and Native American, and most lived at or near poverty level. They were not about to write nice, family stories for the rich, White lady. Evans changed her instruction to focus on writing that "took place in a context that was interesting to students and served a specific purpose" (p. 268), such as writing to prepare for literature discussion groups or on self-selected social studies topics.

Lisa Orta (1996) also used writing as a tool to help her and her students make sense of their world. Growing up in California at the height of the women's movement in the 1970s, Orta was teaching diverse students in the 1990s for whom issues of feminism seemed secondary to navigating their complex lives as urban adolescents. Informed by student writing on gender, Orta realized that her take on feminism was coloring the ways she saw her students and that she needed to open herself to a range of perspectives if she wanted to create true learning relationships. In his study of three struggling, urban high school students he taught during the 1988–89 school year, Eli Goldblatt (1995) focused on how they positioned themselves in relation to textual "author-ity." Goldblatt felt that DuBois's (1903) notion of "double consciousness" was evident as these students sought to negotiate a range of public and private discourses. He concluded that educators need to build a composition theory and pedagogy that carefully consider how cultural conditions affect disenfranchised writers.

Struggling past her own sense of dread about writing, Ellen Baru (1985) enlisted a professional children's writer to visit her classroom regularly. By entering the world of the writer, students began to develop a sense of community, freedom, confidence, and the magic of writing. Finding that magic for students in Fine's (1987) junior high remedial classroom meant writing as a collective. She led her students through an extended "oral group rehearsal," let them follow their voices, and stopped trying to impose hers. The text poured out, and the students came to a point where they wanted to do their own writing. She cautioned, however, that the writing agenda must belong to the students. Ownership was also a central premise for Betty Sanford (1988). She studied what happened when students wrote about what they were noticing, what they had learned, what connections they were making, and how they saw the process of writing reflectively. By analyzing samples of student work, Sanford saw the breadth and depth of her students' thinking, far beyond the one-dimensional answers to test questions. Through writing reflectively, her students began to internalize what they learned, take action as learners, and develop their ability to think. Education, as Freire noted, can free people or domesticate them; when students write reflectively, education may become liberatory.

HOW DO TEACHERS TEACH WRITING?

Teacher research has focused on five elements of composition instruction: creating a literate environment, investigating writing genres, writing to learn across content areas, focusing on the writing process, and developing assessments. Researchers profiled in this section ask not "how?" but "what happens when?" Their work chronicles the dynamic interaction of curriculum, instruction, and learners.

Creating a Literate Environment

Nancie Atwell (1984, 1987, 1989, 1990, 1991b, 1998) has had a profound impact on the teaching of writing. Likewise, teachers who have written books about their literacy approaches are among the best-known writers on the teaching of writing. Books by Linda Rief (1999), Carol Avery (1987), Shelley Harwayne (1992, 1999, 2001), Joanne Hindley (1996), Bobbi Fisher (1995), and others are highlighted, dog-eared, and discussed passionately over school-cafeteria lunches. Because of their renown, we do not focus on them in this review, but acknowledge their tremendous influence.

Many teacher researchers have documented specific aspects of writing workshop. Jim Swaim (2002) investigated elementary writing workshops that would be more responsive to the social priorities of children, especially embracing the Bakhtinian (1984) metaphor of carnival. One critique of the applicability of Atwell's work has been the relative homogeneity of her classroom. Countering this concern, Divans-Hutchinson (1995) showed how a more tightly framed version of writers' workshop benefited her diverse urban middle school students. Teaching in a large high school, Laurie Hoff (1994) found that over time and with an emphasis on mini-lessons, her writing workshop helped students "who lacked confidence in themselves as competent students" (p. 43) to become students who felt empowered by writing. Intending her research to critique writing workshop, Bea Johnson (1999) studied her kindergarten classroom, trying to prove that Graves and Calkins were "ivory-tower" academics who had no credibility. She expected her writing program to fail. It didn't, however, and her book is a detailed guide to establishing a writing program in kindergarten and first grade. The workshop approach also was extended successfully by Charles Pearce (1993) in teaching science and by Patricia Collins (1990) in social studies.

Heidi Mills and Jean Anne Clyde (1990) invited teachers with a whole language philosophy at a variety of grade levels to detail a typical day. Tim O'Keefe's (1990) "transitional kindergarten" students wrote throughout the day in their study of dinosaurs: They labeled pictures, wrote what they knew and what they wanted to learn, created graphs, engaged in written conversations, wrote in journals and in response to literature, and created number stories with dinosaur information. Third-grade teacher Margaret Grant (1990) described an immersion in art and poetry using a print by Pieter Brueghel, demonstrating that "direct instruction has a critical place: at the point of the writers' need" (p. 155). Phyllis Whitin (1990) involved middle school students in family history projects that honed research skills such as interviewing, studying artifacts, and writing engagingly from multiple sources. High school teacher Donelle Blubaugh (1990) reached students in a lower track classroom through personalized exams, photograph-inspired poetry, and engagement in meaningful social issues.

In a rare control group study by a teacher researcher, Vicki Tabachnick (1992) "hypothesized that students in the composition course who constructed knowledge for themselves rather than rely on teacher direction would learn course concepts more effectively" (p. 25). Tabachnick taught an experimental group using a constructivist approach while another teacher taught a control group using a teacher-directed approach. At the end of the semester, both groups took an unannounced, ungraded test on the identifying features for different types of essays they wrote. The experimental group recalled, on average, three times more features than the control group.

Investigating Writing Genres

A number of teacher studies focused on using journals in a range of contexts, with various incarnations of dialogue journals getting the most attention. Christine Cziko

(1996), worried about the dehumanizing effects of learning in an urban high school of more than 4,000 students, used literature dialogue journals to create community and help students connect text to their lives. Cynthia Shelton's (1990) analysis of student journals indicated that students wrote longer and in more depth when they had something important to their lives to write about.

Anne Thompson (1990) analyzed the thinking evident in students' learning logs. She determined seven categories: focusing, gathering, remembering, organizing, predicting and elaborating, integrating, and evaluating. A study by Karen Scales (2000) showed the use of journals in third and fourth grades. On the plus side, Scales noted that supportive teacher comments in journals helped to clarify student understanding and motivate students. However, difficulties with writing limited the usefulness of these journals as an assessment tool, especially for students with writing difficulties. Studies by Jean Hannon (1999), Barbara Roth (1990), and Nancy Wheeler (1990) indicated that the use of journals needs to be refined depending on the contexts.

Many teachers used journals to gain insight into the lives of children. Nancy Hudson (1995) taught at a rural vocational technical center where violence permeated the community. Hudson decided to listen to the students' lives instead of ignoring the disturbing aspects. She employed "no rules" journaling similar to freewriting, spent more time outside class with her students, and called their homes regularly. Two boys Hudson dialogued with in their journals related feelings of hatred for the school and authority. As a trusting bond developed over time, these students revealed the worlds of gangs and abuse in which they lived and began to recognize how violence in their lives affected their behavior. Scott Peterson (2000) reflected on and illustrated how using a writer's notebook could act as a lens through which a writer views the world. Similarly, Michelle Toch (1997) kept her own writer's notebook and modeled for students how to keep a range of entries. Using examples of three students' work, Toch illustrated her students' writing development. Although notebook writing did not spark all of her students' interests, it allowed her to connect to some she might not have otherwise.

A number of teacher researchers explored more traditional academic genres, such as essays and research writing. William Winston's (1987) students inquired into a range of writing models that moved them away from one-dimensional structures into more vivid writing. Derek Furr's (2003) students who struggled with expository writing became more independent after mining their own experiences to start their essays. Likewise, Denise Standiford (1992), in working with "unmotivated, academically unprepared, and economically disadvantaged students," documented how having students write on the same topic in four different styles helped them to develop their writing. Taking a more informal tack, Bill Martin (2003) argued for what he called "occasional papers," short, quickly written pieces that were shared and discussed in class as a meaning-making activity of possibility rather than an academic chore.

Research writing also received the attention of teacher researchers. Mary Lou Hess (1989) showed fourth-grade students how to write narratives that included facts, leading to better understanding of their research topics. Jack Wilde (1988) tackled report writing with his fifth-grade class by engaging them in a study of the range of informational genres in order to widen their options as authors. Similarly, Colleen Ruggieri's (2002) students explored a range of formats to open them to multigenre response. Students who previously struggled in class were able to increase their averages, some by as much as a letter grade. In two studies of research writing, Sally

Randall (1996) showed that students valued information charts as useful tools to support their writing, and Alan Perry (2003) demonstrated that when he required a related PowerPoint presentation 3 weeks before the final research paper was due, more students turned in papers. However, the PowerPoint seemed to be more valued by college prep than technical prep students.

In looking at other genres, Franki Sibberson (1997) used picture books with fourth graders to help them connect reading to writing. When they saw the picture books as appropriate to their level, students were able to inquire into the genre and see how such books often flowed out of the lives of authors. Finally, Ellen Karalitz (1988a) looked at over 400 notes written by students for students. As she observed, "Note writing created an extra layer of discourse in my classroom that allowed children to experiment with argumentation, persuasion, and regulation" (p. 107).

Writing to Learn Across Content Areas

We found more studies connecting writing to art than to any other content area. In our introduction we noted how Gee (1990) felt she was shortchanging her upper-grade elementary students by not doing more art as part of the academic curriculum. This theme of art enhancing visualization echoed through other studies. Whether helping young writers in conferences via drawing (Bridge, 1988), conducting artists' workshop to parallel writers' workshop (Ernst, 1994), having students respond to literature through drawing (Manchey, 1999), or using sketching to push student questioning (Whitin, 1994), teachers found that students showed greater capacity to visualize their writing through artistic endeavors. As Ernst aptly put it, "My kids don't know where writing ends and art begins. Both art and writing were essential to the learning here—theirs and mine" (p. 47).

Of the major content areas, science was most strongly represented in the studies we found. Suzanne Beutler (1988), a sixth-grade teacher, designed individual and team writing activities with cooperative elements to enable all her students to participate in learning astronomy by writing, with the writing procedures ensuring active participation. Writing helped learners read their texts with a goal in mind; to transact with the text; to use their prior knowledge, experience, and metacognitive skills; and to share their learning with others through their astronomy fair. Karen Hume's (2001) knowledge wall, Jo Haney's (1990) puffin project, and Leslie Franks's (2001) writing and drawing about weather investigation further illustrate the ways writing can be effectively drawn into science classrooms. Examples from other content areas include Stan Pesick's (1996) reflective use of portfolios with writing exercises that challenged his students to think like historians, interpreting history rather than feeding back facts; and Christine Evans (1984) having her fifth-grade students explain in writing their methods, definitions, and struggles, which led to improved attitudes about math.

Looking at writing across the curriculum in general, Cudd and Roberts (1989) devised an elaborate scheme of paragraph frames that acted as models for writing in different subject areas; their use facilitated understanding and retention of material. In Sheila Friedman's (1986) first-grade class, almost all learning activities involved writing, which seemed to promote linguistic growth and concept development. In studies focused on ESL classrooms, Cynthia Oei (1995) and Eloise Laliberty (2001) demonstrated how giving English-language learners options to write in home or school languages, and helping them bring their culture into the classroom, resulted in increased understanding of content.

Focusing on Writing Processes

Many teacher researchers investigate strategies that help writers develop their craft. Tom Romano (1987) has written insightfully about helping adolescents write to learn and write about literature. Using vivid stories and case studies, Romano argued that "talk is essential in a writing class" (p. 85); he used student examples to show how teacher–student conferencing resulted in engaged adolescent writers.

Revising and editing have been the focus of several studies. Karyn Schweiker-Marra, Mary Broglie, and Elizabeth Plumer (1997) raised ethical questions about ownership, privacy, and authority when working with students. Despite these concerns, Shawni McBride (2000) guided students through the maze of editing, focusing them on one or two glitches and tracking those concerns over time. She concluded that students need some say in what writing goals they pursue, yet also must be assisted in imagining the larger picture. Frustrated by story endings that fell flat, Pamela Murphy (2003) found that giving students frameworks and getting them to inquire into the dynamics of endings improved their ability to write more satisfying finishes.

Some research pointed toward strategies to help students imagine and re-imagine writing. Working from five strategies developed by Lane (1993)—questions, snapshots, exploding a moment, thoughtshots, and making a scene—Laura Harper (1997) enabled her middle school students to imagine and develop greater detail in their written work. Similarly, Gina Cowin (1986) used a variety of image-provoking activities to move her students from prewriting to a completed effort. Dan Walker (1991) used alternative versions of passages from famous authors to help students key in on stylistic differences. Carol Collins and Barbara Everson (1993) encouraged students to use improvisation and role play to extend first drafts of stories.

Helping students develop their own writing processes also extended to special education classrooms. D'Alessandro (1987) found it helpful for her students with emotional disorders to express their feelings first before worrying about polished writing. In a parent/teacher research collaboration, Connie Mayer (1994) and Evie, her son's teacher, worked for 4 years integrating hearing and deaf students into a writing classroom, finding that the developmental steps through which deaf children moved, paralleled those of hearing children. Teaching second through fourth graders with learning disabilities, Connie Broderick (1996) used activities that, except for her students with perceptual visual deficits, helped them to discover correct spellings through repeated experimentation and verification.

Highlighting the importance of reflection, Kim Douillard (2002) and Robert Griffith (1997) were both concerned about what Griffith termed "a first-draft society," and created space in their teaching days for elementary and middle school students, respectively, to reflect on their learning. Griffith installed daily, weekly, biweekly, quarterly, and yearly reflective routines that gave students insight into their writing process. Griffith's students seemed more able to assess their own work, develop meaningful and insightful writing, and transfer their reflection skills to reading and math. Due to her reflective Friday activities, Douillard's young students subtly showed more signs of reflective thought throughout the year. Douillard discussed eight different types of thinking that students engaged in: recounting, observation, generating questions, making connections, evaluating, being aware of their own learning, recognizing new information, and adding details to information. Students moved from a simple statement in their reflection to a more thoughtful description of their thinking, drawing conclusions, connecting their writing to their own interests and experiences, making observations, and evaluating their own learning.

Teachers also researched written and oral responses to student writing. The dynamics of a teacher–student conference was Mark Smith's (1992) focus. When a student wrote an essay on her schizophrenic sister that, although expressively written, failed to meet the requirements for the assigned argumentative essay, Smith focused on vivid passages she had written, helping her to build an argument around them. Examining the dynamics of an elementary class doing peer conferences, Connie Russell (1983) conceded that it took negotiation and structure to get the conferences working effectively, and argued that her students took greater ownership and were more engaged in their writing as a result. Roger Green (2000) tried out two different types of peer response groups: reading/writing groups, in which the writer was present and received immediate feedback, and publishing committees, in which papers from one class were exchanged with another class and a week's time was given for feedback. He at first cringed when he overheard groups in the latter situation make unkind remarks about the work. Stifling his urge to interfere, he let the process unfold. To his relief, the letters from these committees to the authors were couched in supportive and insightful language. Students came to understand that reading/writing groups gave them quick response and dialogue; the publications committees gave them considered response and deeper insight.

Developing Assessments

Faced with a mandated assessment of his seventh-grade students' growth and competencies, Michael Coughlan (1988) was in a quandary: "The very nature of the exam setting, which isolates the writer from the support of peer conferencing, imposes an assigned topic, and allows a limited time for writing, stood contrary to the kind of environment I had struggled so hard to develop in my writing class" (p. 375). After implementing a writing workshop, Coughlan created a test that consisted of a single question: "Show me what you have learned about writing this year" (p. 375). This evaluation was more than a test to pass or fail; "it was a powerful learning experience for the students" (p. 378), one that forced them to reflect on what they had learned.

Linda Rief (1992) and Joseph Quattrini (1996) explored the educative possibilities of portfolios, she with eighth-grade students and he with high schoolers. In a case study of Nahanni, Rief detailed how involving students in reflection on their work resulted in students who took greater control over their writing. Quatrini saw working with students as working with colleagues. As a group they negotiated five criteria for their portfolio assessment: range, flexibility, connectedness, independence, and conventions. Through these lenses, students were able to play greater roles in their own evaluations.

Self-evaluation was a powerful idea for teachers. When students asked Marion MacLean (1983) to allow them more responsibility in evaluating their work in advanced placement English classes, MacLean documented how writing about their choices regarding their ready-to-be-submitted essays helped them call their internal judgments to the surface. MacLean argued that three critical voices—"the voice of an imagined external audience, the voice of the student as writer, and the voice of the student as audience" (p. 63)—formed the writer's audience.

In other work on self-evaluation, Shirley McPhillips (1985) argued that her fifth-grade students' collaborative inquiry into their writing resulted in higher expectations for their writing, a deeper reach into their creative wells, and greater control over the work. Philip Rhea (1986) discovered that, when allowed to write in nontraditional ways, the 49 students he queried tended to ask more incisive and process-oriented questions about their writing and to possess more intrinsic motivation. While implementing an after-school project with 9 sixth graders, Cynthia Biery (1993) wondered what writings were self-perpetuating and found that each of the students had experienced writing at some time that had been nourished with attention, appreciation, and time. Teri Beaver (1998) described how development of rubrics had allowed elementary students to grow as writers and had created a means for teachers to document that growth over time.

Although the individual import of each of the studies in this section is significant, what might be more critical to the educational community is what messages these studies send collectively. Chiefly, we see throughout this work a kind of productive skepticism on the part of teachers. Rather than just accepting the advice of educational researchers about the use and usefulness of such approaches as writers' workshop, journaling, or portfolio assessment, the teachers who conducted the studies in this section sought to better understand writing instruction in the context of their own teaching. The result is a complexity of understanding that, rather than being daunting, invites other teachers to see their own classrooms as places of inquiry. In doing so, teachers begin to see that rather than trying to fit the square peg of some educational approach into the round hole of their classrooms, they instead might ask what is occurring there and use the resulting data to sand some softer corners into that academic projectile.

HOW DO STUDENTS USE WRITING TO MAKE MEANING OF AND ACT UPON THEIR WORLDS?

Primary-grade students in Laura Siemens's (1996) class were immersed in poetry all year. One student, Au, wrote to his favorite poet, only to discover from her editor that she died recently. Saddened, Au wrote a poem about the poet and sent it to the editor. The poet's daughter responded, indicating that she would put Au's poem on her mother's grave and that her mother would read it from heaven. As the power of language to connect human beings across time and space settled into their collective consciousness, the children became "poets who knew that writing was one way to slow down, to stop and notice the world, and to save the wonders they were discovering" (p. 240).

In this section we focus on studies in which teacher researchers tried to understand how writing helped students to do as Siemens's (1996) class had done: inquire into, connect with, act upon, and make meaning of their worlds. We discuss ways students employed writing in developing self- and cultural identities; connecting families, language, culture, and school; deepening and expanding content understanding; and inquiring into and acting upon social issues.

Developing Self- and Cultural Identities

In learning about others, writers often learn about themselves, as Barbara Michalove (1999) and the team of Nancy Krim and Sandra Worsham (1993) learned. Disturbed by the intolerance her predominantly African American fourth-grade students displayed toward Latino/a classmates as well as those with hearing impairments, Michalove created an interdisciplinary immersion into prejudice, involving students and their parents in writing about discrimination in their own lives. Initially resistant to looking at themselves, students eventually "circled in" on their own prejudice and wrote rules for their own classroom as well as an all-inclusive class play. Krim's Scarsdale, NY, class of predominantly European American students with learning disabilities and Worsham's basic English class in southern Georgia exchanged letters and video recordings for a year to connect to other cultures and real audiences. Krim noted that "the writing difficulties that had stigmatized these students . . . weren't hampering their ability to reach out and tell their stories" (p. 18) and that, over time, self-editing increased. Students understood that "the classroom can be an extension of the real world and what you learn there can help you formulate reasoned positions on the issues that mattered" (p. 23).

Illustrating connections between the development of various aspects of one's identity and the act of writing, then-high school teacher Bob Fecho, writing with former high school student Aaron Green (2002), examined the ways in which Aaron used his writing to explore his identities as provocateur, mainstream writer, and outsider. Aaron's writing and his ongoing conversations with Fecho showed the polyphonic nature of identity construction, the ways identity transactions are connected to literacy, and the importance of such transactions in the classroom. Ultimately, Fecho argued, teachers need to see reading and writing as existential acts for helping students create meaning out of the random chaos of their lives. Also interested in identity issues, students in Mollie Blackburn's (1999) middle school "gifted" class used literature and their experiences to inquire into and write about why students are included or excluded from gifted classes.

In separate studies touching on issues of race and class identity, Karen Alford (1999), in a New Orleans Montessori middle school, and Jeffrey Schwartz (1992), in an affluent western Pennsylvania private school, engaged students in dialogue across cultures. Alford studied the way journals fostered deeper understandings and more emotional resonance as her European American and African American students took on roles of slaves and slave owners, writing candidly and with emotion. Often the writing enabled what discussions couldn't—the time to consider the views of another. In one particularly poignant exchange, Rose—an African American student—wrote, "If you want the negro history/You will get it/ From somebody who wore/ the shoe" (p. 138). Rose's poem prompted Angela, a European American student, to respond that although she could empathize, she couldn't fully understand the African American experience, not having lived it, nor could she "express such feeling as strongly as Rose" (p. 138). Schwartz, in coupling his private school students with others from a high school in Pittsburgh's rust belt, studied how students explored class differences. Students saw not only how writing opened up communication, but also how writing was limited in terms of expressing one's identity.

In addition to race and socioeconomic class, teacher researchers were interested in issues of gender. Using questionnaires, interviews, and essays, Maureen Barbieri

(1987) studied choices her middle school male students made regarding topic and genre of writing. Countering traditional conceptions that boys tend to write about sports, action, and violence, she noticed that male students in the study often wrote to understand or represent themselves better. While teaching at an independent girls' secondary school, Norma Greco (1999) noticed that despite having the cultural capital to compete for the finest universities, many of her students restrained their own writing voices and granted authority to the authors of other texts. After writing in more personal ways, students felt they enjoyed greater freedom as writers, but also felt that they lost some of the control and security that go with formulaic academic writing.

Connecting Families, Language, Culture, and School

Teacher researchers often have found it important to study the complex transactions among family, language, culture, and school. Describing a year-long thematic unit titled "Coming to America," Laura Schiller (1996) invited students and families in her multicultural middle school community to write and read about ancestry, immigration, heritage, and slavery, culminating in a collection of stories about families and immigration. The experience helped students develop an understanding that discrimination against immigrants was not an abstract concept; it affected them personally. Similarly, Krogness (1987) employed family folklore to encourage students to discover the richness of diversity, even though that frequently meant touching "the pain of acknowledging that we were not only different, but unequal" (p. 810).

Herself an "immigrant child," Cristina Igoa (1995) learned about the inner world of her students—the silent state, culture shock, stages of uprooting, isolation, exhaustion, loneliness, and struggle to adjust to a school's culture—in order to teach them in her fifth/sixth-grade sheltered English classroom. She integrated the cultural, academic, and psychological dimensions of children's lives through innovative teaching practices that included helping children explore and represent experiences from their home cultures, families, and religion using art, reading, music, and writing. She created partnerships with parents through home visits, homework notebooks, and other culturally sensitive communications. Igoa included compelling case studies (five of which include follow-up information on the children as adults) as well as group progress data to show the effectiveness of these personalized learning relationships.

One issue of the *Bread Loaf Rural Teacher Network Magazine* focused on the complex relations between language and culture. On Tununak, an isolated island in Alaska, all 90 students and many of their parents and grandparents created the Yup'ik encyclopedia project, a bilingual, multimedia archive of tribal stories, knowledge, and skills that engaged students in inquiry into the power of language in their changing society (Dyment, 1997). Rural teachers designed several electronic, cross-site research projects, such as "the language of power" by secondary teachers Stephen Schadler, Sharon Lander, and Gary Montaño (1997) of New Mexico, Mississippi, and Arizona, respectively. Students discussed their home languages in relation to the "language of power" to make informed decisions about the uses and value of both in oral and written venues.

In helping students understand power relationships in their lives, Linda Christensen (1999), Nancy Lubarsky (1987), and Janet Irby (1993) investigated the role of writing. Christensen used writing to help students understand that their lives count and are part of a history that most school textbooks ignore, to take a critical stance on their world, and to write of their own lives in their "home language" (p. 214). Centering her project on the reappearance of Haley's Comet, Lubarsky and her students interviewed senior citizens and produced writing that enabled them to consider both their past and future. Irby's summer school English class founded a newsletter aimed at informing the school board about problems in the lives of students. Irby wrote, "When they connected their own experiences and opinions with a meaningful purpose and an important audience that wielded some power over their lives, the learning of vocabulary, writing structures, revision, and appropriate rhetorical choices made sense" (p. 54).

Writing as a way of reaching out to parents is evident in the work of Deborah Jumpp (1996), Carole Chin (1996), and Betty Shockley (1993), all of whom involved parents more directly in the life of the classroom. Through portfolio response in Jumpp's inner-city high school classes, suggested writing in Chin's urban elementary school, and dialogue journals in Shockley's first-grade classroom, parents were invited to contribute to the curriculum in meaningful ways. As Jumpp's parents responded to their children's work, they became "mediators in their children's learning" and consequently empowered to tell her "what they felt their children needed from [the teacher] to improve their writing" (p. 141). Chin, known as "the teacher who gives parents homework," documented the ways parents, many first-generation immigrants, saw these writing assignments as ways to take part in the learning of their children, but also to advance their own study of English. Shockley invited parents—who responded with overwhelming levels of involvement in this "low-SES" school—to write family stories and to read and write with their children three times a week in family reading journals.

Concerned with helping students evoke a sense of place especially in terms of identity, *Rural Voices* (Brooke, 2003) contains studies done primarily by K–12 teachers. For many, poetry fostered explorations of place, as when Sharon Bishop's (2003) students used "Where I'm From" poems that enabled them to value their local communities and to locate the community concerns within the global society. The students in Bev Wilhelm's (2003) classes explored a variety of poetic forms to find out about "the past of their hometown" in order to construct "a promise for the future" (p. 101). The authors argued that writing enhances students' understanding of place and their identity within place if teachers help channel their work in those directions.

Deepening and Expanding Content Understanding

In some studies, teachers documented how they helped students push to deeper understandings of what it meant to be a learner in a particular content area or in school generally. Karen Jorgensen (1993) studied how students in third-, fourth-, and fifth-grade classrooms connected language-thinking processes and history through history workshop, an extension of the principles of writing workshop. Transcripts showed students' thoughtfully exploring primary and secondary sources, writing personal narratives as history, and writing history. Case studies illustrated individual growth, issues for English-language learners, and students with different learning histories.

Denise Stavis Levine (1985), Ginnie Schroder (1996), and Leah Richards (1990) were each interested in deepening students' immersion in math or the sciences. Levine wondered "what kind of writing is it that fosters thinking and problem solving, that paves the way for conceptual development?" (p. 43). She studied how both function and audience affected students' writing as it related to learning and intellectual development, discovering that, for her urban middle school students, writing lab reports based on observations and intended for peers resulted in more concrete detail than did other forms of writing. Schroder showed how devising picture books for a younger audience enabled her chemistry students to develop understandings of the basic elements through control of the text and writing at their current level of understanding. Finally, Richards's year 7 classroom in South Australia emphasized that when writing and math intersected, writing allowed students to celebrate their successes, develop and understand their use of mathematical language and its symbols, and demonstrate insight into their thinking process, all of which contributed to their growing confidence as mathematicians.

Inquiring into and Acting upon Social Issues

Vivian Vazquez (1994, 2000, 2004) studied how her multiethnic students, ages 3–8, engaged in critical literacy for social action. She created observational narratives and gathered artifacts, including photographs of the learning wall her students produced each year as an audit trail of their learning. Students researched and wrote about their own questions: Why do we have French class when no one in our class is French, but we have lots of kids who speak Chinese? Why are there no females in this poster of the Royal Canadian Mounted Police? Students sent a letter to the school barbeque committee requesting vegetarian choices, gave a poster to lumberyards reminding them not to buy wood from companies that violate rain forests, and created a chart to show how fast-food companies entice children to buy their food, action that led to a McDonalds boycott.

Also working with young children, Karen Gallas (2001, 2003) explored imagination and its role in discourse acquisition. She collected data for 5 years from the student-directed "incidents of imagination" in her classroom environment where her students "had an unusual amount of room to flex their imaginative muscles" (2001, p. 467). Gallas proposed an "inside-out" theory of literacy learning that allows readers to rethink the role of the imagination in identity development, appropriation of various disciplinary discourses, and the authoring process. She defined authoring as "the process of metaphorically writing the world in a way that gives that interpretation of the world weight, voice, and agency—a way that has the ability to influence the thinking, feelings, and actions of others" (p. 477).

Gallas (2001) also analyzed examples of children across different settings. First and second graders in progressive, diverse, urban Brookline, MA, classrooms "moved easily into storytelling and performance," while kindergartners in a more traditional, less diverse rural California classroom were initially more silent and passive. Gallas noted performative aspects of composing, especially during sharing time. For example, Sophia's stories were always inclusive of her classmates and often included violence that "delighted and horrified the boys in her audience" (p. 479); Joe, on the other hand, controlled and informed his audience through illustrations. Gallas concluded that "dynamic, dialogic communities cannot be created unless I, as a teacher, embrace the authoring process and all its risks. The process of creating improvised, collaborative texts served as a gateway to the development of my students' public identities who influenced the thinking, feeling, and imaginative worlds of their peers" (p. 487).

The Bread Loaf Teachers Network has pioneered the use and study of electronic messaging among students and teachers distanced by geography and culture. As a middle school teacher in Alaska, Scott Christian (1997) connected his students via Web messaging to other Alaskan classrooms, as well as some in Mississippi, Vermont, and New Mexico. In widening the classroom this way, Christian enabled his students to use writing to gain multiple perspectives on literature as well as a deeper and more complex understanding of diversity.

Now a university administrator, Christian joined with Chris Benson, Dixie Goswami, and Walter Gooch (2002) to collect teachers' investigations into writing as a means to social activism. Although not focused solely on electronic forms of writing, much of the work revolved around e-mail exchanges among students within and across school districts. For example, Rosie Roppel (2000), a teacher in Ketchikan, Alaska, described an on-line "Gang Conference" that linked her students with students from other parts of the country who were grappling with issues of gang-related crime. As Roppel's students shared their issues online, they became more candid about their roles in and fears concerning gangs. Susan Miera (2002), a teacher at Pojoaque High School in New Mexico, told of the ways her telecommunications course excited the largely Latino and Native American population of the school, particularly when they created a poetry anthology with students from another New Mexico school. The collaboration helped her students to become more involved in writing both efferently and aesthetically. Lauren Schneider VanDerPloeg and Beth Steffen (2002) electronically united students across their two Wisconsin schools in a project called Write for Your Life that explored, among other subjects, issues of racism. Fueled by local marches of the KKK, students at the schools wrote emotional responses to one another's e-mails on the power of racism and ways to combat that social disease. As the authors noted, "Participation in this exchange developed and strengthened student voices, helping them negotiate their identities and experiences through the dynamic give and take of the situation" (p. 103).

Jennifer Tendero's (1998) Write for Your Life Project involved 14 middle school girls investigating a major social issue in their lives, teen pregnancy. These Hispanic and African American girls from one of the poorest, most violent, and least educationally successful areas of the country read articles, novels, and informational books; wrote poems, short stories, and "tips"; and published a 40-page booklet encouraging teens to wait until they are ready for babies. Similarly, Bronx sixth-grade teacher Marceline Torres (1998) involved her students in self-selected projects investigating "important questions and concerns about the world in which they live" (p. 59), such as drugs, AIDS, teen pregnancy, and homelessness. She also got parents involved, first by having students dialogue with their parents in "letters home," and second by holding monthly "celebrations" where students presented their research findings to their parents.

In two edited volumes (Calkins, 2001; Calkins & Christian, 2000) Alaskan teachers formed a community of practice to explore the influence of state educational standards and assessment on teaching and learning. Among the many strong examples of how students used writing to make meaning of community situations (see Bruce, 2001; Christian, 2000; McLeod, 2001; Roppel, 2000) is work done by Maria Offer (2000), her students, and community members. Offer connected her Inupiaq Eskimo high school students with Priscilla Kelly's Pelion, SC, teens in on-line written dialogues about their lives. One issue was gambling in the Shishmaref Island's Bingo

Hall and in South Carolina video poker venues. Students wrote with great passion—even bitterness—about the effects of gambling on their lives.

Teachers, passionate about both writing and teaching, often write about their teaching lives. Eliot Wigginton's (1986) frustrations as an English teacher in rural Georgia led him to create the Foxfire approach. His book included (1) the story of how his students came to research, write, and publish Foxfire publications based on community history and knowledge; (2) the tenets of the Foxfire philosophy; and (3) a detailed description of a grammar/composition course based on Foxfire principles. Gregory Michie (1999) also built from his students' cultures to encourage writing and learning. Part memoir, part student vignette, his book illustrates how Michie and his students used writing and a wide range of media in their lives to make meaning of the social worlds they were constructing.

Both Maria Sweeney (1997) and Sharon Miller (2001) studied the way writing can sensitize people to the lives of others. Sweeney, challenged by Edelsky's (1994) concept of "education *for* democracy" (p. 252; emphasis in original), asked her fourth-grade suburban students "to consider alternative views of events past and present . . . to look for missing or silenced voices" (Edelsky, 1994, p. 279) in their reading. An interdisciplinary, multimedia study of the end of apartheid in South Africa led the class to write a play that they performed for the rest of the school and the community, and urged the audience to fight racism by actions such as giving money to the Africa Fund and joining anti-racist groups. Miller's work was directed at a relationship she had with an 18-year-old student with cerebral palsy who frequently had denied the use of his work in her teacher research. Through his writing and their discussions, Miller came to understand that writing and research relations must be based on trust, integrity, and mutual respect.

CONTEMPLATING THE PAST, CONSIDERING THE FUTURE

There is a compelling body of teacher research, only some of which we have been able to include herein, that addresses questions about composition that teachers have asked of themselves and their students over the past 2 decades. This research has elucidated how students develop as writers, as well as how teachers use writing to learn about students in order to teach them, create literate environments, and help students make meaning and act upon their worlds through writing.

As we contemplate the rich findings of teacher research on composition, we agree with Ballenger (1999), who emphasized that inquiry in her teacher research community involved "a personal theorizing of the community life" in classrooms. "Teacher research in this tradition tells stories, stories that like all good stories have to do with love and friendship, family and exclusion, truth and fantasy, but these stories also contain data" (p. 98). As we reflected on the themes of the past 20 years, we simultaneously wondered what stories teachers might tell when the next review of composition is published. It would be presumptuous to suggest what inquiries teacher researchers should undertake. However, like Ballenger, we anticipate that teacher research will remain grounded in theorized narratives of students and teachers. We wonder, What deeply human stories will teachers write? What might the issues be?

In reflecting on what we've learned about how students develop as writers, we return to classrooms as sociocultural playgrounds. Teacher researchers have helped readers observe up close the dynamic playground interactions, to see how teachers and children created spaces of collaboration and to listen with new insights to the linguistic diversity of children at work and play. We have learned noteworthy accommodations to make the playground accessible to all learners. As we look to the future, we may rely more and more on teachers to study literacy learning in complex classroom communities. It will be increasingly necessary, in a world of children who are reduced to statistical means, for teachers to share their understandings of the learner as a complex cultural being, in a dynamic classroom full of equally complex learners in interaction with one another, and in an increasingly diverse social context. It will be equally necessary, to counter policy and programs that seek to make teaching a scripted superficial act, for teachers to show classrooms in all their innate messiness, layered density, and issue-laden possibility.

In the majority of studies we reviewed, teachers conducted inquiries with a clear focus on changing their practices to reach students more effectively. Writing became a portal for learning about students as people and as literacy learners; this portal often led teachers to new teaching–learning relationships and instructional strategies. Through studying individual learners and analyzing practices and children over time, teachers painted detailed portraits of children who sailed ahead, as well as the faces of the children left behind on the shoals of failure. These studies made visible issues of language, culture, power, and access. If educational policy continues its centripetal standardization of what and how we teach, teacher researchers we suspect (and hope) will find it necessary to document sociocultural, sociopolitical, and sociohistorical concerns ignored by that policy. By providing this centrifugal tension, will teacher researchers be able to keep dialogue open where silence is expected, diversity vital where monoculturalism is assumed, and educational equity in play where narrow standards are mandated?

The past 2 decades have seen a healthy debate on the establishment, questioning, and revision of instructional orthodoxies. A major trend has been away from viewing reading and writing as separate from each other, and as divorced from other disciplines. However, as seems evident in more-recent studies in this chapter, teachers are concerned about the narrow definition of literacy currently constraining curriculum, pedagogy, and assessment in the United States. The current emphasis in federal legislation and thus state standards on reading often excludes writing. Reading First is Reading Only. What will teachers learn from studying the effects of this remarginalization of writing?

And finally, perhaps the most critical area of inquiry of all: Literacy for what? Teachers documented the myriad ways students employed writing to interrogate, interpret, and act upon their worlds within and beyond the classroom. To turn a Freirian phrase, these students were "writing the word and the world" as actors, not objects. Through writing, students explored issues of identity and culture; they connected with their families and challenged their communities. This literacy for acting on the world is critical at least in part because federally funded research is not asking these questions. The current focus is on comparing instructional practices on discrete aspects of reading (e.g., fluency, vocabulary, phonemic awareness). We believe that teachers will continue to ask the more complex, locally situated questions that, rather than compare, seek to illuminate, explore, and foster more questions.

We argued at the start of this chapter that teacher research is inevitable and necessary. However, we believe that the increased publication of teacher research in the past 2 decades is threatened in today's highly restricted arena of literacy research. With "scientifically based" research demanded by NCLB (http://nclb2.ecs.org), and defined as experimental and quasi-experimental designs, "stated hypotheses," "valid and reliable" measures, published only after "rigorous, objective and scientific review," teacher research of the kind we have documented overwhelmingly here is increasingly marginalized. So the question may be broader than, "What will literacy teachers research in the next 2 decades?" We might be asking, How will teacher research remain a shared source of knowledge? Will schools and review boards eventually outlaw this type of inquiry? Will more teachers form or seek established networks of teacher researchers like those mentioned in this chapter? Such communities of inquiry are highly valued by participants, but should not preclude teachers from membership in the broader research community.

As university-based and school-based researchers, we need the emic perspectives of teachers and their students. We count on teacher researchers to show us the processes and potential, the idiosyncrasies and evolving identities, and, above all, the stories—told through data and theorized by teachers—of students as they write the word and the world.

ACKNOWLEDGMENT

The authors would like to thank the National Writing Project for their generosity in allowing such free and useful access to back issues of *The Quarterly*.

REFERENCES

Aker, D. (1992). From runned to ran: One journey toward a critical literacy. *Journal of Reading, 36*, 104–112.

Alford, K. (1999). "Yes, girl, you understand": History logs and the building of multicultural empathy. In S. W. Freedman, E. R. Simons, J. S. Kalnin, A. Casareno, & the M-CLASS Teams, *Inside city schools: Investigating literacy in multicultural classrooms* (pp. 126–141). New York: Teachers College Press.

Anderson, M. (2003). Reading violence in boys' writing. *Language Arts, 80*, 223–230.

Ashton-Warner, S. (1967). *Teacher*. New York: Simon & Schuster.

Atwell, N. (1984). Writing and reading literature from the inside out. *Language Arts, 61*, 240–252.

Atwell, N. (1987). *In the middle: Writing, reading, and learning with adolescents*. Montclair, NJ: Boynton/Cook.

Atwell, N. (1989). *Workshop 1: Writing and literature*. Portsmouth, NH: Heinemann.

Atwell, N. (1990). *Workshop 2: Beyond the basal*. Portsmouth, NH: Heinemann.

Atwell, N. (1991a). A special writer at work. In N. Atwell (Ed.), *Side by side: Essays on teaching to learn* (pp. 19–36). Portsmouth, NH: Heinemann.

Atwell, N. (1991b). *Workshop 3: The politics of process*. Portsmouth, NH: Heinemann.

Atwell, N. (1998). *In the middle: New understandings about writing, reading, and learning*. Portsmouth, NH: Heinemann.

Aubry, V. S. (1995). Audience options for high school students with difficulties in writing. *Journal of Reading, 38*, 434–443.

Avery, C. S. (1987). Traci: A learning-disabled child in a writing-process classroom. In R. Bullock & G. Bissex (Eds.), *Seeing for ourselves: Case-study research by teachers of writing* (pp. 59–75). Portsmouth, NH: Heinemann.

Bakhtin, M. M. (Ed.). (1984). *Rabelais and his world* (I. Iswolsky, Trans.). Bloomington: Indiana University Press.

Ballenger, C. (1996). Learning the ABCs in a Haitian preschool: A teacher's story. *Language Arts, 73*, 317–323.

Ballenger, C. (1999). *Teaching other people's children: Literacy and learning in a bilingual classroom*. New York: Teachers College Press.

Banford, H. (1996). The blooming of Maricar: Writing workshop and the phantom student. In H. Banford, M. Berkman, C. Chin, C. Cziko, B. Fecho, D. Jumpp, et al. (Eds.), *Cityscapes: Eight views from the urban classroom* (pp. 3–24). Berkeley: National Writing Project.

Barbieri, M. (1987). Writing beyond the curriculum: Why seventh grade boys write. *Language Arts, 64,* 497–504.

Baru, E. (1985). Finding the writer's magic. *Language Arts, 62,* 730–739.

Beaver, T. (1998). *The author's profile: Assessing writing in context.* York, ME: Stenhouse.

Benson, C., Christian, S., Goswami, D., & Gooch, W. (Eds.). (2002). *Writing to make a difference: Classroom projects for community change.* New York: Teachers College Press.

Berkman, M. (1995). Quoc Tin and Sona: The story of a peer journal project. *The Quarterly of the National Writing Project 17*(4), 6–11.

Beutler, S. A. (1988). Using writing to learn about astronomy. *The Reading Teacher, 41,* 412–417.

Biery, C. (1993). When all the right parts don't run the engine: A teacher-researcher project reflects on practice. *Language Arts, 70,* 12–17.

Bishop, S. (2003). A sense of place. In R. Brooke (Ed.), *Rural voices: Place-conscious education and the teaching of writing* (pp. 65–82). New York: Teachers College Press.

Blackburn, M. (1999). Studying privilege in a middle school gifted class. In J. Allen (Ed.), *Class actions: Teaching for social justice in elementary and middle school* (pp. 72–83). New York: Teachers College Press.

Blubaugh, D. (1990). "I have never read five books before in my life": Reading and writing naturally in high school. In H. Mills & J. A. Clyde (Eds.), *Portraits of whole language classrooms: Learning for all ages* (pp. 259–274). Portsmouth, NH: Heinemann.

Borgman, D. (1986). "Whose writing is it anyway?": Kids love to write . . . don't wait until they read. *The Quarterly of the National Writing Project, 8*(3), 13–17.

Boutwell, M. A. (1983). Reading and writing process: A reciprocal agreement. *Language Arts, 60,* 723–730.

Bridge, S. (1988). Squeezing from the middle of the tube. In T. Newkirk & N. Atwell (Eds.), *Understanding writing: Ways of observing, learning, and teaching. K–8* (2nd ed.; pp. 80–87). Portsmouth, NH: Heinemann.

Broderick, C. (1996). "How do you spell 'caught'?" *The Quarterly of the National Writing Project, 17*(4), 24–28.

Brooke, R. (Ed.). (2003). *Rural voices: Place-conscious education and the teaching of writing.* New York: Teachers College Press.

Bruce, C. (2001). Lyrics to lyrics. In A. Calkins (Ed.), *Standard implications II: Classroom truths and consequences* (pp. 61–68). Juneau: University of Alaska Southeast.

Buchanan, J. (1993). Listening to the voices. In M. Cochran-Smith & S. L. Lytle (Eds.), *Inside/outside: Teacher research and knowledge* (pp. 212–220). New York: Teachers College Press.

Burkhardt, R. M. (1984). Becky: A case study in composition. *Language Arts, 61,* 717–721.

Calkins, A. (Ed.). (2001). *Standard implications II: Classroom truths and consequences.* Juneau: University of Alaska Southeast.

Calkins, A., & Christian, S. (Eds.). (2000). *Standard implications: Alaskans reflect on a movement to change teaching.* Juneau: University of Alaska Southeast.

Calkins, L. (1978). Children write and their writing becomes their textbook. *Language Arts, 55,* 804–815.

Calkins, L. (1986). *The art of teaching writing.* Portsmouth, NH: Heinemann.

Chin, C. (1996). "Are you the teacher who gives parents homework?" In H. Banford, M. Berkman, C. Chin, C. Cziko, B. Fecho, D. Jumpp, et al. (Eds.), *Cityscapes: Eight views from the urban classroom* (pp. 145–163). Berkeley: National Writing Project.

Christensen, L. M. (1999). Critical literacy: Teaching reading, writing, and outrage. In C. Edelsky (Ed.), *Making justice our project: Teachers working toward critical whole language practice* (pp. 209–225). Urbana, IL: National Council of Teachers of English.

Christian, S. (1997). *Exchanging lives: Middle school writers online.* Urbana, IL: National Council of Teachers of English.

Christian, S. (2000). Standards in middle school language arts program: One student, one writing assignment. In A. Calkins & S. Christian (Eds.), *Standard implications: Alaskans reflect on a movement to change teaching* (pp. 8–25). Juneau: University of Alaska Southeast.

Clyde, J. A. (1994). Lessons from Douglas: Expanding our visions of what it means to "know." *Language Arts, 71,* 22–33.

Cochran-Smith, M., & Lytle, S. L. (Eds.). (1993). *Inside/outside: Teacher research and knowledge.* New York: Teachers College Press.

Collins, P. J. (1990). Bridging the gap. In N. Atwell (Ed.), *Coming to know: Writing to learn in the intermediate grades* (pp. 17–31). Portsmouth, NH: Heinemann.

Collins, C., & Everson, B. (1993). Writing and performing across cultures. *The Quarterly of the National Writing Project, 15*(3), 6–9.

Coughlan, M. (1988). Let the students show us what they know. *Language Arts, 65,* 375–378.

Cowin, G. (1986). Implementing the writing process with sixth graders: "Jumanji," literature unit. *The Reading Teacher, 40,* 156–161.

Crepps, S. (1993). Journal, what journal? *The Quarterly of the National Writing Project, 15*(2), 7–9.

Crouse, P., & Davey, M. (1989). Collaborative learning: Insights from our children. *Language Arts, 66,* 756–766.

Crowell, C. (1991). Becoming biliterate in a whole language classroom. In Y. Goodman, W. Hood, & K. Goodman (Eds.), *Organizing for whole language* (pp. 95–111). Portsmouth, NH: Heinemann.

Cudd, E. T., & Roberts, L. (1989). Using writing to enhance content area learning in the primary grades. *The Reading Teacher, 42,* 392–404.

Cziko, C. (1996). Dialogue journals: Passing notes the academic way. In H. Banford, M. Berkman, C. Chin, C. Cziko, B. Fecho, D. Jumpp, et al. (Eds.), *Cityscapes: Eight views from the urban classroom* (pp. 99–110). Berkeley: National Writing Project.

D'Alessandro, M. E. (1987). "The ones who always get the blame": Emotionally handicapped children writing. *Language Arts, 64,* 16–22.

DeCristofaro, D. S. (2001). Author to author: How text influences young writers. *The Quarterly of the National Writing Project, 23*(2), 8–29.

Deshon, J. (1997). Innocent and not-so-innocent contributions to inequality: Choice, power, and insensitivity in a first-grade writing workshop. *Language Arts, 74,* 12–16.

Divans-Hutchinson, Y. (1995). Reading/writing in the urban classroom. In M. Carter & A. Mack (Eds.), *Active learning through teacher research: Studies by teacher-researchers UCLA writing project* (pp. 42–61). Los Angeles: UCLA Graduate School of Education & Information Studies.

Douillard, K. (2002). Going past done: Creating time for reflection in the classroom. *Language Arts, 80,* 92–99.

DuBois, W. E. B. (1903). *The souls of black folk.* New York: Washington Square Press.

Duthie, C. (1994). Nonfiction: A genre study for the primary classroom. *Language Arts, 71,* 588–595.

Dyment, H. (1997, Spring/Summer). The Yup'ik encyclopedia of the Paul T. Albert Memorial School. *The Breadloaf Rural Teachers Network Magazine,* pp. 6–7.

Edelsky, C. (1994). Education for democracy. *Language Arts, 71,* 252–257.

Erickson, F. (1986). Qualitative methods in research on teaching. In M. C. Wittrock (Ed.), *Handbook of research on teaching* (pp. 119–161). New York: Macmillan.

Ernst, K. (1994). Writing pictures, painting words: Writing in an artists' workshop. *Language Arts, 71,* 44–52.

Evans, C. S. (1984). Writing to learn in math. *Language Arts, 61,* 828–835.

Evans, K. S. (1995). Teacher reflection as a cure for tunnel vision. *Language Arts, 72,* 266–271.

Fecho, B., & Green, A. (2002). Madaz publications: Polyphonic identity and existential literacy transactions. *Harvard Educational Review, 72,* 93–119.

Fine, E. S. (1987). Marbles lost, marbles found: Collaborative production of text. *Language Arts, 64,* 474–487.

Fine, E. S. (1991). Interrogating silences. In S. Stires (Ed.), *With promise: Redefining reading and writing for "special" students* (pp. 19–26). Portsmouth, NH: Heinemann.

Fisher, B. (1995). *Thinking and learning together: Curriculum and community in a primary classroom.* Portsmouth, NH: Heinemann.

Fracareta, P., & Phillips, D. J. (2000). Working with a writer's notebook. *English Journal, 89*(6), 105–113.

Franks, L. (2001). Charcoal clouds and weather writing: Inviting science to a middle school language arts classroom. *Language Arts, 78,* 319–324.

Freedman, R. A. (1995). The Mr. and Mrs. club: The value of collaboration in writers' workshop. *Language Arts, 72,* 97–104.

Friedman, S. (1986). How well can first graders write? *The Reading Teacher, 40,* 162–167.

Furr, D. (2003). Struggling readers get hooked on writing. *The Reading Teacher, 56,* 518–525.

Gallas, K. (1994). *The languages of learning: How children talk, write, dance, draw, and sing their understanding of the world.* New York: Teachers College Press.

Gallas, K. (2001). "Look, Karen, I'm running like Jell-o": Imagination as a question, a topic, a tool for literacy research and learning. *Research in the Teaching of English, 35,* 457–492.

Gallas, K. (2003). *Imagination and literacy: A teacher's search for the heart of learning.* New York: Teachers College Press.

Gee, K. (1990). Seeing to write: The influence of visual arts on children's writing. In F. Peitzman (Ed.), *The power of context: Studies by teacher-*

researchers (Vol. 1, pp. 139–154). Los Angeles: Center for Academic Interinstitutional Programs.

Goldblatt, E. (1995). 'Round my way: Authority and double consciousness in three urban high school writers. Pittsburgh, PA: University of Pittsburgh Press.

Grant, M. (1990). Mind games: Discovering poetry through art. In H. Mills & J. A. Clyde (Eds.), Portraits of whole language classrooms: Learning for all ages (pp. 133–158). Portsmouth, NH: Heinemann.

Graves, D. H. (1983). Writing: Teachers and children at work. Portsmouth, NH: Heinemann.

Greco, N. (1999). Reinventing Portia: A reading and writing pedagogy for adolescent women. English Journal, 88(6), 70–76.

Green, R. (2000). Behind their backs: Proximity and insult in student response. The Quarterly of the National Writing Project, 22(1), 24–28.

Griffith, R. K. (1997). A first-draft society: Self-reflection and slowing down. In D. Barnes, K. Morgan, & K. Weinhold (Eds.), Writing process revisited: Sharing our stories (pp. 12–31). Urbana, IL: National Council of Teachers of English.

Gunkel, J. (1991). "Please teach America": Keisuke's journey into a language community. Language Arts, 68, 303–310.

Haney, J. (1990). A puffin is a bird, I think. In N. Atwell (Ed.), Coming to know: Writing to learn in the intermediate grades (pp. 139–148). Portsmouth, NH: Heinemann.

Hannon, J. (1999). Talking back: Kindergarten dialogue journals. The Reading Teacher, 53, 200–203.

Hanson, J., Newkirk, T., & Graves, D. (Eds.). (1985). Breaking ground: Teachers relate reading and writing in the elementary school. Portsmouth, NH: Heinemann.

Harper, L. (1997). The writer's toolbox: Five tools for active revision instruction. Language Arts, 74, 193–200.

Hartry, C. (1990). Becoming film reviewers: Learning disabled students tackle analytical writing. In F. Peitzman (Ed.), The power of context: Studies by teacher-researchers (Vol. 2, pp. 119–138). Los Angeles: Center for Academic Interinstitutional Programs.

Harwayne, S. (1992). Lasting impressions. Portsmouth, NH: Heinemann.

Harwayne, S. (1999). Going public: Priorities and practice at the Manhattan New School. Portsmouth, NH: Heinemann.

Harwayne, S. (2001). Writing through childhood: Rethinking process and product. Portsmouth, NH: Heinemann.

Hauser, C. M. (1982). Encouraging beginning writers. Language Arts, 59, 681–686.

Hess, M. L. (1989). All about hawks or Oliver's disaster: From facts to narrative. Language Arts, 66, 304–308.

Hilliker, J. (1988). Labeling to beginning narrative: Four kindergarten children learn to write. In T. Newkirk & N. Atwell (Eds.), Understanding writing: Ways of observing, learning, and teaching. K–8 (2nd ed.; pp. 14–22). Portsmouth, NH: Heinemann.

Himley, M., with Carini, P. F. (2000). From another angle: Children's strengths and school standards. New York: Teachers College Press.

Hindley, J. (1996). In the company of children. York, ME: Stenhouse.

Hoff, L. R. (1994). From omnipotent teacher-in-charge to co-conspirator in the classroom: Developing lifelong readers and writers. English Journal, 83(6), 42–50.

hooks, b. (1994). Teaching to transgress: Education as the practice of freedom. New York: Routledge.

Hubbard, R., & Power, B. (1999). Living the questions: A guide for teacher researchers. York, ME: Stenhouse.

Hudson, N. A. (1995). The violence of their lives: The journal writing of two high school freshmen. English Journal, 84(5), 65–69.

Hume, K. (2001). Seeing shades of gray: Developing a knowledge-building community through science. In G. Wells (Ed.), Action, talk, and text: Learning and teachings through inquiry (pp. 99–117). New York: Teachers College Press.

Igoa, C. (1995). The inner world of the immigrant child. New York: St. Martin's Press.

Irby, J. (1993). Empowering the disempowered: Publishing student voices. English Journal, 82(7), 50–54.

Johnson, A. (1995). Life after death: Critical pedagogy in an urban classroom. Harvard Educational Review, 65, 213–230.

Johnson, B. (1999). Never too early to write: Adventures in the K–1 writing workshop. Gainesville, FL: Maupin House.

Jorgensen, K. (1993). History workshop: Reconstructing the past with elementary students. Portsmouth, NH: Heinemann.

Jumpp, D. (1996). Extending the literate community: Literacy over a life span. In H. Banford, M. Berkman, C. Chin, C. Cziko, B. Fecho, D. Jumpp, et al. (Eds.), Cityscapes: Eight views from the urban classroom (pp. 133–144). Berkeley: National Writing Project.

Karalitz, E. B. (1988a). Note writing: A neglected genre. In T. Newkirk & N. Atwell (Eds.), Understanding writing: *Ways of observing, learning, and teaching. K–8* (2nd ed.; pp. 88–113). Portsmouth, NH: Heinemann.

Karalitz, E. B. (1988b). The rhythm of writing development. In T. Newkirk & N. Atwell (Eds.), *Understanding writing: Ways of observing, learning, and teaching. K–8* (2nd ed.; pp. 40–46). Portsmouth, NH: Heinemann.

Kimbrell-Lee, J., & Wood, T. (1995). Teaching, learning, and partnerships: Strategies for including special needs students. In J. Allen, M. Cary, & L. Delgado (Eds.), *Exploring blue highways: Literacy reform, school change, and the creation of learning communities* (pp. 55–67). New York: Teachers College Press.

Kitagawa, M. (1982). Expressing writing in Japanese elementary schools. *Language Arts, 59,* 18–22.

Krim, N., & Worsham, S. E. (1993). Team-teaching long distance: Making connections across the Mason-Dixon line. *English Journal, 82*(4), 16–23.

Krogness, M. M. (1987). Folklore: A matter of the heart and the heart of the matter. *Language Arts, 64,* 808–818.

Krogness, M. M. (1995). *Just teach me, Mrs. K: Talking, reading, and writing with resistant adolescent learners.* Portsmouth, NH: Heinemann.

Laliberty, E. A. (2001). Hooked on writing: Linking literacy to students' lived experiences. In M. Reyes & J. Halcon (Eds.), *The best for our children: Critical perspectives on literacy for Latino students* (pp. 142–150). New York: Teachers College Press.

Lancia, P. J. (1997). Literary borrowing: The effects of literature on children's writing. *The Reading Teacher, 50,* 470–475.

Lane, B. (1993). *After the end: Teaching and learning creative revision.* Portsmouth, NH: Heinemann.

Levine, D. S. (1985). The biggest thing I learned but it doesn't have to do with science. *Language Arts, 62,* 43–47.

Lew, A. (1999). Writing correctness and the second language student. In S. W. Freedman, E. R. Simons, J. S. Kalnin, A. Casareno, & the M-CLASS Teams, *Inside city schools: Investigating literacy in multicultural classrooms* (pp. 165–178). New York: Teachers College Press.

Lubarsky, N. (1987). A glance at the past, a glimpse of the future. *Journal of Reading, 30,* 520–529.

MacLean, M. S. (1983). Voices within: The audience speaks. *English Journal, 72*(7), 62–66.

Manchey, T. (1999). Drawing: Another path to understanding. *The Quarterly of the National Writing Project, 21*(1), 28–35.

Mansukhani, P. (2002). The explorers club: The sky is no limit for learning. *Language Arts, 80,* 31–39.

Martin, A. (1973). Writing in first grade. *Teachers & Writers Collaborative Newsletter, 4,* 139–150.

Martin, A. (1975). The other side: The teacher as student. *Teachers & Writers Collaborative Newsletter, 7,* 8–10.

Martin, A. (1981). *The words in my pencil: Considering children's writing* (Monograph of the North Dakota Study Group on Evaluation). Grand Forks: University of North Dakota.

Martin, B. (2003). A writing assignment: A way of life. *English Journal, 92*(6), 52–56.

Mayer, C. (1994). Action research: The story of a partnership. In G. Wells (Ed.), *Changing schools from within: Creating communities of inquiry* (pp. 151–170). Portsmouth, NH: Heinemann.

McBride, S. (2000). "Why are you so worried about it?" Struggles and solutions toward helping students improve as writers. *English Journal, 89*(6), 45–52.

McConaghy, J. (1985). Once upon a time and me. *Language Arts, 62,* 349–354.

McLeod, G. (2001). Use your words. In A. Calkins (Ed.), *Standard implications II: Classroom truths and consequences* (pp. 77–87). Juneau: University of Alaska Southeast.

McPhillips, S. P. (1985). The spirit of revision: Listening for the writer's conscience. *Language Arts, 62,* 614–618.

Merrill, C. S. (2000). Following a child's lead toward literacy. *Language Arts, 77,* 532–536.

Michalove, B. (1999). Circling in: Examining prejudice in history and in ourselves. In J. Allen (Ed.), *Class actions: Teaching for social justice in elementary and middle school* (pp. 21–33). New York: Teachers College Press.

Michie, G. (1999). *Holler if you hear me: The education of a teacher and his students.* New York: Teachers College Press.

Miera, S. L. (2002). Beyond e-mail: Writing and publishing for the cybernet community—a scenario. In C. Benson, S. Christian, D. Goswami, & W. Gooch (Eds.), *Writing to make a difference: Classroom projects for community change* (pp. 124–140). New York: Teachers College Press.

Mills, H., & Clyde, J. A. (Eds.). (1990). *Portraits of whole language classrooms: Learning for all ages.* Portsmouth, NH: Heinemann.

Miller, S. K. (2001). Lessons from Tony: Betrayal and trust in teacher research. *The Quarterly of the National Writing Project, 23*(2), 23–29.

Murphy, P. (2003). Discovering the ending in the beginning. *Language Arts, 80,* 461–469.

Newkirk, T., & Atwell, N. (1982). *Understanding writing: Ways of observing, learning, and teaching.* Portsmouth, NH: Heinemann.

Newkirk, T., & Atwell, N. (1988). *Understanding writing: Ways of observing, learning, and teaching* (2nd ed.). Portsmouth, NH: Heinemann.

Nickel, J. (2001). When writing conferences don't work: Students' retreat from teacher agenda. *Language Arts, 79,* 136–147.

Nicolescu, N. (1985). Please disturb: Work in progress. *Language Arts, 62,* 500–508.

Oei, C. (1995). Yours, mine, and ours: Using first language skills to develop writing fluency in the second language. In M. Carter & A. Mack (Eds.), *Active learning through teacher research: Studies by teacher-researchers UCLA writing project* (pp. 1–13). Los Angeles: UCLA Graduate School of Education & Information Studies.

Offer, M. (2000). Listening to voices: Interacting with community and students. In A. Calkins & S. Christian (Eds.), *Standard implications: Alaskans reflect on a movement to change teaching* (pp. 83–90). Juneau: University of Alaska Southeast.

O'Keefe, T. (1990). A day with dinosaurs. In H. Mills & J. A. Clyde (Eds.), *Portraits of whole language classrooms: Learning for all ages* (pp. 65–92). Portsmouth, NH: Heinemann.

Orta, L. (1996). Real world feminism: A teacher learns from her students' writing. *The Quarterly of the National Writing Project, 18*(3), 21–28.

Parker, D. (1997). *Jamie, a literacy story.* York, ME: Stenhouse.

Pearce, C. (1993). "What if . . . ?" In W. Saul, J. Gordon, A. Schmidt, C. Pearce, D. Blockwood, & M. Bird (Eds.), *Science workshop: A whole language approach* (pp. 53–94). Portsmouth, NH: Heinemann.

Perry, A. E. (2003). PowerPoint presentations: A creative addition to the research process. *English Journal, 92*(6), 64–69.

Pesick, S. (1996). Writing history: Before and after portfolios. *The Quarterly of the National Writing Project, 18*(1), 20–29.

Peterson, S. (2000). The writer's eye: Using the writer's notebook as a lens to view the world. *The Quarterly of the National Writing Project, 22*(4), 27–37.

Phillips, A. (1997). Feeling expressed: Portrait of a young poet. *Language Arts, 74,* 325–332.

Powell, J. (1990). Young fluent readers, young developing writers. In F. Peitzman (Ed.), *The power of context: Studies by teacher-researchers* (Vol. 2, pp. 23–34). Los Angeles: Center for Academic Interinstitutional Programs.

Quattrini, J. A. (1996). Hearing voices: Colleagues in the classroom. *English Journal, 85*(6), 62–66.

Racicot, M. (2002). Write from the start: A teacher research project. *The Quarterly of the National Writing Project, 24*(1), 16–19.

Randall, S. N. (1996). Information charts: A strategy for organizing student research. *Journal of Adolescent and Adult Literacy, 39,* 536–542.

Read, S. (2001). "Kid mice hunt for their selfs": First and second graders writing research. *Language Arts, 78,* 333–342.

Rhea, P. L. (1986). Writing for natural purposes. *English Journal, 75*(2), 43–50.

Richards, L. (1990). "Measuring things in words": Language for learning mathematics. *Language Arts, 67,* 14–25.

Rief, L. (1992). Eighth grade: Finding the value in evaluation. In D. Graves & B. Sunstein (Eds.), *Portfolio portraits* (pp. 45–60). Portsmouth, NH: Heinemann.

Rief, L. (1999). *Vision and voice: Extending the literacy spectrum.* Portsmouth, NH: Heinemann.

Romano, T. (1987). *Clearing the way: Working with teenage writers.* Portsmouth, NH: Heinemann.

Roppel, R. (2000). Writing from the heart: Peer revision on the Web. In A. Calkins & S. Christian (Eds.), *Standard implications: Alaskans reflect on a movement to change teaching* (pp. 111–126). Juneau: University of Alaska Southeast.

Roth, B. (1990). The literature journal and student writing. In F. Peitzman (Ed.), *The power of context: Studies by teacher-researchers* (Vol. 2, pp. 79–95). Los Angeles: Center for Academic Interinstitutional Programs.

Ruggieri, C. A. (2002). Multigenre, multiple intelligences, and transcendentalism. *English Journal, 92*(2), 60–68.

Russell, C. (1983). Putting research into practice: Conferencing with young writers. *Language Arts, 60,* 333–340.

Sanford, B. (1988). Writing reflectively. *Language Arts, 65,* 652–657.

Scales, K. (2000). Using math journals in a grade 3 and 4 classroom. *Networks: An On-Line Journal for Teacher Research, 3*(2), 1–10. Retrieved from http://www.oise.utoronto.ca/%7Ectd/networks/journal/Vol%203%282%29.2000sept/article2.html

Schadler, S., Ladner, S., & Montaño, G. (1997, Spring/Summer). Inquiring into a language of power. *Bread Loaf Rural Teacher Network Magazine,* 20–22.

Schiller, L. (1996). Coming to America: Community from diversity (teacher's notebook). *Language Arts, 73,* 46–51.

Schroder, G. (1996). The elements of story writing: Using picture books to learn about the elements of chemistry. *Language Arts, 73,* 412–418.

Schwartz, J. (1992). On the move in Pittsburgh: When students and teachers share research. In A. Branscombe, D. Goswami, & J. Schwartz (Eds.), *Students teaching, teachers learning* (pp. 107–119). Portsmouth, NH: Boynton/Cook Heinemann.

Schweiker-Marra, K. E., Broglie, M., & Plumer, E. (1997). Who says so? Ownership, authorship, and privacy in process writing classrooms. *English Journal, 86*(6), 16–26.

Shelton, C. (1990). Who's that kid in the back row? Dialogue journals in high school. In F. Peitzman (Ed.), *The power of context: Studies by teacher-researchers* (Vol. 1, pp. 77–89). Los Angeles: Center for Academic Interinstitutional Programs.

Shockley, B. (1993). Extending the literate community: Reading and writing with families. *New Advocate, 6*(1), 11–24.

Sibberson, F. (1997). Picture this: Bridging the gap between reading and writing with picture books. In D. Barnes, K. Morgan, & K. Weinhold (Eds.), *Writing process revisited: Sharing our stories* (pp. 111–129). Urbana, IL: National Council of Teachers of English.

Siemens, L. (1996). "Walking through the time of kids": Going places with poetry. *Language Arts, 73*, 234–240.

Smith, M. E. (1992). From expressive to transactional: A case study. *English Journal, 81*(8), 42–46.

Standiford, D. M. (1992). In the process: Using the four modes to develop a layered composition. *English Journal, 81*(8), 47–53.

Starr, P. (1993). Finding our way: A deaf writer's journey. In M. Cochran-Smith & S. L. Lytle (Eds.), *Inside/outside: Teacher research and knowledge* (pp. 184–194). New York: Teachers College Press.

Stires, S. (1991a). First things first: Conditions and connections to literacy. In S. Stires (Ed.), *With promise: Redefining reading and writing for "special" students* (pp. 89–114). Portsmouth, NH: Heinemann.

Stires, S. (1991b). Growing as a writer: L. D. and all. In S. Stires (Ed.), *With promise: Redefining reading and writing for "special" students* (pp. 53–64). Portsmouth, NH: Heinemann.

Stires, S. (Ed.). (1991c). *With promise: Redefining reading and writing for "special" students*. Portsmouth, NH: Heinemann.

Stumbo, C. (1992). Giving their words back to them: Cultural journalism in eastern Kentucky. In A. Branscombe, D. Goswami & J. Schwartz (Eds.), *Students teaching, teachers learning* (pp. 124–142). Portsmouth, NH: Boynton/Cook Heinemann.

Sumida, A. Y. (2000). Reading a child's writing as a social text. *Language Arts, 77*, 309–314.

Swaim, J. (1998). In search of an honest response. *Language Arts, 75*, 118–125.

Swaim, J. F. (2002). Laughing together in carnival: A tale of two writers. *Language Arts, 79*, 337–346.

Sweeney, M. (1997). "No easy road to freedom": Critical literacy in a fourth-grade classroom. *Reading and Writing Quarterly, 13*, 279–290.

Tabachnick, V. (1992). Composition through construction: A less teacher-directed approach. *English Journal, 81*(8), 24–27.

Tendero, J. (1998). Worth waiting for: Girls writing for their lives in the Bronx. *Teacher Research, 5*(2), 10–25.

Thompson, A. (1990). Thinking and writing. In N. Atwell (Ed.), *Coming to know: Writing to learn in the intermediate grades* (pp. 35–51). Portsmouth, NH: Heinemann.

Throne, M. J. (1991). Nazar. In S. Stires (Ed.), *With promise: Redefining reading and writing for "special" students* (pp. 73–80). Portsmouth, NH: Heinemann.

Toch, M. (1997). "ThiiNG I Do'T, WoT To FGeT". In D. Barnes, K. Morgan, & K. Weinhold (Eds.), *Writing process revisited: Sharing our stories* (pp. 52–79). Urbana, IL: National Council of Teachers of English.

Torres, M. (1998). Celebrations and letters home: Research as an ongoing conversation among students, parents and teacher. In A. Egan-Robertson & D. Bloome (Eds.), *Students as researchers of culture and language in their own communities* (pp. 59–68). Cresskill, NJ: Hampton Press.

Van Wyhe, T. (2000). A passion for poetry: Breaking rules and boundaries with online relationships. *English Journal, 90*(2), 60–67.

VanDerPloeg, L. S., & Steffen, B. (2002). Writing for community awareness and change: Two schools talk about race. In C. Benson, S. Christian, D. Goswami, & W. Gooch (Eds.), *Writing to make a difference: Classroom projects for community change* (pp. 83–104). New York: Teachers College Press.

Vasquez, V. (1994). A step in the dance of critical literacy. *UKRA Reading, 28*(1), 39–43.

Vasquez, V. (2000). Our way: Using the everyday to create a critical literacy curriculum. *Primary Voices K-6, 9*(2), 8–13.

Vasquez, V. (2004). *Negotiating critical literacies with young children*. Mahwah, NJ: Erlbaum.

Walker, D. (1991). Teaching critical concepts with our own writing. *English Journal, 80*(7), 77–82.

Weir, C. (1998). Using embedded questions to jump-start metacognition in middle school remedial readers. *Journal of Adolescent and Adult Literacy, 41*, 458–467.

Wells, C. (1990). Audience: Key to writing about reading. In N. Atwell (Ed.), *Workshop by and for teachers: Beyond the basal* (pp. 65–74). Portsmouth, NH: Heinemann.

Werderich, D. E. (2002). Individualized responses: Using journal letters as a vehicle for differentiated reading instruction. *Journal of Adolescent and Adult Literacy, 45,* 746–754.

Wheeler, N. S. (1990). Showing the way: Using journal writing to develop learning and teaching strategies. In N. Atwell (Ed.), *Coming to know: Writing to learn in the intermediate grades* (pp. 129–138). Portsmouth, NH: Heinemann.

Whitin, P. E. (1990). Language learning through family history. In H. Mills & J. A. Clyde (Eds.), *Portraits of whole language classrooms: Learning for all ages* (pp. 229–242). Portsmouth, NH: Heinemann.

Whitin, P. (1994). Opening potential: Visual response to literature. *Language Arts, 71,* 101–107.

Whitshaw, I. (1994). Translation project: Breaking the "English only" rule. *English Journal, 84*(5), 28–30.

Wigginton, E. (1986). *Sometimes a shining moment: The Foxfire experience.* Garden City, NY: Anchor Press/Doubleday.

Wilde, J. (1988). The written report: Old wine in new bottles. In T. Newkirk & N. Atwell (Eds.), *Understanding writing: Ways of observing, learning, and teaching. K–8* (2nd ed.; pp. 179–190). Portsmouth, NH: Heinemann.

Wilhelm, B. (2003). "Common threads": A writing curriculum centered in our place. In R. Brooke (Ed.), *Rural voices: Place-conscious education and the teaching of writing* (pp. 83–101). New York: Teachers College Press.

Winston, L., & Low, D. (1990). Devin's daybook. *Language Arts, 67,* 35–46.

Winston, W. (1987). Teaching writing: Analyzing the craft of professional writers. *The Quarterly of the National Writing Project, 9*(4), 20–25.

CHAPTER 6

Second-Language Composition Teaching and Learning

Ilona Leki, Alister Cumming, and Tony Silva

SECOND-LANGUAGE writers abound worldwide, responding to writing demands in contexts from kindergarten to graduate school, from professional publishing to community literacy and adult education programs. The past 20 years have seen an increasing amount of basic research on these second-language (L2) writers and several disciplinary firsts, among others, the first journal devoted exclusively to L2 writing; the first book linking L2 reading and writing; the first book focusing on adult education and L2 English; and the first book on what is being called Generation 1.5, that is, recent immigrant students in secondary schools in North America.

For many years writing played only a minor role in second/foreign-language classrooms, often primarily as a means of supporting oral or reading skill development. L2 English writing in North America began drawing the attention of researchers in the 1960s as increasing numbers of international students turned up in postsecondary classrooms, including first-year writing courses. Around the same time, the centrality of literacy started to be acknowledged in theories and research on language acquisition, educational achievement, and cultural diversity. Most English-language teachers were not writing teachers, and most writing teachers were not English-language teachers. Both groups felt themselves somewhat ill equipped to help L2 writers navigate the writing demands of tertiary education in English. Increasing numbers of special English as a Second Language (ESL) sections of first-year writing classes appeared in North American postsecondary classrooms, often taught not by writing teachers but by language teachers or applied linguists with backgrounds in second/foreign-language instruction that informed their approaches to pedagogy. As researchers in the 1970s and 1980s turned their attention to these classrooms, writers, and texts in pragmatic efforts to inform instruction, the quest to understand L2 writing began.

From relatively few studies in the 1980s there has been rapid and continuing growth in research since the early 1990s, particularly in regard to ESL (i.e., in English-dominant contexts). This research has become progressively better informed, theoretically and methodologically, drawing on research traditions in applied linguistics, education, and first-language (L1) English composition studies. Early in the

20 years since the 1980s, the central concerns of L2 writing research included needs analyses (analyses of the types of writing required in particular contexts), instructional interventions (such as teacher response to students' papers, teacher–student conferencing, and grammar correction), text analyses (studies of the linguistic and rhetorical features of L2 texts), and learner processes (strategies for composing or learning to compose in an L2).

Each of these research strands continues. But research concerns have expanded over the years, from simple to more complex perspectives, with researchers now typically using mixed designs (qualitative and quantitative), reflecting an increased breadth and depth of knowledge. Sophisticated, cognitively oriented explorations continue into such issues as the effects of L1 writing proficiency on L2 writing; of L2 language proficiency on L2 writing; and of knowledge storage in one language and knowledge retrieval in another. Broad-based, social understandings and culturally inclusive images of L2 writing and writers have converged in investigations of such issues as bilingual identities in L2 writing; learning to write in former colonial languages; the effects on L2 writing development of interruptions to formal schooling for refugees during resettlement; and writing by particular populations like children and graduate students. The overall effect of English-language teaching worldwide also has come under critical scrutiny as researchers have probed the (often negative) effects of the spread of English on other cultures and languages.

Attempting to account fully for the vast research efforts in L2 writing over the past 20 years would warrant a book rather than a chapter. For this reason, our purpose here is merely to capture the major strands of these investigations to provide an overview of findings on L2 writing research. Limiting this review primarily to academic contexts, we have elected to focus on three major aspects of L2 writing research:

- Core issues in pedagogy and assessment
- Contextual factors influencing ESL writers in academic contexts
- Characteristics of L2 writers, writing processes, and texts

ISSUES IN PEDAGOGY AND ASSESSMENT

Curriculum Policies

The teaching of L2 writing typically involves the organization of learning activities that allow students to develop their abilities to (a) produce meaningful, accurate written texts, (b) compose effectively, and (c) engage in the discourse appropriate to specific social contexts and purposes. As observed in previous reviews of L2 writing research, these three aspects of learning are informed by different theoretical foundations, each of which has ascended progressively to prominence in research over the past 2 decades (Cumming, 1998, 2001; Grabe & Kaplan, 1996; Hyland, 2003; Matsuda, 2003; Raimes, 1991, 1998; Silva, 1990). Linguistic or rhetorical theories provide tools and terms to describe the texts and language forms that L2 students produce or might need to learn. Theories from psychology provide tools and terms to describe the ways L2 students think or act while composing written texts, suggesting how these might be improved. Sociocultural, pragmatic, or critical theories provide tools and terms that describe the qualities of interaction and the cultural values that shape L2 students' writing within specific social contexts, seeking explanations for, or reasons to challenge, their actions or societal conditions. Although analyses of social contexts have predominated in recent years, research on all three aspects of L2 writing has persisted, seemingly because these three perspectives are perceived to be complementary in view of the pragmatic purpose of L2 writing instruction—helping students develop their textual, cognitive, and discoursal abilities (Santos, 1992; Silva & Brice, 2004).

Curriculum Contexts

Curricula for teaching L2 writing are circumscribed primarily by the purposes for which people are learning, which in turn reflect the status of the language being learned, the functions and value of literacy in that language, as well as the characteristics and status of the learners. The majority of research on teaching L2 writing has involved learning English for *academic purposes*, so we have reviewed research from these settings in detail. In English-dominant countries, courses in L2 writing are organized for young adults whose strongest language is not English, in order to ensure their academic success, either in preparation for higher education, to pass entrance exams for colleges or universities, or as a requirement upon entry to such institutions (Leki, 2001; Powers & Nelson, 1995; Rosenfeld, Leung, & Oltman, 2001; Williams, 1995). Likewise, in situations of immigrant settlement, L2 writing instruction features prominently in the education of children or adolescents whose home language differs from that of the dominant language in society (Carrasquillo & Rodriguez, 1996; Harklau, Losey, & Siegel, 1999; Hudelson, 1989). Settlement programs for recent adult immigrants also teach L2 writing, although often for the purposes of *cultural adaptation* to the host society or for *specific purposes*, such as training for employment (Burnaby & Cumming, 1992; Feez, 1998; Spener, 1994).

These contexts contrast with the many circumstances internationally in which L2 writing is taught as a *foreign language* (i.e., not widely used in the local community). Such curricula may have the purposes of preparation for future travel, work, or academic studies, particularly in internationally prevalent languages, such as English, French, German, Italian, Japanese, Mandarin, and Spanish, about which a distinctive body of research on L2 writing is starting to emerge (Reichelt, 1999). L2 writing also features in curricula that have the purposes of *language maintenance*, for example, of aboriginal, ancestral, religious, or community languages, for either children or adults (Edelsky, 1986; Hornberger, 2003; Martin-Jones & Jones, 2000).

ORGANIZATION OF L2 WRITING CURRICULA

Language Standards and Tests

Many curricula for L2 writing are shaped by the requirements of tests of L2 proficiency and, increasingly in recent years, curriculum standards that specify expected levels of student achievement. Tests such as IELTS (International English Language Testing System) or TOEFL (Test of English as a Foreign Language) exert a powerful role of gatekeeping internationally to higher education in English-medium universities, requiring demonstrations of writing proficiency in English that in turn influence curricula around the world for students preparing for these tests (Cumming, 1997; Hamp-Lyons, 1991; Kroll, 1998; Weigle, 2002). Following general trends for accountability in education, many educational jurisdictions and professional associations recently have articulated language standards to define the outcomes expected of students at particular points in their education as well as relevant content for teaching. The explicit, describable nature of writing performance has foregrounded writing as a symbolically important aspect of L2 student ability, although these language standards have tended to be specified by professional consensus rather than by empirical or theoretical inquiry (Cumming, 2001; McKay, 2000; TESOL, 2001). Indeed, surprisingly little research exists that relates curriculum content directly with L2 students' writing achievements (Cumming & Riazi, 2000; Mohan & Lo, 1985; Valdes, Haro, & Echevarriarza, 1992), and comparative research into L2 writing assessments tends to show variability according to assessors' cultural backgrounds and educational and professional experiences (Brindley, 2000; Connor-Linton, 1995; Kobayashi & Rinnert, 1996; Li, 1996; Shi, 2001; Shohamy, Gordon, & Kraemer, 1992; Song & Caruso, 1996).

Options for Curriculum Organization

Cumming (2003) identified three sets of options that distinguish the organization of curricula for L2 writing internationally. The first curriculum option concerns whether L2 writing is taught as a separate subject or is integrated with other aspects of language or content study. For example, courses in ESL composition exist at most universities in North America, but at the same time, many curricula value the integration of instruction in reading and writing together as complementary aspects of L2 literacy (Belcher & Hirvela, 2001; Carson & Leki, 1993; Zamel, 1992). The second curriculum option concerns whether L2 writing is taught (a) for specific purposes related to one job function or communication situation (e.g., business letters, reports in a particular format) or (b) to develop general capacities and full L2 literacy. Many L2 writing courses are designed to serve specific purposes or fields (e.g., Jacoby, Leech, & Holten, 1995), often based on extensive analyses of the writing required in target situations (e.g., Bridgeman & Carlson, 1983; Carson, 2001; Hale, Taylor, Bridgeman, Carson, Kroll, & Kantor, 1996). In contrast, theorists such as Widdowson (1983) and Leki and Carson (1997) have argued compellingly that language education should help students develop broad, creative capacities. Extensions of this view appear in courses that foster critical analyses in L2 writing (Belcher, 1995; Benesch, 1996) or students' assumption of individual responsibilities to define and monitor personal goals for writing improvement (Cumming, 1986; Frodesen, 1995; Hoffman, 1998).

The third curriculum option concerns the focus of instructional activities. Curricula tend to focus on various conceptualizations of L2 writing, each of which may overlap in practice, but that also represent relatively distinct theoretical positions about L2 writing as well as conventional repertoires of pedagogical practices in respect to, for example, composing processes (Susser, 1994; Urzua, 1987; Zamel, 1982), genre theory (Feez, 1998; Hyon, 1996; Johns, 1997), grammar teaching (Byrd & Reid, 1998; Frodesen & Holten, 2003; Shih, 2001), or content-based language instruction (Mohan, 1986; Sheppard, 1994; Shih, 1986; Snow & Brinton, 1997). As observed above, these conceptualizations may represent complementary aspects of L2 writing rather than competing pedagogical methods that produce wholly different outcomes. Indeed, as

Cumming and Riazi (2000) concluded, evaluating the outcomes of L2 writing curricula is highly contingent on contextual factors, particularly in situations of cultural diversity; thus, such curricula might best be considered as a set of variable achievements that arise from the interaction of diverse types of instruction and opportunities for learning experienced by students of varying characteristics and backgrounds with differing intentions for L2 writing.

Other alternatives for the organization of L2 curricula arise from the nature of learner populations and their social contexts. One fundamental issue is whether curricula should separate L2 learners from their mother-tongue counterparts. Although comparative research on this point is limited, several studies highlight the differences in cultural environments for learning, and their sometimes stigmatizing consequences, that appear when curricula segregate ESL students from their mainstream peers in separate classes in universities (Atkinson & Ramanathan, 1995; Braine, 1996; Zamel, 1995) or in schools (Carrasquillo & Rodriguez, 1996; Harklau, 1994a; Sheppard, 1994). (See later discussion of L2 high school writers.) A radically different basis for curriculum organization appears in innovative literacy programs for minority populations, which have foregrounded the cultural values of minority communities as the basis of relevance and purposes for writing in their home language and that of the dominant society (Auerbach, 1992; Cumming & Gill, 1991; Maguire, 1997; Moll, 1989; Walsh, 1994; Wilson-Keena, Willett, & Solsken, 2001). A third issue concerns curricula in postcolonial countries, where teaching and learning alike may resist developing L2 writing because of perceptions about the ex-colonial language and values associated with it, for example, in settings such as Sri Lanka (Canagarajah, 1993b, 2002a) or Hong Kong (Pennington, Brock, & Yue, 1996).

ISSUES IN INSTRUCTION, INTERACTION, AND LEARNING

Research on instructional practices for L2 writing has inquired into optimal ways of organizing L2 writing activities, as evidenced by the patterns of discourse and improvements in written texts that appear in natural classroom contexts, as well as psychological and political issues central to L2 learners. In contrast to these naturalistic studies, surprisingly little research has evaluated particular approaches to L2 writing instruction, although training studies have reported on explicit instruction in, for example, rhetorical structures (Connor & Farmer, 1990; Yeh, 1998) or grammar (Frantzen, 1995; Shih, 2001).

Teachers' Knowledge and Classroom Interactions

Studies documenting how L2 writing instructors organize their classroom interactions have pointed toward the value of combining regular routines for writing practice with explicit instruction on text forms and composing processes and individualized responses to written drafts (Cumming, 1992; Shi, 1998; Weissberg, 1994; Yeh, 1998). Various studies have started to document the knowledge that teachers have about L2 writing, identifying key differences in their individual orientations to teaching and writing (Cumming, 2003; Li, 1996; Shi & Cumming, 1995). Such information specifically about L2 writing is integral to guide teacher education (Blanton & Kroll, 2002; Winer, 1992), the accommodation of curriculum innovations (Clachar, 2000;

Cumming, 1993; Pennington, Brock, & Yue, 1996; Pennington, Costa, So, Shing, Hirose, & Niedzielski, 1997), as well as the long-term professional development of educators, particularly in cross-cultural contexts (Belcher & Connor, 2001; Braine, 1999; Crandall, 1993; Leki, 1992). In an effort to validate assessment practices, much detailed information has been accumulated about the criteria and decision-making processes that experienced instructors and evaluators use to assess ESL compositions (Cumming, Kantor, & Powers, 2002; Lumley, 2002; Milanovic, Saville, & Shen, 1996; Weigle, 2002).

Responding to Students' Writing

A highly controversial issue in L2 writing instruction concerns the nature of responses that teachers provide to students' writing. Debate has centered on Truscott's (1996) argument that grammar correction has no positive benefit on L2 students' writing development (cf. Krashen, 1984), to which researchers such as Ferris (1999, 2002) and Goldstein (2001) have responded by synthesizing diverse evidence to demonstrate the value of judicious, purposeful error correction as well as principles to guide such pedagogy. Research on this topic has, with increasing sophistication, described L2 instructors' responding practices (Ferris, Pezone, Tade, & Tinti, 1997; Hyland & Hyland, 2001; Zamel, 1985), surveyed students about their preferences for feedback on their writing (Hedgcook & Lefkowitz, 1994, 1996; Radecki & Swales, 1988; Saito, 1994), and evaluated the effects of specific types of response on students' revisions or attitudes (Chandler, 2003; Cohen & Cavalcanti, 1990; Conrad & Goldstein, 1999; Fathman & Whalley, 1990; Ferris, 1995, 1997; Ferris & Roberts, 2001; Hyland, 1998; Kepner, 1991; Robb, Ross, & Shortreed, 1986). The upshot of this inquiry has been to illuminate the variable range of factors that influence instructors' responding behaviors and students' utilization of them, defying the expectation that there might be any one "proper" way to respond, or not to respond, to L2 students' writing. Whereas survey research initially attempted to identify error types and their degrees of perceived severity (Janopoulos, 1992; Santos, 1988), inquiry that is more sensitive to pedagogical, discoursal, and cultural contexts and intentions has prevailed in recent years (Goldstein, 2001), and sociohistorical analyses have put such issues into local cultural perspectives (Li, 1996; Prior, 1998).

Sociocultural Theories of Learning and Multiliteracies

Analyses of alternative contexts for L2 writing instruction have focused on two theoretical conceptualizations. One concerns explaining the value of instruction for the learning of L2 writing in terms of sociocultural theory. Verbal interactions of instructors and students focused jointly on their writing enact optimal circumstances to observe learning in the Vygotskian zone of proximal development, as demonstrated in contexts of tutoring L2 writing (Aljaafreh & Lantolf, 1994; Cumming & So, 1996), teacher–student conferences (Blanton, 2002; Conrad & Goldstein, 1999; Goldstein & Conrad, 1990; Patthey-Chavez & Clare, 1996; Patthey-Chavez & Ferris, 1997), dialogue journals (Nassaji & Cumming, 2000; Peyton & Staton, 1993), or reflective analyses on portfolios of writing (Donato & McCormick, 1994; Hamp-Lyons & Condon, 2000). Similar principles emerge from studies of interaction in L2 peer writing groups, demonstrating how such activities build local communities of writers while producing particular styles of spoken discourse in groups that may influence L2 learning or text revisions (de Guerrero & Villamil, 1994; Franken & Haslett, 2002; Liu & Hansen, 2002; Lockhart & Ng, 1995; McGroarty & Zhu, 1997; Mendonca & Johnson, 1994; Nelson & Carson, 1998; Shi, 1998; Storch, 2002; Swain & Lapkin, 1995; Tsui & Ng, 2000). The second conceptualization concerns new technologies and expanded notions of literacy as multiliteracies (Cope & Kalantzis, 2000). Computer technologies not only facilitate the means by which L2 writing is produced, for example, enabling revisions through word processing and spelling and grammar checkers, but they also expand definitions of multimedia forms of literate design, of the resources available through Internet sites and communications with various communities of respondents internationally, and of students' potentials and capacities for learning (Cummins & Sayers, 1995; Hyland, 2003; Lam, 2000; Pennington, 1993, 1996; Warschauer, 1999).

Political and Ideological Issues

The political and ideological discussions surrounding L2 writing research that have emerged in the past 20 years have centered on the role of a critical perspective in L2 writing instruction (Santos, 1992), on the hegemony of English and its current academic writing preferences (Canagarajah, 1993a), and the politics of English for academic purposes (EAP). On one hand, a pragmatic argument asserted the needs of L2 learners, especially in BANA countries (Britain, Australia, North America), to quickly improve their writing skills in order to fit into and survive in these English-medium systems (Allison, 1996; Ramanathan, 2002; Santos, 2001; Silva, 1997). The argument on the other side noted that failing to overtly frame English teaching as ideological affirmed the status quo, one that often worked against students' educational, and therefore, material interests and was characterized by social injustices more broadly (Benesch, 1993, 1995, 1996; Severino, 1993). Discussion in the 1990s and 2000s explored issues in critical pedagogy (Benesch, 2001; Canagarajah, 2002a; Hammond & Macken-Horarik, 1999; Pennycook, 1997, 1999), critical literacy (Pennycook, 2001), and the negotiation of competing discourses inherent in the integration of multilingual literacies (Belcher & Connor, 2001; Canagarajah, 2002c).

Ideological concerns about the hegemonic impact of Western notions of professional participation (i.e., academic and professional writing) on scholars, researchers, and writers from nonmetropole countries prompted counterclaims about the importance of local knowledge (Canagarajah, 2002b; Casanave, 2002; Flowerdew, 1999; Gosden, 1996). A budding exploration begun in the 1990s continued in the 2000s into ethnicity, class, and to a lesser degree gender and sexual orientation (Belcher, 1997, 2001; Benesch, 1998; Johnson, 1992; Kubota, 2003; Vandrick, 1994, 1995, 1997).

ESL WRITERS IN ACADEMIC CONTEXTS

The central players in research, pedagogy, or theorizing about L2 writing are the writers themselves. We have limited our review of research here to L2 writers in English-language academic contexts, primarily in North America. Limiting this discussion to writing in academic settings excludes large bodies of literature on L2 professional writing, adult literacy, and workplace writing, as well as extensive research specifically on bilingual education.

Child Writers

Research on L2 child writers conveys a generally hopeful image of capable and enthusiastic learners. (See, however, darker pictures of how schooling is experienced by young L2 learners in Toohey, 2000, and of how programs influence beginning writers in Edelsky, 1996.) Contrary to pedagogical practices of the 1980s that constructed these writers as quite different from L1 beginning writers and as incapable of using text to convey meanings, research findings have suggested that in supportive, meaning-oriented writing contexts, L2 beginning writers bring with them and draw upon a variety of resources and strategies to successfully create expressive, communicative, meaningful texts (Blanton, 1998; Edelsky, 1983, 1986; Han & Ernst-Slavit, 1999; Hudelson, 1989; Urzua, 1987), exhibiting awareness of audience (Edelsky, 1986; Hudelson, 1984; Urzua, 1987), the ability to critically evaluate text (Samway, 1993), and even a general sense that different languages use different script systems (Buckwalter & Lo, 2002; Huss, 1995). In the 1980s this research supported a pedagogical drive away from copying texts and filling in blanks and away from encouraging (or forcing) children to function in only the target language instead of making use of L1 borrowing or code-switching strategies (Carlisle, 1989; Edelsky, 1986; Saville-Troike, 1984). Perrotta (1994) offered a useful summary of the positions that researchers were taking for granted by the beginning of the 1990s.

Recurring themes from the 1990s to 2003 centered around the importance of influential social relations with peers and teachers (Blanton, 2002; Day, 2002; Hunter, 1997; Huss, 1995; Nassaji & Cumming, 2000) and the possibility writing provided children of exploring and making connections between home/native cultures and school/target cultures (Edelsky, 1996; Han & Ernst-Slavit, 1999; Hunter, 1997; Maguire & Graves, 2001; Patthey-Chavez & Clare, 1996), leading as well to a growing awareness of the frustrations sometimes experienced by these children, which resulted in a loss of interest in extended reading and writing in school (Han & Ernst-Slavit, 1999).

Trends in the early 2000s have converged around the examination of how writing develops in biliterate children, and how being bilingual affects literacy development in both languages (Buckwalter & Lo, 2002; Durgunoglu, 1998; Durgunoglu, Mir, & Arino-Martin, 2002; Reynolds, 2002).

High School Students

L2 writing in junior and senior high school generally has suffered from a lack of attention (Harklau, 1999a, 2000, 2001), and, unlike the predominantly optimistic tone of research on child or adult L2 writers, research on high school ESL students and their writing context is permeated with pessimistic reports of their general predicament: the personal sadness, loneliness, embarrassment, struggle with identity, and social isolation of many of these students. A basic reality of high school ESL learners is their enormous variability in background, particularly in literacy education (Fu, 1995; Welaratna, 1992). Furthermore, evidence points to surprisingly limited improvement of L2 writing skills between eighth grade and first year of college, even in English-dominant environments (Tarone, Downing, Cohen, Gillette, Murie, & Dailey, 1993; Valdes, 1999).

The central debate around these students concerns the question of whether and when to "mainstream" them. Potentially supportive, high school ESL classes also have been characterized as the "ESL ghetto" (Valdes, 2001), an isolating, chaotic, stigmatized, self-perpetuating space that keeps students in a holding pattern until graduation and focuses them on minutia of grammatical form (Derwing, DeCorby, Ichikawa, & Jamieson, 1999; Duff, 2001; Garcia, 1999; Harklau, 1994a, 1994b, 1999a; Valdes, 1999, 2001). Under optimal conditions, most negative features of ESL classes can be corrected except one—isolation from peers at a time when peer interaction is crucial (Duff, 2001; Kanno & Applebaum, 1995; McKay & Wong, 1996; Valdes, 2001). However, even L2 students who exit the ESL ghetto may find themselves tracked into low-level, noncollege preparatory English classes less likely to provide academic skills expected for college work (Harklau, 1994b; Losey, 1997). And when these students do continue on to college, many are disappointed to find themselves again placed into segregated ESL classes (Frodesen & Starna, 1999; Harklau, 2000; Holmes & Moulton, 1995).

Despite some reports of successful programs (Derwing et al., 1999; Faltis & Wolfe, 1999; Harklau, 1994a; Valdes, 2001; Walqui, 2000), researchers focusing on high school students generally lament the failure of high schools to accommodate L2 students (Harklau, 1994a) and these students' continued high dropout rates (Derwing et al., 1999). Rare instances in the research literature on teens' L2 writing focus on forms of literacy that students engage in independently outside the school context, for example, poems, letters (Guerra, 1998), or electronic communications (Lam, 2000), but such nonacademic genres carry little cultural capital.

Undergraduates

The bulk of research on ESL writing has explored the undergraduate context. Review articles in 1987 and 1993 (Connor, 1987; Silva, 1993; Zamel, 1987) reflected interests in research on L2 texts, composing processes, and pedagogical issues such as debate over the nature of ESL writing courses and writing demands across university or college curricula (Braine, 1989, 1995; Bridgeman & Carlson, 1984; Carson, Chase, Gibson, & Hargrove, 1992; Hale et al., 1996; Horowitz, 1986; Spack, 1988). The focus later shifted to more ecological approaches, sounding L2 writers' opinions, beliefs, perceptions, goals, attitudes, preferences, and interactions in specific courses, initially by quantitative means and recently in more richly individualized portraits (Basturkmen & Lewis, 2002; Betancourt & Phinney, 1988; Carson & Nelson, 1994, 1996; Cumming, Busch, & Zhou, 2002; Cumming & Riazi, 2000; Currie, 1993, 1998; Ferris, 1995; Fishman & McCarthy, 2001; Frodesen & Starna, 1999; Hedgcock & Lefkowitz, 1994; Holmes & Moulton, 1995; Katznelson, Perpignan, & Rubin, 2001; Kobayashi & Rinnert, 2002; Leki, 1991a, 1995; Leki & Carson, 1994, 1997; Nelson & Carson, 1998; Radecki & Swales, 1988; Saito, 1994; Storch & Tapper, 1997; Zamel, 1990, 1995; Zhu, 2001). Beyond the writing class itself, research into contexts for undergraduate L2 writing has included faculty responses to L2 writing and writers (Janopoulos, 1992; Johns, 1991a; Santos, 1988; Vann, Lorenz, & Meyer, 1991; Vann, Meyer, & Lorenz, 1984; Zamel, 1995).

Discussions continue over the efficacy of separate or combined classes for L1 and L2 English undergraduate writers, and visa and immigrant students (Braine, 1996; Harklau, Losey, & Siegal, 1999; Reid, 1997; Silva, 1994). Interestingly, despite heavy use of writing centers by ESL writers, relatively little research has focused on L2 writers and writing centers, individual tutoring, or writing conferences with their teachers (Conrad & Goldstein, 1999; Goldstein & Conrad, 1990; Harris, 1997; Harris & Silva, 1993). Writing exams are an especially charged aspect of the undergraduate context, including the issues surrounding institutional gatekeeping entrance and exit exams (Braine, 1996; Haswell, 1998; Janopoulos, 1995; Ruetten, 1994).

Research on plagiarism in L2 writing has examined students' familiarity with the concept and attempted to explain instances of plagiarism in L2 writing (Angelil-Carter, 2000; Currie, 1998; Deckert, 1993; Fox, 1994; Matalene, 1985) and to challenge Western assumptions about plagiarism (Bloch, 2001; Pennycook, 1996; Scollon, 1995). Pedagogical and cross-institutional responses to plagiarism raised the issue of how plagiarism interacts with learning in L2 academic contexts (Angelil-Carter, 2000; Barks & Watts, 2001; Pecorari, 2001, 2003).

Increasing numbers of case studies of undergraduate L2 writers have complexified understandings of how a variety of factors interact to produce a particular experience of L2 literacy development (Adamson, 1993; Currie, 1993; Fishman & McCarthy, 2001; Harklau, 1999b, 2000; Hyland, 1998; Johns, 1991b; Leki, 1995, 1999; Losey, 1997; Mlynarczyk, 1998; Rodby, 1999; Spack, 1997). Other studies have focused more pointedly on the intersection of educational and cultural backgrounds with L2 writing (Carson, Carrell, Silberstein, Kroll, & Kuehn, 1990; Newman, Trenchs-Parera, & Pujol, 2003; Tarone et al., 1993), including more recently analyses of the variety of agentive stances these writers take (Angelil-Carter, 1997; Canagarajah, 2002a; Norton, 2000; Thesen, 1997).

To understand the literacy backgrounds of L2 writing students in the aggregate, researchers also have examined literacy practices and preferences in other languages, nations, and cultures, and the ways those practices were taken up through education (Brock & Walters, 1993; Canagarajah, 1993b, 1999, 2002a, 2002b; Carson, 1992; Dong, 1999; Dubin & Kuhlman, 1992; Duszak, 1997; Erbaugh, 1990; Kaplan, 1995; Kobayashi & Rinnert, 2002; Li, 1996; Muchiri, Mulamba, Myers, & Ndoloi, 1995; Parry & Su, 1998; Pennington, Brock, & Yue, 1996; Purves, 1988; Street, 1993; Tarnopolsky, 2000). The most widely cited initial efforts to contextualize L2 writers' literacy development revolved around the notion of contrastive rhetoric (Kaplan, 1966), which later prompted considerable and ongoing controversy for its potential to essentialize L2 writers (Kubota, 1997, 1999; Leki, 1991b; Mohan & Lo, 1985; Susser, 1998). Other work has developed more complex treatment of contrastive rhetoric (Connor, 1996) and fully contextualized and historically and institutionally grounded explorations of cultural differences in literacy practices and preferences (Canagarajah, 2002b; Li, 1996; Ramanathan, 2003; Thatcher, 2000). The role of cultural background and target cultural values continued to be debated, however (Atkinson, 1997; Ramanathan & Atkinson, 1999; Ramanathan & Kaplan, 1996), most extensively the issue of voice in L2 writing (Hirvela & Belcher, 2001; Ivanic & Camps, 2001; Lam, 2000; Matsuda, 2001), an issue of special poignancy for ESL graduate students required to produce an alien voice in their English writing (Fox, 1994; Hirvela & Belcher, 2001; Ivanic & Camps, 2001).

Graduate Students

Research in the 1980s and early 1990s on L2 graduate student writing examined these students' bid to join target disciplinary communities through conformity to disciplinary genre, language, and discourse conventions (Canseco & Byrd, 1989; Casanave & Hubbard, 1992; Cooley & Lewkowicz, 1997; Gosden, 1996; Huckin & Olsen, 1984; Jenkins, Jordan, & Weiland, 1993; Swales, 1990). Later research focused on the kinds of resources such students accessed in meeting disciplinary requirements (Riazi, 1997), including reliance on L1 educational and disciplinary experience (Connor & Kramer, 1995; Connor & Mayberry, 1996), and the types and degrees of difficulty they faced (Angelova & Riazantseva, 1999; Cadman, 1997; Casanave & Hubbard, 1992; Cooley & Lefkowicz, 1997; Dong, 1996; Raymond & Parks, 2002; Riazi, 1997). ESL graduate students were shown to experience disparity between their disciplinary knowledge and sophistication and their ability to write in English (Hirvela & Belcher, 2001; Ivanic & Camps, 2001; Schneider & Fujishima, 1995; Silva, 1992) when called upon to respond to disciplinary writing requirements that often remained implicit, armed with the curricular aid of only elementary and general-focus L2 writing courses (Carson, 2001; Hansen, 2000; Raymond & Parks, 2002).

In addition, these graduate students sometimes suffered a considerable loss in status from social, professional, and familial positions they occupied at home (Fox, 1994; Hirvela & Belcher, 2001; Ivanic & Camps, 2001) and were sensitive to the fact that their domestic peers had a greater understanding of the educational context (Beer, 2000). Their frustration with the expectations and assumptions of the target community (Fox, 1994) sometimes led to resistance, which was variably successful (Belcher, 1994, 1997; Canagarajah, 1999; Casanave, 1992; Li, 1999). Increasingly recognized was the importance of social factors, as represented in both the disciplinary community (Beer, 2000; Braine, 2002; Casanave, 1995, 2002; Li, 1999; Prior, 1991, 1995, 1998; Riazi, 1997; Stein, 1998) and in local, personal connections, such as with thesis and dissertation advisors (Belcher, 1994).

L2 Writing and Its Impact on Identity

Linked to the issue of voice in writing, identity issues became increasingly prominent during the 1990s and early 2000s, raising questions such as how L2 English literacy intersected with established identities and constrained or enhanced the construction of new identities. Researchers investigated the multiliteracies of ESL users, as well as the failure of the mainstream English-speaking world to recognize and credit non-mainstream literacies (Fox, 1994; Fu, 1995; Guerra, 1998; Nero, 2000). Particularly for stabilized dialects of English, or World Englishes, this kind of research led to questions like, Who owns English? and How long is a learner still an ESL student or a language learner? (Chiang & Schmida, 1999; Peirce, 1997).

At the individual level as well, ESL writers, especially in high school and graduate school, questioned the problematic relationships among their literate identities: the one they intuited and the one projected or threatened by English writing (Angelil-Carter, 1997; Belcher & Connor, 2001; Braine, 1999; Cadman, 1997; Canagarajah, 1993b, 2002a; Chiang & Schmida, 1999; Cmejrkova & Danes, 1997; Harklau, 1999b, 2000; Hirvela & Belcher, 2001; Ivanic & Camps, 2001; Kramsch & Lam, 1999; Lam, 2000; Li, 1999; Norton, 2000; Peirce, 1997; Shen, 1989; Stein, 1998; Thesen, 1997) or by their L1 writing after many years with English (Connor, 1999) as they struggled to inhabit desired identities or resisted unwanted transformations. Identity issues surfaced even for the youngest L2 writers (Day, 2002; Maguire & Graves, 2001).

BASIC RESEARCH ON L2 COMPOSING

What do these writers' texts look like? How do these writers' cognitive, educational, and cultural characteristics influence their L2 writing? How do these writers orchestrate the complex processes necessary to create texts in an L2? From 1984 to 2003, a great deal of basic empirical research (both quantitative and qualitative), that is, studies focusing on the phenomenon of L2 writing, has been published. The body of knowledge generated by this research can be placed into three broad categories. One is the characteristics of L2 writers, such as L2 writing ability, L2 proficiency, L2 writing background, and the influence of the L1 on L2 writing. Another is composing processes (and subprocesses), including planning, thinking, translating, rereading, revising, and editing. The third is written text produced by L2 writers, the foci here being on genre, text quality, text length, and syntactic and lexical features.

Writer Characteristics

With regard to writer characteristics, a high level of L2 writing ability was positively related to writer variables like L1 writing ability (Doushaq, 1986; Sasaki & Hirose, 1996), L2 proficiency (Sasaki & Hirose, 1996), awareness of audience (Skibniewski & Skibniewska, 1986), a flexible view of composing (Victori, 1999), writing fluency and confidence in writing (Sasaki & Hirose, 1996), and a positive attitude toward writing (Khaldieh, 2000); ability was related to process variables like effective task assessment and elaborate goal setting (Sasaki, 2000), problem solving, decision making, and control strategies (Cumming, 1989), and reviewing and evaluating (Blaya, 1997); to textual variables like better text quality, content, and organization (Cumming, 1989); and to more words and longer sentences (Zhang, 1987). A low level of L2 writing ability was associated with writing anxiety and frustration (Khaldieh, 2000) and apprehension (Skibniewski & Skibniewska, 1986); low-level revision (Wong & Lam, 1993); a focus on lexis, syntax, spelling, and punctuation (Skibniewski & Skibniewska, 1986); and more linguistic errors (Zhang, 1987).

A high level of L2 proficiency was related to better L2 writing ability (Carson et al., 1990; Kiany & Nejad, 2001), more effective problem-solving behaviors (Cumming, 1989), and application of L1 strategies (Kamimura, 1996); proficiency was related to higher quality (Cumming, 1989; Flahive & Bailey, 1993) and longer (Grant & Ginther, 2000; Kiany & Nejad, 2001) and more complex texts (Yau, 1991); to longer and more unique words (Grant & Ginther, 2000; Kiany & Nejad, 2001); and to greater use of nominalization (Manchon, Roca de Larios, & Murphy, 2000), subordination, complementation, and passives (Grant & Ginther, 2000). However, greater L2 proficiency was not necessarily related to quality of planning (Jones & Tetroe, 1987), revision (Kobayashi & Rinnert, 2001), cognitive processing (Yau, 1991), and strategy use (Sasaki, 2000). Lower L2 proficiency was associated with a less effective L2 composing process (Jones & Tetroe, 1987), greater use of L1 in L2 writing (Wang & Wen, 2002), more translation and slower writing (Sasaki, 2000), and less textual complexity (Yau, 1991).

The L2 writer's background had a substantial influence on development of L2 writing ability (Mohan & Lo, 1985); transfer of L1 skills (Lanauze & Snow, 1989; Carson, Carrell, Silberstein, Kroll, & Kuehn, 1990) and rhetorical patterns (Kubota, 1998); differential performance in L1 and L2 writing (Yu & Atkinson, 1988); and the parallel development of fluency, complexity, and accuracy (Torras & Celaya, 2001); it also influenced approach to a writing task (Lanauze & Snow, 1989), task representation (Connor & Kramer, 1995) or interpretation (Dong, 1998), composing strategies (Raimes, 1987), organizational ability (Mohan & Lo, 1985), directness and specificity (Dong, 1998), and attention to grammar (Liebman, 1992).

L1 influence on L2 writing varied with composing activity and declined with the development of L2 proficiency (Wang & Wen, 2002), helped in L2 word and phrase choice, and aided composing for those with lower levels of L2 proficiency (Cumming, 1990; Jones & Tetroe, 1987), but inhibited the writing of those with higher L2 proficiency (Gosden, 1996). L1 influence was manifested in L2 writing style (Park, 1988) and sophistication (Shaw, 1991), L1 vocabulary use in L2 writing (Jones & Tetroe, 1987), lexical and grammatical errors in the L2 (Connor & Mayberry, 1996), and the qualities of indirectness and assertiveness and the use of anecdotes and proverbs (Wu & Rubin, 2000).

Composing Processes

In terms of composing processes, planning in L1 and L2 involved use of the same patterns (Jones & Tetroe, 1987), although L2 planning involved a more elaborate planning model (Parkhurst, 1990; Whalen & Menard, 1995). L2 planning was virtually nonexistent as a separate stage (Smith, 1994), was not done extensively before writing (Kelly, 1986), and was accorded little time (Raimes, 1987). Lower L2 proficiency reduced the effectiveness and quantity of planning, but not its quality (Jones & Tetroe, 1987). More skilled L2 writers planned more often (Blaya, 1997; Skibniewski, 1988), more consistently (Raimes, 1987), more globally (Sasaki, 2000), and more effectively (Blaya, 1997), and did more elaborate and flexible goal setting and task assessment (Sasaki, 2000).

Thinking processes were fundamentally similar in L1 and L2 and varied with level of L1 writing ability, but not with L2 proficiency level (Cumming, Rebuffot, & Ledwell, 1989). A great deal of thinking was done in the L1 while composing in the L2 (Uzawa & Cumming, 1989). Higher order thinking processes resulted in longer sentences, more syntactic coordination and subordination, more words, and fewer errors (Zhang, 1987).

L1 to L2 translation in L2 writing was common (Gosden, 1996) but not as successful in communicating meaning as was writing directly in the L2 (Wong, 1992). Translation was done phrase by phrase or sentence by sentence (Gosden, 1996). Less skilled L2 writers benefited from translation more than more skilled L2 writers in terms of quality of content, organization, style, and linguistic accuracy (Kobayashi & Rinnert, 1992).

Rereading was different in L1 and L2 (Fagan & Hayden, 1988). It led to rehearsal as well as to editing (Raimes, 1987) and triggered revision (Kelly, 1986). More skilled L2 writers reread more consistently and interactively (Raimes, 1987) and more effectively (Blaya, 1997) than their less skilled counterparts.

Revising was similar across languages, although done more often in the L2, and L2 revising involved transferring L1 processes and entailed processes unique to L2 writing (Hall, 1990). Revising was neither global nor extensive (Kelly, 1986), did not involve consideration of audience (Arndt, 1987), was more common in cognitively demanding operations and done primarily at the sentence level (St. John, 1987), involved mostly surface changes (Hall, 1990; Lai, 1986; Porte, 1997), and focused on words (Arndt, 1987; Hall, 1990; Lai, 1986). More skilled L2 writers spent less time revising and focused more on global and rhetorical issues, while less skilled L2 writers revised more frequently and focused more on lexis, syntax, spelling, and punctuation (Skibniewski & Skibniewska, 1986), and made fewer changes in organization (St. John, 1987).

Editing, which was done by both more and less skilled L2 writers (Wong & Lam, 1993), often was done prematurely (Betancourt & Phinney, 1988). More skilled L2 writers were able to identify and correct errors on their own (Doushaq, 1986), use respondents as resources for editing (Connor & Mayberry, 1996), and identify errors when hearing someone read their writing aloud (Chandrasegaran, 1986).

Written Text

In terms of genre, in contrast to their narrative texts, L2 writers' expository texts were more syntactically complex (Yau & Belanger, 1984) and exhibited less variety in the use of linguistic devices to engage readers' attention and help readers identify participants, objects, and events (Scarcella, 1984). The expository texts had organizational structures similar to those in narratives (Norment, 1986). In argumentative texts, cross-cultural differences were found in organizational patterns, rhetorical appeals, diction, and cultural influences (Kamimura & Oi, 1998). Also, in argumentative essays, L2 writers had difficulties making claims and providing support for them (Oi, 1999) and in elaborating their arguments (Granger & Tyson, 1996).

In some studies it was reported that L2 writers' problems with text organization were caused by transfer of L1 organizational patterns (Doushaq, 1986; Johns, 1984; Kamimura & Oi, 1998); however, in other studies it was claimed that patterns of L2 writing did not differ markedly from those in L1 and were a result of educational experience (Mohan & Lo, 1985), and that no one pattern represented L2 writing (Choi, 1988; Wu & Rubin, 2000).

L2 text quality was positively related to L2 proficiency (Carson et al., 1990; Cumming, 1989; Ferris, 1994; Kamimura & Oi, 2001; Kiany & Nejad, 2001), L2 reading comprehension and L2 grammar test scores (Flahive & Bailey, 1993), writing instruction (Skibniewski & Skibniewska, 1986), lexical variation (Engber, 1995), number of *t*-units (Schneider & Connor, 1990), percentage of error-free *t*-units (Flahive & Bailey, 1993) and L1 writing ability (Carson et al., 1990; Kamimura, 1996). L2 text quality was negatively related to writing apprehension (Skibniewski & Skibniewska, 1986) and percentage of lexical error (Engber, 1995). There was no clear relation between text quality and quantity of L1 or L2 pleasure reading (Flahive & Bailey, 1993) and L1 or L2 reading habits, frequency of reading in different genres, and self-assessment of reading and writing abilities (Hedgcock & Atkinson, 1993).

Text length was greater in L1 than in L2 (Fagan & Eagan, 1990; Hall, 1990), in revisions than in first drafts (Lai, 1986), and when planning was done in the language in which germane information was acquired (Friedlander, 1990). Text length was affected by writing topics (Park, 1988) and related positively to L2 proficiency (Grant & Ginther, 2000) and L1 and L2 writing ability (Kamimura, 1996). Differences in text length between more and less skilled L2 writers were more dramatic in higher order than in lower order cognitive processing (Zhang, 1987).

Syntax was less complex in the writing of beginning L2 writers (Yau, 1991), L2 writers at lower grade levels (Yau & Belanger, 1984), and L2 writers with high anxiety levels (Hall, 1991). L2 writers' syntactic complexity was greater in expository texts (Yau & Belanger, 1984), translations of L1 texts (Kobayashi & Rinnert, 1992), and nontest writing situations (Hall, 1991). The ability to write with grammatical accuracy was positively related to the ability to write more syntactically complex sentences (Ruiz-Funes, 2001).

Finally, L2 writers' texts exhibited restricted use of lexical items (Johns, 1984) and lexical choice was one of the most common foci for revision in L2 texts (Ventola & Mauranen, 1991). Lexical problems typically involved inappropriateness, wordiness, and redundancy (Doushaq, 1986). L2 writing quality was related to lexical variation and lexical error (Engber, 1995). As their L2 proficiency level increased, L2 writers composed longer essays with more unique word choices and made greater use of lexical features that connect text and enable qualification of claims (Grant & Ginther, 2000). Less skilled L2 writers focused more on lexical issues (Skibniewski & Skibniewska, 1986).

CONCLUSION

Over the past 2 decades, studies have revealed much about the contexts of teaching, learning, and composition associated with L2 writing. The prevailing images are of variability—among educational purposes, learner populations, sociopolitical issues, and writing performances—as well as complexity. Our review necessarily has been selective, attempting to highlight major trends and notable findings, rather than to address comprehensively the full range of issues emerging from the extensive recent research on L2 writing. Nonetheless, we can assert several useful findings that have emerged from this inquiry.

First, L2 writers form a particular population, distinct from majority or English-dominant students, thus warranting unique educational considerations and specific forms of curriculum organization and assessment practices. As the previous section of the chapter demonstrates, L2 writers produce unique types and qualities of texts; vary in their literate abilities, proficiency in the L2, composing processes, and familiarity with written genres; and have unique resources of linguistic and cultural knowledge from their first languages and experiences to apply to their L2 writing. For these and other reasons, populations of L2 writers exhibit a wide range of variability, arising from differences in learners' cultural backgrounds, conditions for learning, stages in their lifespans, and statuses and cultural histories in society or educational institutions.

In turn, the situations of L2 writers differ according to their positions in educational programs at particular ages. Whereas bilingual children may seem to have bountiful opportunities for writing development, L2 adolescents may experience various stigmatizing, emotional constraints, L2 undergraduate students must accommodate themselves to prevailing conventions for academic writing, and L2 graduate students must adapt their established writing practices creatively to those of their specialized disciplines. Factors that shape the development of L2 writing, while they resemble those that influence all students' writing, also need to be appreciated for their unique manifestations, for example, with respect to practices for curriculum organization, teaching, responding to writing, and prompting learners' development and particular identities. Finally, political and ideological issues are pervasive with respect to L2 writing and may even be a characteristic that defines the uniqueness of such student populations and educational programs for them.

In sum, the situation of L2 writers brings to the fore many issues that are intrinsic to all student writers but that become acutely visible under situations of cultural and linguistic diversity. For this reason, studies of L2 writing have much potential to inform research on English-dominant writers and educational practices for them. We look forward to future studies that go beyond basic descriptions of L2 writing to explain fundamental relationships, for example, the effects of particular teaching or curriculum options on learner development; differences across various first and second languages, student groups, and their statuses worldwide; or factors that influence development in L2 writing. Research also needs to demonstrate convincingly and from theoretically informed perspectives how to improve the situations of L2 writers and the education offered to such learners. The cultural complexity of these issues calls for research that involves mixed methods (e.g., combining analyses of emergent texts, composing processes, and contextual factors) in naturally occurring settings, attends to emic as well as etic viewpoints with the rigor and detail of ethnographic inquiry, adopts and evaluates innovative pedagogical actions to promote bilingual writing and multiliteracies, challenges issues of equity and opportunity in status quo settings, and adopts a comparative and longitudinal perspective on specific cases while also illuminating trends among sample populations that are representative of well-defined larger populations. The research to date on L2 writing makes it all the more evident how crucial, complex, and pervasive the issues are, and the growing numbers of L2 English writers in North America and worldwide make continued research into L2 writing both fascinating and necessary.

REFERENCES

Adamson, H. D. (1993). *Academic competence: Theory and classroom practice: Preparing ESL students for content courses.* New York: Longman.

Aljaafreh, A., & Lantolf, J. (1994). Negative feedback as regulation and second language learning in the zone of proximal development. *Modern Language Journal, 78,* 465–483.

Allison, D. (1996). Pragmatist discourse and English for academic purposes. *English for Specific Purposes, 15,* 85–103.

Angelil-Carter, S. (1997). Second language acquisition of spoken and written English: Acquiring the skeptron. *TESOL Quarterly, 31,* 263–287.

Angelil-Carter, S. (2000). *Stolen language? Plagiarism in language.* Reading, MA: Pearson.

Angelova, M., & Riazantseva, A. (1999). "If you don't tell me, how can I know?": A case study of four international students learning to write the U.S. way. *Written Communication, 16,* 491–525.

Arndt, V. (1987). Six writers in search of texts: A protocol based study of L1 and L2 writing. *ELT Journal, 41,* 257–267.

Atkinson, D. (1997). A critical approach to critical thinking in TESOL. *TESOL Quarterly, 31,* 71–94.

Atkinson, D., & Ramanathan, V. (1995). Cultures of writing: An ethnographic comparison of L1 and L2 university writing/language programs. *TESOL Quarterly, 29,* 539–568.

Auerbach, E. (1992). *Making meaning, making change: Participatory curriculum development for adult ESL literacy.* Washington, DC: Center for Applied Linguistics and Delta Systems.

Barks, D., & Watts, P. (2001). Textual borrowing strategies for graduate-level ESL writers. In D. Belcher & A. Hirvela (Eds.), *Linking literacies: Perspectives on L2 reading–writing connections* (pp. 246–267). Ann Arbor: University of Michigan Press.

Basturkmen, H., & Lewis, M. (2002). Learner perspectives of success in an EAP writing course. *Assessing Writing, 8,* 31–46.

Beer, A. (2000). Diplomats in the basement: Graduate engineering students and intercultural communication. In P. Dias & A. Pare (Eds.), *Transitions: Writing in academic and workplace settings* (pp. 61–88). Cresskill, NJ: Hampton Press.

Belcher, D. (1994). The apprenticeship approach to advanced academic literacy: Graduate students and their mentors. *English for Specific Purposes, 13,* 23–34.

Belcher, D. (1995). Writing critically across the curriculum. In D. Belcher & G. Braine (Eds.), *Academic writing in a second language: Essays on research and pedagogy* (pp. 135–154). Norwood, NJ: Ablex.

Belcher, D. (1997). An argument for nonadversarial argumentation: On the relevance of the feminist critique of academic discourse to L2 writing pedagogy. *Journal of Second Language Writing, 6,* 1–21.

Belcher, D. (2001). Does second language writing theory have gender? In T. Silva & P. Matsuda (Eds.), *On second language writing* (pp. 59–71). Mahwah, NJ: Erlbaum.

Belcher, D., & Connor, U. (Eds.). (2001). *Reflections on multiliterate lives.* Buffalo, NY: Multilingual Matters.

Belcher, D., & Hirvela, A. (Eds.). (2001). *Linking literacies: Perspectives on L2 reading–writing connections.* Ann Arbor: University of Michigan Press.

Benesch, S. (1993). ESL, ideology, and the politics of pragmatism. *TESOL Quarterly, 27,* 705–717.

Benesch, S. (1995). Genres and processes in sociocultural context. *Journal of Second Language Writing, 4,* 191–195.

Benesch, S. (1996). Needs analysis and curriculum development in EAP: An example of a critical approach. *TESOL Quarterly, 30,* 723–738.

Benesch, S. (1998). Anorexia: A feminist EAP curriculum. In T. Smoke (Ed.), *Adult ESL: Politics, pedagogy, and participation in classroom and community programs* (pp. 101–114). Mahwah, NJ: Erlbaum.

Benesch, S. (2001). *Critical English for academic purposes: Theory, politics, and practice.* Mahwah, NJ: Erlbaum.

Betancourt, F., & Phinney, M. (1988). Sources of writing block in bilingual writers. *Written Communication, 5,* 461–479.

Blanton, L. (1998). *Varied voices: On language and literacy learning.* Boston: Heinle & Heinle.

Blanton, L. (2002). Seeing the invisible: Situating L2 literacy acquisition in child–teacher interaction. *Journal of Second Language Writing, 11,* 295–310.

Blanton, L., & Kroll, B. (Eds.). (2002). *ESL composition tales: Reflections on teaching.* Ann Arbor: University of Michigan Press.

Blaya, M. V. (1997). EFL composing skills and strategies: Four case studies. *RESLA, 12,* 163–184.

Bloch, J. (2001). Plagiarism and the ESL student: From printed to electronic texts. In D. Belcher & A. Hirvela (Eds.), *Linking literacies: Perspectives on L2 reading–writing connections* (pp. 209–228). Ann Arbor: University of Michigan Press.

Braine, G. (1989). Writing in science and technology: An analysis of assignments from ten undergraduate courses. *English for Specific Purposes, 8,* 3–15.

Braine, G. (1995). Writing in the natural sciences and engineering. In D. Belcher & G. Braine (Eds.), *Academic writing in a second language: Essays on research and pedagogy* (pp. 113–135). Norwood, NJ: Ablex.

Braine, G. (1996). ESL students in first-year writing courses: ESL versus mainstream classes. *Journal of Second Language Writing, 5,* 91–107.

Braine, G. (Ed.). (1999). *Non-native educators in English language teaching.* Mahwah, NJ: Erlbaum.

Braine, G. (2002). Academic literacy and the nonnative speaker graduate student. *Journal of English for Academic Purposes, 1,* 59–68.

Bridgeman, B., & Carlson, S. (1983). *Survey of academic writing tasks required of graduate and undergraduate students* (TOEFL Research Report 15). Princeton, NJ: Educational Testing Service.

Bridgeman, B., & Carlson, S. (1984). Survey of academic writing tasks. *Written Communication, 1,* 247–280.

Brindley, G. (2000). Task difficulty and task generalisability in competency-based writing assessment. In G. Brindley (Ed.), *Studies in immigrant English language assessment* (Vol. 1, pp. 125–157). Sydney, Australia: National Centre for English Language Teaching and Research, Macquarie University.

Brock, M., & Walters, L. (1993). *Teaching composition around the Pacific rim.* Philadelphia: Multilingual Matters.

Buckwalter, J., & Lo, Y. (2002). Emergent literacy in Chinese and English. *Journal of Second Language Writing, 11,* 269–293.

Burnaby, B., & Cumming, A. (Eds.). (1992). *Sociopolitical aspects of ESL in Canada.* Toronto: OISE Press.

Byrd, P., & Reid, J. (Eds.). (1998). *Grammar in the composition classroom: Essays on teaching ESL for college-bound students*. Boston: Heinle & Heinle.

Cadman, K. (1997). Thesis writing for international students: A question of identity? *English for Specific Purposes, 16*, 3–14.

Canagarajah, S. (1993a). Comment on Ann Raimes's "Out of the woods: Emerging traditions in the teaching of writing": Up the garden path: Second language writing approaches, local knowledge, and pluralism. *TESOL Quarterly, 27*, 301–306.

Canagarajah, S. (1993b). Critical ethnography of a Sri Lankan classroom: Ambiguities in student opposition to reproduction through ESOL. *TESOL Quarterly, 27*, 601–626.

Canagarajah, S. (1999). *Resisting linguistic imperialism in English teaching*. Oxford, UK: Oxford University Press.

Canagarajah, S. (2002a). *Critical academic writing and multilingual students*. Ann Arbor: University of Michigan Press.

Canagarajah, S. (2002b). *The geopolitics of academic writing and knowledge production*. Pittsburgh, PA: University of Pittsburgh Press.

Canagarajah, S. (2002c). Multilingual writers and the academic community: Towards a critical relationship. *Journal of English for Academic Purposes, 1*, 29–44.

Canseco, G., & Byrd, P. (1989). Writing required in graduate courses in business administration. *TESOL Quarterly, 23*, 305–316.

Carlisle, R. (1989). The writing of Anglo and Hispanic elementary school students in bilingual, submersion, and regular programs. *Studies in Second Language Acquisition, 11*, 257–280.

Carrasquillo, A., & Rodriguez, V. (1996). *Language minority students in the mainstream classroom*. Clevedon, UK: Multilingual Matters.

Carson, J. (1992). Becoming biliterate: First language influences. *Journal of Second Language Writing, 1*, 37–60.

Carson, J. (2001). A task analysis of reading and writing in academic contexts. In D. Belcher & A. Hirvela (Eds.), *Linking literacies: Perspectives on L2 reading–writing connections* (pp. 48–83). Ann Arbor: University of Michigan Press.

Carson, J., Carrell, P., Silberstein, S., Kroll, B., & Kuehn, P. (1990). Reading-writing relationships in first and second language. *TESOL Quarterly, 24*, 245–266.

Carson, J., Chase, N., Gibson, S., & Hargrove, M. (1992). Literacy demands of the undergraduate curriculum. *Reading Research and Instruction, 31*, 25–50.

Carson, J., & Leki, I. (Eds.). (1993). *Reading in the composition classroom: Second language perspectives*. Boston: Heinle & Heinle.

Carson, J., & Nelson, G. (1994). Writing groups: Cross-cultural issues. *Journal of Second Language Writing, 3*, 17–30.

Carson, J., & Nelson, G. (1996). Chinese students' perceptions of ESL peer response group interaction. *Journal of Second Language Writing, 5*, 1–19.

Casanave, C. (1992). Cultural diversity and socialization: A case study of a Hispanic woman in a doctoral program in sociology. In D. Murray (Ed.), *Diversity as resource: Redefining cultural literacy* (pp. 148–180). Washington, DC: TESOL.

Casanave, C. (1995). Local interactions: Constructing contexts for composing in a graduate sociology program. In D. Belcher & G. Braine (Eds.), *Academic writing in a second language: Essays on research and pedagogy* (pp. 83–110). Norwood, NJ: Ablex.

Casanave, C. (2002). *Writing games*. Mahwah, NJ: Erlbaum.

Casanave, C., & Hubbard, P. (1992). The writing assignments and writing problems of doctoral students: Faculty perceptions, pedagogical issues and needed research. *English for Specific Purposes, 11*, 33–49.

Chandler, J. (2003). The efficacy of various kinds of error feedback for improvement in the accuracy and fluency of L2 student writing. *Journal of Second Language Writing, 12*, 267–296.

Chandrasegaran, A. (1986). An exploratory study of ESL students' revision and self correction skills. *RELC Journal, 17*, 26–40.

Chiang, Y.-S., & Schmida, M. (1999). Language identity and language ownership: Linguistic conflicts of first-year university writing students. In L. Harklau, M. Siegal, & K. Losey (Eds.), *Generation 1.5 meets college composition* (pp. 81–96). Mahwah, NJ: Erlbaum.

Choi, Y. (1988). Text structure of Korean speakers' argumentative essays in English. *World Englishes, 7*, 129–142.

Clachar, A. (2000). Opposition and accommodation: An examination of Turkish teachers' attitudes toward Western approaches to the teaching of writing. *Research in the Teaching of English, 35*, 66–100.

Cmejrkova, S., & Danes, F. (1997). Academic writing and cultural identity: The case of Czech academic writing. In A. Duszak (Ed.), *Culture and styles of academic discourse* (pp. 41–61). New York: Mouton de Gruyter.

Cohen, A., & Cavalcanti, M. (1990). Feedback on written compositions: Teacher and student verbal reports. In B. Kroll (Ed.), *Second language writing: Research insights for the classroom* (pp. 155–177). Cambridge, UK: Cambridge University Press.

Connor, U. (1987). Research frontiers in writing analysis. *TESOL Quarterly, 21,* 677–696.

Connor, U. (1996). *Contrastive rhetoric: Cross-cultural aspects of second-language writing.* New York: Cambridge University Press.

Connor, U. (1999). Learning to write academic prose in a second language: A literacy autobiography. In G. Braine (Ed.), *Non-native educators in English language teaching* (pp. 29–42). Mahwah, NJ: Erlbaum.

Connor, U., & Farmer, M. (1990). The teaching of topical structure analysis as a revision strategy for ESL writers. In B. Kroll (Ed.), *Second language writing: Research insights for the classroom* (pp. 126–139). New York: Cambridge University Press.

Connor, U., & Kramer, M. (1995). Writing from sources: Case studies of graduate students in business management. In D. Belcher & G. Braine (Eds.), *Academic writing in a second language: Essays on research and pedagogy* (pp. 155–182). Norwood, NJ: Ablex.

Connor, U., & Mayberry, S. (1996). Learning discipline-specific academic writing: A case study of a Finnish graduate student in the United States. In E. Ventola & A. Mauranen (Eds.), *Academic writing: Intercultural and textual issues* (pp. 231–253). Philadelphia: John Benjamins.

Connor-Linton, J. (1995). Cross-cultural comparisons of writing standards: American ESL and Japanese EFL. *World Englishes, 14,* 99–115.

Conrad, S., & Goldstein, L. (1999). ESL student revision after teacher-written comments: Text, contexts, and individuals. *Journal of Second Language Writing, 8,* 147–179.

Cooley, L., & Lewkowicz, J. (1997). Developing awareness of the rhetorical and linguistic conventions of writing a thesis in English: Addressing the needs of EFL/ESL postgraduate students. In A. Duszak (Ed.), *Culture and styles of academic discourse* (pp. 113–129). New York: Mouton de Gruyter.

Cope, B., & Kalantzis, M. (Eds.). (2000). *Multiliteracies: Literacy learning and the design of social futures.* London: Routledge.

Crandall, J. (1993). Professionalism and professionalization of adult ESL literacy. *TESOL Quarterly, 27,* 497–515.

Cumming, A. (1986). Intentional learning as a principle for ESL writing instruction: A case study. *TESL Canada Journal, 1,* 69–83.

Cumming, A. (1989). Writing expertise and second language proficiency. *Language Learning, 39,* 81–141.

Cumming, A. (1990). Metalinguistic and ideational thinking in second language composing. *Written Communication, 7,* 482–511.

Cumming, A. (1992). Instructional routines in ESL composition teaching. *Journal of Second Language Writing, 1,* 17–35.

Cumming, A. (1993). Teachers' curriculum planning and accommodations of innovations: Three case studies of adult ESL instruction. *TESL Canada Journal, 11,* 30–52.

Cumming, A. (1997). The testing of second-language writing. In D. Corson (Series Ed.) & C. Clapham (Vol. Ed.), *Language assessment: Vol. 7. Encyclopedia of language and education* (pp. 51–63). Dordrecht, Netherlands: Kluwer.

Cumming, A. (1998). Theoretical perspectives on writing. *Annual Review of Applied Linguistics, 18,* 61–78.

Cumming, A. (2001). Learning to write in a second language: Two decades of research. In R. Manchon (Ed.), *Writing in the L2 classroom: Issues in research and pedagogy* [Special issue] (pp. 1–23). *International Journal of English Studies, 1*(2).

Cumming, A. (2003). Experienced ESL/EFL writing instructors' conceptualization of their teaching: Curriculum options and implications. In B. Kroll (Ed.), *Exploring the dynamics of second language writing* (pp. 71–92). New York: Cambridge University Press.

Cumming, A., Busch, M., & Zhou, A. (2002). Investigating learners' goals in the context of adult second-language writing. In G. Rijlaarsdam, S. Ransdell, & M. Barbier (Eds.), *New directions for research in L2 writing* (pp. 189–208). Boston: Kluwer.

Cumming, A., & Gill, J. (1991). Learning ESL literacy among Indo-Canadian women. *Language, Culture and Curriculum, 4,* 181–200.

Cumming, A., Kantor, R., & Powers, D. (2002). Decision making while rating ESL/EFL writing tasks: A descriptive framework. *Modern Language Journal, 86,* 67–96.

Cumming, A., Rebuffot, J., & Ledwell, M. (1989). Reading and summarizing challenging texts in first and second languages. *Reading and Writing, 2,* 201–219.

Cumming, A., & Riazi, A. (2000). Building models of adult second-language writing instruction. *Learning and Instruction, 10,* 55–71.

Cumming, A., & So, S. (1996). Tutoring second language text revision: Does the approach to instruction or the language of communication make a difference? *Journal of Second Language Writing, 5*, 197–226.

Cummins, J., & Sayers, D. (1995). *Brave new schools: Challenging cultural illiteracy*. Toronto: OISE Press/University of Toronto Press.

Currie, P. (1993). Entering a disciplinary community: Conceptual activities required to write for one introductory university course. *Journal of Second Language Writing, 2*, 101–117.

Currie, P. (1998). Staying out of trouble: Apparent plagiarism and academic survival. *Journal of Second Language Writing, 7*, 1–18.

Day, E. (2002). *Identity and the young English language learner*. Clevedon, UK: Multilingual Matters.

Deckert, G. (1993). Perspectives on plagiarism from ESL students in Hong Kong. *Journal of Second Language Writing, 2*, 131–148.

de Guerrero, M., & Villamil, O. (1994). Social-cognitive dimensions of interaction in L2 peer revision. *Modern Language Journal, 78*, 484–496.

Derwing, T. M., DeCorby, E., Ichikawa, J., & Jamieson, K. (1999). Some factors that affect the success of ESL high school students. *Canadian Modern Language Review, 55*, 532–547.

Donato, R., & McCormick, D. (1994). A sociocultural perspective on language learning strategies: The role of mediation. *Modern Language Journal, 78*, 453–464.

Dong, Y. (1996). Learning how to use citations for knowledge transformation: Non-native doctoral students' dissertation writing in science. *Research in the Teaching of English, 30*, 428–457.

Dong, Y. (1998). From writing in their native language to writing in English: What ESL students bring to our writing classrooms. *College ESL, 8*, 87–105.

Dong, Y. (1999, March 26). The need to understand ESL students' native language writing experiences. *Teaching English in the Two Year College*, 277–285.

Doushaq, M. (1986). An investigation into stylistic errors of Arab students learning English for academic purpose. *English for Specific Purposes, 5*, 27–39.

Dubin, F., & Kuhlman, N. (Eds.). (1992). *Cross-culture literacy: Global perspectives on reading and writing*. Englewood Cliffs, NJ: Prentice-Hall.

Duff, P. (2001). Language, literacy, content, and (pop) culture: Challenges for ESL students in mainstream courses. *Canadian Modern Language Review, 58*, 103–132.

Durgunoglu, A. (1998). Acquiring literacy in English and Spanish in the United States. In A. Durgunoglu

& L. Verhoeven (Eds.), *Literacy development in a multilingual context* (pp. 135–145). Mahwah, NJ: Erlbaum.

Durgunoglu, A., Mir, M., & Arino-Martin, S. (2002). The relationships between bilingual children's reading and writing in their two languages. In S. Ransdell & M. Barbier (Eds.), *New directions for research in L2 writing* (pp. 81–100). Boston: Kluwer.

Duszak, A. (1997). Cross cultural academic communication: A discourse-community view. In A. Duszak (Ed.), *Culture and styles of academic discourse* (pp. 11–39). New York: Mouton de Gruyter.

Edelsky, C. (1983). Writing in a bilingual program: The relation of L1 and L2 texts. *TESOL Quarterly, 16*, 211–228.

Edelsky, C. (1986). *Writing in a bilingual program: Habia una vez*. Norwood, NJ: Ablex.

Edelsky, C. (1996). *With literacy and justice for all*. Bristol, PA: Taylor & Francis.

Engber, C. (1995). The relationship of lexical proficiency to the quality of ESL compositions. *Journal of Second Language Writing, 4*, 139–155.

Erbaugh, M. (1990). Taking advantage of China's literary tradition in teaching Chinese students. *Modern Language Journal, 74*, 15–27.

Fagan, W. T., & Eagan, R. L. (1990). The writing behavior in French and English of grade three French immersion children. *English Quarterly*, pp. 157–168.

Fagan, W., & Hayden, H. (1988). Writing processes in French and English of fifth grade immersion students. *The Canadian Modern Language Review, 44*, 653–688.

Faltis, C., & Wolfe, P. (Eds.). (1999). *So much to say: Adolescents, bilingualism, and ESL in the secondary school*. New York: Teachers College Press.

Fathman, A., & Whalley, E. (1990). Teacher response to student writing: Focus on form versus content. In B. Kroll (Ed.), *Second language writing: Research insights for the classroom* (pp. 178–190). Cambridge, UK: Cambridge University Press.

Feez, S. (1998). *Text-based syllabus design*. Sydney, Australia: National Centre for English Language Teaching and Research, Macquarie University.

Ferris, D. (1994). Lexical and syntactic features of ESL writing by students at different levels of L2 proficiency. *TESOL Quarterly, 28*, 414–420.

Ferris, D. (1995). Student reactions to teacher response in multiple-draft composition classrooms. *TESOL Quarterly, 29*, 33–53.

Ferris, D. (1997). The influence of teacher commentary on student revision. *TESOL Quarterly, 31*, 315–339.

Ferris, D. (1999). The case for grammar correction in L2 writing classes: A response to Truscott (1996). *Journal of Second Language Writing, 8*, 1–10.

Ferris, D. (2002). *Treatment of error in second language student writing*. Ann Arbor: University of Michigan Press.

Ferris, D., Pezone, S., Tade, C., & Tinti, S. (1997). Teacher commentary on student writing: Descriptions and implications. *Journal of Second Language Writing, 6*, 155–182.

Ferris, D., & Roberts, B. (2001). Error feedback in L2 writing classes: How explicit does it need to be? *Journal of Second Language Writing, 10*, 185–212.

Fishman, S., & McCarthy, L. (2001). An ESL writer and her discipline-based professor: Making progress even when goals don't match. *Written Communication, 18*, 181–228.

Flahive, D., & Bailey, N. (1993). Exploring reading/writing relationships in adult second language learners. In J. Carson & I. Leki (Eds.), *Reading in the composition class: Second language perspectives* (pp. 128–140). Boston: Heinle & Heinle.

Flowerdew, J. (1999). Problems in writing for scholarly publication in English: The case of Hong Kong. *Journal of Second Language Writing, 8*(3), 243–264.

Fox, H. (1994). *Listening to the world: Cultural issues in academic writing*. Urbana, IL: National Council of Teachers of English.

Franken, M., & Haslett, S. (2002). When and why talking can make writing harder. In G. Rijlaarsdam (Series Ed.) & S. Ransdell & M. Barbier (Vol. Eds.), *Studies in writing: Vol. 11. New directions for research in L2 writing* (pp. 209–229). Dordrecht, Netherlands: Kluwer.

Frantzen, D. (1995). The effects of grammar supplementation on written accuracy in an intermediate Spanish content course. *Modern Language Journal, 79*, 329–344.

Friedlander, A. (1990). Composing in English: Effects of a first language on writing in English as a second language. In B. Kroll (Ed.), *Second language writing: Research insights for the classroom* (pp. 109–125). New York: Cambridge University Press.

Frodesen, J. (1995). Negotiating the syllabus: A learning-centered, interactive approach to ESL graduate writing course design. In D. Belcher & G. Braine (Eds.), *Academic writing in a second language: Essays on research and pedagogy* (pp. 331–350). Norwood, NJ: Ablex.

Frodesen, J., & Holten, C. (2003). Grammar and the ESL writing class. In B. Kroll (Ed.), *Exploring the dynamics of second language writing* (pp. 141–161). New York: Cambridge University Press.

Frodesen, J., & Starna, N. (1999). Distinguishing incipient and functional bilingual writers: Assessment and instructional insights gained through second-language writer profiles. In L. Harklau, K. Losey, & M. Siegal (Eds.), *Generation 1.5 meets college composition* (pp. 61–79). Mahwah, NJ: Erlbaum.

Fu, D. (1995). *My trouble is my English*. Portsmouth, NH: Boynton/Cook.

Garcia, O. (1999). Educating Latino high school students with little formal schooling. In C. Faltis & P. Wolfe (Eds.), *So much to say: Adolescents, bilingualism, and ESL in the secondary school* (pp. 61–82). New York: Teachers College Press.

Goldstein, L. (2001). For Kyla: What does the research say about responding to ESL writers. In T. Silva & P. Matsuda (Eds.), *On second language writing* (pp. 73–89). Mahwah, NJ: Erlbaum.

Goldstein, L., & Conrad, S. (1990). Student input and negotiation of meaning in ESL writing conferences. *TESOL Quarterly, 24*, 443–460.

Gosden, H. (1996). Verbal reports of Japanese novices' research writing practices in English. *Journal of Second Language Writing, 5*, 109–128.

Grabe, W., & Kaplan, W. (1996). *Theory and practice of writing: An applied linguistic perspective*. Harlow, UK: Longman.

Granger, S., & Tyson, S. (1996). Connector usage in the English essay writing of native and non-native EFL speakers in English. *World Englishes, 15*, 17–27.

Grant, L., & Ginther, A. (2000). Using computer-tagged linguistic features to describe L2 writing differences. *Journal of Second Language Writing, 9*, 123–145.

Guerra, J. C. (1998). *Close to home: Oral and literate practices in a transnational Mexicano community*. New York: Teachers College Press.

Hale, G., Taylor, C., Bridgeman, B., Carson, J., Kroll, B., & Kantor, R. (1996). *A study of writing tasks assigned in academic degree programs* (TOEFL Research Report 54). Princeton, NJ: Educational Testing Service.

Hall, C. (1990). Managing the complexity of revising across languages. *TESOL Quarterly, 24*, 43–60.

Hall, E. (1991). Variations in composing behaviors of academic ESL writers in test and non-test situations. *TESL Canada Journal, 8*, 9–33.

Hammond, J., & Macken-Horarik, M. (1999). Critical literacy: Challenges and questions for ESL classroooms. *TESOL Quarterly, 33*, 528–544.

Hamp-Lyons, L. (Ed.). (1991). *Assessing second language writing in academic contexts*. Norwood, NJ: Ablex.

Hamp-Lyons, L., & Condon, W. (2000). *Assessing the portfolio: Practice, theory and research*. Cresskill, NJ: Hampton Press.

Han, J. W., & Ernst-Slavit, G. (1999). Come join the literacy club: One Chinese ESL child's literacy experience in a 1st grade classroom. *Journal of Research in Childhood Education, 13*, 144–154.

Hansen, J. (2000). Interactional conflicts among audience, purpose, and content knowledge in the acquisition of academic literacy in an EAP course. *Written Communication, 17*, 27–52.

Harklau, L. (1994a). ESL versus mainstream classes: Contrasting L2 learning environments. *TESOL Quarterly, 28*, 241–272.

Harklau, L. (1994b). Tracking and linguistic minority students: Consequences of ability grouping for second language learners. *Linguistics and Education, 6*, 217–244.

Harklau, L. (1999a). The ESL learning environment in secondary school. In C. Faltis & P. Wolfe (Eds.), *So much to say: Adolescents, bilingualism, and ESL in the secondary school* (pp. 42–60). New York: Teachers College Press.

Harklau, L. (1999b). Representing culture in the ESL writing classroom. In E. Hinkel (Ed.), *Culture in language teaching and learning* (pp. 109–130). New York: Cambridge University Press.

Harklau, L. (2000). From the "good kids" to the "worst": Representations of English language learners across educational settings. *TESOL Quarterly, 34*, 35–67.

Harklau, L. (2001). From high school to college: Student perspectives on literacy practices. *Journal of Literacy Research, 33*, 33–70.

Harklau, L., Losey, K., & Siegal, M. (Eds.). (1999). *Generation 1.5 meets college composition*. Mahwah, NJ: Erlbaum.

Harris, M. (1997). Cultural conflicts in the writing center: Expectations and assumptions of ESL students. In C. Severino, J. Guerra, & J. Butler (Eds.), *Writing in multicultural settings: Research and scholarship in composition* (pp. 220–233). New York: Modern Language Association.

Harris, M., & Silva, T. (1993). Tutoring ESL students: Issues and options. *College Composition and Communication, 44*, 525–537.

Haswell, R. (1998). Searching for Kiyoko: Bettering mandatory ESL writing placement. *Journal of Second Language Writing, 7*, 133–174.

Hedgcock, J., & Atkinson, D. (1993). Differing reading-writing relationships in L1 and L2 literacy development. *TESOL Quarterly, 27*, 329–333.

Hedgcock, J., & Lefkowitz, N. (1994). Feedback on feedback: Assessing learner receptivity to teacher response in L2 composing. *Journal of Second Language Writing, 3*, 141–163.

Hedgcock, J., & Lefkowitz, N. (1996). Some input on input: Two analyses of student response to expert feedback on L2 writing. *Modern Language Journal, 80*, 287–308.

Hirvela, A., & Belcher, D. (2001). Coming back to voice: The multiple voices and identities of mature multilingual writers. *Journal of Second Language Writing, 10*, 83–106.

Hoffman, A. (1998). An exploratory study of goal setting and the nature of articulated goals in second language writing development. *New Zealand Studies in Applied Linguistics, 4*, 33–48.

Holmes, V., & Moulton, M. (1995). A contrarian view of dialogue journals: The case of a reluctant participant. *Journal of Second Language Writing, 4*, 223–251.

Hornberger, N. (Ed.). (2003). *Continua of biliteracy: An ecological framework for educational policy, research, and practice in multilingual settings*. Clevedon, UK: Multilingual Matters.

Horowitz, D. (1986). What professors actually require: Academic tasks for the ESL classroom. *TESOL Quarterly, 20*, 445–462.

Huckin, T., & Olsen, L. (1984). The need for professionally oriented ESL instruction in the United States. *TESOL Quarterly, 18*, 273–294.

Hudelson, S. (1984). Kan yu ret an rayt en Ingles: Children become literate in English as a second language. *TESOL Quarterly, 18*, 221–238.

Hudelson, S. (1989). *Write on: Children writing in ESL*. Englewood Cliffs, NJ: Prentice-Hall.

Hunter, J. (1997). Multiple perceptions: Social identity in a multilingual elementary classroom. *TESOL Quarterly, 31*, 603–611.

Huss, R. (1995). Young children becoming literate in English as a second language. *TESOL Quarterly, 29*, 767–774.

Hyland, F. (1998). The impact of teacher-written feedback on individual writers. *Journal of Second Language Writing, 7*, 255–286.

Hyland, F., & Hyland, K. (2001). Sugaring the pill: Praise and criticism in written feedback. *Journal of Second Language Writing, 10*, 185–212.

Hyland, K. (2003). *Teaching second language writing*. New York: Cambridge University Press.

Hyon, S. (1996). Genre in three traditions: Implications for ESL. *TESOL Quarterly, 30*, 693–722.

Ivanic, R., & Camps, D. (2001). I am how I sound: Voice as self-representation in L2 writing. *Journal of Second Language Writing, 10*, 3–33.

Jacoby, S., Leech, D., & Holten, C. (1995). A genre-based developmental writing course for undergraduate ESL science majors. In D. Belcher & G. Braine (Eds.), *Academic writing in a second language: Essays on research and pedagogy* (pp. 351–373). Norwood, NJ: Ablex.

Janopoulos, M. (1992). University faculty tolerance of NS and NNS writing errors: A comparison. *Journal of Second Language Writing, 1,* 109–121.

Janopoulos, M. (1995). Writing across the curriculum, writing proficiency exams, and the NNS college student. *Journal of Second Language Writing, 4,* 43–50.

Jenkins, S., Jordan, M., & Weiland, P. (1993). The role of writing in graduate engineering education: A survey of faculty beliefs and practices. *English for Specific Purposes, 12,* 51–67.

Johns, A. (1984). Textual cohesion and the Chinese speaker of English. *Language Learning and Communication, 3,* 69–74.

Johns, A. (1991a). Faculty assessment of ESL student literacy skills: Implications for writing assessment. In L. Hamp-Lyons (Ed.), *Assessing second language writing in academic contexts* (pp. 167–179). Norwood, NJ: Ablex.

Johns, A. (1991b). Interpreting an English competency examination: The frustration of an ESL science student. *Written Communication, 8,* 379–401.

Johns, A. (1997). *Text, role, and context.* New York: Cambridge University Press.

Johnson, D. (1992). Interpersonal involvement in discourse: Gender variation in L2 writers' complimenting strategies. *Journal of Second Language Writing, 1,* 195–215.

Jones, S., & Tetroe, J. (1987). Composing in a second language. In A. Matsuhashi (Ed.), *Writing in real time* (pp. 34–57). Norwood, NJ: Ablex.

Kamimura, T. (1996). Composing in Japanese as a first language and English as a foreign language: A study of narrative writing. *RELC Journal, 27,* 47–69.

Kamimura, T., & Oi, K. (1998). Argumentative strategies in American and Japanese English. *World Englishes, 17,* 307–323.

Kamimura, T., & Oi, K. (2001). The effects of differences in point of view on the story production of Japanese EFL students. *Foreign Language Annals, 34,* 118–130.

Kanno, Y., & Applebaum, S. D. (1995). ESL students speak up: Their stories of how we are doing. *TESL Canada Journal, 12,* 32.

Kaplan, R. (1966). Cultural thought patterns in inter-cultural education. *Language Learning, 16,* 1–20.

Kaplan, R. (Ed.). (1995). *The teaching of writing in the Pacific basin, 6* (1/2).

Katznelson, H., Perpignan, H., & Rubin, B. (2001). What develops *along with* the development of second language writing? Exploring the "by-products". *Journal of Second Language Writing, 10,* 141–159.

Kelly, P. (1986). How do ESL writers compose? *Australian Review of Applied Linguistics, 9,* 94–119.

Kepner, C. G. (1991). An experiment in the relationship of types of written feedback to the development of second-language writing skills. *Modern Language Journal, 75,* 305–313.

Khaldieh, S. A. (2000). Learning strategies and writing processes of proficient vs. less-proficient learners of Arabic. *Foreign Language Annals, 33,* 522–534.

Kiany, G. R., & Nejad, M. K. (2001). On the relationship between English proficiency, writing ability, and the use of conjunctions in Iranian EFL learners' compositions. *ITL Review of Applied Linguistics, 133/134,* 227–241.

Kobayashi, H., & Rinnert, C. (1992). Effects of first language on second language writing: Translation versus direct composition. *Language Learning, 42,* 183–215.

Kobayashi, H., & Rinnert, C. (1996). Factors affecting composition evaluation in an EFL context: Cultural rhetorical pattern and readers' background. *Language Learning, 46,* 397–437.

Kobayashi, H., & Rinnert, C. (2001). Factors relating to EFL writers' discourse level revision skills. In R. M. Manchon (Ed.), *Writing in the L2 classroom: Issues in research and pedagogy* (pp. 71–102). Murcia, Spain: Universidad de Murcia.

Kobayashi, H., & Rinnert, C. (2002). High school student perceptions of first language literacy instruction: Implications for second language writing. *Journal of Second Language Writing, 11,* 91–116.

Kramsch, C., & Lam, W. (1999). Textual identities: The importance of being non-native. In G. Braine (Ed.), *Non-native educators in English language teaching.* Mahwah, NJ: Erlbaum.

Krashen, S. (1984). *Writing: Research, theory, and application.* Oxford, UK: Pergamon Press.

Kroll, B. (1998). Assessing writing abilities. *Annual Review of Applied Linguistics, 18,* 219–240.

Kubota, R. (1997). A reevaluation of the uniqueness of Japanese written discourse. *Written Communication, 14,* 460–480.

Kubota, R. (1998). An investigation of L1–L2 transfer in writing among Japanese university students: Implications for contrastive rhetoric. *Journal of Second Language Writing, 7,* 69–100.

Kubota, R. (1999). Japanese culture constructed by discourses: Implications for applied linguistics research and ELT. *TESOL Quarterly, 33*, 9–35.

Kubota, R. (2003). New approaches to gender, class, and race in second language writing. *Journal of Second Language Writing, 12*, 31–47.

Lai, P. (1986). The revision processes of first year students at the National University of Singapore. *RELC Journal, 17*, 71–84.

Lam, W. S. E. (2000). L2 literacy and the design of the self: A case study of a teenager writing on the internet. *TESOL Quarterly, 34*, 457–482.

Lanauze, M., & Snow, C. (1989). The relation between first- and second-language writing skills: Evidence from Puerto Rican elementary school children in bilingual programs. *Linguistics and Education, 1*, 323–339.

Leki, I. (1991a). The preferences of ESL students for error correction in college-level writing classes. *Foreign Language Annals, 24*, 203–218.

Leki, I. (1991b). Twenty-five years of contrastive rhetoric: Text analysis and writing pedagogies. *TESOL Quarterly, 25*, 123–143.

Leki, I. (1992). *Understanding ESL writers: A guide for teachers.* Portsmouth, NH: Boynton/Cook.

Leki, I. (1995). Coping strategies of ESL students in writing tasks across the curriculum. *TESOL Quarterly, 29*, 235–260.

Leki, I. (1999). "Pretty much I screwed up": Ill-served needs of a permanent resident. In L. Harklau, K. Losey, & M. Siegal (Eds.), *Generation 1.5 meets college composition* (pp. 17–43). Mahwah, NJ: Erlbaum.

Leki, I. (Ed.). (2001). *Academic writing programs.* Alexandria, VA: TESOL.

Leki, I., & Carson, J. (1994). Students' perceptions of EAP writing instruction and writing needs across the disciplines. *TESOL Quarterly, 28*, 81–101.

Leki, I., & Carson, J. (1997). "Completely different worlds": EAP and the writing experiences of ESL students in university courses. *TESOL Quarterly, 31*, 39–69.

Li, X.-M. (1996). *"Good writing" in cross-cultural context.* Albany: State University of New York Press.

Li, X.-M. (1999). Writing from the vantage point of an outside/insider. In G. Braine (Ed.), *Nonnative educators in English language teaching* (pp. 43–56). Mahwah, NJ: Erlbaum.

Liebman, J. (1992). Toward a new contrastive rhetoric: Differences between Arabic and Japanese rhetorical instruction. *Journal of Second Language Writing, 1*, 141–165.

Liu, J., & Hansen, J. (2002). *Peer response in second language writing classrooms.* Ann Arbor: University of Michigan Press.

Lockhart, C., & Ng, P. (1995). Analyzing talk in ESL peer response groups: Stances, functions, and content. *Language Learning, 45*, 605–655.

Losey, K. (1997). *Listen to the silences: Mexican American interaction in the composition classroom and the community.* Norwood, NJ: Ablex.

Lumley, T. (2002). Assessment criteria in a large-scale writing test: What do they really mean to the raters? *Language Testing, 19*, 246–276.

Maguire, M. (1997). Shared and negotiated territories: The socio-cultural embeddedness of children's acts of meaning. In A. Pollard, D. Thiessen, & A. Filer (Eds.), *Children and their curriculum: The perspectives of primary and elementary school children* (pp. 51–80). Washington, DC: Falmer Press.

Maguire, M., & Graves, B. (2001). Speaking personalities in primary school children's L2 writing. *TESOL Quarterly, 35*, 561–593.

Manchon, R. M., Roca de Larios, J., & Murphy, L. (2000). An approximation to the study of backtracking in L2 writing. *Learning and Instruction, 10*, 13–35.

Martin-Jones, M., & Jones, K. (Eds.). (2000). *Multilingual literacies: Reading and writing different worlds.* Amsterdam: John Benjamins.

Matalene, C. (1985). Contrastive rhetoric: An American writing teacher in China. *College English, 47*, 789–807.

Matsuda, P. K. (2001). Voice in Japanese written discourse: Implications for second language writing. *Journal of Second Language Writing, 10*, 35–53.

Matsuda, P. (2003). Second language writing in the twentieth century: A situated historical perspective. In B. Kroll (Ed.), *Exploring the dynamics of second language writing* (pp. 15–34). New York: Cambridge University Press.

McGroarty, M., & Zhu, W. (1997). Triangulation in classroom research: A study of peer revision. *Language Learning, 47*, 1–43.

McKay, P. (2000). On ESL standards for school-age learners. *Language Testing, 17*, 185–214.

McKay, S. L., & Wong, S. C. (1996). Multiple discourses, multiple identities: Investment and agency in second-language learning among Chinese adolescent immigrant students. *Harvard Educational Review, 66*, 577–608.

Mendonca, C., & Johnson, K. (1994). Peer review negotiations: Revision activities in ESL writing instruction. *TESOL Quarterly, 28*, 745–769.

Milanovic, M., Saville, N., & Shen, S. (1996). A study of the decision-making behaviour of composition markers. In M. Milanovic & N. Saville

(Eds.), *Performance testing, cognition and assessment* (pp. 92–114). Cambridge, UK: Cambridge University Press.

Mlynarczyk, R. (1998). *Conversations of the mind.* Mahwah, NJ: Erlbaum.

Mohan, B. (1986). *Language and content.* Reading, MA: Addison-Wesley.

Mohan, B., & Lo, W. (1985). Academic writing and Chinese students: Transfer and developmental factors. *TESOL Quarterly, 19,* 515–534.

Moll, L. (1989). Teaching second language students: A Vygotskian perspective. In D. Johnson & S. Roen (Eds.), *Richness in writing* (pp. 55–69). New York: Longman.

Muchiri, M., Mulamba, N., Myers, G., & Ndoloi, D. (1995). Importing composition: Teaching and researching academic writing beyond North America. *College Composition and Communication, 46,* 175–198.

Nassaji, H., & Cumming, A. (2000). What's in a ZPD? A case study of a young ESL student and teacher interacting through dialogue journals. *Language Teaching Research, 4,* 95–121.

Nelson, G., & Carson, J. (1998). ESL students' perceptions of effectiveness in peer response groups. *Journal of Second Language Writing, 7,* 113–131.

Nero, S. (2000). The changing faces of English: A Caribbean perspective. *TESOL Quarterly, 34,* 483–510.

Newman, M., Trenchs-Parera, M., & Pujol, M. (2003). Core academic literacy principles versus culture-specific practices: A multi-case study of academic achievement. *English for Specific Purposes, 22,* 45–71.

Norment, N. (1986). Organizational structures of Chinese subjects writing in Chinese and ESL. *Journal of the Chinese Language Teachers Association, 21,* 49–72.

Norton, B. (2000). *Identity and language learning: Gender, ethnicity and educational change.* New York: Pearson Education.

Oi, K. (1999). Comparison of argumentative styles: Japanese college students vs. American college students—An analysis using the Toulmin Model. *JACET Bulletin, 30,* 85–102.

Park, Y. (1988). Academic and ethnic background as factors affecting writing performance. In A. Purves (Ed.), *Writing across languages and cultures: Issues in contrastive rhetoric* (pp. 261–272). Newbury Park, CA: Sage.

Parkhurst, C. (1990). The composition process of science writers. *English for Specific Purposes, 9,* 169–180.

Parry, K., & Su, X. (Eds.). (1998). *Culture, literacy, and learning English.* Portsmouth, NH: Boynton/Cook.

Patthey-Chavez, G., & Clare, L. (1996). Task, talk, and text: The influence of instructional conversation on transitional bilingual writers. *Written Communication, 13,* 515–563.

Patthey-Chavez, G., & Ferris, D. (1997). Writing conferences and the weaving of multi-voiced texts in college composition. *Research in the Teaching of English, 31,* 51–90.

Pecorari, D. (2001). Plagiarism and international students: How the English-speaking university responds. In D. Belcher & A. Hirvela (Eds.), *Linking literacies: Perspectives on L2 reading–writing connections* (pp. 229–245). Ann Arbor: University of Michigan Press.

Pecorari, D. (2003). Good and original: Plagiarism and patchwriting in academic second-language writing. *Journal of Second Language Writing, 12,* 317–345.

Peirce, B. N. (1997). Language, identity, and the ownership of English. *TESOL Quarterly, 31,* 409–429.

Pennington, M. (1993). A critical examination of word processing effects in relation to L2 writers. *Journal of Second Language Writing, 2,* 227–255.

Pennington, M. (1996). *The computer and the non-native writer: A natural partnership.* Cresskill, NJ: Hampton Press.

Pennington, M., Brock, M., & Yue, F. (1996). Explaining Hong Kong students' response to process writing: An exploration of causes and outcomes. *Journal of Second Language Writing, 5,* 227–252.

Pennington, M., Costa, V., So, S., Shing, J., Hirose, K., & Niedzielski, K. (1997). The teaching of English-as-a-Second-Language writing in the Asia-Pacific region: A cross-country comparison. *RELC Journal, 28,* 120–143.

Pennycook, A. (1996). Borrowing others' words: Text, ownership, memory and plagiarism. *TESOL Quarterly, 30,* 201–230.

Pennycook, A. (1997). Vulgar pragmatism, critical pragmatism, and EAP. *English for Specific Purposes, 16,* 253–269.

Pennycook, A. (Ed.). (1999). Critical approaches to TESOL [Special issue]. *TESOL Quarterly, 33.*

Pennycook, A. (2001). *Critical applied linguistics: A critical introduction.* Mahwah, NJ: Erlbaum.

Perrotta, B. (1994). Writing development and second language acquisition in young children. *Childhood Education, 70,* 237–241.

Peyton, J., & Staton, J. (Eds.). (1993). *Dialogue journals in the multilingual classroom: Building fluency and writing skills through written interaction.* Norwood, NJ: Ablex.

Porte, G. (1997). The etiology of poor second language writing: The influence of perceived teacher preferences on second language revision strategies. *Journal of Second Language Writing, 6,* 61–78.

Powers, J., & Nelson, J. (1995). L2 writers and the writing center: A national survey of writing center conferencing at graduate institutions. *Journal of Second Language Writing, 4,* 113–138.

Prior, P. (1991). Contextualizing writing and response in a graduate seminar. *Written Communication, 8,* 267–310.

Prior, P. (1995). Redefining the task: An ethnographic examination of writing and response in graduate seminars. In D. Belcher & G. Braine (Eds.), *Academic writing in a second language: Essays on research and pedagogy* (pp. 47–82). Norwood, NJ: Ablex.

Prior, P. (1998). *Writing/disciplinarity: A socio-historic account of literate activity in the academy.* Mahwah, NJ: Erlbaum.

Purves, A. (Ed.). (1988). *Writing across languages and cultures: Issues in contrastive rhetoric.* Newbury Park, CA: Sage.

Radecki, P., & Swales, J. (1988). ESL students' reaction to written comments on their written work. *System, 16,* 355–365.

Raimes, A. (1987). Language proficiency, writing ability, and composing strategies: A study of ESL college student writers. *Language Learning, 37,* 439–468.

Raimes, A. (1991). Out of the woods: Emerging traditions in the teaching of writing. *TESOL Quarterly, 25,* 407–430.

Raimes, A. (1998). Teaching writing. *Annual Review of Applied Linguistics, 18,* 142–167.

Ramanathan, V. (2002). *The politics of TESOL education.* New York: Routledge Falmer.

Ramanathan, V. (2003). Written textual production and consumption (WTPC) in vernacular and English-medium settings in Gujarat, India. *Journal of Second Language Writing, 12,* 125–150.

Ramanathan, V., & Atkinson, D. (1999). Individualism, academic writing, and ESL writers. *Journal of Second Language Writing, 8,* 45–75.

Ramanathan, V., & Kaplan, R. (1996). Audience and voice in current L1 composition texts: Some implications for ESL student writers. *Journal of Second Language Writing, 5,* 21–34.

Raymond, P., & Parks, S. (2002). Transitions: Orienting to reading and writing assignments in EAP and MBA contexts. *Canadian Modern Language Review, 59,* 152–180.

Reichelt, M. (1999). Toward a comprehensive view of L2 writing: Foreign language writing in the U.S. *Journal of Second Language Writing, 8,* 181–204.

Reid, J. (1997). Which non-native speaker? Differences between international students and U.S. resident (language minority) students. *New Directions for Teaching and Learning, 70,* 17–27.

Reynolds, D. (2002). Learning to make things happen: Causality in the writing of middle-grade English language learners. *Journal of Second Language Writing, 11,* 311–328.

Riazi, A. (1997). Acquiring disciplinary literacy: A social-cognitive analysis of text production and learning among Iranian graduate students of education. *Journal of Second Language Writing, 6,* 105–137.

Robb, T., Ross, S., & Shortreed, I. (1986). Salience of feedback on error and its effect on ESL writing quality. *TESOL Quarterly, 20,* 83–95.

Rodby, J. (1999). Contingent literacy: The social construction of writing for nonnative English-speaking college freshman. In L. Harklau, K. Losey, & M. Siegal (Eds.), *Generation 1.5 meets college composition* (pp. 45–60). Mahwah, NJ: Erlbaum.

Rosenfeld, M., Leung, S., & Oltman, P. (2001). *The reading, writing, speaking, and listening tasks important for academic success at the undergraduate and graduate levels* (TOEFL Monograph 21). Princeton, NJ: Educational Testing Service.

Ruetten, M. (1994). Evaluating ESL students' performance on proficiency exams. *Journal of Second Language Writing, 3,* 85–96.

Ruiz-Funes, M. (2001). Task representation in foreign-language reading-to-write. *Foreign Language Annals, 34*(12), 226–234.

Saito, H. (1994). Teachers' practices and students' preferences for feedback on second language writing: A case study of adult ESL learners. *TESL Canada Journal, 11,* 46–70.

Samway, K. (1993). "This is hard, isn't it?": Children evaluating writing. *TESOL Quarterly, 27,* 233–257.

Santos, T. (1988). Professors' reactions to the academic writing of nonnative-speaking students. *TESOL Quarterly, 22,* 69–90.

Santos, T. (1992). Ideology in composition: L1 and ESL. *Journal of Second Language Writing, 1,* 1–15.

Santos, T. (2001). The place of politics in second language writing. In T. Silva & P. Matsuda (Eds.), *On second language writing* (pp. 173–190). Mahwah, NJ: Erlbaum.

Sasaki, M. (2000). Toward an empirical model of EFL writing processes: An exploratory study.

Journal of Second Language Writing, 9, 259–291.

Sasaki, M., & Hirose, K. (1996). Explanatory variables for EFL students' expository writing. *Language Learning, 46,* 137–174.

Saville-Troike, M. (1984). What really matters in second language learning for academic achievement? *TESOL Quarterly, 18,* 199–219.

Scarcella, R. (1984). How writers orient their readers in expository essays: A comparative study of native and non-native English writers. *TESOL Quarterly, 18,* 671–688.

Schneider, M., & Connor, U. (1990). Analyzing topical structure in ESL essays: Not all topics are equal. *Studies in Second Language Acquisition, 12,* 411–427.

Schneider, M., & Fujishima, N. (1995). When practice doesn't make perfect. The case of an ESL graduate student. In D. Belcher & G. Braine (Eds.), *Academic writing in a second language: Essays on research and pedagogy* (pp. 3–22). Norwood, NJ: Ablex.

Scollon, R. (1995). Plagiarism and ideology: Identity in intercultural discourse. *Language and Society, 24,* 1–28.

Severino, C. (1993). The sociopolitical implications of response to second language and second dialect writing. *Journal of Second Language Writing, 2,* 181–201.

Shaw, P. (1991). Science research students' composing processes. *English for Specific Purposes, 10,* 189–206.

Shen, F. (1989). The classroom and the wider culture: Identity as key to learning English composition. *College Composition and Communication, 40,* 459–465.

Sheppard, K. (1994). *Content-ESL across the USA: A technical report.* Washington, DC: Center for Applied Linguistics.

Shi, L. (1998). Effects of prewriting discussions on adult ESL students' compositions. *Journal of Second Language Writing, 7,* 319–345.

Shi, L. (2001). Native and nonnative-speaking EFL teachers' evaluation of Chinese students' English writing. *Language Testing, 18,* 303–325.

Shi, L., & Cumming, A. (1995). Teachers' conceptions of second language writing instruction: Five case studies. *Journal of Second Language Writing, 4,* 87–111.

Shih, M. (1986). Content-based approaches to teaching academic writing. *TESOL Quarterly, 20,* 617–648.

Shih, M. (2001). A course in grammar-editing for ESL writers. In J. Murphy & P. Byrd (Eds.), *Understanding the courses we teach: Local perspectives on English language teaching* (pp. 346–363). Ann Arbor: University of Michigan Press.

Shohamy, E., Gordon, C., & Kraemer, R. (1992). The effect of raters' background and training on the reliability of direct writing tests. *Modern Language Journal, 76,* 27–33.

Silva, T. (1990). Second language composition instruction: Developments, issues, and directions in ESL. In B. Kroll (Ed.), *Second language writing: Research insights for the classroom* (pp. 11–23). Cambridge, UK: Cambridge University Press.

Silva, T. (1992). L1 vs. L2 writing: ESL graduate students' perceptions. *TESL Canada Journal, 10,* 27–47.

Silva, T. (1993). Toward an understanding of the distinct nature of L2 writing: The ESL research and its implications. *TESOL Quarterly, 27,* 657–677.

Silva, T. (1994) An examination of writing program administrators' options for the placement of ESL students in first year writing classes. *Writing Program Administration, 18*(1/2), 37–43.

Silva, T. (1997). On the ethical treatment of ESL writers. *TESOL Quarterly, 31,* 359–363.

Silva, T., & Brice, C. (2004). Research in teaching writing. *Annual Review of Applied Linguistics, 24,* 70–106.

Skibniewski, L. (1988). The writing process of advanced foreign language learners in their native and foreign languages: Evidence from thinking aloud and behavior protocols. *Studia Anglica Posnaniensia, 21,* 177–186.

Skibniewski, L., & Skibniewska, M. (1986). Experimental study: The writing processes of intermediate/advanced foreign language learners in their foreign and native languages. *Studia Anglica Posnaniensia, 19,* 142–163.

Smith, V. (1994). *Thinking in a foreign language: An investigation into essay writing and translation by L2 learners.* Tubingen, Germany: G. Narr.

Snow, M., & Brinton, D. (Eds.). (1997). *The content-based classroom: Perspectives on integrating language and content.* New York: Longman.

Song, B., & Caruso, I. (1996). Do English and ESL faculty differ in evaluating the essays of native English-speaking and ESL students? *Journal of Second Language Writing, 5,* 163–182.

Spack, R. (1988). Initiating ESL students in the academic discourse community: How far should we go? *TESOL Quarterly, 22,* 29–51.

Spack, R. (1997). The acquisition of academic literacy in a second language. *Written Communication, 14,* 3–62.

Spener, D. (Ed.). (1994). *Adult biliteracy in the United States.* McHenry, IL: Delta Systems and Center for Applied Linguistics.

Stein, P. (1998). Reconfiguring the past and the present: Performing literacy histories in a Johannesburg classroom. *TESOL Quarterly*, *32*, 517–528.

St. John, M. (1987). Writing processes of Spanish scientists' publishing in English. *English for Specific Purposes*, *6*, 113–120.

Storch, N. (2002). Patterns of interaction in ESL pair work. *Language Learning*, *52*, 119–158.

Storch, N., & Tapper, J. (1997). Student annotations: What NNS and NS university students say about their own writing. *Journal of Second Language Writing*, *6*, 245–264.

Street, B. (Ed.). (1993). *Cross-cultural approaches to literacy*. New York: Cambridge University Press.

Susser, B. (1994). Process approaches in ESL/EFL writing instruction. *Journal of Second Language Writing*, *3*, 31–47.

Susser, B. (1998). EFL's othering of Japan: Orientalism in English language teaching. *JALT Journal*, *20*, 49–82.

Swain, M., & Lapkin, S. (1995). Problems in output and the cognitive processes they generate: A step towards second language learning. *Applied Linguistics*, *16*, 371–391.

Swales, J. (1990). Nonnative speaker graduate engineering students and their introductions: Global coherence and local management. In U. Connor & A. Johns (Eds.), *Coherence in writing: Research and pedagogical perspectives* (pp. 189–206). Alexandria, VA: TESOL.

Tarnopolsky, O. (2000). Writing English as a foreign language: A report from Ukraine. *Journal of Second Language Writing*, *9*, 209–226.

Tarone, E., Downing, B., Cohen, A., Gillette, S., Murie, R., & Dailey, B. (1993). The writing of Southeast Asian-American students in secondary school and university. *Journal of Second Language Writing*, *2*, 149–172.

TESOL (Teachers of English to Speakers of Other Languages). (2001). *Scenarios for ESL standards-based assessment*. Alexandria, VA: Authors.

Thatcher, B. (2000). L2 professional writing in a US and South American context. *Journal of Second Language Writing*, *9*, 41–69.

Thesen, L. (1997). Voices, discourse, and transition: In search of new categories in EAP. *TESOL Quarterly*, *31*, 487–511.

Toohey, K. (2000). *Learning English in schools: Identity, social relations, and classroom practice*. Clevedon, UK: Multilingual Matters.

Torras, M. R., & Celaya, M. L. (2001). Age-related differences in the development of written production. An empirical study of EFL school learners. In R. M. Manchon (Ed.), *Writing in the L2 classroom. Issues in research and pedagogy* (pp. 103–126). Murcia, Spain: Universidad de Murcia.

Truscott, J. (1996). The case against grammar correction in L2 writing classes. *Language Learning*, *46*, 327–369.

Tsui, A., & Ng, M. (2000). Do secondary L2 writers benefit from peer comments? *Journal of Second Language Writing*, *9*, 147–170.

Urzua, C. (1987). "You stopped too soon": Second language children composing and revising. *TESOL Quarterly*, *21*, 279–304.

Uzawa, K., & Cumming, A. (1989). Writing strategies in Japanese as a foreign language: Lowering or keeping up the standards. *Canadian Modern Language Review*, *46*, 178–194.

Valdes, G. (1999). Incipient bilingualism and the development of English language writing abilities in the secondary school. In C. Faltis & P. Wolfe (Eds.), *So much to say: Adolescents, bilingualism, and ESL in the secondary school* (pp. 138–175). New York: Teachers College Press.

Valdes, G. (2001). *Learning and not learning English: Latino students in American schools*. New York: Teachers College Press.

Valdes, G., Haro, P., & Echevarriarza, M. (1992). The development of writing abilities in a foreign language: Contributions toward a general theory of L2 writing. *Modern Language Journal*, *76*, 333–352.

Vandrick, S. (1994). Feminist pedagogy and ESL. *College ESL*, *4*, 69–92.

Vandrick, S. (1995). Privileged ESL university students. *TESOL Quarterly*, *29*, 375–381.

Vandrick, S. (1997). The role of hidden identities in the postsecondary ESL classroom. *TESOL Quarterly*, *31*, 153–157.

Vann, R., Lorenz, F., & Meyer, D. (1991). Error gravity: Faculty response to errors in the written discourse of nonnative speakers of English. In L. Hamp-Lyons (Ed.), *Assessing second language writing in academic contexts* (pp. 181–195). Norwood, NJ: Ablex.

Vann, R., Meyer, D., & Lorenz, F. (1984). Error gravity: A study of faculty opinion of ESL errors. *TESOL Quarterly*, *18*, 427–440.

Ventola, E., & Mauranen, A. (1991). Non-native writing and native revising of scientific articles. In E. Ventola (Ed.), *Functional and systemic linguistics: Approaches and uses* (pp. 457–492). Berlin: Mouton de Gruyter.

Victori, M. (1999). An analysis of writing knowledge in EFL composing: A case study of two effective and two less effective writers. *System*, *27*, 537–555.

Walqui, A. (2000). *Access and engagement: Program design and instructional approaches for immigrant students in secondary school.* Washington, DC: Center for Applied Linguistics.

Walsh, C. (1994). Engaging students in learning: Literacy, language, and knowledge production with Latino adolescents. In D. Spener (Ed.), *Adult biliteracy in the United States* (pp. 211–237). Washington, DC: Center for Applied Linguistics.

Wang, W., & Wen, Q. (2002). L1 use in the L2 composing process: An exploratory study of 16 Chinese EFL writers. *Journal of Second Language Writing, 11,* 225–246.

Warschauer, M. (1999). *Electronic literacies: Language, culture, and power in online education.* Mahwah, NJ: Erlbaum.

Weigle, S. (2002). *Assessing writing.* Cambridge: Cambridge University Press.

Weissberg, B. (1994). Speaking of writing: Some functions of talk in the ESL composition class. *Journal of Second Language Writing, 3,* 121–139.

Welaratna, U. (1992). A Khmer perspective: Connections between Khmer students' behavior, history, and culture. In D. Murray (Ed.), *Diversity as resource: Redefining cultural literacy* (pp. 135–147). Washington, DC: TESOL.

Whalen, K., & Menard, N. (1995). L1 and L2 writers' linguistic knowledge: A model of multiple-level discourse processing. *Language Learning, 45,* 381–418.

Widdowson, H. (1983). *Learning purpose and language use.* Oxford: Oxford University Press.

Williams, J. (1995). ESL composition program administration in the United States. *Journal of Second Language Writing, 4,* 157–179.

Wilson-Keena, J., Willett, J., & Solsken, J. (2001). Families as curriculum partners in an urban elementary inclusion classroom. In J. Murphy & P. Byrd (Eds.), *Understanding the courses we teach: Local perspectives on English language teaching* (pp. 92–114). Ann Arbor: University of Michigan Press.

Winer, L. (1992). "Spinach to chocolate": Changing awareness and attitudes in ESL writing teachers. *TESOL Quarterly, 26,* 57–80.

Wong, R., & Lam, Y. (1993). Strategies for construction of meaning: Chinese students in Singapore writing in English and Chinese. *Language, Culture, and Curriculum, 6,* 291–301.

Wong, S. (1992). Contrastive rhetoric: An exploration of proverbial references in Chinese student L1 and L2 writing. *Journal of Intensive English Studies, 6,* 71–90.

Wu, S.-Y., & Rubin, D. L. (2000). Evaluating the impact of collectivism and individualism on argumentative writing by Chinese and North American college students. *Research in the Teaching of English, 35,* 148–178.

Yau, M. S. S. (1991). The role of language factors in second language writing. In W. M. Malave & G. Duquette (Eds.), *Language, culture, and cognition* (pp. 266–283). Clevedon, UK: Multilingual Matters.

Yau, M. S. S., & Belanger, J. (1984). The influence of mode on syntactic complexity of EFL students at three grade levels. *TESL Canada Journal, 2,* 65–76.

Yeh, S. (1998). Empowering education: Teaching argumentative writing to cultural minority middle-school students. *Research in the Teaching of English, 33*(1), 49–83.

Yu, V., & Atkinson, P. (1988). An investigation of the language difficulties experienced by Hong Kong secondary school students in English medium schools: I. The problems. *Journal of Multilingual and Multicultural Development, 9,* 267–284.

Zamel, V. (1982). Writing: The process of discovering meaning. *TESOL Quarterly, 16,* 195–209.

Zamel, V. (1985). Responding to student writing. *TESOL Quarterly, 19,* 79–101.

Zamel, V. (1987). Recent research on writing pedagogy. *TESOL Quarterly, 21,* 697–715.

Zamel, V. (1990). Through students' eyes: The experiences of three ESL writers. *Journal of Basic Writing, 9,* 83–97.

Zamel, V. (1992). Writing one's way into reading. *TESOL Quarterly, 26,* 463–485.

Zamel, V. (1995). Strangers in academia. *College Composition and Communication, 46,* 506–521.

Zhang, S. (1987). Cognitive complexity and written production in English as a second language. *Language Learning, 37,* 469–481.

Zhu, W. (2001). Interaction and feedback in mixed peer response groups. *Journal of Second Language Writing, 10,* 251–276.

CHAPTER 7

Research in Rhetoric

Victor Villanueva, C. Jan Swearingen, and Susan McDowall

AROUND 1984, growing numbers of community college and high school teachers in the audiences for National of Council of Teachers of English (NCTE) and Conference on College Composition and Communication (CCCC) panels were dealing with the history of rhetoric. Why would they be checking in for a tune-up on rhetorical tropes, ethos, outlines of political speeches, and other elements in the classical canon? The answer was surprising, and it illuminated new links between the sociolinguistics and multicultural movements of the early 1980s, and the revival of historical studies in rhetoric. Community college teachers, high school teachers, and most college-level teachers were realizing that they could assume very little about their students' familiarity with argumentation, logic, the conventions of expository prose, and even the concepts basic to rhetoric: audience, ethos/voice, and attention to crafting the style and articulation of ideas within a text.

RHETORIC, COMPOSITION, AND SOCIOLINGUISTICS: AN INTEGRATED FIELD?

Teachers in the history of rhetoric sessions wanted to review classical rhetorical traditions because they realized, due to the presentation in some textbooks, that the ancestors of most composition pedagogies reside in one version or another of earlier rhetorics (see Applebee, 1974; deBeaugrande, 1980; Hairston, 1981). Aristotle is still cited as the honorable grandparent of many elements of composition: persuasion, argumentation, logic, style, and invention (Beason, 2000; Berlin, 1984; Gage, 2000). To know more about origins, many teachers believed, would help them explain the rationale to their students. Even if, in the end, teachers and their students decided that they did not agree with the content of the curriculum or its rationale, they would be more knowledgeable about the origins of conventions that people encounter almost daily in classroom and courtroom, newspaper and talk show, public and private debate and conversation.

Twenty years later compositionists are still debating the relevance of historical studies in rhetoric to the teaching of composition (Bacon, 2000; Conley, 1987; Connors, 1997; Connors & Lunsford, 1993; Crowley, 1990, 1998; Crowley & Hawhee, 2003;

Dawkins, 1995; Horner, 1990; Horner & Leff, 1995) and the relation of sociolinguistics to both of these fields (Harris, 1993; Smitherman & Villanueva, 2003; Stillar, 1998). And yet it should not be so complicated: To ask about literacy is to ask not only rhetorical questions but sociolinguistic and, from another perspective, historical questions. The sociolinguistic studies by Tannen (1994) and Heath (1983), among others, have documented predictable differences in uses of argumentation and narrative genres within different demographic groups and regions of the United States. Some U.S. students are as unfamiliar with the forms and uses of argument as Korean students, who may be better versed in persuasive uses of narrative, like many African Americans. The literacy narratives that have been composed by Rose (1989), Gilyard (1991), and Villanueva (1993), among others, represent the rise of a new narrative genre: an account of entry into schooling and academia told in the voice of the outsider about the experience of the outsider who gradually learns to talk the talk of the academy and, however ambivalently, accepts its ways and uses. These are only a few of the ways in which historical studies in rhetoric and sociolinguistics have come to work together, even though they continue to politely and sometimes not so politely disagree.

The late 1970s and early 1980s saw a groundswell in two related areas: the integration of historical and theoretical studies in rhetoric with composition pedagogy, and the growth of graduate programs in rhetoric and composition. Hairston (1982) promised a paradigm shift relocating composition as a bona fide area of scholarship more central to English departments than literature. Histories of rhetoric began to include more material on pedagogy in different periods, not simply as a basis for modern textbooks or courses in rhetoric, composition, and argumentation (Bizzell, 1994; Clark, 2003; Crowley & Hawhee, 2003; Lindemann & Tate, 1991; Tate, Rupiper, & Schick, 2001; Villanueva, 2003), but as a field of scholarship that would draw upon sociolinguistics, ethnography, histories of language, and literary genre studies (Bawarshi, 2003; Berthoff, 1991; Horner, 1983; Odell, 2003; Schilb, 1996). Where Corbett (1965) had provided a textbook pure and simple, highlighting a dignified ancestry for modern composition in classical rhetoric, new historical studies of composition and rhetoric encompassed comparisons of ancient with modern pedagogy (Murphy, 1990); studies of literary, literate, and oral genres taught in the schools of different periods (Swearingen, 1991); cultural analyses of rhetoric, gender, class, and race (Berlin, 1984, 1987; Brody, 1993; Buck, 1996; Villanueva, 1993, 1999a); institutional histories of universities and English departments (Berlin, 1987; Crowley, 1990; Miller, 1993); and redefinitions of the intersections between rhetorical and critical theory (Clifford & Schilb, 1994). Historiography became a featured topic in rhetorical studies (Vitanza, 1994). One of the results was a rehabilitation of the sophists and then their adoption as models for contemporary understandings and practices of discourse (Enos, 1976; Jarratt, 1991; Poulakos & Poulakos, 1999). The status of composition within English departments has been likened to the status of the sophists in Athenian Greek rhetorical culture, even though some question the analogy. Histories of women in rhetoric, like the revival of the sophists, have encouraged reconsiderations of how the historical canon was formed, a question that now extends to all previously marginalized groups in different periods and cultures (Clark, 1995; Glenn, 1994, 1997, 2000). Pedagogical models for composition have continued to be amplified by theoretical, linguistic, and historical studies; it is now mandatory that composition faculty have some understanding of the history and theory of their discipline, which entails some study of the history of rhetoric. Debates about pedagogy, based on theoretical and historical issues, concern the origin, effectiveness, and value of different composition pedagogies: those based on self-expression, creative writing, and personal essays (Bartholomae & Elbow, 1995); those based on argumentation and exposition (Crowley & Hawhee, 2003); those based on social and cultural critique (Bizzell, 1992); and those based on social constructionist and civic discourse models (Bruffee, 1986). Each of these areas of composition pedagogy has developed its own history, new definitions of its relation to other pedagogies, and new understandings of older historical models that it resembles and can draw upon.

Both sociolinguistics and rhetorical studies have answered questions from the postmodern criticisms of foundationalism, the belief in firm foundations for epistemology (knowledge and the study of knowledge), and agency, the belief in an individual subject, a person who initiates actions and ideas. For sociolinguists and social constructionists, the movement away from foundationalism sometimes has brought with it a return to determinism: an implicit and often unstated belief that language, thoughts, and identities are handed down by culture or society. In this model, most language is approached as already set, as imitative, and most constructions of identity and social organization as dictated by culture. Studying what is already there, the purpose of sociolinguistics, coexists in an uneasy relation with the purposes of pedagogy: to bring new understanding into students' repertoires of language and its use. Similarly, the utility of knowing what has been taught in past courses in rhetoric and composition is not always clear. Are compositionists studying the past only to disassemble it or define its irrelevance? Do they believe they can know the past, much less the present? Will they be able to incorporate what they know about the past and present into an energetic and enthusiastic classroom practice? What are some models for that future? The following sections describe the past 20 years of scholarship in each area, concluding with some of the most recent models for future pedagogies (see, for example, Applebee, 1974; Bartholomae & Elbow, 1995; Berlin, 1984; Miller, 2004; Ohmann, 1974; White, 1989).

HISTORICAL STUDIES IN RHETORIC

The starting point for historical studies in rhetoric and composition often has been located in the debates that emerged in response to Corbett (1965). At the same time English departments were challenging both the Cold War milieu in which the debates were immersed and New Criticism. Just as critics of logocentrism challenged the neutral descriptive objectivism of New Criticism in literary studies, the value and even the possibility of teaching students classical or civic democratic logic and persuasion were called into question. In both cases, the formalism of product/text production was rejected in favor of methods less dry, less mechanical, and more in tune with the social and intellectual world of the 1970s and 1980s. Classical argumentation-based composition pedagogy began to be challenged on historical as well as social-cultural grounds and rejected as "current traditional" for its focus on product rather than process, the form of the finished essay rather than the creative, cognitive, and critical modes of thinking that it required and encouraged (Berlin, 1994; Crowley, 1990; Flower & Hayes, 1981). It is telling that a database search for titles of articles and books containing "rhetoric and composition" as a pair takes a quantum leap in 1983 and shows a continuing steady pace since that time (CCCC, 1990–1999). What grew out of a critique of one composition pedagogy generated a new field of historical and pedagogical scholarship that links the history of rhetoric, the history of the class-room in different periods, and sociolinguistic studies of linguistic variety in different places and periods. Hairston (1982) celebrated this paradigm shift and inaugurated the movement toward defining graduate-level curriculum to study and make known the new composition and rhetoric pedagogies.

In the process of criticizing and revising classical rhetoric-based composition, a number of comparative studies illuminated points of similarity among classical, medi-eval, Renaissance, 18th-century, and modern concepts of rhetoric. Many historical studies emphasized that inasmuch as rhetoric until the mid-20th century *was* the "com-position" course, the history of composition could be seen as identical with that of rheto-ric. While classical Aristotelian rhetoric was undergoing much criticism as elitist and logocentric, a revival of the concepts of the Greek sophists introduced historical bases for teaching many of the principles of contemporary critical language theories: contin-gency, antifoundationalism, the illusoriness of language and meaning, the "always al-ready situated" relativism of meaning. The sophists also were compared with many outsider groups in subsequent periods, individuals and groups whose discourses were shunned by dominant and elite cultures. As symbols of subverting dominant and hege-monic discourses, the sophists also became discursive models in composition courses focused on social and political critique (Crowley & Hawhee, 2003).

Historians of rhetoric and compositionists converged in an agreement that classi-cal rhetoric-based courses in rhetoric and argumentation should be replaced by alter-native models. "Current traditional rhetoric," as it came to be called, was deemed too formalist, too context-independent, too focused on prefabricated logical and argumen-tative outlines, too focused on product and not enough on process. Historians of re-cent composition pointed out that the return to classical models as a common if artificial/academic language was precipitated in large part by the G.I. Bill post-World War II and parallel enfranchisements for veterans after the Korean and Vietnam Wars (Ber-lin, 1994). The emphasis on the value and status of Aristotelian models for rhetorical instruction gave way to a critique of historically based models, first and foremost Corbett (1965). Since 1983, research and pedagogy continue to develop a number of variations on the theme of this criticism, including the following:

1. Anything based on classical or historical models is deemed elitist or "enlight-enment" or based on a now bankrupt model of epistemology, agency, and speaker–audience or author–reader relations (Berlin, 1984, 1987).
2. Any relevance of historical materials, partly because of their "elitist" base, is questionable if not automatically rejected (Knoblauch & Brannon, 1984).
3. Yet the repudiation of, rather than the replacement of, classical and other historical models has prevailed in many studies. The field has thrown the baby out with the bathwater and failed to replace both of them. The critique of classical and modernist epistemologies in some cases has become the subject of the composition course. Some view this as a shifting of the balance away from composition and toward literary theory, toward a reading of theory rather than a pedagogy centered in the writing process. A number of social critique and historical critique pedagogies now lay down, define, and defend the valid-ity of critique without replacing the rejected models with an alternative method for the writing process and its purposes.

4. Going back at least to the 1940s and the movement toward more inclusive admissions and standards to define them, the base line has been set on a common culture defined in historical and traditional terms. The repudiation of tradition has become a part of the content of more recent pedagogies, often leaving students and teachers alike with confusion about the subject, purposes, and outcomes of pedagogy in composition and rhetoric. Should students become self-expressionists, exploring their innermost feelings and private thoughts? Should students follow the leader and become junior cultural critics, writing essays that denounce existing social, political, and intellectual structures as oppressive? Should students be encouraged to write in their own authentic voices, repudiating the artificiality of academic language and conventional prose? Each of these goals for composition pedagogy has evolved out of various critiques of the historical legacies. What remain to be developed are more positive paradigms for the methods and the content of pedagogy, particularly the latter. In the rush to repudiate current traditional and enlightenment humanist models, the concepts of knowing and of content often have been abandoned, a development that may not be useful to teachers or students. Just as often, a process pedagogy coexists with a product definition of the essay that does not differ significantly from the models taught in current traditional curricula.

During the early 1990s a number of book-length revisionist histories of rhetoric appeared (Buck, 1996; Connors, 1997; Crowley, 1990; Glenn, 1997; Jarratt, 1991; Lunsford, 1995; Swearingen, 1991). Journal articles joined in the reappraisal of historical studies in rhetoric in general, and classical rhetorical "traditions" in particular (Berthoff, 1991; Chordas, 1992; Clark, 1995; Crowley, 1985; Cushman, 1996; Dawkins, 1995; Glenn, 1994; Ratcliffe, 1999). Studies of individual rhetorical canons were expanded to develop, among other themes, comparisons of classical with modern models of invention, style, memory, delivery, and arrangement. These comparisons continue to be fruitful bases for studying not only past and present Western traditions but also similarities to and differences from non-Western traditions (Berlin, 1984; Crowley, 1998; Horner, 1983; Jarratt, 1991; Swearingen, 1991, 2002; Welch, 1990).

A look at recent composition and rhetoric textbooks reflects the rich historical resources that have emerged during the past 20 years. Instead of a single model of "the" classical tradition, compositionists have reclaimed alternative traditions even within Greek or Roman rhetoric. Rereadings of Isocrates emphasize the pluralism of Athenian Greek culture and define rhetoric as a way of creating common places to provide for discussions across different identities and boundaries (Poulakos & Poulakos, 1999; Welch, 1990). Rereadings of Plato see him not only as a critic of rhetoric but also as one of its first practitioners, in defining the rhetorics of dialogue and narrative that are practices in the *Dialogues*. Many studies of the progymnasmata (classroom exercise) traditions that developed within Greek and Latin rhetorical schools note their similarities to later pedagogies in the medieval, Renaissance, and later modern periods (see Binkley & Lipson, 2004; Crowley, 1998; D'Angelo, 2000; Poulakos & Poulakos, 1999; Smith, 2003; Welch, 1990). Additional historical resources now provide ample material for graduate and advanced undergraduate courses in the history of rhetoric and its relation to composition (Bizzell & Herzberg, 2004; Horner & Leff, 1995; Miller, 1993; Smith, 2003).

The return to traditional canonical literature and revolts against multiculturalism are among the most notable recent developments in many school curricula. With the growing belief that writing ability is waning among college-bound U.S. students, the SAT has begun requiring a writing sample that conforms to traditional, "current-traditional" standards. Many home school and charter school curricula are teaching traditional essay forms and genres. These movements suggest a renewed interest in the 1960s model for civic discourse based on classical rhetorical models. Alternatives to these pedagogies, at both the K–12 and college levels, include multicultural readers, emphasis on multicultural literacies, and invitations to use a wide variety of Englishes in classroom speech and writing. The study of contemporary speech genres by sociolinguists, and the study of rhetorical forms and pedagogies, dance a sometimes uneasy duet in the work of many historians, scholars, and teachers. Teaching tolerance and respect for all languages and language variants is sometimes at odds with defining and teaching correct usage, and the rationale for a shared, common language that is not perceived or experienced as elitist (Smitherman & Villanueva, 2003).

RHETORIC AND SOCIOLINGUISTICS

The uses of Freire's (1970) liberatory pedagogy among social constructionists illustrate how difficult it is to focus on political and social critique in the classroom, to work toward developing critical consciousness in students, while at the same time adhering to the antifoundationalist position that there is no basis for seeking, acquiring, and producing knowledge. Disbelief in foundations also has resulted in a weakened concept of agency, and without a clear concept of agency, encouraging students to develop a voice, much less to engage in political or civic action, becomes much more difficult. Adapting Freire's original work among rural farmers in Latin America to fit rural and marginalized U.S. student populations, many liberatory and empowerment-based pedagogies borrowed Freire's Marxism, but not his religious concerns for the soul. Without the latter, and lacking any model of interior selfhood that can be inspired to agency, some liberatory pedagogies have fostered classrooms centered in producing social or political critique, and teachers who encourage their students to imitate the language and stance of critical consciousness without having a clear sense of where such resistance can or should go (Villanueva, 1991).

Language and society scholars versed in Russian linguistics observed that the earlier Bakhtin (1973), who emphasized "inner speech" and "inner voices" and "dialogue," was replaced by a determinist Bakhtin (1979/1986), describing case after case of the always already written, a closed linguistic loop in which agency, invention, and change barely exist (see Wertsch, 1991, for a more fluid interpretation of Bakhtin). Along with Freire and Bakhtin, source materials for social constructionist views of identity-voice have emphasized that society constructs voice, that identity is shaped by social forces beyond any individual's control. Sociolinguistics in some sense assumes this view of language and identity, for it looks for and finds broadly practiced and statistically documentable forms of language use. In this conception, sociolinguistics overlaps with studies of rhetoric in earlier centuries, with the important difference that sociolinguistics rarely emphasizes correct usage, and rhetoric nearly always does. How can values-neutral, nonprescriptive research in language and society be employed productively in composition classrooms? This question no doubt will continue to occupy scholars for some time.

On several fronts developments in historical and theoretical rhetoric have converged with developments in linguistics and sociolinguistics during the past 20 years, particularly in discussions of the purposes and forms of classroom learning in relation to the larger society that surrounds students and classrooms. Sociolinguistic work on classroom dialogues and discourses and studies of students' home languages now join contemporary rhetorics for multicultural student populations and for a multicultural society. Providing linguistic descriptions of the languages of home and classroom has always been a primary contribution of linguistics to the language classroom, but the uses of the descriptions are very different in a freshman composition classroom and in a junior or graduate-level course in sociolinguistics. Knowing that everyone code switches is one thing; knowing what to do about it, is another, as the extended and continuing Ebonics debates illustrate (Baugh, 2002). Knowing that there are many variants of spoken English is one thing. Knowing what to do about that as a teacher or learner, is another. How can knowledge that choices exist help in the formulation of which choices to make? This question is further complicated by the movement toward questioning the bases and possibilities of knowledge itself.

Current research in sociolinguistics returns in some ways to the sociolinguistic movement of the early 1970s that eventually resulted in the Conference on College Composition and Communication's "Students' Right to Their Own Language" (1974) document. The myth of Standard English was widely debunked, and instances of what is now known as *linguistic profiling* were widely documented. Other than insisting on tolerance and respect for all language variants, sociolinguistics' contribution to composition pedagogy has remained conflicted on several issues: agency, prescriptivism, and tensions between academic and social initiatives to which linguistic research contributes.

THE RETURN TO THE (SOCIO)LINGUISTIC TURN

The agency crisis is especially troubled among rhetorical and language theorists who take as their primary purpose to denounce normative standard language hierarchies at all levels: lexicon, syntax, discourse, and genre. Joining affirmations of students' rights to their own languages and dialects, and values-neutral writing process composition pedagogies, adapted antifoundationalist theories have extended social constructionist models to assist in the formulation of a critical language pedagogy. The student's role as a scholar-writer is defined as it is in cultural critique theory and pedagogy; the teacher's role continues to be defined as a peer-critic and sometimes guerilla coach, encouraging the student to look outward at a culture in need of analysis and political/ethical critique (Fox, 1990). Language-critical pedagogy added to social critique pedagogy a focus on language as the instrument of social and political oppression, specifically Standard English, which was refined in 1969 as the *language of wider communication* (Fishman, 1972). In its singular focus on language as the object of analysis and source of consciousness, critical-language theory and pedagogy come very close to returning to the linguistic turn, if not to orthodox deconstruction. The linguistic turn was a call to recognize that everything is linguistically constructed and that language itself is an arbitrary system of signs and is culturally constructed. The sociolinguistic turn of the early 1970s became a call for tolerance and diversity much like today's multicultural and language diversity initiatives in curriculum and pedagogy.

The development of current language-critical pedagogy may be regarded not only as a direct descendant of 1970s sociolinguistics, but also as a subset of social critique and civic discourse models. Some may want to "flip the script," in Gilyard's (1996) phrase, and see language-critical pedagogy as perhaps the most important, or prior, development, the big brother as it were of other critical pedagogies. Historians and theorists of rhetoric and composition are now re-examining the relation between the current uses of descriptive sociolinguistics and discourse theory in a new revision of the CCCC language policy, and Students' Right to Their Own Language documents. Paradoxically, critical language pedagogy can place the student even further outside the practices of standard language and culture, even when the languages encouraged by critical pedagogy are themselves consonant with academic discourse. The agency taught in such pedagogies is agency against, from the outside, and not from within.

The immediate sociolinguistic tasks of equalizing the status among English-language variants, and of affirming linguistic diversity in the United States, may provide surprisingly common ground for dialogue with the culture wars and theory wars within rhetoric and composition. The practical difficulties that have emerged from antifoundationalist social critique models affect the implementation of tolerance- and diversity-based language pedagogies. It is nothing new to ask, if everything is equal, what is it equal to? Tolerance can be a low-level goal, akin to tolerating a food or drug that is not particularly agreeable. Linguists' recent responses to the Oakland Ebonics incident are revisiting many of the sites that were examined in the wake of the Ann Arbor "Black English" trial of 1978: the King decision. Theory and pedagogy have yet to define methods of accomplishing the goal of pluralism alongside the goal of empowering students to succeed individually and socially in the language of wider communication: Standard English and its written form, edited American English.

It is not too early to observe the institutional consequences of strained relations between rhetorical theory and composition practice. The controversy over Linda Brodkey's freshman English social-critique curriculum at the University of Texas at Austin brought to the surface tensions between the practicalities of running and maintaining a writing program and the theories that have so richly informed the improvement and diversification of writing curricula during the past 20 or more years. As institutions, and institutional practices, rhetoric and composition seem poised for resegregation, or divorce. Many rhetorical theorists now want nothing to do with writing programs and have joined the theory elite within English departments more generally. Writing program administration, with its own national organization and graduate courses, functions increasingly as a distinct professional venue for compositionists. Many universities have resisted the pressure to develop remedial courses staffed by English departments and other units internal to the university. However, most universities are moving toward a model in which a writing center, sometimes along with the writing program, resides in a unit almost entirely separate from the English department. At UT-Austin, post-Brodkey, this unit has become the Division of Rhetoric and Composition, a semi-independent entity with its own faculty and a large number of adjuncts, both full- and part-time, teaching writing courses and working in the writing center alongside teaching assistants. Similar structures are being developed in other universities, with variations. It will be very ironic indeed if 20 years after the founding of graduate courses and programs in rhetoric and composition, the Ph.D.s produced by those programs have no professional prospects outside largely nontenure track ghettos: the "projects" from which rhetoric and composition emerged in the first place.

Although seemingly distinct from each other, rhetoric and composition intersect at many points, with sociolinguistics as a field in language studies within English departments and English teaching. Literacy studies is an area that illustrates the intersection.

HISTORICAL RHETORIC, LINGUISTICS, AND THE CULTURAL

The connection between rhetoric and linguistics becomes explicit in the development of applied linguistics, that branch of linguistics that looks to the pedagogical. Within applied linguistics Kaplan (1966) first established a connection between the linguistic and the rhetorical with his term "contrastive rhetoric." Contrastive rhetoric conceptualizes language and language practices in ways that are embedded in culture, ways that recall the sophists. Connor (1996) characterizes contrastive rhetoric as "an area of research in second language acquisition that identifies problems in composition encountered by second language writers and, by referring to the rhetorical strategies of the first language, attempts to explain them" (p. 5). She retells the narratives of many students who have difficulty composing in English because they are attempting to translate words, phrases, and organization from their home languages into English. Connors tells of students trying to recreate jokes and stories that are widely known in their home discourses, but who fail to make their points in translation not because of an inability to move between the two languages but because discursive tropes familiar to them are not familiar to the audience they are writing for. We read the words, understand the words, but fail to gather the meaning, the import. Yet rather than see the problems as rhetorical, teachers still read students as steeped in "error," if not misunderstood completely. Contrastive rhetoric tries to account for rhetorical differences between languages by seeking to understand language and writing as culturally bound phenomena, and not as universal constructs. As such, contrastive rhetoric endeavors to understand language as differently identified within particular contexts.

Contrastive rhetoric began with Kaplan (1966), in which he drew on the Sapir-Whorf hypothesis (Sapir, 1949), specifically the assertion that logic is culturally bound. Kaplan argued that because of language's ability to communicate and shape culture, native speakers of different languages compose and make meaning using different rhetorical structures. For example, Kaplan argued that English is particularly linear in its construction—that the paragraph in English begins with a topic sentence and then "by a series of subdivisions of that topic statement, each supported by example and illustrations, proceeds to develop that central idea in its proper relationship with the other ideas in the whole essay" (p. 297). In contrast, he writes, Asian rhetoric is constructed as a spiral, circling the main idea, "showing it in a variety of tangential views, but the subject is never looked at directly" (p. 302). The upshot of his argument is that rhetoric should be seen as viable and recognizable parts of given languages, as different among languages as are grammatical structures.

Following its publication, contrastive rhetoric received very little attention (or little positive attention) until the early 1980s. Most comments to that time pointed to contrastive rhetoric's limitations—its overarching claims, its questionable methodology, and its stereotyping and essentializing of large sweeps of cultures as monolithic. Yet in 1982, the *Annual Review of Applied Linguistics* was devoted to contrastive rhetoric and matters of text-based study. Articles included rather detailed analyses of several languages and their relation to English, and particularly featured articles on English and American Indian Languages (Leap, 1982), English and German (Clyne, 1982), English and Hindi (Kachru, 1982), English and Japanese (for a related article, see Hinds, 1983), English and Korean (Chang, 1982), English and Mandarin (Tsao, 1982), and English and Marathi (Pandharipande, 1982). This volume, along with deBeaugrande (1980), rekindled interest in whole-text analysis and issues of contrastive rhetoric. Connor and Kaplan (1987) further augmented the study of contrastive rhetoric, using its framework to investigate the different rhetorical patterns of other languages that previously had not been studied. Purves continued the theoretical and linguistic considerations of contrastive rhetoric, again contrasting different rhetorical styles to those of English. Purves also engaged theoretical considerations of curricula, the selection of writing tasks, and assessment issues.

In the 1990s, contrastive rhetoric moved away from a strict linguistic perspective. Connor (1996) contends that "a broader definition that considers cognitive and socio-cultural variables of writing in addition to linguistic variables has been substituted for a purely linguistic framework" (p. 18). Connor sees many reasons for this shift, including the realization within linguistics of the limitations of feature-oriented research, as well as external pressures in first-language composition research. She points to cognitive models of writing (Flower & Hayes, 1981) and the increasingly large body of work that views writing and learning as inherently social (Bartholomae, 1999; Bizzell, 1994; Heath, 1983; Rose, 1989). The problem remained, however, that the literature was Anglocentric. The focus, according to Land and Whitely, should not be on assimilation of U.S. English rhetorical patterns; the focus should be complementary, investigating the textual rhetorical patterns of students, but also negotiating those rhetorical patterns. This strategy of active negotiation of meaning between students and teacher in a conference setting has been shown to facilitate the writing and revision processes for second-language speakers (Goldstein & Conrad, 1990).

Although contrastive rhetoric and its applications should always be viewed with some skepticism, given its history and some of its practitioners' propensity to reify culturally accepted notions of racist essentialism, it is a promising field of pedagogical theory because it does not view language as universal, but as inherently social—and as rhetorical. As Panetta (2000) has argued, even though teachers may not have been trained specifically in the home language and culture of each student, contrastive rhetoric allows teachers to frame students' knowledge and knowledge making in a less prescriptive, less error-centered manner. Doing so would change what too often has been the case among ESL students and among "basic writers," most often conceived of as underprepared college students who are often people of color. Contrastive rhetoric also assists teachers in acknowledging our own culturally formed notions of knowledge making—allowing us to complicate notions of power as they are related to language—and allowing us to make these conventions explicit to students. As discourses and rhetorical conventions are made explicit, students begin to understand what are sometimes ephemeral rules for what they are: socially derived conventions. Panetta argues that as students are taught how to identify rhetorical conventions for what they are, they are able more readily to understand the nuances of a particular language. They gather greater metalinguistic awareness (Hartwell, 1985).

As contrastive rhetoric moves out of the scientific, taxonomizing culture of linguistics and becomes more informed by postcolonial and poststructuralist notions of discourse, it broadens and becomes more applicable not only to students in ESL classes, but to all students of writing. This shift currently is moving contrastive rhetoric from its initial position of contrasting other, foreign languages with English, to contrasting other English discourses with English academic discourse. This move fosters the transfer of sound pedagogical theory from second-language classrooms to other classrooms within the university as a way to empower and understand students whose first discourse is not academic English. Panetta (2000) seeks to theorize contrastive rhetoric from within contexts other than an ESL classroom, engaging the possible uses of contrastive rhetoric for students of color more generally and for women, African American women, and gay men. Still, just as Leki (1997) has cautioned scholars not to be too reckless in their embrace of contrastive rhetoric for its use with nonnative speakers of English, and to be constantly aware of the potential colonizing effects of learning English, we need to recognize that the warning should be heeded with regard to other students as well. Bliss, for example, argues that students from diverse cultural backgrounds across the United States may have problems with composition because they are unfamiliar with the rhetorical structure. She contends that these difficulties could be overcome by using contrastive rhetoric and examining the rhetorical structures of academic prose.

Delpit argues that teachers, because of differences in discourse, fail to understand what students are saying and react based on that misunderstanding. Smitherman shows the link between the use of Black English (now recognized as African American Language) and the education of Black students. Smitherman (1992) finds that Black students use their rich rhetorical history to aid them in the production of high-quality writing. Through a contrastive rhetoric students negotiate between conventions consciously, using their already well-honed rhetorical skills in ways that help them. Contrastive rhetoric helps students and teachers negotiate questions of assimilation and empowerment—a negotiation that must happen when students learn the discourse of current power. Although the theories of contrastive rhetoric certainly will not be a cure for all the issues of literacy and power that go on inside and outside classrooms, they do offer a "way in" that values both the student's rhetorical and discourse communities and the material need that students have to master the discourse of those having the greatest sets of social and material options.

What's more, contrastive rhetoric can become more clearly ensconced within rhetoric as conventionally understood. Villanueva (1999a) returns to the history of rhetoric, now tied to the histories of Greek, Roman, and Byzantine imperialism, to explain how these rhetorical differences came about and to clarify "Greek" from "Roman" as sophistic rhetorics (given to students from Arabic backgrounds and Spanish backgrounds) and Aristotelian rhetorics (the rhetoric of the schools and the logic of Standard English and edited American English). It was a move to what would become a concern with the "postcolonial."

The 1980s and 1990s show a greater desire to understand "rhetorics" in their broader context. Lu writes about a comparative (rather than contrastive) rhetoric.

Using Burke (1969) as a touchstone, Lu compares the ideological stances of both China and the United States as reflected in the ways composition is taught in those countries. Berlin (1984) makes the connections between rhetoric and ideology more overt, although he remains tied to his taxonomy of epistemological fields (now refined to cognitive rhetorics, expressionist rhetorics, and social epistemic rhetorics). Drawing on Valesio and on Burke, Berlin argues that rhetoric is always culturally and socially imbued, bringing the idea of socially constructed ways of knowing within the realm of rhetoric, although the social construction already had been a part of composition's discussions (cf. Bruffee, 1986). For all that, "epistemic rhetoric" had known a series of debates (Leff, 1978). The early 1980s saw a series of debates on the intersections between rhetoric and epistemology, with the assertion of a cultural connection among rhetorics sustained (e.g., Cherwitz & Hikins, 1982).

The result of asserting a connection between rhetoric and ways of knowing affects not only what is in the classroom but how those who traditionally have not been in positions of power are not reflected in historical studies of rhetoric. A number of works emerge that argue for the rhetorics of women (both historically and contemporarily), of Black men and women, of American Indians, of Mexicans, and of the AmerInd who preceded Mexicans and South Americans (Gilyard, 1999; Glenn, 1997; Jarratt & Worsham, 1998; Logan, 1999; Lunsford, 1995; Lyons, 2000; Miller, 1992; Pough, 2002; Powell, 2002; Royster, 2000; Swearingen, 1991; Villanueva, 1999b). The past 20 years marked the rise of ancient and contemporary rhetorics that do not necessarily arise from Athens and Rome (with those that do being wrestled into different social and cultural contexts).

Just as discussions concerning the resurrection of the sophists led to assertions from classicists that the sophists were being recast within a contemporary mindset, the introduction of women rhetoricians of ancient Athens also met with resistance (Gale, 1996). Yet what matters most is the need to break free from the counterintuitive yet long-held assertion that rhetoric was solely Greek (or Athenian, more accurately) and solely male (Swearingen, 1991). Glenn (1997) recaps and develops the discussion concerning women rhetoricians. Jacqueline Jones Royster (2000) reviews 19th-century African American women rhetors, noting that those she presents were not "unique and exceptional" but "typical and representative" of African American women (pp. 4–5). She argues that "African American women have understood with great clarity two things: the power of language and learning and the inherent hostility of the context within which people of African descent must live in the United States" (p. 108), so that only occasionally have African American women rhetors' "talents . . . flowed past the barriers, reconstituted themselves, and become noticeable as 'traces of a stream'" (p. 4). Logan (1995, 1999) provides examples of these African American women rhetors, analyzing the rhetorics displayed in the public discourse of African American club and church women of the later 19th century. Although she provides no explicit connection to contemporary writing instruction, she offers a glimpse into the rhetorical strategies of African American discourse, ways beyond the often reductive pedagogies of teaching "English as a Second Dialect" for African American students. In like manner, Gilyard (2003) studies the rhetoric of John Oliver Killens, and Miller (1992) provides a rhetorical study of Martin Luther King, Jr.

Gilyard also introduces the rhetorics of others of color in *Race, Rhetoric, and Composition* (1999). Within that collection Powell (1999) introduces the rhetoric of the Mixed-Blood and the American Indian rhetor. In Diné and Hopi terms, American

Indian rhetoric is that of the kachina of the trickster, a rhetoric of compliance with and a simultaneous resistance to the dominant discourse, a rhetoric also discussed by Villanueva (1999a) in terms of the Puerto Rican rhetor. Wardi (1999) calls on Said (1978) to describe an orientalist rhetoric, an anti-Arab racism. Others within the collection make the connections between rhetoric and the teaching of writing. Cintron (1997) discusses the rhetoric of violence in a Chicano area in Chicago. Villanueva (1999a) calls for a reconsideration of rhetoric beyond the classical Western tradition. Calling on the work of Enrique Dussel (1995), Villanueva notes the rhetorics used by 16th-century Incans and Aztecs, noting the degree to which rhetoric played as central a role in the lives of these ancient cultures as it had among the Athenians—without any knowledge of ancient Athenian or Roman rhetorics.

By the beginning of 2004, writings of the traditional rhetorics of the southern part of the Western hemisphere begin to show up in print. In the meanwhile, Bizzell, Schroeder, and Fox (2002) gather together the discussions from linguistics and from rhetoric to argue, as Bizzell has argued throughout the past 20 years, that teachers of writing must look to alternative rhetorics if they are to prepare students for all that constitutes intellectual and social work.

RHETORIC, 1983–2003, OR BACK TO THE FUTURE

In 1914, academic rhetoricians walked out of the annual meeting of the Modern Language Association in protest against the trend away from rhetoric within the relatively new departments of English. The protestors returned to their home institutions to create new departments of speech. Although interest in rhetoric in what became departments of speech communications or departments of communications diminished as interest in rhetoric was revived in departments of English, the study of rhetoric has continued to inform both disciplines (as well as classics and philosophy). The connections among rhetoric, linguistics, and the teaching of writing form one rich area of inquiry in rhetoric. Rhetorics of science, economics, politics, protest, feminism, racism, the postcolonial, the visual, and the technological are as prevalent in communications—which looks to public speeches, television, and pop culture—as they are in English studies.

Our richness as a discipline is relatively recent, with the tensions between the rhetoricians and the literary critics remaining to some extent. It was not until the mid-1960s that rhetorical studies resumed within English departments, almost exclusively within first-year composition programs. Because of this history a tension persists between those who "teach writing" and those who "teach literature," even though the two activities in most cases are combined in various ways. Understanding the history of this tension can help English teachers combine the "two disciplines" in a variety of ways, especially now that the rhetorics of different disciplines and the rhetorical traditions of different cultures have become a staple of multicultural and diversity-based curriculum. Although the sources cited in this chapter focus primarily on research in rhetoric since 1983, it will be most useful if read in the context of the longer history that has shaped the teaching of English in American schools (Coe, Lingard, & Teslenko, 2002; Enos, 1996; Harkin & Schilb, 1991; Horner, 1990).

REFERENCES

Applebee, A. (1974). *Tradition and reform in the teaching of English*. Urbana, IL: National Council of Teachers of English.

Bacon, N. (2000). Building a swan's nest for instruction in rhetoric. *College Composition and Communication, 51,* 589–609.

Bakhtin, M. M. (1973). *Problems of Dostoevsky's poetics* (R. W. Rotsel, Trans.). Ann Arbor: Ardis.

Bakhtin, M. M. (1986). *Speech genres and other essays* (C. Emerson & M. Holquist, Eds.; V. W. McGee, Trans.). Austin: University of Texas Press. (Original work published 1979)

Bartholomae, D. (1999). Inventing the university. In R. Connors & C. Glenn (Eds.), *The new St. Martin's guide to teaching writing* (pp. 443–457). Boston: Bedford/St. Martin's.

Bartholomae, D., & Elbow, P. (1995). Writing with teachers: A conversation with Peter Elbow. *College English, 46,* 84–92.

Baugh, J. (2002). *Beyond Ebonics: Linguistic pride and racial prejudice*. New York: Oxford University Press.

Bawarshi, A. S. (2003). *Genre and the invention of the writer: Reconsidering the place of invention in composition*. Logan: Utah State University Press.

Beason, G. B. (2000). *Using Aristotle to recover an art of dialectic for composition*. Mahwah, NJ: Erlbaum.

Berlin, J. A. (1984). *Writing instruction in nineteenth-century American colleges*. Carbondale: Southern Illinois University Press.

Berlin, J. A. (1987). *Rhetoric and reality: Writing instruction in American colleges, 1900–1985*. Carbondale: Southern Illinois University Press.

Berlin, J. A. (1994). *Writing instruction in nineteenth-century American colleges*. Carbondale: Southern Illinois University Press.

Berthoff, A. E. (1991). Rhetoric as hermeneutic. *College Composition and Communication, 42,* 279–287.

Binkley, R. A., & Lipson, C. S. (Eds.). (2004). *Rhetoric before and beyond the Greeks*. Albany: State University of New York Press.

Bizzell, P. (1992). *Academic discourse and critical consciousness*. Pittsburgh, PA: University of Pittsburgh Press.

Bizzell, P. (1994). "Contact zones" and English studies. *College English, 56,* 163–169.

Bizzell, P., & Herzberg, B. (Eds.). (2004). *The rhetorical tradition*. New York: Bedford/St. Martins.

Bizzell, P., Schroeder, C., & Fox, H. (2002). *Alt dis: Alternative discourses and the academy*. Portsmouth, NH: Heinemann.

Brody, M. (1993). *Manly writing: Gender, rhetoric, and the rise of composition*. Carbondale: Southern Illinois University Press.

Bruffee, K. A. (1986). Social construction, language, and the authority of knowledge: A bibliographical essay. *College English, 48,* 773–790.

Buck, G. (1996). *Toward a feminist rhetoric: The writing of Gertrude Buck* (J. Campbell, Ed.). Pittsburgh, PA: University of Pittsburgh Press.

Burke, K. (1969). *A rhetoric of motives*. Berkeley: University of California Press.

CCCC bibliography of composition and rhetoric. (1990–1999). Carbondale: Southern Illinois University Press.

Chang, S-J. (1982). English and Korean. *Annual Review of Applied Linguistics, 3,* 85–98.

Cherwitz, R. A., & Hikins, J. W. (1982). Toward a rhetorical epistemology. *Southern Speech Communication Journal, 47,* 135–162.

Chordas, N. (1992). Classrooms, pedagogies, and the rhetoric of equality. *College Composition and Communication, 43,* 214–224.

Cintron, R. (1997). *Angels' town: Chero ways, gang life, and rhetorics of the everyday*. Boston: Beacon.

Clark, I. L. (2003). *Concepts in composition: Theory and practice in the teaching of writing*. Mahwah, NJ: Erlbaum.

Clark, S. (1995). Women, rhetoric, teaching. *College Composition and Communication, 46,* 108–122.

Clifford, J., & Schilb, J. (1994). *Writing theory and critical theory*. New York: Modern Language Association.

Clyne, M. G. (1982). English and German. *Annual Review of Applied Linguistics, 3,* 38–49.

Coe, R., Lingard, L., & Teslenko, T. (Eds.). (2002). *The rhetoric and ideology of genre: Strategies for stability and change*. Cresskill, NJ: Hampton.

Conference on College Composition and Communication. (1974). Students' right to their own language. *College Composition and Communication, 25,* 1–32.

Conley, T. M. (1987). *Philo's rhetoric: Studies in style, composition, and exegesis*. Berkeley: Center for Hermeneutical Studies in Hellenistic and Modern Culture.

Connor, U. (1996). *Contrastive rhetoric: Cross-cultural aspects of second-language writing*. New York: Cambridge University Press.

Connor, U., & Kaplan, R. B. (Eds.). (1987). *Writing across languages*. Reading, MA: Addison-Wesley.

Connors, R. J. (1997). *Composition-rhetoric: Backgrounds, theory, and pedagogy*. Pittsburgh, PA: University of Pittsburgh Press.

Connors, R. J., & Lunsford, A. A. (1993). Teachers' rhetorical comments on student papers. *College Composition and Communication, 44*, 200–223.

Corbett, E. P. J. (1965). *Classical rhetoric for the modern student*. New York: Oxford University Press.

Crowley, S. (1985). Invention in nineteenth-century rhetoric. *College Composition and Communication, 36*, 51–60.

Crowley, S. (1990). *Methodical memory: Invention in current-traditional rhetoric*. Carbondale: Southern Illinois University Press.

Crowley, S. (1998). *Composition in the university: Historical and polemical essays*. Pittsburgh, PA: University of Pittsburgh Press.

Crowley, S., & Hawhee, D. (2003). *Ancient rhetorics for contemporary students*. New York: Longman.

Cushman, E. (1996). The rhetorician as an agent of social change. *College Composition and Communication, 47*, 7–28.

D'Angelo, F. (2000). *Composition in the classical tradition*. Needham Heights, MA: Allyn & Bacon.

Dawkins, J. (1995). Teaching punctuation as a rhetorical tool. *College Composition and Communication, 46*, 533–548.

deBeaugrande, R. (1980). *Text, discourse, and process: Toward a multidisciplinary science of texts*. Norwood, NJ: Ablex.

Dussel, E. (1995). *The invention of the Americas: Eclipse of "the other" and the myth of modernity* (M. D. Barber, Trans.). New York: Continuum.

Enos, R. L. (1976). The epistemology of Gorgias' rhetoric: A re-examination. *Southern Speech Communication Journal, 42*, 35–51.

Enos, T. (Ed.). (1996). *Encyclopedia of rhetoric and composition: Communication from ancient times to the information age*. New York: Garland.

Fishman, J. A. (1972). *Language in sociocultural change*. Stanford: Stanford University Press.

Flower, L., & Hayes, J. R. (1981). A cognitive process theory of writing. *College Composition and Communication, 32*, 365–387.

Fox, T. (1990). *The social uses of writing: Politics and pedagogy*. Norwood, NJ: Ablex.

Freire, P. (1970). *Pedagogy of the oppressed* (M. B. Ramos, Trans.). New York: Herder and Herder.

Gage, J. (2000). *The shape of reason: Argumentative writing in college*. New York: Longman.

Gale, X. L. (1996). *Teachers, discourses, and authority in the postmodern composition classroom*. Albany: State University of New York Press.

Gilyard, K. (1991). *Voices of the self: A study of language competence*. Detroit: Wayne State University Press.

Gilyard, K. (1996). *Let's flip the script: An African American discourse on language, literature, and learning*. Detroit: Wayne State University Press.

Gilyard, K. (Ed.). (1999). *Race, rhetoric, and composition*. Portsmouth, NH: Heinemann Boynton/Cook.

Gilyard, K. (2003). *Liberation memories: The rhetoric and poetics of John Oliver Killens*. Detroit: Wayne State University Press.

Glenn, C. (1994). Sex, lies, and manuscript: Refiguring Aspasia in the history of rhetoric. *College Composition and Communication, 45*, 180–199.

Glenn, C. (1997). *Rhetoric retold: Regendering the tradition from antiquity through the renaissance*. Carbondale: Southern Illinois University Press.

Glenn, C. (2000). Truth, lies, and method: Revisiting feminist historiography. *College English, 62*, 387–389.

Goldstein, L. M., & Conrad, S. M. (1990). Student input and negotiation of meaning in ESL writing conferences. *TESOL Quarterly, 24*, 443–460.

Grabe, W., & Kaplan, R. B. (1996). *Theory and practice of writing: An applied linguistic perspective*. New York: Longman, 1996.

Hairston, M. (1981). *Successful writing: A rhetoric for advanced composition*. New York: Norton.

Hairston, M. (1982). The winds of change: Thomas Kuhn and the revolution in the teaching of writing. *College Composition and Communication, 33*, 76–88.

Harkin, P., & Schilb, J. (Eds.). (1991). *Contending with words: Composition and rhetoric in a postmodern age*. New York: Modern Language Association.

Harris, J. D. (1997). *A teaching subject: Composition since 1966*. Upper Saddle River, NJ: Prentice-Hall.

Hartwell, P. (1985). Grammar, grammars, and the teaching of grammar. *College English, 47*, 105–127.

Heath, S. B. (1983). *Ways with words: Language, life, and work in communities and classrooms*. New York: Cambridge University Press.

Hinds, J. (1983). Contrastive rhetoric: Japanese and English. *Text, 3*, 183–195.

Horner, W. B. (1983). *Composition and literature: Bridging the gap*. Chicago: University of Chicago Press.

Horner, W. B. (Ed.). (1990). *The present state of scholarship in historical and contemporary rhetoric.* Columbia: University of Missouri Press.

Horner, W. B., & Leff, M. (Eds.). (1995). *Rhetoric and pedagogy: Its history, philosophy, and practice: Essays in honor of James J. Murphy.* Mahwah, NJ: Erlbaum.

Jarratt, S. (1991). *Rereading the sophists: Classical rhetoric refigured.* Carbondale: Southern Illinois University Press.

Jarratt, S. C., & Worsham, L. (1998). *Feminism and composition studies: In other words.* New York: Modern Language Association.

Kachru, Y. (1982). English and Hindi. *Annual Review of Applied Linguistics, 3,* 50–77.

Kaplan, R. B. (1966). Cultural thought patterns in inter-cultural education. *Language Learning, 16,* 294–309.

Knoblauch, C. H., & Brannon, L. (1984). *Rhetorical traditions and the teaching of writing.* Portsmouth, NH: Boynton/Cook.

Leap, W. L. (1982). English and American Indian language. *Annual Review of Applied Linguistics, 3,* 24–37.

Leff, M. C. (1978). In search of Ariadne's thread: A review of the recent literature on rhetorical theory. *Central States Speech Journal, 29,* 73–91.

Leki, I. (1997). Cross-talk: ESL issues and contrastive rhetoric. In C. Severino, J. C. Guerra, & J. E. Butler (Eds.), *Writing in multicultural settings* (pp. 234–244). New York: Modern Language Association.

Lindemann, E., & Tate, G. (Eds.). (1991). *An introduction to composition studies.* New York: Oxford University Press.

Logan, S. W. (Ed.). (1995). *With pen and voice: A critical anthology of nineteenth-century African American women.* Carbondale: Southern Illinois University Press.

Logan, S. W. (1999). *"We are coming": The persuasive discourse of nineteenth-century black women.* Carbondale: Southern Illinois University Press.

Lunsford, A. A. (Ed.). (1995). *Reclaiming rhetorica: Women in the rhetorical tradition.* Pittsburgh, PA: University of Pittsburgh Press.

Lyons, S. R. (2000). Rhetorical sovereignty: What do American Indians want from writing? *College Composition and Communication, 51,* 447–468.

Miller, K. D. (1992). *Voice of deliverance: The language of Martin Luther King, Jr. and its sources.* Athens: University of Georgia Press.

Miller, S. (1993). *Textual carnivals: The politics of composition.* Carbondale: Southern Illinois University Press.

Miller, S. (2004). *Rescuing the subject: A critical introduction to rhetoric and the writer.* Carbondale, IL: Southern Illinois University Press.

Murphy, J. J. (Ed.). (1990). *A short history of writing instruction from ancient Greece to twentieth-century America.* Davis, CA: Hermagoras.

Odell, L. (Ed.). (2003). *Theory and practice in the teaching of writing: Rethinking the discipline.* Carbondale: Southern Illinois University Press.

Ohmann, R. (1974). *English in America.* New York: Oxford University Press.

Pandharipande, R. (1982). English and Marathi. *Annual Review of Applied Linguistics, 3,* 118–136.

Panetta, C. G. (Ed.). (2000). *Contrastive rhetoric revisited and redefined.* Mahwah, NJ: Erlbaum.

Pough, G. D. (2002). Empowering rhetoric: Black students writing Black Panthers. *College Composition and Communication, 53,* 466–486.

Poulakos, J., & Poulakos, T. (1999). *Classical rhetorical theory.* Boston: Houghton Mifflin.

Powell, M. (1999). Blood and scholarship: One mixed-Blood's Story. In K. Gilyard (Ed.), *Race, rhetoric, and composition* (pp. 1–16). Portsmouth, NH: Heinemann.

Powell, M. (2002). Rhetorics of survivance: How American Indians use writing. *College Composition and Communication, 53,* 396–434.

Ratcliffe, K. (1999). Rhetorical listening: A trope for interpretive invention and a "code of cross-cultural conduct." *College Composition and Communication, 51,* 195–224.

Rose, M. (1989). *Lives on the boundary: The struggles and achievements of America's underprepared.* New York: Free Press.

Royster, J. (2000). *Traces of a stream: Literacy and social change among African American women.* Pittsburgh, PA: University of Pittsburgh Press.

Said, E. (1978). *Orientalism.* New York: Pantheon.

Sapir, E. (1949). *Language: An introduction to the study of speech.* New York: Harcourt Brace Jovanovich.

Schilb, J. (1996). *Between the lines: Relating composition theory and literary theory.* Portsmouth, NH: Boynton/Cook.

Smith, C. (2003). *Rhetoric and human consciousness: A history.* Prospect Heights, IL: Waveland.

Smitherman, G. (1992). Black English: Diverging or converging? The view from the National Assessment of Educational Progress. *Language and Education, 6,* 47–61.

Smitherman, G., & Villanueva, V. (Eds.). (2003). *Language diversity in the classroom: From intention to practice.* Carbondale: Southern Illinois University Press.

Stillar, G. F. (1998). *Analyzing everyday texts: Discourse, rhetoric, and social perspectives.* Thousand Oaks, CA: Sage.

Swearingen, C. J. (1991). *Rhetoric and irony: Western literacy and western lies.* New York: Oxford University Press.

Swearingen, C. J. (2002). Rhetoric and composition as a coherent intellectual discipline: A meditation. In G. A. Olson (Ed.), *Rhetoric and composition as intellectual work* (pp. 12–22). Carbondale: Southern Illinois University Press.

Tannen, D. (1994). *Gender and discourse.* New York: Oxford University Press.

Tate, G., Rupiper, A., & Schick, K. (2001). *A guide to composition pedagogies.* New York: Oxford University Press.

Tsao, F. F. (1982). English and Mandarin. *Annual Review of Applied Linguistics, 3,* 99–136.

Villanueva, V. (1991). Considerations of American Freireistas. In R. Bullock & J. Trimbur (Eds.), *The politics of writing instruction: Postsecondary* (pp. 247–262). Portsmouth, NH: Boynton/Cook.

Villanueva, V. (1993). *Bootstraps: From an American academic of color.* Urbana, IL: National Council of Teachers of English.

Villanueva, V. (1999a). On the rhetoric and precedents of racism. *College Composition and Communication, 50,* 645–662.

Villanueva, V. (1999b). The student of color and contrastive rhetoric. In E. R. Hollins and E. I. Oliver (Eds.), *Finding pathways to success in school: Culturally responsive teaching* (pp. 107–123). Mahwah, NJ: Erlbaum.

Villanueva, V. (2003). *Cross talk in comp theory: A graduate reader* (2nd ed.). Urbana: NCTE.

Vitanza, V. (1994). *Writing histories of rhetoric.* Carbondale: Southern Illinois University Press.

Wardi, A. J. (1999). Terrorists, madmen, and religious fanatics: Revising orientalism and racist rhetoric. In K. Gilyard (Ed.), *Race, rhetoric, and composition* (pp. 31–43). Portsmouth, NH: Boynton/Cook.

Welch, K. (1990). *The contemporary reception of classical rhetoric: Appropriations of ancient discourse.* Mahwah, NJ: Erlbaum.

Wertsch, J. V. (1991). *Voices of the mind: A sociocultural approach to mediated action.* Cambridge, MA: Harvard University Press.

White, E. M. (1989). *Developing successful college writing programs.* San Francisco: Jossey-Bass.

CHAPTER 8

Family and Community Literacies

*Ellen Cushman, Stuart Barbier, Catherine Mazak,
and Robert Petrone*

RESEARCH IN family and community literacy began with a fight. Goody's (1971) ethnophilosophical statement about the psychosocial effects produced when a people are facile (or not) with the technology of the alphabet extended his earlier arguments along these lines (Goody, 1968). Ong (1983), a Jesuit priest, was making parallel arguments about the effects of literacy on the human and on society: "All thought, including that in primary oral cultures, is to some degree analytic; it breaks its materials into various components. But abstractly sequential, classificatory, explanatory examination of phenomena or of stated truths is impossible without writing" (p. 8). Primary oral cultures were less capable of abstract thought, the argument went, and less likely to develop as civilizations because they had fewer means of archiving social practices. Thus the great divide was located between primary oral cultures and literate ones and was made possible by use of the alphabet and writing as means for recording history, listing transactions in trade and commerce, and facilitating the establishment of social institutions.

THE GREAT DIVIDE: WHEN LITERACY BECAME LITERACIES

Weighing in on the effects of the alphabet on ancient culture, Havelock (1976, 1982) attributed high value to alphabet technology for its efficiency, reproducibility, and economy. The alphabet as sign technology was a better tool, especially when used with ink and papyrus, for representing reality than the cuneiform, character, syllabary, or hieroglyph. The alphabet, writing, and the social practices possible with them were viewed as superior to other forms of meaning making. In effect, these scholars were trying to uncover the effects that the use of sign technologies had on human meaning-making activities and the development of social and cultural institutions. Their arguments had implications for the study of the relation between orality and literacy, for the effects of schooling on developing students' abstract reasoning through literacy, and on deficit models of cognition as it relates to orality and literacy. Response to the great divide theory of literacy and orality was swift, detailed, and convincing.

The great divide theorists were critiqued for being ethnocentric, lauding West-ern (literate) cultures for their civilization, and demeaning the meaning-making ac-tivities of non-Western (oral) cultures. These critiques took aim at the epistemological and methodological approaches that great divide scholars used. To begin with the epistemological framework: The alphabet appears to be a remarkable tool for creat-ing and communicating meaning if viewed from the instrumental perspective of technology, as many of the great divide theorists did. Feenberg (1991) argued that "instrumental theory offers the most widely accepted view of technology. It is based on the common sense idea that technologies are 'tools' standing ready to serve the purposes of their users" (p. 5). The letter is indifferent to the ends for which it is employed and to the political ramifications of these uses. Alphabetic technology thus has a "rational character and the universality of the truth it embodies" (p. 6). Given these "understandings of technology, the only rational stance is unreserved commit-ment to its employment" (p. 6). In this way, the alphabet could be viewed as sepa-rate and separable from its use, its effects on readers and writers, and the value systems that attach to the tool and those who use the tool fluently.

Seeing the letter as an instrument, humanities scholars such as Goody, Ong, and Havelock identified its instrumental qualities that have helped in no small measure to secure its ubiquity and social value. They elevated the letter above other sign tech-nologies by looking at its functionality (e.g., its efficiency, economy of production, and ease of production and distribution); its history of refinement (e.g., how it devel-oped into 26 letters); and its potential for continued use (e.g., greater demand for it and greater ease of reproduction with papyrus). Other sign technologies (e.g., cunei-form, hieroglyph, syllabary, and character), when viewed from this instrumentalist approach, appear to be less useful, reproducible, and efficient. This view is partial, limited by its extrication of context, practice, and cultural values from use of tool, and thus it is limiting in its depiction of other practices of meaning making and tool use. That it takes an instrumentalist approach to technologies of literacy should be seen as possibly the greatest strength and weakness of this line of work.

Another critique of great divide theory centered on its methodological flaws. Building their claims with ethnophilosophical methodologies, these theorists often relied on evidence that seemed suspiciously selective. One check to the great divide theories was informed by the qualitative (ethnographic) research that Street (1984) conducted in Iran. Street contested Goody's autonomous model of literacy, saying, "Writers concerned to establish a 'great divide' between the thinking processes of different social groups have classically described them in such terms as logical/pre-logical, primitive/modern and concrete/scientific" (p. 24). Street challenged the meth-odology of those who studied "primitive" cultures: "European commentators of the meaning of what was being said and done . . . were ill-informed in the sense that the conceptual basis for understanding such meaning was not carefully theorized, as well as in the more obvious sense that that the travelers often simply did not know the language and did not spend enough time living in a particular society" (p. 24).

Street (1984) argued further that literacy cannot be seen as a singular activity divorced from the context of its use; literacy is not a neutral tool with social and cognitive consequences, as the "autonomous" view of literacy, as he called it, would hold. Street proposed that literacy should be seen through an ideological model that included a variety of meaning-making activities imbued with cultural values. His ideological model of literacy so influenced the field that most scholars now use the word *literacies*, rather than assuming a singular, autonomous literacy. Scholars who subscribed to this model needed to conduct ethnographic fieldwork that revealed types and kinds of literacies, including their social and cultural values for the families and communities in which these practices were unfolding.

With its methodological problems opened for critique, specific implications of the great divide scholarship also could be explored and complicated. To begin with, researchers questioned the premise that orality and literacy were discrete activities that could be categorized. Heath's (1983) study, based on more than a decade of ethnographic research in the Piedmont Carolinas, did much to debunk the notion that orality was separable from literacy. She proposed instead that literacy and orality be seen as mutually informing and sustaining practices that might better be viewed as being on two separate although interconnected continua, the oral and the written (Heath, 2001). Even in communities that have noted oral traditions, and thus are mistaken too often by scholars as primary oral cultures, rich literate traditions many times can be demonstrated (McHenry & Heath, 2001).

The great divide in literacy achievement also was discussed in terms of national campaigns, literacy crises, economic upheavals, and educational reform. The literacy crisis of the later 1970s prompted many educational researchers to issue calls for reform in the very concept of literacy and the ways it is studied. Lankshear and Knobel (2003) link the literacy crises of the 1970s and early 1980s to the economic movements of postindustrialism. With massive shifts in workplace demands, kinds of products and services provided, and economic underpinnings of society, literacy—its definition, its relation to school and to work, and its social consequences—became increasingly important to understand. Governments of postindustrialized nations demanded educational reform, given the perception of a literacy crisis that they had helped to manufacture (see Berliner & Biddle, 1995).

To address this faulty perception of a literacy crisis, Szwed (2001) argued that a better understanding of literacy practices, rather than educational reform, was in order. He argued for greater methodological diversity in studying the rapidly changing nature of what it meant to be literate in industrialized nations: "Literacy has typically been viewed as a yes-and-no matter, easily determined: either one reads and writes or one doesn't. . . . But a closer look suggests that even among those of privileged background, these abilities are complexly patterned, and not at all equally distributed" (p. 422). The gross view of literacy that searched for and did not find one standard level of literacy for all people (workers) overlooked the ways that knowledge, skills, and meaning-making abilities are distributed among groups. The reports that described the literacy crisis tended to use macro views of societal uses of literacy as evidence of claims. "These shifts in larger societal contexts for literacy are easily and frequently talked about," Heath (2001) finds, "but their specific effects on communities . . . , though occasionally inferred, are very rarely examined" (p. 466). If researchers in the early 1980s were to better understand societal contexts of literacy, they needed to see specific literacy events as data that could indicate larger practices and cultural patterns of behavior; they needed to redefine literacy; and they needed to move away from autonomous models of literacy studies.

To document the robust nature of literacies, Szwed (2001) believes, researchers must account for "five elements of literacy—text, context, function, participants, and motivation" (p. 423). If researchers explored these, they would uncover the "*social meaning of literacy*" and would gather a better understanding of "differences in literacy [among] members of different ethnic groups, age groups, sexes, socioeconomic classes, etc." (p. 422; emphasis in original). This search for differences in practices, beliefs, and values among groups of individuals grew into a research movement earmarked by an explosion of qualitative research. Qualitative methodologies were the best way to see specific literacy events that served as evidence of daily practices, and daily practices indicated something of the larger cultural patterns of behavior (see Heath, 2001, for elaboration on events and practices). Literacy could be best understood as it was situated in events, practices, patterns of behavior, and, ultimately, socioeconomic structures.

With this move to qualitative research, the thinking went, scholars would come to understand that definitions of literacy should be founded on community, not school-based, practices. The problem, in part, was that understandings of literacy often were based on love of the book, or on an ability to decode "extended prose passages or production of expository writing, the two literacy achievements most associated with school success" (Heath, 1983, p. 465), or on "the reification of literacy in itself at the expense of recognition of its location in structures of power and ideology, related to the 'neutrality' of the object of study" (Street, 1984, p. 431). Scholastic literacy was the baseline of judgment against which all other forms of literacy were to be measured, tested, and achieved. Rather than seeing a singular literacy that is tacitly based on schooled literacy, Street (1984) and Szwed (2001) sought to understand literacies in societal contexts; to acknowledge that more than one literacy practice takes place in homes, communities, and cultures; and to uncover the value systems attached to this multiplicity of literacies.

CURRENT TRENDS, ISSUES, AND QUESTIONS

These calls for redefining literacy through qualitative research methods were situated within a growing body of work that was taking place in education and sociolinguistics in the 1970s and 1980s: Freire (1970), Labov (1972), Gumperz and Hymes (1972), Hymes (1974), Smitherman (1977/1986), Scribner and Cole (1981), Scollon and Scollon (1981), Gumperz (1982a, 1982b), Heath (1983), Taylor (1983), Geertz (1983), Bereiter and Scardamalia (1987), and Farr (1981). These important studies, often cited, were foundational to a trajectory of cross-disciplinary, qualitative research that developed over the past 20 years. This work has contributed to educational reform movements from critical pedagogy to Ebonics to multiliteracies; it has contributed to the development of activist research and community literacy initiatives; and it has been central to developing understandings of identity politics and multiculturalism that inform classroom practices. Family and community literacy studies explore the types of oral and literate practices taking place in homes and neighborhoods, often with the expectation that such study will benefit educators: The more educators know about their students' home-based knowledge, skills, and practices, the better prepared they will be to shape curricular practices, especially for preschool and young children.

To visualize the immense body of research that developed in relation to these early studies, it might be helpful to view family and community literacies as the context in which individuals develop identities as they engage in cultural, social, generational, and institutional practices of meaning making. The overall context of family and community literacies is discussed in Jennings and Purves's (1991) book of collected essays, which provides an overview of the theory of culture, language studies, and literacy that has shaped the study of family and community literacy. Wagner's (1991) essay also offers a conceptual framework that allows scholars to see etic and emic perspectives on literacy. While etic perspectives on literacy studies (psychometric analyses of discrete, decontextualized literacy skills) are useful, they are incomplete. Emic perspectives on literacy, which explore literacy events as they unfold in cultural and social symbolic systems, yield important information about the adaptation of new and emergent literacies in society. "If literacy is culture, then interventions in or 'tampering' with literacy (i.e., through campaigns of any kind, and even schooling) is to change, sometimes forcibly, the way people live" (p. 17). Family literacy studies often are centered on tracing the complex, value-laden interactions between home and school-based literacies.

Central among works in family literacy is Taylor's (1983) study that revealed how influential literacy practices from wider society come to be adopted and adapted in family literacy. Her fieldwork on six families, conducted between 1977 and 1979, explored how these families transmitted to their children cultural and social values associated with literacy. These British, mostly middle-class families transmitted literacy learning "indirectly, at the very margins of awareness through the continuously diffuse use of written language in ongoing life of the family" (p. 7). Literacy is developed and integrated into a child's life, she found, in proportion to the ways that the parents need and use literacy. Taylor later explored the relation between family and adult literacies and schooled literacies (1993, 1996; Taylor & Dorsey-Gaines, 1988), the role of special education in addressing the needs of learning disabled and exceptional children (1991), and the role of family literacy programs in promoting early childhood literacy and learning (1997).

Heath (1983) also developed a seminal line of ethnographic research, the cornerstone of which showed that White middle-class American families transmitted schooled literacy to their children through direct instruction and recreation of the kinds of activities that children might take part in at school. For example, they would ask their young children to identify objects, signs, and words in their environment—to abstract literacy from its context of use, in ways one might in school. Heath subsequently studied children's literacy (Heath & Wolf, 1992), after-school and community-based literacy programs (Heath & Flower, 2000), and linguistically and culturally diverse learners in school (Heath, Mangiola, Schecter, & Hull, 1991).

One area of this research on family literacy explores early literacy practices and the development of literacy in preschool and K–6 years both at home and in school (see, for instance, Dyson, 1989, 1997, 2003; Snow, 1991). Handel (1999) interviewed African American women over an 8-year study of a school-based family literacy program. She found that "family literacy is a complex concept that refers to at least three types of activities: intergenerational family literacy programs . . . ; parent involvement activities that may or may not be structured programs; and naturally occurring literacy process within families as studied by researchers" (p. 8). She describes the institutional structures and resources that facilitate (or hinder) the implementation of family literacy programs in schools.

Another line of research in family literacies explores the transfer of literacy practices from schools to homes (see Hull & Shultz, 2002; Morro, 1995; Paratore, 2001; Snow & Tabors, 1996). Snow and Tabors's (1996) work identifies four types of literacy transfer among intergenerational family members: the transfer of literacy through daily functional literacy practices, orchestrated literacy practices, parents' metacommunication about literacy, and positive experiences with literacy (p. 79). Note that these transfer activities are not unidirectional but work in reciprocity with one another, particularly in immigrant families. The transfer of literacy skills from one context to another, especially when those contexts are imbued with asymmetrical power relationships, becomes crucial to understanding the dynamics of family and community literacies.

Still another line of family literacy research explores the cross-cultural influences on the integration of family and school literacy practices (e.g., Ah Nee-Benham & Stein, 2003; Delgado-Gaitan, 1988, 1990, 1996, 2001; Ladson-Billings, 1992; Mahiri, 1991, 1996, 1998; Moll, 1992, 2002; Perez, 1998, 2004; Slaughter & Epps, 1987). Many of these works share the goals of Gregory and Williams (2000), whose work was "born out of the wish to dispel deep-seated myths concerning the teaching and learning of reading in urban, multicultural areas" (p. xvi).

This research points to a number of questions related to family and community literacies as they develop in the home and community, transfer to public realms, and influence language policy and standards, curricular development, and identity formation. These questions include but are not limited to the following:

- In what ways do individuals and communities use language and literacy to negotiate with and work within public institutions, standard language mandates, and educational policies?
- How does the acquisition of various literacies impact identity formation? In what ways do communities use linguistic difference to shape their culture and social organization?
- In what ways might universities and schools apply this research in the day-to-day activities of knowledge making and teaching?

These questions circle around the most recent iteration of the great divide, the divide between definitions of literacy that arise from differential valuations of school and community literacies (Hull & Shultz, 2002). Cook-Gumperz and Gumperz (1981) prophetically pointed to this growing great divide in a review of literacy scholarship: "By narrowing the definition . . . we make the literacy experience discontinuous with the practices of everyday life for most people" (p. 108). The discontinuity between school-based, standardized, and testable definitions of literacy and the kinds of literate and discursive practices taking place in homes and communities is the basis for Gee's (1996, 2001) theoretical differentiation between secondary and primary Discourses. This discontinuity also has been seen in recent work around the topic of borderlands, contact zones, and gatekeeping interactions, and identity formation within these. Finally, this discontinuity has played out in language policies applied from top-down mandates and the ways these applications and mandates are contested, resisted, and obviated. The study of discontinuities has been central to the research done on family and community literacies, and these studies might be grouped loosely in terms of power, identity, and pedagogy.

POWER IN FAMILY AND COMMUNITY LITERACY: MANDATES, PROGRAMS, AND RESISTANCE

The focus of research into adult literacy developed into two interrelated lines of work: research into top-down literacy mandates, language policies, and adult literacy education programs, and research into local, situated, literacy practices. Armed with Street's (1984) ideological model, work investigating adult literacy revealed how ideologies of literacy that come from top-down policies were often in conflict with the ideologies of groups "on the ground." Research into adult literacy in the past 20 years reveals the ways that language and literacy are used to negotiate structures (and ideologies) of power. This research helps scholars in family and community literacy to understand why many adult literacy programs fail and how those programs and literacy policy might be re-imagined to better meet the needs of those they are meant to serve.

This new concern with power was related to larger theoretical movements in language studies. The social turn in linguistics led to a concern with how language is related to a society's hierarchies of power. In addition, across language-related disciplines such as literature and cultural studies, the "posts" (postmodernism, post-structuralism, postcolonialism) began to deconstruct accepted notions of the way the world worked. Postcolonialism and studies of colonialism and its effects on language influenced researchers' understandings of language and power.

Thus, the past 20 years of adult literacy research have revealed a push–pull dynamic between top-down and bottom-up ideologies of literacy. As researchers have investigated adult literacy programs and policies, many of which are well-intentioned, research has revealed ideologies of literacy that rely on a certain construction of adult "illiterates," one that views the very people it is trying to help as "deficient." Situated research into local practices of literacy around the world has revealed quite the opposite: that communities have ideologies and practices of literacy that meet their social needs. Imposition of other ideologies of literacy often has led to resistance by those local communities. Literacy programs, as ambassadors of top-down literacy ideologies, would be more successful if they were in tune with local literacy practices. Situated knowledge of how literacy is patterned by different cultural needs and gender roles is key, then, to the success of adult literacy programs. Some questions of concern to adult literacy researchers include, but are not limited to the following:

- Who defines literacy? For what purposes? In what situations?
- Who is calling for improved adult literacy, for whom, and why?
- How might a group's literacy level increase that group's access to structures of power, and how might it not matter?
- How do "illiterate adults" access literacy through unsanctioned means?
- How do literacy practices differ across cultures, by gender, and between school and home, and whose literacy practices are valued by mainstream society?
- How might issues of power, gender, and culture be at work in adult literacy programs, and how can these programs be re-imagined with a focus on equity and justice?

Constructing Adult Illiteracy

Top-down ideologies of literacy tend to be based on the definition of literacy of those in government, educational institutions, and popular media. In this view from above, literacy is constructed as essential to economic development, equality, liberty, freedom, and democracy. Far from being a socially situated practice, literacy is seen as a skill that can be acquired much like any other "thing." In this ideology of literacy, simply becoming literate will give one access to structures of power, including increased economic opportunity.

Through study of adults developing literacy, this ideology has been critiqued. Rockhill (1993) explores common beliefs about literacy in light of her ethnographic research with Hispanic immigrant women in southern California. She looks at how literacy has been constructed by media and the government as having power (as if it is an autonomous thing, something that one get can get, something that exists outside people, cultures, economies, etc.) and contrasts this with the lived experience of the women in her study. She finds that this dominant definition of literacy characterizes those who do not obtain literacy as having a lack of motivation and threatening freedom and democracy by undermining economic productivity and civic participation. Rockhill critiques this conceptualization of literacy as a kind of "moral panic" because it relies on a characterization of "illiterates" as immoral, lazy, and, at worst, threatening.

From the perspective of those who study adult literacy development, though, this negative characterization is problematic. Lytle (2001) worked in adult literacy programs and studied adult literacy development to complicate the current public conceptions of "illiterate adults" as lost, shamed, deficient people. She describes how adults that enter literacy programs come with their own experiences and strategies for teaching themselves to read and write for their own purposes. Lytle recommends that literacy researchers "question prevailing assumptions about the capabilities and lifestyles of less-than-literate adults, unpack conflicting conceptions of literacy, and explore what adult learners and educators count as learning" (p. 378). Adult literacy happens in a complex social context, as part of a community or network of people living their lives. Rather than looking at literacy as "skills and tasks," Lytle explains how one must see literacy as "practices and critical reflection/action." As researchers explore what "counts as learning," they must look beyond school practices and into cultural and social patterns of interaction that adults bring to literacy learning (p. 386). The purpose of this work is to challenge dominant definitions of literacy.

The Deficit/Difference Model in Adult Literacy Studies

The conflict between dominant and marginalized ideologies of literacy relies, in part, on the construction of adults learning literacy as "less than." The assumption here is that "illiterate" adults either have no literacy practices (they are a blank slate) or value and practice reading and writing in ways that are less likely to ensure their success in school and the economy. In the late 1960s and through the 1970s, many researchers, looking for an answer to why minority students did poorly in schools, compared cultural differences between mainstream and minority family and community language practices. They asserted that White, mainstream children did well in schools because their family and community's cultural practices were similar to those found in school learning. Minority students' families and culture, on the other hand, did not support and, in fact, undermined school success. This well-intentioned line of thinking gave rise to programs such as Head Start, which attempted to make up for this cultural "difference" through early childhood education. It also gave rise to many adult and family literacy programs that, again, sought to improve the chances of minority students by educating parents out of the "culture of poverty" (see Lewis [1959, 1961] for a discussion of this concept). The goal was school success for minority students—a noble one.

Although noble in its goals, the deficit/difference model was dangerous because it spurred misconceptions of "adult illiterates" and was culturally biased, and research since the early 1980s has helped to show why. Ethnographic research into non-mainstream communities (e.g., Heath, 1983) began to reveal how definitions of literacy matter. With a more practice-based focus in research, scholars began to see the dangers in the deficit model. In addition, much Chicano/a and Latino/a research in the past 20 years has focused on how this model devalues the parenting styles of Mexican American families. To the participants in Valdés's (1996) ethnographic study of Mexican American families living in a Texas border town, raising "successful" children meant they were to get a job in which they did not have to do physical labor and were able to contribute back to the success of the family as a unit. This value stood in opposition to mainstream goals that emphasize higher education for children and individual achievement. In addition, Valdés showed how the parents' definition of being "bien educado" was to be well-mannered (of which schooling was just a part), while the mainstream definition was to be academically successful. Valdés showed the cultural mismatch between school and home and how the cultural beliefs of the families were important and, although different, by no means "deficient."

By hanging all hopes for minority children's school success on their parents' literacy practices, programs that were aimed at changing the literacy practices of parents ignored the other important literacy practices that children learned at home. Gregory and Williams (2000) studied literacy acquisition in two socioeconomically distinct communities in London: Spitalfields and the City. This qualitative study of more than 50 people gathered data from across generations to see how literacy was acquired as historical, economic, and community changes occurred. Gregory and Williams found that their study challenged four myths about literacy: (1) economic poverty means poor literacy skills, (2) reading success in children is a result of parental literacy practices, (3) a difference between home and school language will mean early reading failure, and (4) there is one correct way to teach literacy. This qualitative study provided evidence that all four of these myths are false. The message of the study is that although parents might not be following a literacy practice at home that educators accept as helpful to children's literacy development (e.g., reading stories), they are adding to the literacy repertoire of students in other important ways, ways that may be specific to their family's cultural background. The deficit model ignores and devalues these ways by defining literacy *only* as the type of literacy valued by schools.

Local Literacy Practices

Hand-in-hand with research that has critiqued dominant ideologies of literacy for their reliance on the deficit model, has been research that focuses on understanding local literacy practices around the world. Documenting local literacy practices that meet the literacy needs of communities complicates the top-down ideology that advocates one type of literacy for all (Street, 1995). A chief advocate of this type of research is Street (2001a), who argues that "research . . . has a task to do in making visible the complexity of local, everyday, community literacy practices and challenging dominant stereotypes and myopia" (p. 7). Using ethnographies of communities around the world, Street argues against the assumptions that literacy automatically will empower, facilitate jobs, or create social mobility (Street, 1993, 2001b).

Aikman (2001) studied Harakmbut people of the Amazonian region of Peru. The Harakmbut recognize their need for Spanish literacy in certain domains, especially in dealing with legal issues related to protecting their community boundaries from settlers. The Harakmbut reject development based on capitalist models of production, which the United Nations advocates. Instead they try to promote their own "self-development" based on their indigenous values.

In situations such as this, literacy programs become places where dominant ideologies and discourses are resisted by local people. People appropriate texts for their own purposes, learning literacy in specific domains for specific economic or legal ends, rather than becoming literate for participation in the world market or the dominant economy. Thus, "local participants . . . pick out from the official dominant development program those items which they feel will be 'really useful' to them, while rejecting the whole package with its power implications" (Street, 2001a, pp. 215–216). He concluded by saying that as long as the literacy programs of dominant groups impose their idea of literacy on subaltern groups, those programs will not be successful. New literacy programs need to enhance what local people's literacy practices already are, not impose a different kind of literacy.

Learning Literacy Outside School

In resisting dominant ideologies of literacy, there is not always a clear rejection of imposed forms of literacy. As mentioned earlier, there is a push–pull between dominant and marginalized ideologies of literacy. Oppressed groups may simultaneously resist and call for access to dominant genres of power, as the Harakmbut did in Aikman's (2001) study (cf. Marshall, 1993). Besnier (1995) terms these "incipient literacies," an emerging use of literacy that is not to be confused with "restricted literacy" but is to be seen as a "multifarious phenomenon right from its inception, upon which members of the 'receiving' group can exert agentive control by shaping it and defining its meaning in novel and locally relevant ways" (p. 173). Often this complex resistance/insistence involves finding routes to literacy acquisition that subvert dominant means of delivering that literacy instruction, such as in schooling and formal literacy programs.

Various unsanctioned paths to literacy emerge as individuals seek entry into the literate world. Brandt's (2001a, 2001b) work identifying sponsors of literacy shows the process by which individuals learn literacy from others outside of school. Brandt studied the life histories of 80 participants. She defines her concept of "sponsors" of literacy as: "any agents, local or distant, concrete or abstract, who enable, support, teach, model, as well as recruit, regulate, suppress, or withhold literacy—and gain advantage by it in some way" (2001a, p. 19). Sponsors can be people or other entities, including market forces.

Key to research in this area of adult literacy acquisition is the notion that literacy is used for communicative purposes and, when needed, will develop on its own accord (Cook-Gumperz & Gumperz, 1981; Moss, 1994, 2003; Purcell-Gates & Waterman, 2000; Szwed, 2001). Farr (2001) documented one such case when she studied a social network of Mexican immigrants in Chicago. Farr explores the ways in which the men in the community learned literacy *lírico*, or outside school. Many first began this process when they were taken out of school in Mexico to work on a ranch or farm. A friend would teach them the alphabet, and the boys would use materials such as cigarette cartons to practice reading. In Chicago as adults, they needed to write letters home as an important way to maintain social ties. With the help of another community member, the men would develop their literacy skills in order to write home. Farr stresses that if literacy is needed for a certain social function, some way to meet this need will be created with or without the help of formal schooling, as happened with the men in her study. Although these literacy practices may emerge spontaneously from the social roles of men, the social roles of women actually may mitigate against the development of spontaneous literacy practices among women.

Gender and Adult Literacy

Researchers have been seeking to understand how literacy practices might be different for men and women, and how these differences might be overlooked by literacy programs and policies that see literacy learning as "one size fits all." Gender roles may indeed affect adult literacy development in a variety of ways. Power relationships within families as well as a group's sanctioned gender roles may limit women's access to literacy learning. In her life history study of approximately 50 Spanish-speaking immigrant women and men, Rockhill (1993) found that although the women wanted to learn English literacy, several factors severely limited their ability to do so. Women's confinement to the home limited their access to social situations and to school, where they would have opportunities to practice English. Many women were forced to be home-bound because of their husbands, who often were physically abusive. The husbands did not want their wives to have contact with the outside world, or to be in situations where they might meet men—especially American men—and thus prevented their wives from learning English as a form of control. Although women tried to resist by attending school, often their obligations at home kept them from coming to class.

For those women who can attend adult literacy programs, their reasons for doing so may be very different from what program designers anticipate. Literacy programs can function as sanctioned places for adult women to meet outside the home, and thus may provide opportunities for social interaction that otherwise may be limited by work, household, and child-rearing obligations. Stromquist (1997) studied an adult literacy program in São Paulo, Brazil, called MOVA (Movimento de Alfabetizacão de Jovens e Adultos). She found that a major function of the literacy class in the lives of the female students was as a sanctioned place to socialize, talk about their problems, and build relationships. Cuban (2003) found similar results in an in-depth study of women in a Hawaiian adult education program that attempted to re-educate its students for a new service-based economy. The program was a social space and a place where the women could learn to become "somebody." The women in Cuban's study sought literacy learning and stayed in the program not for "re-education," but because they felt they needed literacy in their roles as caregivers. Finally, Handel's (1999) study of seven mothers who participated in the Newark family literacy program found similar motivations for literacy learning. While program directors thought that the motivation for participation in the program would be literacy development, the motivation cited by most women was social/relational, meaning they came to socialize with others in the group and then develop their relationships with their family at home through literacy activities. Thus, top-down notions of the purposes and goals of literacy programs are altered by participants on the ground level and, ultimately, can be reinvented by participants to meet gender-specific needs.

Because factors such as gender are not considered in dominant ideologies of literacy, research into gender and literacy seems to reveal surprising results. Women use literacy programs in ways that differ greatly from the intentions of program designers. The local will always transform, appropriate, and resist dominant ideologies of literacy. This shift in thinking from a focus on top-down literacy demands to situated attention to adults' need for literacy and their motivations for seeking it, would create programs that better served women and culturally diverse students.

Adult Literacy Policy and Programs

As we have seen, literacy is expected of adults and especially parents, yet adult literacy programs often fail to meet the needs of students. This disjuncture obtains partially because dominant ideologies of literacy have been imposed on adults who may have very different literacy ideologies and practices of their own. Research in the field of adult literacy in the past 20 years has shown that these practices are affected by culture and gender. Because adult literacy programs often focus on literacy-as-skills, they often miss issues of differential access to literacy practices by men and women. Also, they often overlook culturally or linguistically different, although no less valuable, practices.

As research has uncovered the ways that adult literacy varies by language, gender, and culture, so, too, has it exposed structures of power reified in seemingly benign calls for adult and family literacy. The relation between literacy and power is far more complex than the common ideology that "literacy = power." This simple belief obscures the way that literacy has different uses and purposes for women and men, and across different cultural groups, and ultimately may blame the marginalized (labeled "illiterates") for their own marginalization. The research referenced here shows how calls for literacy need examination. The question, "Whose literacy?" is ultimately one of power, and those who define literacy are often the powerful. As the field of adult literacy moves forward, these issues of gender, culture, and power will be at its heart.

How researchers think about family and community literacy has much to do with their conceptions of adult literacy. Constructions of adult literacy (or illiteracy) illustrate the ways in which families and communities with other-than-mainstream literacy practices are conceived of in dominant ideologies of literacy. At the same time, research into adult literacy suggests that communities are not passive in their responses to these dominant ideologies. Quite the opposite: Certain literacy practices, demands for access to dominant discourses, and rejections of dominant ideologies of literacy can be forms of resistance. Literacy practices, like language, are one way that people in different groups construct and perform their identity. The relationship between literacy practices and identity is explored in the next section.

IDENTITY IN FAMILY AND COMMUNITY LITERACIES

As qualitative research expanded significantly between 1983 and 2003 in the area of family and community literacies, much of it emphasized the impact that identity formation has on literacy acquisition and vice versa. When people identify with mainstream cultural attitudes toward literacy, they're more motivated to learn fluency with these; they're more likely to feel comfortable in contexts outside the home and community; and they're likely to gain a foothold in economic structures where fluency with mainstream literacy is demanded. To couple Gee's (1996) idea of an identity tool kit with Ogbu and Simon's (1998) idea of voluntary and involuntary minorities, fluency in various secondary discourses can be gained more easily if the person values the mainstream culture, wants to be fluent in the predominant discursive conventions, and wants to identify with mainstream discourse communities. The extent to which a person identifies with a discourse community might well influence the extent to which that person is able to adopt and adapt the discursive conventions of that community.

The concept of identity politics strives to explain how and why people define themselves publicly and privately as they do, including consideration of the contexts in which they form such identities. Identity is constantly shifting—both the identity one chooses to have as well as the identity one chooses to display, identities that both influence and are influenced by the actions, attitudes, and identities of others. Identity is displayed in various ways, including through literacy practices. What one reads and writes is influenced by one's identity, as well as by one's concept—conscious or not—of how this identity fits into various contexts.

The idea of identity politics as it relates to family and community literacy research between 1983 and 2003 begins with Heath (1983; Heath & McLaughlin, 1993). She explores the question, "What are the effects of the preschool home and community environments on the learning of those language structures and uses which were needed in classrooms and job settings?" (p. 4). A subquestion explores "why habitual ways of talking and listening did not always seem to work" in the schools and the mills of the communities she studied (p. 2). These questions relate to identity formation in that they begin to explore how one's literacy both impacts and is impacted by one's identity, an idea that has pedagogical implications. Her book represents 10 years of work conducting an ethnography in two working-class communities of Blacks and Whites, whom she compared with "townspeople"—the "blacks and whites of the mainstream middle class" (p. 10). She saw her main job as accounting for "the ways of living, eating, sleeping, worshiping, using space, and filling time which surrounded these language learners" (p. 3). She found very different uses of language in the homes of preschool children, a result of differing cultural patterns. Also, "the language socialization process" is multifaceted and cultural patterns greatly affect using written and oral language (p. 344). Thus, the children were prepared for school in quite different ways.

The concept of identity politics is central to family and community literacies. How people learn to read and write their lives depends very much on how they see themselves in contextualized experiences. How people construct themselves with text helps scholars understand family and community literacies, especially as it relates to the ideas of dual consciousness and alliance building, while maintaining different ways of negotiating personalities and power.

Such power negotiation, however, is complicated and takes time. For example, class, gender, and sexuality composition researchers Gibson, Marinara, and Meem (2000) explain that "identity is constructed of memory and experience" (p. 91). And teacher educators/researchers Huber and Whelan (1999) discuss identity as a "story to live by" (p. 382). They state that "a sense of fluidity shapes our story to live by as it is composed over time, recognizing the multiplicity of situations and experiences we embody" (p. 382). Qualitative studies in family and community literacies try to understand the various contexts in which people acquire literacy and the various stories that people live by, and try to characterize how these contexts influence and are influenced by power relationships and identity. For example, Hesford (1999) asserts that identity politics "has put autobiography and self-representation at the center of campus" (pp. xxiii–xxiv). This idea of self-representation is taken a step further by researchers who study communities that historically have been marginalized and whose literacy practices have been undervalued.

Several of the family and community literacy studies reviewed below demonstrate the complications of performed identities as they relate to literate practices. The idea that people perform multiple and changing identities, an important concept for literacy educators to understand, is echoed by Gibson and colleagues (2000), Clarke (1994), Spack (1997), and Chaput (2000). It is important for literacy educators and researchers to keep in mind Kerby's assertion that "nowadays, identity formation is conceived as an ongoing process that involves the interpretation and reinterpretation of experiences as one lives through them" (quoted in Beijaard, Verloop, & Vermunt, 2000, p. 750). Personal experiences, shaped as they are by social and cultural contexts, are interpreted by individuals who, in the process of doing so, shape their identities. The importance of context is central in the study of community and family literacies. Moss (1994) asserts and demonstrates the ways that literacy must be defined in context. Like Heath (1983), Moss (2003) argues that schools, let alone scholars in composition and rhetoric, "must understand the role of community" (p. 4). She argues that "teachers and administrators concerned with literacy and language instruction, [must] . . . find bridges between the community and the classroom . . . [and] cannot place the burden on the students alone to recognize and find strategies to negotiate their ways through sites of conflict and common ground" (p. 158). Her claims concern the relation of power and literacy discussed in the preceding section, especially as the issues relate to the idea of negotiating resistance and solidarity. Part of this negotiation is grounded in identity politics.

In short, identity politics is integral to development of literacy skills because it enables people to find a place to speak in hegemonic systems. As Cook-Gumperz (1993, p. 340) points out, "Language is always spoken (and written for that matter) out of a particular *social identity* (or social role), an identity that is a composite of words, actions, and (implied) beliefs, values, and attitudes" (quoted in Cushman, 1998, p. 17; emphasis in original). Cushman (1998) asserts that identity politics combines with cultural politics to enable people to negotiate "the vast middle ground between domination and resistance" (p. 230). Several researchers in family and community literacies drew on identity politics in this way between 1983 and 2003, particularly as it relates to individuals and communities. In the main, this research was published as autobiography and ethnography, and each provides important insights into family and community literacies.

Many have written narratives to discuss teaching, learning, and the acquisition of literacy (e.g., Belcher & Connor, 2001; Bishop, 1997; Canagarajah, 1997; Holdstein & Bleich, 2001; Rodriguez, 1982). Rose's (1989) "autobiography, case study—commentary" (p. 8) is "a book about the abilities hidden by class and cultural barriers" (p. xi); it is about those who cross "educational boundaries" (p. 9). He discusses his own education and introduction to teaching via the Teacher Corps, which required teacher aids to know the communities and homes of their students. His main contention that "hope fosters . . . learning" (p. 242) shows how a strong sense of identity—current and growing—as evidenced by a "hopeful" outlook, leads to increased literacy, and that increased literate activities concurrently can increase one's hope, especially in marginalized socioeconomic classes (cf. Anzaldua's [1987] exploration of similar class identity politics from a *mestiza* feminist perspective).

How students shape and forge their identities within the influence of those around them, including school systems, is explored also by Gilyard (1991), whose autobiographical narrative analyzes how he acquired Standard English skills and sociolinguistic competence, which he defines, quoting Philips, as "knowledge of when and in what style one must present one's utterances" (p. 12). He uses his experiences in acquiring his various voices to assert that "a pedagogy is successful only if it makes knowledge or skill achievable while at the same time allowing students to maintain their own sense of identity" (p. 11). How one perceives oneself in relation to others affects how one will interact with others, whether exerting agency, resisting authority, or acquiescing to the status quo. Learning literacy has a lot to do with understanding one's relationship to authority within families and communities. In Gilyard's case, this was manifested in the following way: "What has been commonly referred to by educators as 'failure' to learn Standard English is more accurately termed an act of resistance: Black students affirming, through Black English, their sense of self in the face of a school system and society that deny the same" (p. 164).

Gilyard's exploration of sociolinguistic competence also is taken up by Villanueva (1993). A major theme of his narrative is the rhetorical power play of code switching, using "different rules in different places" (p. 8). As he relates his honing of different literacies, Villanueva asserts that people "need to cling to [their] various collectives— Puerto Rican, Latino, of color, academic, American—and they need not be mutually exclusive if we consider them critically, and if we accept that we carry contradictions" (p. 143). Villanueva's (1993), Gilyard's (1991), and Rose's (1989) books are all concerned with how a disenfranchised person learns to grapple with a powerful code. In other words, one can keep one's cultural identity, yet succeed outside one's culture.

Studies such as these are important to understanding identity politics and family and community literacies, especially in illustrating how this sense of dual consciousness can be a tool of empowerment and encouraged and built upon in the classroom. As N. Scott Momaday asserts, "We are what we imagine. Our very existence consists in our imagination of ourselves. Our best destiny is to imagine, at least, completely, who and what, and *that* we are" (quoted in Powell, 2002, p. 399; emphasis in original). Viewing work in family and community literacies through the theoretical lens of identity politics allows literacy acquisition to be seen as intimately and intricately related to identity politics.

How one perceives who one is greatly affects how one will use and acquire literacy. However, Akinnaso (2001) argues that studies of people's and specific societies' choices of literacy uses are more relevant and important than research that seeks an all-encompassing or universal answer. He argues that literacy changes one's identity with oneself and others, supporting his argument by relating how he became literate and how it affected his family and village in Nigeria. Various researchers have heeded his call by going beyond the individual autobiography to explore community literacy via ethnography, a move that makes sense as an individual's literacy is developed within discursive communities. His study also links to Smitherman's (1977/1986) and those of others discussed below in that it explores the give-and-take of literacy transfer and acquisition and its effects on how one comes to identify with peer and new groups. Gee (1996) argues that when people use language, they need to "say or write the right thing in the right way while playing the right social role and (appearing) to hold the right values, beliefs, and attitudes" (p. 526). Thus, fluency with literacy and social discourses is all about identity politics—negotiating our own and others' perceptions of who we are and how that enables us to use literacy to our advantage. While the individual is an important site of study for family and community literacies—because through these accounts, scholars can learn up close the personal stakes involved in gaining prestige dialects—studies of community literacies are also important.

Smitherman (1977/1986) discusses Black English, its origins, and its implications for teaching. She asserts that Black English has enabled African Americans to "create a culture of survival in an alien land, and as a by-product has served to enrich the language of all Americans" (pp. 2–3). She discusses how Black speech is essential to identity formation. Smitherman (1977/1986) declares that "in thus taking the subject of Black Language off the library shelves and out of ivory and ebony towers into the public domain, this celebration of Black Language has influenced popular discussion and debate about Black English and the role of language in the formation of positive identity and self-esteem" (p. 244). Smitherman (2000) extends her inquiry in a collection of essays that focuses on "the interrelationship between language, education, and culture in African America (p. xii).

Moss (2003) also explores the language of a particular identity and culture as she looks at "the use of language and texts in the church" (p. 1), thereby "extending the discussion of literacy acquisition among African Americans" by exploring "the relation between how language is used and what counts as literacy" (p. 2), two important concepts in identity politics, as they affect literacy acquisition, especially in what counts as literacy. She points out that "what constitutes 'community literacy' . . . does not necessarily match what is known as *school literacy*" (p. 3; emphasis in original). Mentioning several important ethnographic studies of literacy in nonacademic settings (including Weinstein-Shr's [1994] study of Philadelphia Hmong, Philips's [1983] study of the Warm Springs Indian Reservation, and Taylor & Dorsey-Gaines's [1988] study of poor, urban New Jersey African American families), Moss calls for additional studies of community literacies. She points out that now, more scholars recognize that the use of literacy differs from one community to another, but not many see that the definition of literacy also varies. Like many of the other researchers described here, she also calls on schools to better recognize communities' roles in literacy development. Schools should draw on the family and community literacies that students bring to the classroom in order to help them understand the identity politics involved in negotiating power and in acquiring additional literacies.

Mahiri (1998) shares this emphasis, "especially regarding marginalized groups" (p. 1). He argues that teachers

> have considerable agency to transform key aspects of schooling by instituting classroom curricula and teaching practices that can help students to more clearly understand, effectively negotiate, and ultimately critique and change the sociocultural, economic, and political conditions that contextualize and often constrain their lives and learning. (p. 4)

Students thus will better grasp how an understanding of identity politics will add to their literacies. Directing his suggestions at high school and college writing courses, Mahiri draws "on findings and implications from four research projects to suggest ways that classroom discourse, curricula, and culture can be changed to enhance processes of teaching and learning by building more powerfully on authentic experiences of students" (p. 4). To support his points, he draws on four studies, three of which are classroom-based. Mahiri indicates that some of these findings can be used in schools "to help students develop their unique personal voices in learning to write and in using writing to learn" (p. 53), which the rest of the book explores (he does point out that his study is of men and boys outside school, especially in a coaching situation, which may not be transferable to school situations or to women and girls; however, he feels that some transfer is possible). Helping students develop their personal voices would foster a better understanding of how they could use literacy to accomplish their goals, which relates to Rose's concept of "hope," discussed earlier. Another male-oriented study is Cintron's (1997) ethnography in which he explores "how a variety of people made or displayed themselves and how these markings were influenced by systemic power differences" and "how [they] . . . were received by different audiences" (p. x).

Other studies focused on the community literacies of women and girls (some of which were discussed earlier) as these related to identity politics and literacy development, such as Cushman's (1998, 1999) activist ethnographic study of a community of African American women, young adults, and children who used oral, literate, and analytic strategies—the "deep games of power inner city residents played with their language and critical consciousness" (1988, p. x)—"in their day-to-day efforts to obtain food, shelter, resources, and respect from [the] wider society's institutions" (p. xi). Other studies in family and community literacies include Lindquist's (1999, 2002, 2004) ethnographic study of a working-class bar and class-influenced rhetorics in the Chicago area; Guerra's (1998) ethnography of transnational Mexicanos; and Herr and Anderson's (1997) study of "the student–school relationship from a cross-national perspective" in terms of identity formation (p. 45). Along the lines of making meaning in public spaces, Powell (2002) shows how "some of us read and listen from a different space, and . . . as a discipline, it is time we all learned to hear that difference" (p. 398). Highlighting that difference, Pough (2002) discusses helping students develop empowering rhetoric using Black Panther Party documents (thereby bridging community and classroom). Furthermore, Lyons (2000) defines "rhetorical sovereignty" as "the inherent right and ability of *peoples* to determine their own communicative needs and desires[:] the goals, modes, styles, and languages of public discourse" that suit them (p. 449; emphasis in original). Likewise, Jacqueline

Jones Royster (1996) explores cross-boundary discourse and personal challenge as one negotiates identity, establishes authority, and develops "strategies for action, carrying forth intent with a particular type of agency" (p. 29). She further (2000) discusses how "the merging . . . of . . . identities (personal, historical, social, professional, even political) gave rise to a particular type of process for the formation of ethos among these women as writers and speakers in public domains" (p. 210).

Overall, such studies in family and community literacies help to better understand identity politics: how and why people define themselves publicly and privately within various contexts as they do. In turn, identity politics helps to understand how one acquires and uses literacy. The researchers reviewed in this section all demonstrate that schools need to understand the transformative power of community literacies and reflect that understanding in classroom pedagogies.

IMPLICATIONS FOR TEACHERS, TEACHER EDUCATORS, AND LITERACY RESEARCHERS

Thus far, this chapter has chronicled the research done during the past 20 years on the literacy practices of various groups of people in a variety of out-of-school contexts. Whether focused on African American males in an urban area (Mahiri, 1998), *Mexicano* families in a Latino/a community (Cintron, 1997), or a family in a White working-class community (Purcell-Gates, 1995), virtually every study has one common finding: Complex and multiple literacy practices flourish in out-of-school contexts, regardless of gender, race, or class. However, despite this central finding, a great divide exists. Much as the area of research in family and community literacy began as a result of another divide, this time between the sophisticated literacy practices of individuals, families, and communities, and those of their school and academic achievement. The divide necessitates a shift in the discussion. This section, therefore, moves from a discussion about the research that has been done in out-of-school contexts to one about the implications, limitations, and possibilities of this body of research for teachers, teacher educators, literacy researchers, and curriculum policy makers.

At the core of the divide between out-of-school literacy skills and school achievement is the following question: How is it that students come into classrooms with the literacy abilities to perform complex literacy tasks in certain contexts and consistently fail in school literacy tasks, many of which often do not even require as sophisticated an aptitude and performance as are needed in the out-of-school contexts (Au, 1993; Barton & Hamilton, 1998; Dyson, 2003; Gee, 1996, 2003; Morrell, 2004; Perez, 1998)? This question has particular relevance for students whose individual, home, and cultural literacy practices differ significantly from the literacy practices legitimized in schools and other mainstream institutions. Much of the research chronicled throughout this chapter has worked to debunk many of the myths and misperceptions educators may hold toward their language-minority students, and, as Hull and Schultz (2002) note, this research has the potential to help teachers and teacher educators see students who have linguistic and literacy practice "differences" as "as capable [of] learn[ing] and do[ing] in the world" (p. 1) as their peers whose linguistic and literacy backgrounds more closely match those of school.

An essential element for students' academic success is teachers' attitudes toward students' home languages, literacy practices, and cultural experiences (Au, 1993;

Cook-Gumperz & Gumperz, 1981; Gregory & Williams, 2000; Heath, 1983). Moll and Gonzalez (2001) note that the households and communities of language-minority students "are often viewed solely as places from which children must be saved or rescued, rather than places that, along with problems (as in all communities), contain valuable knowledge and experiences that can foster the children's development" (pp. 161–162). This perspective potentially can limit language-minority students' performances. Synthesizing much literacy research done in multicultural settings, Au (1993) writes, "The negative attitudes some teachers have toward students' home languages may cause students to feel alienated and resentful and eventually lead them to refuse to participate in school literacy activities" (p. 130). Through their attitudes toward their students' experiences and language—whether transmitted overtly or tacitly—teachers have the power to either draw students into the educational system or push them away from it, causing students to resist the teacher and eventually much, if not all, of the educational system. Au states, "Rejecting students' home languages can be tantamount to rejecting the students themselves. When students feel that their language is being denigrated by teachers, their resistance to teachers' negative attitudes increases, their school literacy learning slows, and they eventually drop out of school" (p. 132). Many students who perform poorly in school often are seen as deficient by their society, teachers, families, and even themselves (Perez, 1998).

Conversely, students whose home languages, cultural experiences, and literacy practices are valued and used as resources in academic contexts are more apt to succeed in school. Based on her work with Bangladeshi children in homes and schools in metropolitan England, Blackledge (2000) writes, "Children who find continuity between school and home literacy practices are more likely to become literate in the terms prescribed by the school. The literacy interactions which occur in the learning process are crucial in determining whether or not literacy learning is culturally meaningful for the child" (p. 10). In addition to teacher attitudes toward students of nonmainstream linguistic backgrounds, curricular and pedagogical practices that work to lessen the mismatch between home and school literacy and cultural practices have become a central focus for literacy researchers and educators at all levels.

This approach, often termed "culturally responsive teaching," starts with the assumption that linguistic-minority students are rich users of literacies that are different from, or "contrasting" with (Gregory & Williams, 2000), academic literacy, but not deficient. From there, culturally responsive teaching draws on students' experiences and backgrounds as resources in order to develop meaningful and congruent pedagogical practices that will foster student academic achievement. Gay (2000) defines culturally responsive teaching as "using the cultural knowledge, prior experiences, and performance styles of diverse students to make learning more appropriate and effective for them; it teaches to and through the strengths of these students" (p. 29). In their study of Navajo students in Arizona, McCarty and Dick (2003) articulate, without using the term, a purpose for their research closely aligned with that of culturally responsive teaching. Influenced by participatory action research, ESL theory and research, critical anthropological theories, and language-as-resource approaches to curricular theory, they "begin with the assumption that the Navajo Language is a tremendous intellectual, social, cultural, and scientific resource to its speakers and humankind . . . to support and capitalize on local linguistic and cultural resources, and to incorporate them into the school curriculum in transformative and liberatory ways" (p. 104).

Alongside much of the research discussed thus far in the chapter is a growing body of research that intersects out-of-school literacy practices and in-school practices and achievement (Au, 1993; Moll, 2000; Moll & Gonzalez, 2001; Morrell, 2004; Perez, 1998). Building on the work of Vygotsky (1978), many educational and literacy researchers investigate how knowledge of particular groups' literacy and cultural practices ("funds of knowledge") can inform and transform what happens in classrooms. Social constructivist theories of learning and teaching have been at the foreground of this body of research, much of which highlights the importance of drawing on the experiences and practices students bring with them into classrooms, resources often ignored or even devalued. Lee (1993), who studied African American secondary students, writes, "I propose that novice African American adolescent readers bring into classrooms a powerful intellectual tool which goes unnoticed, devalued, and untapped" (p. 13). And, as quoted in Hull and Schultz (2002), Dewey wrote over 100 years ago, "From the standpoint of the child, the great waste in the school comes from his inability to utilize the experiences he gets outside of school in any complete and free way within the school itself; while on the other hand, he is unable to apply in daily life what he is learning at school" (p. 4).

As research continues to explore various community, family, and cultural groups and unearths their literacy practices, teachers gain a sense of the funds of knowledge of various groups of people and can develop pedagogical practices that will help scaffold the experiences and skills students bring with them in order to teach them school literacy skills (Barton, Hamilton, & Ivanic, 2000). Lee's (1993) work in literary studies and pedagogical practices demonstrates how this relationship could work. Specifically, she shows how knowledge of the literacy practice of signifying in African American communities leads to pedagogical practices that draw on this knowledge to help students develop critical thinking, reading, and writing skills, particularly dealing with the concepts of metaphor and irony.

Some studies also have focused on the possibilities of bridging the gap between homes and schools by looking at how parents can become more responsive to school literacy. In her work with Bangladeshi children in homes and schools, Blackledge (2000) "investigat[ed] the specific strategies used by minority-language parents as they respond to the task of helping their children to read school books at home" (p. 61). She observed home and school literacy events of 18 families whose children were enrolled in a primary school in an inner-city area of a large metropolitan area of England (cf. Delgado-Gaitan, 1990). Blackledge shows the various strategies parents used to work around their gaps in linguistic knowledge, saying, "We have seen reports of best practice indicate that the divide between home and school is reduced when culturally appropriate texts are used, when teachers have a good knowledge of the home literacy environments of the children's families, and when parents have a definite understanding of what the school expects of them as literacy tutors" (p. 84).

The work of Moll (1992, 2000) and Moll and Gonzalez (2001) has been vital to the development of attitudes, curricular and instructional practices, and methods to ascertain students' funds of knowledge, which, they write, "can form the basis for an education that addresses broader social, academic, and intellectual issues than simply learning basic, rudimentary skills" (Moll & Gonzalez, 2001, pp. 157–158). Focusing on the education of Latino/a students in Tucson, AZ, Moll (1992) explains an interdisciplinary research project, which he calls a "'model system' for the study of literacy-related issues in both community and school settings" (pp. 211–212). His model brings together theory, research, and practice by simultaneously implementing the following three components: (1) ethnographic analysis of literacy practices and skills in a Hispanic community; (2) an after-school "lab" where teachers use the home and community literacy practices ascertained by the ethnographies in order to experiment with literacy instruction; and (3) analysis of current literacy classroom instructional methods and exploration of possible changes to instruction based on the "lab" experiments. In their work with American Indian and Alaska Native communities, McCarty and Watahomigie (2001) discuss several ways teachers "can enhance their ability to build on indigenous students' cultural, linguistic, and personal resources" (p. 497). Part of what they suggest is the development of partnerships between teachers and schools and family and community members. Drawing from the work of Lipka and Ilutsik (1996), they write that for "teachers who are from the community, and especially for those who are not, it is necessary, from time to time, to become students themselves and to explore the community together with parents, elders, and children" (pp. 499–500).

This research shows how literacy research can directly intervene in the social world it is investigating. Also, it extends the roles of teachers and researchers. Both of these points are key factors in what is needed in further research in closing the achievement gap: institutional critique and change. Even though much of the work over the past 20 years has helped to eliminate the "deficit-model" attitude and labeling and to describe the cultural practices of various cultural, familial, and community groups that can lead to pedagogical practices to help remedy the achievement gaps, the gaps still remain and in some cases are getting worse. The issue of the achievement gap is, to a large extent, political and institutional, and a persistence of looking at this gap from primarily the micro level of teacher attitudes and pedagogical practices puts a blind eye toward other, larger issues that work to perpetuate the gap in achievement and ultimately marginalize language-minority students. By their very nature, institutions impose a certain kind of literacy, particularly one that often contrasts with the literacies of nonmainstream students. Therefore, the next divide that the adult, family, and community literacy research of the past 20 years can bridge is that which exists between what the research reveals about these groups' literacy abilities and the institutions that marginalize them.

Although some literacy researchers have suggested that it is important for more attention to be given to the macro-level, institutional structures that continually promote this achievement gap, not as much research in this area actually has been done. In their study with low-income students, Barnes, Chandler, Goodman, Hemphill, and Snow (1991) acknowledge that while improved conditions either at home or at school should produce improved literacy achievements, in order to have a significant impact on literacy achievement for low-income children, intervention must occur in many sites and on many levels—homes, schools, curriculum, policy, and increased community, state, and federal support for education. In his study with African American urban high school students, Morrell (2004) notes, "In order to bring about large-scale urban educational reform that builds upon the findings of this study, several implications must be accepted by a variety of participants including educators, administrators, teacher educators, and educational policymakers" (p. 146). And even in their work with teachers, Moll and Gonzalez (2001) agree that change will not occur if teachers are not able to go beyond their classrooms.

Too narrowly focused on the micro-level issues of curriculum and instruction, perhaps researchers, teachers, and teacher educators need to look toward the institutions and sociocultural factors within which they teach and research and continue to consider how praxis, intervention, and social and institutional change might work to close the achievement gap. As Street (1984) writes:

> Research and experience in both the UK and the USA . . . is suggesting that, whatever governments may say, the only long-term way of dealing with the defined "problem" of literacy levels is to change the institutions themselves. Some radical literacy teachers, however, despairing of achieving such a goal, have opted in the short term for changing the "victims." (pp. 215–216)

And nearly 20 years later, Grabill (2001), as he theorizes a way to understand and ultimately change institutions, particularly those aimed at fostering technologically enhanced literacy skills in their participants, writes, "as Street argues, we have too long been limited to changing the 'victims' of institutional systems. To change a theory of literacy isn't difficult and changes very little. To change a literacy institution might change everything" (p. 161).

Viewing the issue of "literacy hierarchy," manifested in a variety of visible and invisible ways, most noticeably in this chapter as an achievement gap in education, as, in large part, institutional rather than pedagogical, demands the following questions: What, then, can actually be done? How does one go about changing an institution? And how might a process of institutional critique and change obviate the problems discussed throughout this chapter? No clear, easy answers exist for these questions, and the questions themselves certainly suggest possible areas for further inquiry and research. However, much work done within the past 20 years offers several generative places to begin.

Grabill's (2001) theory shows how to better understand institutions by making them more "visible" and how institutional change through participatory work from community members can not only lead to more empowered participants but also make institutions better suited to meet the needs of the people whom they are meant to help. Fundamentally, Grabill's work offers a view of literacy and literacy practices beyond the micro level of classroom practices and literacies to the macro level of the discursive structures that create the spaces for these literacies. For Grabill any change in the values of literacy and literate practices has to be done on the level of institutional change (Porter, Sullivan, Blythe, Grabill, & Miles, 2000); in fact, not pursuing institutional critique, or continuing to pursue inquiry only at the level of classrooms, teachers, and students, actually might be damaging for members of communities that are served by autonomous, detached institutions that legitimize and marginalize certain literacies.

What Grabill's (2001) work offers, then, is a "critical rhetoric" for institutional critique and (re)design that values and draws on local, vernacular knowledge and literacies in order to co-construct, through a dialogic relationship with outside people, the institutions meant to serve them. This co-construction of knowledge and dialogic relationship necessitates that those who work with community members enter the conversations as learners and not solely as the ones with all the answers. Drawing on the work of Barton and Hamilton (1998), Grabill makes the point that "those participating in the construction of community-based programs must be open to seeing and understanding the everyday literacies of their communities and local institutions" (p. 104). Only through this collaborative process and "solidarity" can institutional redesign work to empower its participants and also better serve the community for which it is designed. Freire (2001), in his work in adult literacy programs, also sees this collaboration as an essential element for effective literacy programs. He explains how one of the most difficult aspects of the programs is the training of the teams of coordinators, "the creation of a new attitude—that of dialogue (a relationship between two Subjects), so absent in our own upbringing and education" (p. 625). Participation of local community members, a valuing of their literacies by those who work with them, and a dialogic relationship are essential elements to effective institutional critique and change.

Perhaps the clearest examples of possibilities for and realities of institutional change during the past 20 years of scholarship, particularly in composition studies, have been in the areas of service learning and action research (Adler-Kassner, Crooks, & Watters, 1997; Bacon, 1994; Cooper & Julier, 1995; Cushman, 2003; Deans, 2000; Flower, Higgins, & Peck, 2001; Flower, Long, & Higgins, 2000; Green, 2003; Herzberg, 1994; Schine, 1997; Wade, 1997). Service learning in composition studies offers various ways of bridging the gap between institutions and the literacy practices they legitimize, and the literacy practices of those they are meant to serve. As Adler-Kassner and colleagues assert, "The most immediate effect of service-learning is to rearticulate the college or university as part of rather than opposed to the local community" (p. 4). Specifically, service learning and action research exemplify the necessity of principles that make institutional critique and change, social change, praxis, and meaningful intervention possible: co-construction of knowledge, dialogic relationships, breakdown of division between academics and real-world situations, and the use and value of all knowledges to solve real-world problems.

The work of Flower, Higgins, and Peck (2001) with a community literacy program in Pittsburgh has proven to be generative in this area of scholarship. The Community Literacy Center is the site in Pittsburgh for a service learning, community and university project with a goal of collaborative problem solving in the community in which it resides. One example of social and institutional change through this work involves the student community group that investigated reasons for increased suspensions in public schools. The result of this project was a community conversation with local politicians, school board officials, students, media, and eventually a newsletter that became mandatory reading for teachers and students. One of the goals of the conversations and newsletter was to help create a new vision of education in cities, a vision that "centers on building productive intercultural relationships in which equity is established through mutual learning and the transactional practices of writing and dialogue" (p. 573).

As in Freire's (2001) work, intervention at the local, often individual level is of prime significance. Freire explains the necessity for educators in such a context to be in "solidarity" with those with whom they work and utilize a dialogic pedagogy that engages students in conversation in which they begin to "discover the value of [their] person." Or, as one man said, " 'I make shoes, and now I see that I am worth as much as the Ph.D. who writes books'" (p. 622). As one illiterate from São Paulo said, "'I want to learn to read and write so I can change the world,' for whom to know quite correctly meant to intervene in his reality" (p. 623). This literacy is not simply reading and writing but "rather an attitude of creation and re-creation, a self-transformation producing a stance of intervention in one's context" (p. 622). There-fore, the educator's role is to engage in dialogue with the illiterates about their ma-terial conditions and concrete situations and then offer them the instruments with which "they can teach themselves to read and to write" (p. 622).

The activist research that often accompanies service learning programs uses tech-niques involving dialogue and reciprocity. It avoids the traditional top-down model of education and strives to make knowledge with individuals and scholars. For Grabill (2001) action research "demands the co-definition of problems, the co-generation of knowledge, and collaborative action. It is concerned with local or community-based action, it is participatory, and it seeks to solve problems as articulated by those most in need" (p. 148). For Cushman (2003), "Activist ethnographic research insures that, at every level of the ethnographic enterprise—from data collection through the in-terpretation to write-up—the researcher and participants engage in openly negoti-ated, reciprocal, mutually beneficial relations" (p. 824).

As service learning scholarship enters its second generation, research about it continues to extend beyond when and how to implement service learning into com-position courses to questions of who participates in service learning, in what ways, and why they do so. Green (2003) is interested in theorizing how service learning is experienced by those from different groups and argues for an examination of the "gaps" between theories of service learning and those of subject positions, of race, class, gender, sexuality, and writing. Specifically, using theories of multicultural edu-cation and White privilege, Green structures her service learning projects in order to discover what the stories of the participants in those projects signify about race, class, and writing, and ultimately to consider how the explicit teaching of race, particu-larly Whiteness and social class, alters the stories participants tell about service learning and moves service learning toward social change work. Stories are also the focus of the Digital Underground Storytelling for Youth Project (DUSTY), an after-school project founded by Glynda Hull and Michaelangelo James that is housed in schools and community centers in West and East Oakland, CA (Hull & Zacher, 2004). Hull's students mentor and tutor the children and youth in this project as they create digital stories, compilations of image, text, spoken word, and audio. Students and youths alike bring their knowledge, expertise, and stories to the table in this collaborative and produce powerful representations of themselves, their families, and their com-munities. Hull and Zacher write: "What counts as literacy—and how literacy is prac-ticed—are now in historical transition, and young people like Asia [a participant in DUSTY] are at the vanguard of the creation of new cultural forms."

In addition to the potential for immediate social, cultural, and institutional critique and change, service learning programs and action research also offer oppor-tunities for transformation of the role of the public intellectual, what counts as knowl-edge, and university institutional critique. Throughout the work of most service learning scholars is the thread of the relationship and responsibility of researchers to the people they are researching, the community they are a part of, and their own institutional requirements of teaching, research, and service. Within these possibili-ties for transformation also lie limitations to this type of work: institutional limita-tions (course/term structures, discipline/department structures, evaluation procedures for professors), nontransferable consultation (Flower et al., 2001), and program sustainability (Cushman, 2002).

While the past 20 years of scholarship concerning individual, family, and community literacies has vastly broadened knowledge, attitudes, and pedagogical practices and in many ways opened up an entirely new line of scholarship, many places for further inquiry exist. As this chapter suggests, much more needs to be done on the level of institutional critique and change. How can teachers, teacher educators, and literacy researchers put their efforts into not only creating better classrooms but actually creating the larger institutions that create the classroom spaces? How can service learning programs be implemented on various levels in order to democratize the tools of inquiry, critique, and transformation?

The researchers we have reviewed show how understanding the dynamics of family and community literacies requires an understanding of the transfer of literacy skills from one context to another, especially when the discontinuities in contexts—including borderlands, contact zones, and gatekeeping interactions—are imbued with asymmetrical power relationships. These meeting places rely too often on mandated definitions of literacy that mismatch the needs, desires, and goals of the people for whom educative policies and programs are intended. Educators who pay attention to the types of practices, skills, and knowledge that students bring to the classroom can best shape curricular practices for teaching literacy. The researchers we reviewed show how increasing collaboration between community members and academics/schools might well be the ticket to fostering change that demands less identity compromising.

REFERENCES

Adler-Kassner, L., Crooks, R., & Watters, A. (Eds.). (1997). *Writing the community: Concepts and models for service-learning in composition.* Washington, DC: American Association for Higher Education.

Ah Nee-Benham, M. K. P., & Stein, W. (2003). *The renaissance of American Indian higher education: Capturing the dream.* Mahwah, NJ: Erlbaum.

Aikman, S. (2001). Literacy, languages and developments in Peruvian Amazonia. In B. Street (Ed.), *Literacy and development: Ethnographic perspectives* (pp. 103–121). London: Routledge.

Akinnaso, F. N. (2001). Literacy and individual conciousness. In E. Cushman, E. R. Kintgen, B. M. Kroll, & M. Rose (Eds.), *Literacy: A critical sourcebook* (pp. 138–155). Boston: Bedford/St. Martin's.

Anzaldua, G. (1987). *Borderlands = La frontera: The new mestiza.* San Francisco: Aunt Lute Books.

Au, K. (1993). *Literacy instruction in multicultural settings.* Belmont, CA: Wadsworth/Thomson Learning.

Bacon, N. (1994). Community service and writing instruction. *National Society for Experiential Education Quarterly, 14*(2), 47–69.

Barnes, W., Chandler, J., Goodman, I., Hemphill, L., & Snow, C. (1991). *Unfulfilled expectations: Home and school influences on literacy.* Cambridge, MA: Harvard University Press.

Barton, D., & Hamilton, M. (1998). *Local literacies: Reading and writing in one community.* London: Routledge.

Barton, D., Hamilton, M., & Ivanic, R. (Eds.). (2000). *Situated literacies: Reading and writing in context.* London: Routledge.

Beijaard, D., Verloop, N., & Vermunt, J. D. (2000). Teachers' perceptions of professional identity: An exploratory study from a personal knowledge perspective. *Teaching and Teacher Education, 16,* 749–764.

Belcher, D., & Connor, U. (Eds.). (2001). *Reflections on multiliterate lives.* Buffalo, NY: Multilingual Matters.

Bereiter, C., & Scardamalia, M. (1987). *The psychology of written composition.* Mahwah, NJ: Erlbaum.

Berliner, D., & Biddle, B. (1995). *The manufactured crisis: Myths, fraud, and the attack on America's public schools.* Reading, MA: Addison-Wesley.

Besnier, N. (1995). *Literacy, emotion, and authority:*

Reading and writing on a Polynesian atoll. Cambridge, UK: Cambridge University Press.

Bishop, W. (1997). *Teaching lives: Essays and stories.* Logan: Utah State University Press.

Blackledge, A. (2000). *Literacy, power and social justice.* Staffordshire, UK: Trentham Books.

Brandt, D. (2001a). *Literacy in American lives.* Cambridge, UK: Cambridge University Press.

Brandt, D (2001b). Sponsors of literacy. In E. Cushman, E. R. Kintgen, B. M. Kroll, & M. Rose (Eds.), *Literacy: A critical sourcebook* (pp. 555–572). Boston: Bedford/St. Martin's.

Canagarajah, A. S. (1997). Safehouses in the contact zone: Coping strategies of African-American students in the academy. *College Composition and Communication, 48,* 173–196.

Chaput, C. (2000). Identity, postmodernity, and an ethics of activism. *JAC: Journal of Composition Theory, 20*(1), 43–72.

Cintron, R. (1997). *Angels' town: Chero ways, gang life, and rhetorics of the everyday.* Boston: Beacon.

Clarke, C. (1994). "Out" outside the classroom: The co-curricular challenge. *Radical Teacher, 45,* 23–25.

Cook-Gumperz, J. (1993). Dilemmas of identity: Oral and written literacies in the making of a basic writing student. *Anthropology and Education Quarterly 24*(4), 336–356.

Cook-Gumperz, J., & Gumperz, J. (1981). From oral to written culture: The transition to literacy. In M. Farr (Ed.), *Writing: The nature, development, and teaching of written communication* (pp. 89–109). Hillsdale, NJ: Erlbaum.

Cooper, D., & Julier, L. (Eds.). (1995). *Writing in the public interest: Service learning and the writing classroom.* East Lansing: The Writing Center at Michigan State University.

Cuban, S. (2003). "So lucky to be like that, somebody care": Two case studies of women learners. *Adult Basic Education, 13*(1), 19–43.

Cushman, E. (1998). *The struggle and the tools: Oral and literate strategies in an inner city community.* Albany: State University of New York Press.

Cushman, E. (1999). Critical literacy and institutional language. *Research in the Teaching of English, 33,* 245–274.

Cushman, E. (2002). Sustainable service learning programs. *College Composition and Communication, 54,* 40–65.

Cushman, E. (2003). The public intellectual, service learning, and activist research. In V. Villanueva (Ed.), *Cross-talk in comp theory: A reader* (2nd ed.; pp. 819–828). Urbana, IL: National Council of Teachers of English.

Deans, T. (2000). *Writing partnerships: Service-learning in composition.* Urbana, IL: National Council of Teachers of English.

Delgado-Gaitan, C. (1988). *School and society: Learning content through culture.* New York: Praeger.

Delgado-Gaitan, C. (1990). *Literacy for empowerment: The role of parents in children's education.* New York: Falmer.

Delgado-Gaitan, C. (1996). *Protean literacy: Extending the discourse on empowerment.* New York: Falmer.

Delgado-Gaitan, C. (2001). *The power of community: Mobilizing for family and schooling.* Lanham, MD: Rowman & Littlefield.

Dyson, A. Haas (1989). *Multiple worlds of child writers: Friends learning to write.* New York: Teachers College Press.

Dyson, A. Haas (1997). *Writing superheroes: Contemporary childhood, popular culture, and classroom literacy.* New York: Teachers College Press.

Dyson, A. Haas (2003). *The brothers and sisters learn to write: Popular literacies in childhood and school cultures.* New York: Teachers College Press.

Farr, M. (Ed.). (1981). *Writing: The nature, development, and teaching of written communication.* Mahwah, NJ: Erlbaum.

Farr, M. (2001). En los dos idiomas: Literacy practices among Chicago Mexicans. In E. Cushman, E. R. Kintgen, B. M. Kroll, & M. Rose (Eds.), *Literacy: A critical sourcebook* (pp. 376–401). Boston: Bedford/St. Martin's.

Feenberg, A. (1991). *Critical theory of technology.* Oxford, UK: Oxford University Press.

Flower, L., Higgins, L., & Peck, W. C. (2001). Community literacy. In E. Cushman, E. R. Kintgen, B. M. Kroll, & M. Rose (Eds.), *Literacy: A critical sourcebook* (pp. 572–588). Boston: Bedford/St. Martin's.

Flower, L., Long, E., & Higgins, L. (2000). *Learning to rival: A literate practice for intellectual inquiry.* Mahwah, NJ: Erlbaum.

Freire, P. (1970). *Pedagogy of the oppressed.* New York: Herder & Herder.

Freire, P. (2001). The adult literacy process as cultural action. In E. Cushman, E. R. Kintgen, B. M. Kroll, & M. Rose (Eds.), *Literacy: A critical sourcebook* (pp. 616–628). Boston: Bedford/St. Martin's.

Gay, G. (2000). *Culturally responsive teaching: Theory, research, and practice.* New York: Teachers College Press.

Gee, J. P. (1996). *Social linguistics and literacies: Ideology in discourses* (2nd ed.). London: Taylor & Francis.

Gee, J. P. (2001). Literacy, discourse, and linguistics: Introduction and what is literacy? In E. Cushman, E. R. Kintgen, B. M. Kroll, & M. Rose (Eds.), *Literacy: A critical sourcebook* (pp. 525–544). Boston: Bedford/St. Martin's.

Gee, J. P. (2003). *What video games have to teach us about learning and literacy.* New York: Palgrave MacMillan.

Geertz, C. (1983). *Local knowledge: Further essays in interpretative anthropology.* New York: Basic Books.

Gibson, M., Marinara, M., & Meem, D. (2000). Bi, butch, and bar dyke: Pedagogical performances of class, gender, and sexuality. *College Composition and Communication, 52,* 69–95.

Gilyard, K. (1991). *Voices of the self: A study of language competence.* Detroit: Wayne State University Press.

Goody, J. (Ed.). (1968). *Literacy in traditional societies.* Cambridge, UK: Cambridge University Press.

Goody, J. (1971). *The domestication of the savage mind.* Cambridge, UK: Cambridge University Press.

Grabill, J. (2001). *Community literacy programs and the politics of change.* Albany: State University of New York Press.

Green, A. E. (2003). Difficult stories: Service-learning, race, class, and whiteness. *College Composition and Communication, 55*(2), 276–301.

Gregory, E., & Williams, A. (2000). *City literacies: Learning to read across generations and cultures.* London: Routledge.

Guerra, J. C. (1998). *Close to home: Oral and literate practices in a transnational Mexicano community.* New York: Teachers College Press.

Gumperz, J. (Ed.). (1982a). *Discourse strategies.* Cambridge, UK: Cambridge University Press.

Gumperz, J. (Ed.). (1982b). *Language and social identity.* Cambridge, UK: Cambridge University Press.

Gumperz, J., & Hymes, D. (1972). *Directions in sociolinguistics: The ethnography of communication.* New York: Holt, Rinehart & Winston.

Handel, R. (1999). *Building family literacy in an urban community.* New York: Teachers College Press.

Havelock, E. (1976). *Origins of Western literacy.* Toronto: Ontario Institute for Studies in Education.

Havelock, E. (1982). *The literate revolution in Greece and its cultural consequences.* Princeton, NJ: Princeton University Press.

Heath, S. B. (1983). *Ways with words: Language, life, and work in communities and classrooms.* Cambridge, UK: Cambridge University Press.

Heath, S. B. (2001). Protean shapes in literacy events: Ever-shifting oral and literate traditions. In E. Cushman, E. R. Kintgen, B. M. Kroll, & M. Rose (Eds.), *Literacy: A critical sourcebook* (pp. 443–467). Boston: Bedford/St. Martin's.

Heath, S. B., & Flower, L. (2000). *Language and learning across the disciplines, 4*(3), 45–55.

Heath, S. B., Mangiola, L., Schecter, S. R., & Hull, G. A. (Eds.). (1991). *Children of promise: Literate activity in linguistically and culturally diverse classrooms.* Washington, DC: National Education Association.

Heath, S. B., & McLaughlin, M. W. (Eds.). (1993). *Identity and inner-city youth: Beyond ethnicity and gender.* New York: Teachers College Press.

Heath, S. B., & Wolf, S. A. (1992). *The braid of literature: Children's worlds of reading.* Cambridge, MA: Harvard University Press.

Herr, K., & Anderson, G. (1997). The cultural politics of identity: Student narratives from two Mexican secondary schools. *Qualitative Studies in Education, 10*(1), 45–61.

Herzberg, B. (1994). Community service and critical teaching. *College Composition and Communication, 45*(3), 307–319.

Hesford, W. S. (1999). *Framing identities: Autobiography and the politics of pedagogy.* Minneapolis: University of Minnesota Press.

Holdstein, D., & Bleich, D. (Eds.). (2001). *Personal effects: The social character of scholarly writing.* Logan: Utah State University Press.

Huber, J., & Whelan, K. (1999). A marginal story as a place of possibility: Negotiating self on the professional knowledge landscape. *Teaching and Teacher Education, 15,* 381–396.

Hull, G., & Schultz, K. (Eds.). (2002). *School's out: Bridging out-of-school literacies with classroom practice.* New York: Teachers College Press.

Hull, G., & Zacher, J. (2004). What is after-school worth? Developing literacy and identity out of school. *Voices in Urban Education, 3.* Retrieved October 23, 2004, from http://www.annenberginstitute.org/VUE/spring04/Hull.html

Hymes, D. (1974). *Foundations in sociolonguistics: An ethnographic approach.* Philadelphia: University of Pennsylvania Press.

Jennings, E., & Purves, A. (Eds.). (1991). *Literate systems and individual lives: Perspectives on literacy and schooling.* Albany: State University of New York Press.

Labov, W. (1972). *Language in the inner city: Studies in the black English vernacular.* Philadelphia: University of Pennsylvania Press.

Ladson-Billings, G. (1992). Africentrism and multiculturalism: Conflict or consonance. *The Journal of Negro Education, 62*(3), 378–391.

Lankshear, C., & Knobel, M. (2003). *New literacies: Changing knowledge and classroom learning.* Philadelphia: Open University Press.

Lee, C. D. (1993). *Signifying as a scaffold for literary interpretation: The pedagogical implications of an African American discourse genre* (Research Report No. 26). Urbana, IL: National Council of Teachers of English.

Lewis, O. (1959). *Five families: Mexican case studies in the culture of poverty.* New York: Basic Books.

Lewis, O. (1961). *The children of Sanchez.* New York: Vintage.

Lindquist, J. (1999). Class ethos and the politics of inquiry: What the barroom can teach us about the classroom. *College Composition and Communication, 51,* 225–247.

Lindquist, J. (2002). *A place to stand: Politics and persuasion in a working-class bar.* Oxford, UK: Oxford University Press.

Lindquist, J. (2004). Class affects, classroom affectations: Working through the paradoxes of strategic empathy. *College English, 67*(2), 234–267.

Lipka, J., & Ilutsik, E. (1996). Ciulistet and the curriculum of the possible. In N. H. Hornberger (Ed.), *Indigenous literacies in the Americas: Language planning from the bottom up* (pp. 45–67). Berlin: Mouton de Gruyter.

Lyons, S. R. (2000). Rhetorical sovereignty: What do American Indians want from writing? *College Composition and Communication, 51,* 447–468.

Lytle, S. L. (2001). Living literacy: Rethinking development in adulthood. In E. Cushman, E. R. Kintgen, B. M. Kroll, & M. Rose (Eds.), *Literacy: A critical sourcebook* (pp. 376–401). Boston: Bedford/St. Martin's.

Mahiri, J. (1991). Socialization forces affecting the education of African American youth in the 1990s. *The Journal of Negro Education, 60*(3), 305–313.

Mahiri, J. (1996). Writing for their lives: The nonschool literacy of California's urban African American youth. *The Journal of Negro Education, 65*(2), 164–180.

Mahiri, J. (1998). *Shooting for excellence: African American and youth culture in new century schools.* Urbana, IL: National Council of Teachers of English.

Marshall, J. (1993). *Literacy, power, and democracy in Mozambique.* Boulder, CO: Westview.

McCarty, T., & Dick, G. S. (2003). *Telling the people's stories: Literary practices and processes in a Navajo community school.* In A. Willis, G. Garcia, R. Barrera, & V. Harris (Eds.), *Multicultural issues in literacy research and practice* (pp. 101–122). Mahwah, NJ: Erlbaum.

McCarty, T., & Watahomigie, L. (2001). Language and literacy in American Indian and Alaska native communities. In E. Cushman, E. R. Kintgen, B. M. Kroll, & M. Rose (Eds.), *Literacy: A critical sourcebook* (pp. 488–508). Boston: Bedford/St. Martin's.

McHenry, E., & Heath, S. B. (2001). The literate and the literary: African Americans as writers and readers. In E. Cushman, E. R. Kintgen, B. M. Kroll, & M. Rose (Eds.), *Literacy: A critical sourcebook* (pp. 261–274). Boston: Bedford/St. Martin's.

Moll, L. (1992). Literacy research in community and classrooms: A sociocultural approach. In R. Beach, J. L. Green, M. L. Kamil, & T. Shanahan (Eds.), *Multidisciplinary perspectives on literacy research* (pp. 211–244). Urbana, IL: National Council of Teachers of English.

Moll, L. (2000). Inspired by Vygotsky: Ethnographic experiments in education. In C. Lee & P. Smagorinsky (Eds.), *Vygotskian perspectives on literacy research* (pp. 256–258). Cambridge, UK: Cambridge University Press.

Moll, L. (2002). The concept of educational sovereignty. *Penn GSE Perspectives on Urban Education, 1*(2), 1–11.

Moll, L., & Gonzalez, N. (2001). Lessons from research with language-minority children. In E. Cushman, E. R. Kintgen, B. M. Kroll, & M. Rose (Eds.), *Literacy: A critical sourcebook* (pp. 156–172). Boston: Bedford/St. Martin's.

Morrell, E. (2004). *Becoming critical researchers: Literacy and empowerment for urban youth.* New York: Peter Lang.

Morro, L. M. (1995). *Family literacy: Connections in schools and communities.* New Brunswick, NJ: Rutgers University Press.

Moss, B. (1994). *Writing across communities.* Creskill, NJ: Hampton Press.

Moss, B. J. (2003). *A community text arises: A literate text and a literacy tradition in African-American churches.* Cresskill, NJ: Hampton Press.

Ogbu, J., & Simons, H. (1998). Voluntary and involuntary minorities: A cultural-ecological theory of school performance with some implications for education. *Anthropology and Education Quarterly, 29,* 155–188.

Ong, W. (1983). *Orality and literacy.* New York: Mathuen.

Paratore, J. (2001). *Opening doors, opening opportunities: Family literacy in an urban community.* Needham Heights, MA: Allyn & Bacon.

Perez, B. (1998). *Sociocultural contexts of language and literacy.* Mahwah, NJ: Erlbaum.

Perez, B. (2004). *Becoming biliterate.* Mahwah, NJ: Erlbaum.

Philips, S. U. (1983). *The invisible culture: Communication in classroom and community on the Warm Springs Indian Reservation.* New York: Longman.

Porter, J., Sullivan, P., Blythe, S., Grabill, J., & Miles, L. (2000). Institutional critique: A rhetorical methodology for change. *College Composition and Communication, 51,* 610–642.

Pough, G. D. (2002). Empowering rhetoric: Black students writing Black Panthers. *College Composition and Communication, 53,* 466–486.

Powell, M. (2002). Rhetorics of survivance: How American Indians use writing. *College Composition and Communication, 53,* 396–434.

Purcell-Gates, V. (1995). *Other people's words.* Cambridge, MA: Harvard University Press.

Purcell-Gates, V., & Waterman, R. (2000). *Now we read, we see, we speak: Portrait of literacy development in a Freirean-based adult class.* Mahwah, NJ: Erlbaum.

Rockhill, K. (1993). Gender, language and the politics of literacy. In B. Street (Ed.), *Cross-cultural approaches to literacy studies* (pp. 156–175). Cambridge, UK: Cambridge University Press.

Rodriguez, R. (1982). *Hunger of memory.* Boston: Godine.

Rose, M. (1989). *Lives on the boundary: A moving account of the struggles and achievements of America's educationally underprepared.* New York: Penguin.

Royster, J. J. (1996). When the first voice you hear is not your own. *College Composition and Communication, 47,* 29–40.

Royster, J. J. (2000). *Traces of a stream: Literacy and social change among African American Women.* Pittsburgh, PA: University of Pittsburgh Press.

Schine, J. (Ed.). (1997). *Service learning.* Chicago: University of Chicago Press.

Scollon, R., & Scollon, S. (1981). *Narrative, literacy, and face in interethnic communication.* Norwood, NJ: Ablex.

Scribner, S., & Cole, M. (1981). *The psychology of literacy.* Cambridge, MA: Harvard University Press.

Slaughter, D. T., & Epps, E. G. (1987). The Black child's home environment and student achievement. *The Journal of Negro Education, 56*(1), 3–20.

Smitherman, G. (1986). *Talkin and testifyin: The language of Black America.* Boston: Houghton Mifflin. (Original work published 1977)

Smitherman, G. (2000). *Talkin that talk: Language, culture, and education in African America.* New York: Routledge.

Snow, C. (1991). *Unfulfilled expectations: Home and school influences on literacy.* Cambridge, MA: Harvard University Press.

Snow, C., & Tabors, P. (1996). Intergenerational transfer of literacy. In A. Benjamin & J. Lord (Eds.), *Family literacy: Directions in research and implications for practice* (pp. 73–80). Washington, DC: U.S. Department of Education.

Spack, R. (1997). The (in)visibility of the person(al) in academe. *College English, 59,* 9–31.

Street, B. (1984). *Literacy in theory and practice.* Cambridge, UK: Cambridge University Press.

Street, B. (1993). (Ed.). *Cross-cultural approaches to literacy studies.* Cambridge: Cambridge University Press.

Street, B. (1995). *Social literacies: Critical approaches to literacy in development, ethnography, and education.* New York: Longman.

Street, B. (Ed.). (2001a). *Literacy and development: Ethnographic perspectives.* London: Routledge.

Street, B. (2001b). The new literacy studies. In E. Cushman, E. R. Kintgen, B. M. Kroll, & M. Rose (Eds.), *Literacy: A critical sourcebook* (pp. 440–443). Boston: Bedford/St. Martin's.

Stromquist, N. P. (1997). *Literacy for citizenship: Gender and grassroots dynamics in Brazil.* Albany: State University of New York Press.

Szwed, J. (2001). The ethnography of literacy. In E. Cushman, E. R. Kintgen, B. M. Kroll, & M. Rose (Eds.), *Literacy: A critical sourcebook* (pp. 421–430). Boston: Bedford/St. Martin's.

Taylor, D. (1983). *Family literacy: Young children learning to read and write.* Portsmouth, NH: Heinemann.

Taylor, D. (1991). *Learning denied.* Portsmouth, NH: Heinemann.

Taylor, D. (1993). *From the child's point of view.* Portsmouth, NH: Heinemann.

Taylor, D. (1996). *Toxic literacies: Exposing the injustice of bureaucratic texts.* Portsmouth, NH: Heinemann.

Taylor, D. (Ed.). (1997). *Many families, many literacies: An international declaration of principles.* Portsmouth, NH: Heinemann.

Taylor, D., & Dorsey-Gaines, C. (1988). *Growing up literate: Learning from inner-city families.* Portsmouth, NH: Heinemann.

Valdés, G. (1996). *Con respeto: Bridging the distances between culturally diverse families and schools: An ethnographic portrait.* New York: Teachers College Press.

Villanueva, V. (1993). *Bootstraps: From an American academic of color.* Urbana, IL: National Council of Teachers of English.

Vygotsky, L. S. (1978). *Mind in society.* Cambridge, MA: Harvard University Press.

Wade, R. (1997). *Community service learning: A guide to including service in the public school curriculum.* Albany: State University of New York Press.

Wagner, D. (1991). Literacy as culture: Emic and etic perspectives. In E. Jennings & A. Purves (Eds.), *Literate systems and individual lives: Perspectives on literacy and schooling* (pp. 67–92). Albany: State University of New York Press.

Weinstein-Shr, G. (1994). From mountaintops to city streets: An ethnographic investigation of literacy and social process among the Hmong of Philadelphia. In B. J. Moss (Ed.), *Literacy across communities* (pp. 49–83). Cresskill, NJ: Hampton Press.

CHAPTER 9

Writing in the Professions

Anne Beaufort

AS OTHERS in this volume attest, writing research took a turn in the late 1970s and early 1980s. The particular turn that is the subject of this chapter is the interest of composition and rhetoric researchers that leapt beyond rhetorical criticism and theory, beyond English classroom research, to writing outside academic settings. Work in technical writing, particularly engineering writing, had existed for some time (Brockmann, 1998; Connors, 1982) but was a specialty largely apart from the concerns of those in composition or English education. But the new research direction I speak of here is the interest in the writing of college graduates working in business and in various disciplines outside English. Questions that hadn't been asked before began to stir researchers: What kinds of writing did college graduates do? What did they learn in traditional English composition classes that was helpful—or not—for writing beyond college? And setting aside practical issues of improving education, from a research perspective how did writing as a social activity take place in various settings? And could an examination of writing activity in numerous settings add to theories of composing, rhetorical theory, and genre theory?

In this chapter, I examine this body of work of the past 20 years from different angles and for different purposes. One purpose is to aid researchers and theorists in stepping back to gain perspective: What has the trajectory of this body of work been? Where has it led us as a field? The second purpose is to bring this body of work to the attention of teachers of writing who otherwise might not encounter it, so that they might consider its implications for their teaching. The angles from which I've viewed the work and present it here are also twofold: first, looking at the chronological unfolding of the research: What happened first? Next? And then? And second, looking more thematically: What were the kinds of questions being investigated? What were the common themes in the findings? But first a bit of historical grounding: Why did this interest emerge in the first place?

Several publications marked this turn in English and composition studies to an interest in what writers do in workplace and professional settings. Witte and Faigley (1983) studied ways of improving college writing programs. Another landmark publication that signaled this turn, Odell and Goswami's *Writing in Nonacademic Settings* (1985), began as a dispute between the editors as to what they imagined their students did with writing beyond college. They realized, as good researchers, they had no evidence for their views; hence, a book was born that reported the beginnings of workplace writing research and spawned a great deal more research.

Others who were among the early English and composition scholars to turn toward workplace and professional writing as fertile ground for research recount other convergences, in part personal and idiosyncratic, in part indicative of wider social and political forces. Steve Bernhardt (1985a, 1985b), working on his doctorate at the University of Michigan and propelled by the dictum of current language theory that language must be viewed in context and by his love of canoeing, did research in environmental writing on wetland issues in the early 1980s. Chuck Bazerman (1988a), suffering the intellectual and emotional disjunctures between a dissertation on Elizabethan poetry and the language needs of the elementary children in Brooklyn whom he was teaching, started getting interested in ways in which academic research, and in particular literacy research, could be made more accessible and useful to a wider audience. David Jolliffe, teaching mostly students who were working full-time and attending the University of Illinois part-time, wanted to find out why apparent success with literacy demands of the workplace did not guarantee his students' success with academic literacies. He began investigating what it was they were reading and writing at work (1997, 1998).

Cross-fertilizations among departments at various institutions also stimulated the intellectual ferment that led to new directions in composition research. At the University of Michigan, for example, an interest in English for science and technology was spawned at the English Language Institute, bringing together scholars in engineering, English, and linguistics. At Carnegie-Mellon, where faculty had strong ties with industry (U.S. Steel, for example), the Communications Design Center was formed and research looking at the relations between graphics and texts was begun. Another influence on the research at Carnegie-Mellon was President Carter's signing "plain language" legislation (later revoked by President Reagan) that required public documents to be made more readable for average citizens, following an effort that started in Britain. Workplace writing and its effect on readers became a source for government funding and fertile research ground.

What follows, then, is a summary of the high points of 20 years of work. By my own limitations, I no doubt will neglect the work of some that is worthy of mention. I intend no personal slights and hope that I will hear from readers about any egregious omissions. What is captured most fully here is the research on managers' and other professionals' writing activities in business/professional settings. Excluded from this survey for the most part are studies of the writing of blue-collar and shop-floor workers and workplace literacy programs for those with limited English skills (see Chapter 8). Another related strand of research that I will touch on here but not represent in an exhaustive manner is that in technical communications. Nor have I given exhaustive treatment to all of the rhetorical studies of discourses in various professions, but rather have tried to give a small sampling of this important area of scholarship.

THE GENERAL TRAJECTORY

One way of getting a sense of the body of workplace research as a whole is to notice the books published on the subject. Most have been edited collections, gatherings of research, with framing chapters offering theoretical overviews. After Odell and Goswami (1985), similar collections appeared (Hull, 1997; Matalene, 1989; Spilka, 1993; Sullivan & Dautermann, 1996). Interspersed with these edited collections have been a few book-length ethnographies of particular workplace settings (Barabas, 1990; Beaufort, 1999; Brown & Herndl, 1986; Gowen, 1992; Winsor, 1996). In 1995, Petraglia published a critique of freshman composition, somewhat based on research on writing in workplace and other professional settings. In 1998, Garay and Bernhardt published a collection of essays with a more positive view of the possibilities of school-to-work connections for writers. This book was followed by several others with particular educational agendas (Dias, Freedman, Medway, & Pare, 1999; Dias & Pare, 2000).

While the bibliography for this review is not exhaustive, nonetheless it is worth mentioning the numbers of articles reviewed for this chapter in particular time periods: In 1982–1984, 11 articles were noted; in 1985–1987, 17; in 1991–1993, 41 articles. In 2000–2003, 37 articles were reviewed. While these numbers represent only my idiosyncratic reading of the literature, nonetheless the growing and sustained interest of composition scholars in this area of research since Faigley's (1985) and Odell and Goswami's (1985) early work is clear.

But rather than take the reader through a chronological summary of the body of work, perhaps it will be of greater use to look at the work from the standpoint of major themes in the research: (1) studies of writers' composing processes in multiple settings; (2) studies of the influence of technologies on written communication; (3) studies of social contexts and the interrelation of texts and institutions; (4) studies of the interrelation of print and visual texts; and (5) studies of the socialization process, or the learning curve, for writers coming out of academic settings and going into workplace settings. Themes overlap, of course, but for purposes of some orderliness to this review, they appear separately. But first, I discuss the early descriptive studies of workplace writing.

A BEGINNING DESCRIPTION OF WORKPLACE WRITING

Several early descriptive studies had the general purpose of establishing what kinds of writing activities went on in workplace settings and in what quantities. Survey methods were used, and in some cases follow-up interviews were conducted with selected participants. In general, these surveys established the value placed on writing by management-level employees in a variety of professions. Faigley and Miller (1982) reported, for example, that white-collar professionals in six occupations wrote an average of 23% of the work week. Another survey (Harwood, 1982) at the same time found a typical graduate wrote once or twice a day, and, perhaps more important, that as income rose, so did frequency of writing. Bataille's (1982) survey likewise confirmed the importance of on-the-job writing among those he surveyed in the fields of English, mechanical engineering, textile industry, chemistry, industrial administration, and sociology. These surveys were done prior to the widespread availability and use of personal computers. It would be interesting to repeat such surveys now to see how frequency and usage patterns for writing might have changed.

Another survey attempted to get at possible problems in writing on-the-job: Aldrich (1982) found among 254 managers surveyed that writing anxiety was prevalent and there was little evidence of writing process knowledge. Several studies also tried to get at how writing activities and types of writing done might differ from academic writing. Odell, Goswami, and Quick (1983) used discourse-based interviews (questions tied to sample texts) to analyze the differences in conceptions of audience and purpose between undergraduates and legislative analysts, a first step toward articulating the path to context-specific writing expertise (although the researchers didn't frame their study in that way). Paradis, Dobrin, and Miller (1985) interviewed managers at Exxon, also in an attempt to see what the character of workplace writing was. In both studies, researchers were beginning to document the difference that social context makes in both how writers perform and how they perceive writing tasks. In these and other studies (Barabas, 1990; Laruuche & Pearson, 1985) a greater sense of audience in the workplace than among student writers was one of the differences that emerged, as well as a stronger sense among workplace writers of writing as a problem-solving process. Later studies would expand on the early seeds sown in these studies.

COMPOSING PROCESSES ON-THE-JOB

Mainstream composition research focused a great deal of attention in the late 1970s and early 1980s on the composing processes of writers. Flower and Hayes's (1981) model of the composing process became a gauntlet for others to pick up and test in different writing contexts. A number of researchers conducted studies to determine whether the same recursive process of composing was evidenced among seasoned writers in the workplace. A few expanded on Flower and Hayes's model; for example, Doheny-Farina (1986) found what "stored writing plans" meant among writers in a small computer firm—a rich and specific understanding of complex social issues that would affect the writer's decision-making process in composing texts. Blyler's (1989) study expanded the nuances of understanding "purpose" in the composing process. Hovde (2001) documented the extensive generative nature of the research process technical writers needed to undertake as part of the process of writing software documentation, and Spilka (1988) also found generating content to be an important part of the composing process. In a year-long ethnography following six engineers composing a variety of documents, she found more-successful engineers spending more of their energies on content than on arrangement or style. These studies expand on the Flower and Hayes model of the composing processes of writers.

But several studies convincingly argued that claims for a universal model of composing were not valid—composing processes of writers varied depending on the nature of the genre and other situational variables. Broadhead and Freed (1986) documented a very linear composing process of two management consultants who used boilerplate formulas supplied by their company to write proposals to clients. The government proposal, on the other hand, could be a daunting genre to tackle. One writer, after suffering through a very laborious, anxiety-ridden round of proposal writing, approached the same task a year later, wiser for her earlier experiences, in her own methodical way: typing out the RFP (request for proposal) in order to internalize what the grantors were requesting, and creating manila folders for each section of the proposal where she could place notes, relevant information, and rough drafts of the section for later assemblage into the whole. She wrote sections non-sequentially as well, according to what seemed easiest to tackle first (Beaufort, 1999).

Schumacher, Scott, Klare, Cronin, and Lambert (1989), in an experiment with journalism students, found that under one writing condition—composing a news story—the writers needed to spend less time planning, given the pre-established structure of the genre, whereas when writing editorials, which have a more open format, writers spent more time reaching decisions as they wrote.

Couture and Rymer (1993) and Beaufort (1999) documented the influence of situational factors—the amount of time available, and whether or not the writing situation was routine—on writers' degree of attention to planning and revising. And writers in one nonprofit organization (Beaufort, 1999) were found to vary their writing processes depending not only on the nature of the genre, but also on the physical realities of the workplace—one writer wrote easy things on Mondays and Fridays, when there were a lot of interruptions, and more difficult projects on Tuesdays, Wednesdays, and Thursdays, when there were greater opportunities for concentrated effort but still numerous interruptions, which in themselves became part of the writing process.

Several other variables that influenced the writing processes of workplace writers also demonstrate richly varied composing processes. A number of studies (Beaufort, 1999; Johns, 1989; Selzer, 1993; Winsor, 1989) point to the effect of intertextuality in workplace writing (portions of texts freely borrowed from other texts) on writers' processes; one writer in a nonprofit agency, for example, organized various boilerplate texts for business letters she frequently wrote in file folders on her desktop computer, labeled according to type of letter: rejection letter, request for donation, and so forth (Beaufort, 1999). Other studies (Allen, 1993; Dorff & Duin, 1989; Witte & Haas, 2001) further complicate conceptions of the writing process by observing various forms of collaborative writing the Flower and Hayes model cannot account for. For example, Witte and Haas (2001) demonstrate the intertwining of different areas of expertise ("distributed cognition") of city workers and engineers in the process of documenting and revising technical documents, and ways in which gestures and diagrams operated in the composing process as "pre-texts." Allen, Atkinson, Morgan, Moore, and Snow (1987) were able to document specific processes, described as creative conflict, that best facilitated collaborative writing (e.g., preserving divergent points of view of group members, shared decision-making about documents, etc.).

Collaborative writing (sometimes referred to as document cycling) also could lead writers to feel less ownership of texts, and less immediacy in terms of the rhetorical situation. Not only is the image of the solo writer as "creator" often not apropos in workplace writing situations, but the resulting effects on writers' sense of authorship (or lack of it) spawned by these writing practices also has been documented. It seems most writers have to go through a period of psychological adjustment to the loss of control of "their" texts (Anson & Forsberg, 1990; Beaufort, 1999; Doheny-Farina, 1989; Henry, 1995b; Winsor, 1993); in one case (Henry, 1995b), this loss of sense of ownership of text also affected the writers' abilities to imagine the real audience for the texts, as internal readers and editors were the most immediate audience. As a public relations writer in an engineering firm said, "Neither our native tongue nor our professional language is ever entirely our own. We must constitute ourselves in texts that we do not wholly control" (Winsor, 1993, p. 194). For a bibliography of studies on collaboration in technical writing, see Jorn (1993).

Efficiency in the writing process was a factor in workplace settings as well: Front-line supervisors who didn't have a good handle on the writing process were losing money for the company with their inefficiencies (Mabrito, 1997). One Silicon Valley company (McIsaac & Aschauer, 1990) formed a Proposal Operations Center to review proposals as part of the writing process in order to improve not only efficiency in the writing process, but effectiveness of the proposals as well (proposals, in this case, for large military contracts, often involved a 52-step process; anywhere from 42 to 100 individuals could be involved in writing of the proposals). The writing process for these documents included storyboarding ("scribble sheets," i.e., early drafts of sections of text) pinned to walls for viewing and a "Red Team" that simulated readers' reactions to early drafts. In some settings workplace writing processes resembled the proverbial assembly line.

In summary, the research on writers' composing processes in settings other than school or experimental conditions suggests not that the Flower and Hayes cognitive processing model is invalid, or that the individual must not gain awareness and skills in managing the writing process (a cornerstone of writing curriculum today), but rather that there can be many variations on a writer's composing process that are factors of social context, the type of writing being done, and individual idiosyncrasies. Dias (2000) puts it this way: "The research that matters here is a search for finer and fuller accounts of the writing process, with the promise of further elaborations into classroom practice" (p. 13). And perhaps most important for writing teachers from this body of research is the knowledge that the composing process is as much a social process in writing classes as it is in the workplace (Nelson, 1990, 1995).

TECHNOLOGY AND WRITERS' PROCESSES

The impact of technology on composing processes has only begun to be investigated and is not exclusive to workplace research. Studies of students' uses of computers in electronic classrooms have been plentiful (see, e.g., Hawisher & Selfe, 1989). However, as new technologies tend to get started in workplace settings and efficiency is perhaps of greater concern in the workplace, there have been a number of investigations in this arena, generally along two lines of questioning: (1) how technologies affect (or don't affect) writers' processes, and (2) how technologies spawn (or don't spawn) new genres or new communicative patterns.

An experimental study of professionals and advanced graduate students composing press releases on the computer or with paper and pencil, as well as revising and editing press releases under the same conditions, revealed advantages and disadvantages of composing with computers. On the one hand, writers spent less time planning and felt free to write spontaneously and creatively with the computer (Lutz, 1987). They also made five times more changes to the text on the computer than with paper and pencil, and more changes at the whole-sentence level. On the other hand, the physical limitations of the computer screen interfered with making whole-text-level structural changes, which were made more readily on the paper and pencil version, where the whole text could be spread out. Haas (1989) also documented the difficulty for writers of reading their texts on computer screens. Other researchers (Sellen & Harper, 2002), looking at writing at the International Monetary Fund, found that managers drafted and did final editing on computers, but collaborating on revisions was done on paper and accounted for 71% of the writing time. Managers needed to spread papers on tables, mark them, share pages, and so on, before making changes on the computer. Paper also seems to serve other cognitive functions in critical thinking and composing processes. The authors state:

> Knowledge workers rarely store and file paper documents or refer back to the information they do keep. Rather, it is the process of taking notes that is important in helping them to construct and organize their thoughts. The information that they do keep is arranged around their offices in a temporary holding pattern of paper documents that serves as a way of keeping available the inputs and ideas they might have use for in their current projects. (p. 63)

Gladwell (2002) reports on a study by Mackay, a computer scientist, of air traffic controllers making similar use of on-line technologies and paper. The researcher found that air traffic controllers used little strips of paper to make notes on airplane locations and worked with the slips of paper *and* the radar images on their computer screens to manage air traffic. It appears that computers aid aspects of the writing process, and "old-fashioned" paper and pencil aid other aspects of the composing process. On the one hand, digital processing of texts facilitates storing and accessing large amounts of information, display of multimedia documents, fast full-text searches, quick links to related materials, and dynamic modifying or updating of content. But hard copy of text facilitates quick, flexible navigation through and around documents, reading across more than one document at once, marking up a document while reading, and interweaving reading and writing (Daiute, 1983; Sellen & Harper, 2002).

In addition to the influence of technology on reading/writing practices, research has documented the shifting of social roles in relation to written communications in the workplace as a result of technological changes. Dictation nearly has disappeared as even top executives have turned to desktop computers, and, conversely, secretaries have become more than typists, often revising and editing others' documents online (Dautermann, 1996). Other roles, too, have changed as a result of the ready accessibility of digital technologies. Cook-Gumperz with Hanna (1997) found the social status of nurses in the hospital hierarchy increased when they started using bedside computer terminals to chart patients' conditions and accessed database tools for patient assessment.

More radical perhaps than word processing are several other technical media: personal digital assistants (PDAs), structured document processors (SDPs), instant messaging (IM), and hypertext. PDAs, as exemplified in Geisler's (2001) self-study, may blur the boundaries between personal and work-related writing. Geisler's self-study of a 97-minute composing session also demonstrated the multilayered, multitasking possibilities that Internet technology, computers, and PDAs allow: She used all three interchangeably as she composed. IM has transformed written communication to nearly match the synchronicity of oral communication and, like PDAs, is a newer technology warranting further research. Of more limited use are the SDP software programs that create templates for complicated software documentation that allow writers in essence to fill in the blanks in the forms and import boilerplate information from linked databases (Norman & Grider, 1992; Wiering et al., 1996).

Researchers point to the alteration of the concept of "authoring" when writing tools such as these are employed. Reader–writer relationships also are affected by "new" media. Hypertext enables readers, in a sense, to become "co-authors" with writers (Wenger & Payne, 1994) and presents additional organizational possibilities and problems for writers: Nonlinear organizational patterns such as trees, cycles, grids, and stars can be created that verbal rhetorical devices do not allow (Horton, 1991). Also, information can be layered for different audiences. Fortune (1989) also presents a case for the use of computer drawing programs as another tool for aiding critical thinking and prewriting in the composing process.

The second line of investigation of technology/writing connections has been an examination of changes in writing styles, genres, and communication patterns as a result of "new" technologies. Yates's (1989) historical study of the rise of business communications reveals a fascinating intertwining of human and material factors that spawned new genres and new communication practices. Her study helps to put into perspective current technological changes that affect writing. Some predicted the telephone would diminish or eliminate written communications, but the telegraph, the typewriter, carbon paper, and vertical filing cabinets (instead of desk pigeonholes) all increased the ease and functionality of written communications. And the genre of the internal memo evolved, gradually, from the more formal business letter. For example, the standard headings of the memo were created for efficiency of referencing documents and allowed dropping unnecessary courtesies such as "yours very truly" (p. 96).

E-mail, which took off as a communications medium in the late 1980s, has been examined as a "new" genre. Although early on, some researchers raised the question of whether e-mail was really a genre (Spooner & Yancey, 1996), most of the research suggests that e-mail is a hybrid between oral and written communications and that the form has been developing a set of regularized textual features unique enough to warrant considering it a genre in its own right—for example, more use of incomplete sentences, a preference for coordinated rather than subordinated ideas, and use of specialized vocabulary and graphical symbols to convey emotions (Baron, 2000; Gimenez, 2000; Sims, 1996; Yates, Orlikowski, & Okamura, 1999). Yates and colleagues (1999) also found, in an extensive study of organizational culture, a number of e-mail "subgenres," for example, the "official announcement genre" and the "dialogue genre."

Changes in organizational structure and patterns of communication as a result of new computer technologies such as e-mail also have been examined. Researchers found that communications with new customers began as standard business letters, but as relationships became established, e-mail became the preferred medium of communication (Murray, 1987). And, as the memo encouraged more informality than the business letter, e-mail likewise has increased both the informality and personal nature of business communications (Gimenez, 2000). And yet Yates and colleagues (1999), studying use of e-mail in two different divisions of a Japanese manufacturing firm, found that corporate cultures in the divisions differed and as a result "norms" for e-mail communications also differed, suggesting that it is not the medium, but the genre features as shaped by social context, that vary the form of communications. The researchers offer this cautionary note: "The migration of existing communication patterns to new media may, however, lead users simply to apply ineffective habits of use from old technologies to new ones" (p. 100). They call for deliberate consideration of genres and genre repertoires in specific contexts for communication. A final note: Bernhardt (1993) gives a good overview of the ways in which hypertext is changing acts of reading and writing. Although he does not give empirical evidence of readers' and writers' behaviors with hypertext media, he presents a thorough textual analysis, pointing out the features of hypertext that influence the ways writers and readers interact around such texts: Hypertexts are interactive (a reader can be active rather than passively absorbing information); hypertexts are functionally mapped (text is displayed in ways that cues readers what can be done with it); hypertexts are modular; hypertexts are navigable (readers can move across large pools of information in different directions for different purposes); hypertexts are hierarchically embedded; hypertexts are spacious (unconstrained by physicality); and hypertexts are graphically rich. Technology has changed the way we write and what we write, and no doubt there will be more changes to come.

SOCIAL CONTEXTS/WRITING IN THE PROFESSIONS

Since the early 1980s researchers in composition have been applying theories of the social construction of knowledge and discourse community theory to their research. What the research in workplace settings affords is an examination of settings *other than* school settings in which writing takes place, which, by contrast, can shed light back onto classrooms as social sites for composing (Dias, 2000; Freedman, Adam, & Smart, 1994).

A number of studies have enabled an examination of the ways in which organizational culture influences writers' behaviors. Brown and Herndl (1986) found that social hierarchies within an organization influenced writers' sense of what linguistic features, and even genres, were appropriate. Specifically, through interviews and analysis of writing samples of two writing groups (those considered outstanding writers within the organization, and those considered average), the authors found that superfluous use of nominalizations was greater among the average writers, causing their writing to be "muddy" and "verbose," and these traits increased if the writing was for upper management or for powerful people outside the corporation, and decreased when the writing was for those lower in the corporate hierarchy. Nominalizations also increased with a sense of job insecurity: Writers felt such linguistic features conveyed a greater sense of authority. Similarly, Henry (1995b) found writers' use of nominalizations, passive voice, and other less direct stylistic choices in a military organization resulted from the layers of approvals (what they referred to as the "chop chain") that removed them from any sense of audience or personal investment in the writing. Others have documented similar stylistic choices made by writers in response to the social milieu in which they wrote (Odell, Goswami, Herrington, & Quick, 1983; Orlikowski & Yates, 1994).

On the other hand, from the perspective of businesses evaluating their employees' writing, in one study (Beason, 2001) there was consensus among 15 managers interviewed in a variety of corporate settings that mechanical errors reflect negatively on writers' social status in organizations, and another study (Blau, Glantie, & Sherwin, 1989) empirically tested writing samples of nonnative speakers that had lexical or syntactic errors. Managers rated the syntactic errors as the most serious errors in terms of both miscommunication and the writer's status in the organization. Another study of nonnative computer scientists and engineers working in a large U.S. corporation (Belcher, 1991) documented nonnative writers oversimplifying grammar to avoid errors and not understanding the subtle rhetorical purposes of written documentation for self-promotion. Gender differences in written business communications, unfortunately, have not been a subject of research, as far as I could ascertain. Tebeaux (1990) did one study with technical writing students who had workplace experience and found that both men and women who had worked in jobs requiring interpersonal communications used both "masculine" and "feminine" approaches to communication, as warranted by specific situations. From this study and her review of gender research, Tebeaux argues for business writers to have "androgynous" writing strategies in order to meet a variety of communication situations. Barker (1998) argues for a similar position, almost 10 years later, based on studies of oral communications in the workplace.

Turning to more large-scale effects of dialogic relationships between social context and writing practices, nurses' use of bedside computers to chart patients' conditions and access databases for diagnostic purposes (Cook-Gumperz & Hanna, 1997) both depersonalized the writing for the nurses ("I cannot even see my own signature on the chart" [p. 329]) *and* raised the visibility of the nurses' observations to the rest of the medical staff and even enabled patients to be more involved in their own medical planning and healing processes. Social circumstances also can have a negative effect on writers. Pare (2000) documented the ways in which social workers were constrained by, influenced by, and even tried to circumvent legal and social constraints on the types of information they could put into case reports on juvenile delinquents. Similar studies in the field of psychiatry (Berkenkotter, 2001; McCarthy, 1991; McCarthy & Gerrig, 1994) have documented the ways in which the DSM-III or DSM-IV pushes psychiatrists into codifying clients' behaviors for billing and "social accountant" purposes, potentially restricting the actual practice of therapy. And Schryer (1993) documented similar "constraints" on social dynamics between veterinarians and pet owners, given the professional standards for documentation.

A second thread in studies looking at the relationship of social context and writing practices is concerned with the ways in which written texts function socially and culturally within organizations. One of the earliest studies (Doheny-Farina, 1986) documents the ways in which the drafting of a business plan in a small, start-up computer company in fact shaped the direction of the company. Stygall (1991) documents the ways in which jury instructions can interfere with the jury's understanding of the legal process, and Schryer (2000) documents the ways in which boilerplate text in an insurance company's letters turning down clients' disability claims was so dense that it was off the readability charts and led to appeals on over 60% of negative letters. When the researcher presented her evidence to the company (she was hired as a consultant to help them reduce the number of appeals of negative letters), there was a reluctance to turn dense legal prose into plain English. Even more disconcerting, Sauer (1994) demonstrates that the linear, sequential model of cause and effect prose used in accident reports of large government agencies fails to account for the multidimensional nature of accidents. And Herndl, Fennel, and Miller (1991) do a thorough rhetorical analysis of memos that preceded both the Three Mile Island nuclear accident and the deaths of eight astronauts aboard the Challenger flight. They demonstrate, through careful rhetorical analysis of the memos and an examination of the social context of the two divisions of the company involved in the Challenger decision, that the engineering division argued that past performance and some limited data about cold temperatures affecting O-rings warranted canceling the flight, but management discounted the engineers' data. Herndl and colleagues say, "The managers reasoned at the level of contracts and programs—successful flights. The warrants of each set of interests, or social groups, were insufficient to the other" (p. 302). A number of studies also document the complex rhetorical situations that are embedded in professional genres; for example, Beaufort's (1999) study of a writer in a nonprofit agency learning to compose effective press releases revealed the rhetorical challenge of both representing the client in the best possible light and appealing to journalists' views of what counts as "news," and Myers (1985) documents the challenges in science writing of positioning one's research as both continuing the discourse community's ongoing work and at the same time breaking new ground.

A third vein of research on the interrelation of social context and texts concerns the features of texts themselves as they evolve in relation to their social functions within organizations. Bazerman's (1981) pioneering article comparing the rhetorical approaches of three academic disciplines—sociology, biology, and literature—led to a number of other rich analyses of the ways in which genre conventions arise out of socially constrained or socially motivated situations and enact certain epistemological assumptions—what counts as truth, as evidence, and so on. There is a substantial body of work now on the rhetorical (i.e., nonobjective) nature of science writing (Bazerman, 1982; Blakeslee, 2001b; Fahnestock, 1986; Myers, 1985; Paul & Charney, 1995). In addition, Fahnestock and Secor (1991) explicate the rhetorical motives and moves of literary scholars; in business settings, Smart (1993), Orlikowski and Yates (1994), and Devitt (1991) similarly document the interrelation of genre features (evolving, nonstatic, dialogic) and the social purposes to which the texts attend. Segal (1993) analyzed over 200 articles written over a 10-year period, in various medical publications, to examine the rhetoric of medicine. She found medical writing to be paternalistic and that authority was established through extensive use of citations and nominalizations. She concluded, "Physicians are locked within scientific medicine's frame of reference because of the nature of language itself" (p. 84). And Beaufort (1999) found a single genre, the grant proposal, varied considerably in its genre features depending on the goals, values, and communication processes of different discourse communities using the genre: Grant proposals for private foundations had different requirements from those for local government agencies, and those for federal agencies had yet another set of features particular to the communicative context. Social status also can be at issue in formation of text types, as Munger (2000) demonstrates in an historical review of the evolution of reporting forms for emergency medical technicians. The more the form evolved from narrative to checking off boxes or "fill-in-the-blank" type reporting, the less social status EMTs felt they had within the medical profession.

Devitt (1991) broke new ground theoretically by demonstrating the interrelation of "sets" of genres employed by an accounting firm. She found two types of intertextuality—referential (one text referring to another explicitly) and functional (one text linked by function to another). She states, "In examining the genre set of a community, we are examining the community's situations, its recurring activities and relationships" (p. 340). She also observed that "the stabilizing power of genres, through the interaction of texts within the same genre . . . increases the efficiency of creating the firm's products" (p. 342). Others likewise have documented the occurrence of interconnected genres that work in concert within given social contexts: in the legal system (Bazerman, 1994b), in banking (Smart, 1993), and in interoffice e-mail communications (Orlikowski & Yates, 1994).

Other studies examined textual features more microscopic than issues of genre. Popken (1991) analyzed frequency of topic sentences for paragraphs in a variety of technical, journalistic, and academic documents, demonstrating the varying uses of topic sentences within different genres, depending on the overall length of paragraphs and whether graphical elements such as headings were used. Charney, Reder, and Wells (1988) examined, in experimental studies, the effect of degrees of elaboration of information in user manuals (for computer programs) on users' abilities to learn new software. And others (Rivers, 1989; Woolever, 1989) offer general observations about the differences in purpose, structure, and style of academic writing compared with most business-oriented texts. Although such generalizations are perhaps too broad, they nonetheless confirm socially driven textual features and give in broad strokes some of the differences between academic and business writing.

It is perhaps fitting to close this section with Freedman's (1984) fascinating experimental study, as it demonstrates in a reverse way the influence of social context on writing instruction. English teachers were asked, in a blind study, to grade two sets of papers. One set was produced by students; the other, by professional writers. Freedman found that teachers graded the professional writers' texts lower because the discourse conventions were not the ones they held their students to.

In all, studies of writing in the social contexts of business and the professions have yielded a rich basis for understanding (and theorizing) the social features of language, genres, and acts of composing. Olsen's (1993) review of studies of legal and medical writing says it well:

> These studies show that there is indeed an effect—and often a profound effect—of the context and the values of the community of readers and listeners on the content and form of a document. Perhaps more unexpectedly, a few of the studies also suggest that there is sometimes an effect of the content and form of a document on the context, including helping to define the sense of community and to project its set of values and attitudes. (p. 189)

TEXT AND OTHER SIGN SYSTEMS

As mentioned already, the physicality of the new genre of hypertext has altered reading and writing processes and meaning making (Bernhardt, 1993; Haas, 1989). Others have documented the pervasiveness of visual symbols side-by-side with written text in home and workplace settings (Hull, 1997; Medway, 2000; Rose, 2003; Witte, 1992). Witte (1992) even raises the question, What is writing versus nonwriting? From the standpoint of literacy, this reality of richly integrated symbol systems would suggest that students must be trained in verbal and visual rhetoric. Several studies suggest the richness of this area of investigation. Bernhardt (1986) offers an excellent analysis of the interaction of visual and verbal rhetoric in a brochure published by a wetlands agency. Horton (1993) documents research on the culturally specific meanings of graphics, text layouts, and even colors. Brumburger (2002), in an experimental study, found that subjects consistently assigned personality types to certain typefaces. And Medway (2000) analyzes, in an extensive case study, the use of tools—visual and textual—in an architecture student's critical thinking process as he worked on a building design. Early conceptual thinking was done in words, but later design ideas had to be represented with visual symbols.

Document design has become a subspecialty within rhetoric, drawing on perception studies in psychology, reading studies (how readers process texts), and linguistic anthropology (what symbols mean in context). An example of such research is the study by Zimmerman and Schultz (2000) of two medical questionnaires filled out by cancer patients—one a "standard" form and the other asking for the same information, but employing the principles of information design. Ninety percent of the questions in the "designed" form elicited better information than the questions on the standard form, demonstrating the efficacy of applying known principles of document design to strategic documents. It appears, though, that there has been limited empirical research into the effects of other sign systems on writers' processes, on genres themselves, and on the social dynamics of text usage, in spite of calls for such research (Schriver, 1989). There have been advances, however, in research methods for studying the effects of document design: Instead of relying on abstract readability formulas, for example, researchers now examine readers' actual comprehension and use of documents and have expanded their definition of which aspects of documents to evaluate (Schriver, 1997). A small tangential area of research related to texts has concerned the readability of technical documents and audience appeal; for a summary of that research, see Spyridakis, 1989a, 1989b. For a good bibliography on visual design, see Albers and Lisberg, 2002. For an overview of the field of information design, see Redish, 2000; Schriver, 1997.

SOCIALIZATION PROCESSES FOR WRITERS AND SCHOOL-TO-WORK TRANSITIONS

Given the research on workplace writing reported here, the question arises, What does this body of research suggest to educators? There are studies that have looked explicitly at school-to-work transitions for college graduates who must write as part of their professional work. It is worth noting what they learned, how they learned, and what helped or hindered learning. Implicit, too, in these matters is the dynamic of transfer of learning: What knowledge, skills, and behaviors do writers carry with them from one context to another, and with what results?

Much of what I've reported on so far can be considered the "what" of specific writing behaviors and knowledge required in professional settings. Writing process knowledge is certainly key, given the need for efficiency in business contexts. Studies have documented varied composing processes required by the nature of the tasks, physical settings, and other social factors. Rhetorical knowledge—understanding specific audiences and discourse community needs—is critical. And a clear sense of purpose—in business and professional settings, usually action-oriented rather than philosophical or knowledge-for-the-sake-of-knowledge—is paramount. Genres vary across social contexts. Uses of technologies and other symbol systems vary and can require working with state-of-the-art technology in certain settings. And writers' social roles within organizations and social status are also factors influencing writing behaviors. No amount of preparation in school can equip one fully for context-specific writing tasks in professional life.

Some have reflected directly on the differences between school and workplace writing through comparative studies. Dias and colleagues (1999), doing extensive comparisons of school and workplace writing situations in four fields, concluded that the key differences affecting writers moving from school to work settings are (1) the complexity of the social context as it influences writing practices in the workplace, (2) the multifunctionality of texts written in the workplace, and (3) the implications of power relations for writers. In contrast to writing in the workplace, writing for school is generally for evaluative purposes. A sense of audience and purpose is remote, other than the teacher and the teacher's grade book (Dias, 2000). As Russell (1997) says, "Students and professors rightly perceive classroom genres as operating in the genre system of the university more immediately and directly than in the genre system of a discipline. . . . Most students are doing school most of the time, not disciplinary work" (p. 541). At the undergraduate level, writers seldom feel they are participants in any authentic way in a community of writers or colleagues (Beaufort, 2004). Their social status as writers is "novice" or "student" rather than "author." As Tebeaux (1986) reports, one engineer said that all freshman English did for him was teach him to write in freshman English. Writing processes sometimes are prescribed by the assignment, but even then can be circumvented (Nelson, 1990, 1995); almost always, the writing is accomplished without input from others and must be "original" to count. In addition, the range of genres taught (or more likely, "assigned") is limited: the academic essay (reflective, or critical analyses of texts, or syntheses of research), the lab report, the timed essay (short answer or longer), or the research proposal. Freedman, Adam, and Smart (1994), in a comparative study of students preparing for careers in finance and writers in a bank setting, offer this summary of the differences in writers' roles in different contexts for writing:

> For the student, for any piece of writing, closure is only achieved when a grade has been assigned . . . student papers are often thrown out immediately after the grade is assigned. . . . In the workplace however, texts have a continued physical existence (in accessible files within the institution) as well as an ongoing role in the institutional conversation and memory. Workplace writing is characterized by a kind of intertextuality entirely absent from the student writing; workplace writing is resonant with the discourse of colleagues and the ongoing conversation of the institution. (pp. 209–210)

Collaborative processes, appropriating others' texts without citations, and other practices common to workplace writing would be deemed unacceptable in school contexts. And as mentioned earlier, there are important distinctions in general communicative principles between school and workplace writing.

Nor are internships for students in workplace settings or assignments that simulate a workplace environment necessarily effective in helping students to bridge from school to workplace writing. Most research on internships or simulated situations in the classroom document less than successful results (Anson & Forsberg, 1990; Freedman & Adam, 2000b; Freedman et al., 1994; Hill & Resnick, 1995). The cause of these failures seems to be either a lack of explicit instruction in workplace settings (much of workplace knowledge is tacit) or the difficulty in school settings of creating situations that truly "count" beyond the grade in the class and hence replicate or even approximate the social context of workplace writing. One internship assignment reported by Freedman and Adam (2000a) was successful, however, suggesting internships can be effective if carefully orchestrated. Blakeslee (2001a) also argues for the possibility of successful workplace internships for students based on case studies in two different institutional settings.

But also of interest is how writers learn in workplace settings, where "instruction" is informal, or self-motivated and indirect. Although early research in workplace settings captured only what writers were doing or thinking in a given interview or survey, or in single texts, by the late 1980s researchers began to use ethnographic techniques to take a longer view of workplace settings. From these studies came increased awareness of the socialization processes of writers making the transition from academic writing to business and professional writing. Doheny-Farina (1989, 1992) followed a student doing a writing internship in a nonprofit organization and documented her process of coming to realize the importance of understanding the political context of the organization in order for her writing to be useful to the organization. Anson and Forsberg (1990) also documented the psychological adjustment of students doing writing internships—coming to see the community's viewpoint as paramount, rather than their own.

Beaufort (1999) followed the trajectory of four writers at a nonprofit organization over several years, as they gradually adapted their writing behaviors and gleaned knowledge in five areas associated with writing expertise that were crucial to successful written communications both internal and external to the organization. Although there was no formal training program for writers new to the organization, managers observed were teaching as they worked with the writers, staging growth by assigning low-risk tasks (routine business correspondence or small sections of grant proposals) that gradually were replaced by high-risk writing tasks (grant applications, etc.), giving feedback on drafts in face-to-face coaching situations, and treating novices as already part of the professional community they were working in. From the writers' vantage point, learning to write successfully on the job involved constant observation of others' language practices (oral and written), finding out who was the best grammarian to solicit editing help from, and so on. All possible resources for learning-on-the-job were marshaled to accomplish the writing tasks. Although mistakes were made and the learning environment was by no means ideal, in this ethnographic study many of the features of what Lave and Wenger (1991) term "cognitive apprenticeships" or "legitimate peripheral participation" were present. Dias and colleagues (1999) also document the role of cognitive apprenticeships and distributed cognition in workplace learning.

Another interesting question is what transfers from one writing context to another, that is, are "general" writing skills, whatever those might be, transferable across multiple writing tasks and contexts? Dias and colleagues (1999), from their study of four school/workplace contexts for writing, concluded that three skills transfer from school to work settings: using writing for thinking, computer and graphic skills, and oral social skills. Beaufort's (1998, 1999) study of four writers who had successfully taken on considerable writing responsibilities in their jobs at a nonprofit agency showed that critical thinking skill fostered by academic writing tasks, sentence-level skills, and a general fluency in written language were helpful bases for adding context-specific knowledge. There were instances of negative transfer as well—assuming the same standards for "good writing" in business and academe, a reluctance to "manipulate" text for rhetorical effect instead of "just presenting the facts," and a lack of metacognitive awareness of problem-solving frameworks for dealing with new writing challenges.

How much useful experience teachers can give students that will aid with transfer of learning from one context to another is in fact an area of disagreement in the field. Freedman (1993, 1995) argues that little transfer is possible. Others (Beaufort, 1999; Jolliffe, 1995; Lingard & Haber, 2002) suggest that a combination of teaching problem-solving heuristics and concepts such as "genre," "discourse community," "reflective practice," and collaborative skills (skills in group process) can enhance transfer and efficiency of learning in new social contexts. Blakeslee (2001a) and Hill and Resnick (1995) suggest guidelines for effective types of workplace apprenticeships, another approach to preparing students for writing in professional roles: for example, assigning students to do writing that the university can use, or writing assignments in partnerships with corporations, or taking writing expertise into the workplace to assess rhetorical situations and make tacit knowledge explicit.

FROM RESEARCH TO THEORY AND BACK

Theorists in composition studies and literacy studies have drawn from and expanded their work in the past 20 years by looking at the empirical and descriptive research in workplace and professional writing practices reported here. A number of key people come to mind: Bazerman (1994a, 1994b), Berkenkotter and Huckin (1995), Gee (1989, 2000), Russell (1995, 1997), Swales (1990, 1992), and Witte (1988, 1992). The work of Orlikowski and Yates (1994; Yates & Orlikowski, 1992) in management communications theory has followed a similar trajectory. Drawing from social constructionist theories, literary theories, rhetorical theory, sociolinguistics, and the "new" literacy studies, and on their own rhetorical analyses of written communications in these contexts or on ethnographic work (their own and others'), they have, collectively, expanded greatly the understanding of written communications beyond K–12 and undergraduate views of writing. These researchers have added theoretical understanding specifically to matters of writing acquisition and use.

Cope and Kalantzis (2000) employ the term *multiliteracies* to describe the wide variations in "literate" behaviors in out-of-school settings. Here is their definition of the term:

> We decided that the outcomes of our discussions could be encapsulated in one word, multiliteracies—a word we chose because it describes two important arguments we might have with the emerging cultural, institutional, and global order. The first argument engages with the multiplicity of communications channels and media; the second with the increasing salience of cultural and linguistic diversity. (p. 5)

They argue, as do others (Beaufort, 2000; Heath, 1982; Hull & Schultz, 2001; Rose, 2003), that there can be no *one* standard for what counts as writing proficiency, or expertise. In a similar vein, Gee (1989) states that true literacy in a discourse is possible only outside one's primary (home) discourse because literacy requires the metaknowledge of what the discourse is doing socially, and that's not possible until one has a secondary discourse with which to critique the primary discourse. So, in essence, whether a writer is working in a school or workplace setting, s/he is outside the "home" discourse and immersed in other social, political, and cultural contexts that shape the nature of the writing in multiple ways. Plain and simple, teachers no longer have a corner on "correct" or "good" writing. What is "correct" or "good" depends on the social context—the activity system, or discourse community, or genre at hand (Nystrand, 1986).

In order to conceptualize more specifically how writers and the texts they produce function socially, others have applied activity theory to written communications

(Bazerman, 1988b; Russell, 1997), and explored the concept of discourse community (Beaufort, 1997; Killingsworth & Gilbertson, 1992; Olsen, 1993; Swales, 1990, 1992), an activity system that focuses specifically on written communication (and the interface with oral and visual communications). Examining the goals, values, communicative patterns, genre sets, and epistemologies for establishing arguments that particular discourse communities espouse (for example, nonprofit agencies, government agencies, biologists, stamp collectors, physicists, literary scholars, etc.) can illuminate what is going on in individual writers' behaviors and in individual texts and groups of texts within discourse communities. This theoretical work, in turn, has enabled making the familiar strange, that is, stepping back to examine the social systems of writing classes and writing-in-the-disciplines (Bazerman, 1997; Dias, 2000; Russell, 1997). In light of the empirical and theoretical work cited here, the social dynamics of school settings cannot be ignored in the design of writing instruction.

Closely related to theories of activity systems and discourse communities, but not as broad in scope, are the expanded theories of genre, genre systems, and intertextuality that have grown from and been employed in understandings of workplace and professional communications practices. Bazerman's (1982) work in scientific genres, Devitt's (1991) in the genres employed by tax accountants, Berkenkotter's (2001) and McCarthy's (1991; McCarthy & Gerrig, 1994) on the formation of the DSM-III and DSM-IV in psychiatry, Schryer's (1993) examination of veterinary records, and Yates's (1989) historical work on the rise of the business memo, to name a few studies, have added to conceptions of genres as socially situated and interactive with social forces over time, both influencing and being influenced by those forces. How texts function in cultures is now a subject of scholarship in composition studies as much as in linguistic anthropology, in large part as a result of the research in the past 20 years reported here. Arguments for the social construction of knowledge can be instantiated by the research here as well.

Some studies in workplace and professional writing also have taken a cognitive perspective and add to sociocognitive theories of composing and to general understandings of distributed cognition as well. Dias and colleagues (1999), drawing on theories of situated cognition and situated learning, point to the sociocognitive aspect of collaborative writing processes, common in workplace settings. In banking (Smart, 2000) and in engineering (Witte & Haas, 2001) examples abound of overlapping and specialized knowledge that is shared, leading to "robustness of decision making" in connection with written texts. Knowledge and thinking processes in acts of composing are shared and interactive. Collaborative writing is not just a division of labor; rather, it entails interactive cognitive processes among writers, editors, and managers.

In addition to adding to sociocognitive views of composing processes of writers, workplace studies have instantiated socially situated views of learning and, in particular, cognitive apprenticeships and legitimate peripheral participation of novice writers in workplace and professional discourse communities (Beaufort, 2000; Freedman & Adam, 2000b). Interactive composing sessions, employing cultural tools at hand (model texts, electronic resources, etc.) and tangible results from writing projects, are commonplace in workplace and professional settings, and suggest an alternative model of learning processes to those typical of classroom settings. While not all classroom dynamics can be transformed into the types of learning situations profiled in workplace studies, nonetheless studies of writers learning on-the-job add to conceptions of learning processes in the acquisition of writing skills.

In all, the research and the theory building that have taken place, iteratively, in the time span reported here, have expanded greatly understandings of what it means to be a writer, to write for specific purposes, and even to gain writing expertise. A working model of specific areas of knowledge and skill that constitute writing expertise, suggested from one ethnography of communication in a workplace setting (Beaufort, 1999), includes these overlapping areas: discourse community knowledge, subject matter knowledge, genre knowledge, rhetorical knowledge, and writing process knowledge. Writing expertise is many things, and writing literacies—plural—are gained over time, in multiple settings. The writing classroom is only one school for writers.

A review of research such as this makes clear the research/theory connection in composition studies, and I hope will spur further research and theorizing based on empirical findings. What might next steps be for research in workplace and professional settings? Areas that appear important for further investigation include the following:

- Effects of current and evolving technologies on composing processes of writers, reader–writer relations, genres, and discourse community practices
- Interactions of visual and written rhetoric
- Gendered differences in workplace communications
- Transfer of learning issues: what transfers from school to work and what aids or hinders transfer
- Learning/socialization processes in school and workplace settings; for example, how do writers gain skills related to written literacies in campus residence halls and computer labs and in various workplace settings?

There is also the challenge of those in university writing programs, in technical writing, and in management communications to keep abreast of one another's work (Beaufort, 2001).

I also would make a brief comment on research methodologies. Early research in workplace settings typically employed surveys and brief interviews. There was much self-reporting by writers and a lack of triangulation of data to increase validity. As several have pointed out (Faigley & Hansen, 1985; Spilka, 1993; Stratman & Duffy, 1990), analyses of social contexts is important: Looking at a text or talking solely to the individual writer cannot fully explain what is going on in terms of social roles and discourse community goals, purposes, and ideologies as they impact acts of writing. In 1986, two ethnographies of writing in workplace settings were published (Brown & Herndl, 1986; Doheny-Farina, 1986), and numerous others have followed. For a detailed explanation of ethnographic methods employed in a workplace setting, see Beaufort, 1999, Chapter 8.

Odell and Goswami (Odell, Goswami, & Herrington, 1983; Odell, Goswami, Herrington, & Quick, 1983), among the earliest scholars to conduct workplace research, developed a new method for getting at writers' tacit knowledge of social contexts, genres, and so on, that they called "discourse-based interviews." They found examples in the writers' texts of supporting statements for an argument and asked, for example, whether the writer would be willing to eliminate the statement. Writers' answers revealed much about the context for writing and the writer's conceptual thinking. They also tried writing the legislative report their informants were writing and then had the informants (legislative analysts) comment on their writing to get further information on the "norms" in the context for writing. This method is frequently used now in ethnographic studies, usually in combination with interviews, observation, and textual analysis.

Although qualitative and naturalistic studies or textual analyses have been used more commonly in recent years in workplace research, it is worth a reminder that a number of researchers have developed experimental designs that have yielded interesting findings. Think-aloud protocols (Blyler, 1989; Lutz, 1987) also have yielded important findings, and Debs (1993) also recommended visualizing methods (networks, maps, and Q-sorts) as other ways of investigating workplace writing. In addition, Geisler (2001) employed state-of-the-art screen-capture technology (set at 1 frame per second) to capture data for a self-study of her composing process. This and other technologies to come could provide other means for understanding writers' composing processes.

CONCLUSION

Technical and business writing teachers are perhaps more oriented toward the preparation of students for workplace writing than are teachers of freshman composition. And yet, the challenge of making students aware of and equipped for the lifelong learning required of all writers is similar in both contexts for teaching writing. If this review of research has revealed anything, it is just that: Writing expertise is situation-specific and requires writers to be, in a sense, researchers themselves—learning what the values, practices, and purposes of discourse communities are, whether a particular industry's, company's, or professional organization's discourse community. Writers who make successful transitions from one writing context to another both are aware of the need to analyze the immediate context for writing and have the social and critical thinking skills needed to interpret the environment (Beaufort, 1999). Learning for writers, in real-world situations, is communal. So the more teachers can foster an atmosphere of collaborative learning (not just collaborative writing), the better.

Teaching for transfer is a second and equally important conclusion suggested by the research, given that no textbook, no formula, no one class or setting can teach a writer all s/he needs to know. The general literature on transfer of learning suggests that expert problem solvers, in a variety of fields, are able to use concepts at a mid-level of abstraction to organize existing knowledge into a useful frame of reference for analyzing new situations. What this finding translates to, for writing instruction, is teaching students metacognitive skills for reflecting on writing assignments in their social context and for analyzing "model" texts. Concepts such as discourse community and genre and rhetorical analysis can serve writers in studying new writing situations. Teaching meta-awareness of one's composing processes, as well as a range of approaches to different aspects of composing, would serve writers in school-to-work and other transitions as well. Foertsch (1995), who has reviewed the literature on transfer of learning for composition teachers, says, "Research in both the classroom and the lab demonstrates that transfer of learning is most likely to be obtained when general principles and reasoning processes are taught in conjunction with their real-life applications in varied, specific contexts" (p. 374).

Foertsch's comment and Durst's (1999) research suggest a third approach to teaching that will best serve writers over the long term: creating writing projects that are meaningful, as much as possible, beyond the social context of school, that is, beyond goals of achieving grades, diplomas, and so on. Writing internships offer one such avenue (for guidance on setting up writing internships, see Henry, 1995a; Blakeslee, 2001a; Freedman & Adam, 2000a). Another could be creating within classroom contexts a community of writers, engaged in projects both individually and collectively meaningful, for audiences beyond the teacher and purposes in addition to course credits (Bazerman, 1997). Even exposing students to a few of the research reports cited here that demonstrate the critical role writing serves in society would not be a bad idea; for example, the analysis of failed arguments that led to the Challenger accident (Herndl et al., 1991) or candid reactions of recruiters and managers to flawed writing (Beason, 2001).

REFERENCES

Albers, M. J., & Lisberg, B. C. (2002). Information design: A bibliography. *Technical Communication, 47*(2), 170–176.

Aldrich, P. G. (1982). Adult writers: Some reasons for ineffective writing on the job. *College Composition and Communication, 33*(3), 284–287.

Allen, N. J. (1993). Community, collaboration, and the rhetorical triangle. *Technical Communication Quarterly, 2*(2), 63–74.

Allen, N. J., Atkinson, D., Morgan, M., Moore, T., & Snow, C. (1987). What experienced collaborators say about collaborative writing. *Journal of Business and Technical Communication, 1*(2), 70–90.

Anson, C. M., & Forsberg, L. L. (1990). Moving beyond the academic community: Transitional stages in professional writing. *Written Communication, 7*(2), 200–231.

Barabas, C. (1990). *Technical writing in a corporate culture: A study of the nature of information.* Norwood, NJ: Ablex.

Barker, K. (1998). *Comparing work skills analysis tools: Project report.* Vancouver, BC: Forestry Continuing Studies Network.

Baron, N. S. (2000). *Alphabet to e-mail: How written English evolved and where it's headed.* London: Routledge.

Bataille, R. R. (1982). Writing in the world of work: What our graduates report. *College Composition and Communication, 33*(3), 226–283.

Bazerman, C. (1981). What written knowledge does: Three examples of academic discourse. *Philosophy of the Social Sciences, 2,* 361–387.

Bazerman, C. (1982). Scientific writing as a social act. In P. Anderson (Ed.), *New essays in techni-* cal and scientific communication (pp. 156–184). Farmingdale, NY: Baywood.

Bazerman, C. (1988a). Looking at writing, writing what I see. In T. Enos & D. Roen (Eds.), *Living rhetoric and composition* (pp. 15–24). Mahwah, NJ: Erlbaum.

Bazerman, C. (1988b). *Shaping written knowledge: The genre and activity of the experimental article in science.* Madison: University of Wisconsin Press.

Bazerman, C. (1994a). *Constructing experience.* Carbondale: Southern Illinois University Press.

Bazerman, C. (1994b). Systems of genres and the enactment of social intentions. In A. Freedman & P. Medway (Eds.), *Genre and the new rhetoric* (pp. 79–100). London: Taylor & Francis.

Bazerman, C. (1997). The life of genre, the life in the classroom. In W. Bishop & H. Ostrom (Eds.), *Genre and writing: Issues, arguments, alternatives* (pp. 19–26). Portsmouth, NH: Boynton/Cook.

Beason, L. (2001). Ethos and error: How business people react to errors. *College Composition and Communication, 53*(1), 33–64.

Beaufort, A. (1997). Operationalizing the concept of discourse community: A case study of one institutional site of composing. *Research in the Teaching of English, 31*(4), 486–529.

Beaufort, A. (1998). Transferring writing knowledge to the workplace: Are we on track? In M. S. Garay & S. A. Bernhardt (Eds.), *Expanding literacies: English teaching and the new workplace* (pp. 179–199). Albany: State University of New York Press.

Beaufort, A. (1999). *Writing in the real world: Making the transition from school to work.* New York: Teachers College Press.

Beaufort, A. (2000). Learning the trade: A social apprenticeship model for gaining writing expertise. *Written Communication, 17*, 185–223.

Beaufort, A. (2001). Epilogue: Rhetorical studies, communications, and composition studies. In J. Petraglia & D. Bahri (Eds.), *Realms of rhetoric: The prospects for rhetoric education* (pp. 229–246). Albany: State University of New York Press.

Beaufort, A. (2004). Developmental gains of a history major: A case for building a theory of disciplinary writing expertise. *Research in the Teaching of English, 39*(2), 136–185.

Belcher, D. D. (1991). Nonnative writing in a corporate setting. *The Technical Writing Teacher, 18*(2), 104–115.

Berkenkotter, C. (2001). Genre systems at work: DSM-IV and rhetorical recontextualization in psychotherapy paperwork. *Written Communication, 18*(3), 326–349.

Berkenkotter, C., & Huckin, T. N. (1995). *Genre knowledge in disciplinary communication: Cognition/culture/power.* Hillsdale, NJ: Erlbaum.

Bernhardt, S. A. (1985a). Text structure and graphic design: The visible design. In J. D. Benson & W. S. Breaves (Eds.), *Systemic perspectives on discourse* (Vol. 2, pp. 18–38). Norwood, NJ: Ablex.

Bernhardt, S. A. (1985b). The writer, the reader, and the scientific text. *Journal of Technical Writing and Communication, 15*(2), 163–174.

Bernhardt, S. A. (1986). Seeing the text. *College Composition and Communication, 37*(1), 66–78.

Bernhardt, S. A. (1993). The shape of texts to come: The texture of print on screens. *College Composition and Communication, 44*(2), 151–175.

Blakeslee, A. M. (2001a). Bridging the workplace and the academy: Teaching professional genres through classroom workplace collaborations. *Technical Communication Quarterly, 10*(2), 169–192.

Blakeslee, A. M. (2001b). *Interacting with audiences: Social influences on the production of scientific writing.* Mahwah, NJ: Erlbaum.

Blau, E. K., Glantie, F. L., & Sherwin, R. T. (1989). Employment interviewers' judgments of business and technical writing of non-native speakers of English. *The Technical Writing Teacher, 16*(2), 136–146.

Blyler, N. R. (1989). Purpose and professional writers. *The Technical Writing Teacher, 16*(1), 52–67.

Broadhead, G. J., & Freed, R. C. (1986). *The variables of composition: Process and product in a business setting.* Carbondale: Southern Illinois University Press.

Brockmann, R. J. (1998). *From millwrights to shipwrights to the twenty-first century: Explorations in a history of technical communication in the United States.* Cresskill, NJ: Hampton Press.

Brown, R. L., & Herndl, C. G. (1986). An ethnographic study of corporate writing: Job status as reflected in written text. In B. Couture (Ed.), *Functional approaches to writing: Research perspectives* (pp. 11–28). London: Frances Pinter.

Brumburger, E. R. (2002). The rhetoric of typography: The awareness and impact of typeface appropriateness. *Technical Communication, 50*(2), 224–231.

Charney, D. H., Reder, L. M., & Wells, G. W. (1988). Studies of elaboration in instructional texts. In S. Doheny-Farina (Ed.), *Effective documentation: What we have learned from research* (pp. 47–72). Cambridge, MA: MIT Press.

Connors, R. J. (1982). The rise of technical writing instruction in America. *Journal of Technical Writing and Communication, 12*(4), 329–352.

Cook-Gumperz, J., with Hanna, K. (1997). Nurses' work, women's work: Some recent issues of professional literacy and practice. In G. Hull (Ed.), *Changing work, changing workers: Critical perspectives on language, literacy, and skills* (pp. 316–334). Albany: State University of New York Press.

Cope, B., & Kalantzis, M. (Eds.). (2000). *Multiliteracies: Literacy learning and the design of social futures.* London: Routledge.

Couture, B., & Rymer, J. (1993). Situational exigence: Composing processes on the job by writer's role and task value. In R. Spilka (Ed.), *Writing in the workplace: New research perspectives* (pp. 4–20). Carbondale: Southern Illinois University Press.

Daiute, C. (1983). The computer as stylus and audience. *College Composition and Communication, 34*, 134–145.

Dautermann, J. (1996). Writing with electronic tools in midwestern businesses. In P. Sullivan & J. Dautermann (Eds.), *Electronic literacies in the workplace: Technologies of writing* (pp. 3–22). Urbana, IL: National Council of Teachers of English.

Debs, M. B. (1993). Reflexive and reflective tensions: Considering research methods from writing-related fields. In R. Spilka (Ed.), *Writing in the workplace: New research perspectives* (pp. 238–252). Carbondale: Southern Illinois University Press.

Devitt, A. J. (1991). Intertextuality in tax accounting: Generic, referential, and functional. In C. Bazerman & J. Paradis (Eds.), *Textual dynamics of the professions: Historical and contemporary studies of writing in professional communities* (pp. 336–357). Madison: University of Wisconsin Press.

Dias, P. (2000). Writing classrooms as activity systems. In P. Dias & A. Pare (Eds.), *Transitions: Writing in academic and workplace settings* (pp. 11–29). Cresskill, NJ: Hampton Press.

Dias, P., Freedman, A., Medway, P., & Pare, A. (1999). *Worlds apart: Acting and writing in academic and workplace contexts.* Mahwah, NJ: Erlbaum.

Dias, P., & Pare, A. (Eds.). (2000). *Transitions: Writing in academic and workplace settings.* Cresskill, NJ: Hampton Press.

Doheny-Farina, S. (1986). Writing in an emerging organization. *Written Communication, 3,* 158–185.

Doheny-Farina, S. (1989). A case study of one adult writing in academic and nonacademic discourse communities. In C. B. Matalene (Ed.), *Worlds of writing: Teaching and learning in discourse communities of work* (pp. 17–42). New York: Random House.

Doheny-Farina, S. (1992). The individual, the organization, and kairos: Making transitions from college to careers. In S. P. Witte, N. Nakadate, & R. D. Cherry (Eds.), *A rhetoric of doing: Essays on written discourse in honor of James L. Kinneavy* (pp. 293–309). Carbondale: Southern Illinois University Press.

Dorff, D. L., & Duin, A. H. (1989). Applying a cognitive model to document cycling. *The Technical Writing Teacher, 16*(3), 234–249.

Durst, R. (1999). *Collision course: Conflict, negotiation, and learning in college composition.* Urbana, IL: National Council of Teachers of English.

Fahnestock, J. (1986). Accommodating science: The rhetorical life of scientific facts. *Written Communication, 3*(3), 275–296.

Fahnestock, J., & Secor, M. (1991). The rhetoric of literary criticism. In C. Bazerman & J. Paradis (Eds.), *Textual dynamics of the professions: Historical and contemporary studies of writing in professional communities* (pp. 76–96). Madison: University of Wisconsin Press.

Faigley, L. (1985). Nonacademic writing: The social perspective. In L. Odell & D. Goswami (Eds.), *Writing in nonacademic settings* (pp. 231–248). New York: Guilford Press.

Faigley, L., & Hansen, K. (1985). Learning to write in the social sciences. *College Composition and Communication, 34,* 140–149.

Faigley, L., & Miller, T. P. (1982). What we learn from writing on the job. *College English, 44*(6), 555–569.

Flower, L., & Hayes, J. R. (1981). A cognitive process theory of writing. *College Composition and Communication, 32*(4), 365–387.

Foertsch, J. (1995). Where cognitive psychology applies: How theories about memory and transfer can influence composition pedagogy. *Written Communication, 12*(3), 360–383.

Fortune, R. (1989). Visual and verbal thinking: Drawing and word processing in writing instruction. In G. E. Hawisher & C. L. Selfe (Eds.), *Critical perspectives on computers and composition instruction* (pp. 145–161). New York: Teachers College Press.

Freedman, A. (1993). Show and tell? The role of explicit teaching in the learning of new genres. *Research in the Teaching of English, 27*(3), 222–251.

Freedman, A. (1995). The what, where, when, why, and how of classroom genres. In J. Petraglia (Ed.), *Reconceiving writing, rethinking writing instruction* (pp. 121–144). Mahwah, NJ: Earlbaum.

Freedman, A., & Adam, C. (2000a). Bridging the gap: University-based writing that is more than simulation. In P. Dias & A. Pare (Eds.), *Transitions: Writing in academic and workplace settings* (pp. 129–144). Cresskill, NJ: Hampton Press.

Freedman, A., & Adam, C. (2000b). Write where you are: Learning to write in university and workplace settings. In P. Dias & A. Pare (Eds.), *Transitions: Writing in academic and workplace settings* (pp. 31–60). Cresskill, NJ: Hampton Press.

Freedman, A., Adam, C., & Smart, G. (1994). Wearing suits to class: Simulating genres and simulations as genre. *Written Communication, 11*(2), 193–226.

Freedman, S. W. (1984). The registers of student and professional expository writing: Influence on teachers' responses. In R. Beach & L. S. Bridwell (Eds.), *New directions in composition research* (pp. 334–347). New York: Guilford Press.

Garay, M. S., & Bernhardt, S. A. (Eds.). (1998). *Expanding literacies: English teaching and the new workplace.* Albany: State University of New York Press.

Gee, J. P. (1989). Literacy, discourse, and linguistics: Introduction. *Journal of Education, 171*(1), 5–17.

Gee, J. P. (2000). The new literacy studies: From "socially situated" to the work of the social. In D. Barton, M. Hamilton, & R. Ivanic (Eds.), *Situated literacies: Reading and writing in context* (pp. 180–196). London: Routledge.

Geisler, C. (2001). Textual objects: Accounting for the role of texts in the everyday life of complex organizations. *Written Communication, 18*(3), 296–325.

Gimenez, J. C. (2000). Business e-mail communication: Some emerging tendencies in register. *English for Specific Purposes, 19,* 237–251.

Gladwell, M. (2002). The social life of paper: Looking for method in the mess. *The New Yorker,* 92–96.

Gowen, S. G. (1992). *The politics of workplace literacy: A case study.* New York: Teachers College Press.

Haas, C. (1989). Seeing it on the screen isn't really seeing it: Computer writers' reading problems. In G. E. Hawisher & C. L. Selfe (Eds.), *Critical perspectives on computers and composition instruction* (pp. 16–29). New York: Teachers College Press.

Harwood, J. T. (1982). Freshman English ten years after: Writing in the world. *College Composition and Communication, 33*(3), 281–283.

Hawisher, G. E., & Selfe, C. L. (Eds.). (1989). *Critical perspectives on computers and composition instruction.* New York: Teachers College Press.

Heath, S. B. (1982). What no bedtime story means: Narrative skills at home and school. *Language in Society, 11,* 49–76.

Henry, J. (1995a). Teaching technical authorship. *Technical Communication Quarterly, 4*(3), 261–282.

Henry, J. (1995b). Workplace ghostwriting. *Journal of Business and Technical Communication, 9*(4), 425–445.

Herndl, C. C., Fennel, B. A., & Miller, C. R. (1991). Understanding failures in organizational discourse: The accident at Three Mile Island and the Shuttle Challenger disaster. In C. Bazerman & J. Paradis (Eds.), *Textual dynamics of the professions: Historical and contemporary studies of writing in professional communities* (pp. 279–395). Madison: University of Wisconsin Press.

Hill, C. A., & Resnick, L. (1995). Creating opportunities for apprenticeship in writing. In J. Petraglia (Ed.), *Reconceiving writing, rethinking writing instruction* (pp. 145–158). Mahwah, NJ: Erlbaum.

Horton, W. (1991). Is hypertext the best way to document your product? An assay for designers. *Technical Communication Quarterly, 38,* 20–35.

Horton, W. (1993). The almost universal language: Graphics for international documents. *Technical Communication, 40,* 682–693.

Hovde, M. R. (2001). Research tactics for constructing perceptions of subject matter in organizational contexts: An ethnographic study of technical communicators. *Technical Communication Quarterly, 10*(1), 59–95.

Hull, G. (Ed.). (1997). *Changing work, changing workers: Critical perspectives on language, literacy, and skills.* Albany: State University of New York Press.

Hull, G., & Schultz, K. (2001). Literacy and learning out of school: A review of theory and research. *Review of Educational Research, 71*(4), 575–611.

Johns, L. C. (1989). The file cabinet has a sex life: Insights of a professional writing consultant. In C. B. Matalene (Ed.), *Worlds of writing: Teaching and learning in discourse communities of work* (pp. 153–187). New York: Random House.

Jolliffe, D. (1997). Finding yourself in the text: Identity formation in the discourse of workplace documents. In G. Hull (Ed.), *Changing work, changing workers: Critical perspectives on language, literacy, and skills* (pp. 335–349). Albany: State University of New York Press.

Jolliffe, D. (1998). Preparing all students for the new workplace literacy: Avenues for English instruction in high schools and colleges. In M. S. Garay & S. A. Bernhardt (Eds.), *Expanding literacies: English teaching and the new workplace* (pp. 285–297). Albany: State University of New York Press.

Jolliffe, D. A. (1995). Discourse, interdiscursivity, and composition instruction. In J. Petraglia (Ed.), *Reconceiving writing, rethinking writing instruction* (pp. 197–216). Mahwah, NJ: Erlbaum.

Jorn, L. A. (1993). A selected annotated bibliography on collaboration in technical communication. *Technical Communication Quarterly, 2*(1), 105–115.

Killingsworth, M. J., & Gilbertson, M. K. (1992). *Signs, genres, and communities in technical communication.* Amityville, NY: Baywood.

Laruuche, M. G., & Pearson, S. S. (1985). Rhetoric and rational enterprises: Reassessing discourse in organizations. *Written Communication, 2*(3), 246–268.

Lave, J., & Wenger, E. (1991). *Situated learning: Legitimate peripheral participation.* Cambridge, UK: Cambridge University Press.

Lingard, L., & Haber, R. (2002). Learning medical talk: How the apprenticeship complicates current explicit/tacit debates in genre instruction. In R. Coe, L. Lingard, & T. Teslenko (Eds.), *The rhetoric and ideology of genre: Strategies for stability and change* (pp. 155–170). Cresskill, NJ: Hampton Press.

Lutz, J. A. (1987). A study of professional and experienced writers revising and editing at the computer and with pen and paper. *Research in the Teaching of English, 21*(4), 398–421.

Mabrito, M. (1997). Writing on the front line: A study of workplace writing. *Business Communication Quarterly, 60*(3), 58–70.

Matalene, C. B. (Ed.). (1989). *Worlds of writing: Teaching and learning in discourse communities of work.* New York: Random House.

McCarthy, L. (1991). A psychiatrist using DSM-III: The influence of a charter document in psychiatry. In C. Bazerman & J. Paradis (Eds.), *Textual dynamics of the professions: Historical and contemporary studies of writing in professional communities* (pp. 358–377). Madison: University of Wisconsin Press.

McCarthy, L., & Gerrig, J. (1994). Revising psychiatry's charter document, DSM-IV. *Written Communication, 11,* 147–192.

McIsaac, C., & Aschauer, M. A. (1990). Proposal writing at Atherton Jordan, Inc. *Management Communication Quarterly, 3*(4), 527–560.

Medway, P. (2000). Writing and design in architectural education. In P. Dias & A. Pare (Eds.), *Transitions: Writing in academic and workplace settings* (pp. 89–128). Cresskill, NJ: Hampton Press.

Munger, R. (2000). Evolution of the emergency medical services profession: A case study of EMS run reports. *Technical Communication Quarterly, 9*(3), 329–346.

Murray, D. E. (1987). Requests at work: Negotiating the conditions for conversation. *Management Communication Quarterly, 1,* 58–83.

Myers, G. (1985). The social construction of two biologists' proposals. *Written Communication, 2*(3), 219–245.

Nelson, J. (1990). *This was an easy assignment: Examining how students interpret academic writing tasks* (Rep. No. 43). Berkeley, CA: Center for the Study of Writing and Literacy.

Nelson, J. (1995). Reading classrooms as text: Exploring student writers' interpretive practices. *College Composition and Communication, 46*(3), 411–429.

Norman, R., & Grider, D. (1992). Structured document processors: Implications for technical writing. *Technical Communication Quarterly, 1*(3), 5–21.

Nystrand, M. (1986). *The structure of written communication: Studies in reciprocity between writers and readers.* Orlando: Academic Press.

Odell, L., & Goswami, D. (Eds.). (1985). *Writing in nonacademic settings.* New York: Guilford Press.

Odell, L., Goswami, D., & Herrington, A. (1983). The discourse-based interview: A procedure for exploring the tacit knowledge of writers in nonacademic settings. In P. Mosenthal, L. Tamor,
& S. Walmsley (Eds.), *Writing research: Methods and procedures* (pp. 221–236). New York: Longman.

Odell, L., Goswami, D., Herrington, A., & Quick, D. (1983). Studying writing in non-academic settings. In P. B. Anderson, R. J. Brockman, & C. R. Miller (Eds.), *New essays in technical and scientific communication: Research, theory, practice* (Vol. 2, pp. 17–40). Farmingdale, NY: Baywood.

Odell, L., Goswami, D., & Quick, D. (1983). Writing outside the English composition class. In R. W. Bailey & R. M. Forsheim (Eds.), *Literacy for life* (pp. 175–194). New York: Modern Language Association.

Olsen, L. A. (1993). Research on discourse communities: An overview. In R. Spilka (Ed.), *Writing in the workplace* (pp. 181–194). Carbondale: Southern Illinois University Press.

Orlikowski, W. J., & Yates, J. A. (1994). Genre repertoire: The structuring of communicative practices in organizations. *Administrative Science Quarterly, 39*(4), 541–574.

Paradis, J., Dobrin, D., & Miller, R. (1985). Writing at Exxon ITD: Notes on the writing environment of an R&D organization. In L. Odell & D. Goswami (Eds.), *Writing in nonacademic settings* (pp. 281–307). New York: Guilford Press.

Pare, A. (2000). Writing as a way into social work: Genre sets, genre. In P. Dias & A. Pare (Eds.), *Transitions: Writing in academic and workplace settings* (pp. 145–166). Cresskill, NJ: Hampton Press.

Paul, D., & Charney, D. (1995). Introducing chaos (theory) into science and engineering. *Written Communication, 12*(4), 396–438.

Petraglia, J. (Ed.). (1995). *Reconceiving writing, rethinking writing instruction.* Mahwah, NJ: Erlbaum.

Popken, R. (1991). A study of topic sentence use in technical writing. *The Technical Writing Teacher, 18*(1), 49–58.

Redish, J. C. (2000). What is information design? *Technical Communication, 47*(2), 163–166.

Rivers, W. E. (1989). From the garret to the fishbowl: Thoughts on the transition from literary to technical writing. In C. B. Matalene (Ed.), *Worlds of writing: Teaching and learning in discourse communities of work* (pp. 64–79). New York: Random House.

Rose, M. (2003). Words in action: Rethinking workplace literacy. *Research in the Teaching of English, 38*(1), 125–128.

Russell, D. (1995). Activity theory and its implications for writing instruction. In J. Pegralia (Ed.),

Reconceiving writing, rethinking writing instruction (pp. 51–77). Mahwah, NJ: Erlbaum.

Russell, D. R. (1997). Rethinking genre in school and society: An activity theory analysis. *Written Communication, 14*(4), 504–554.

Sauer, B. (1994). The dynamics of disaster: A three-dimensional view of a tightly regulated industry. *Technical Communication Quarterly, 3,* 393–419.

Schriver, K. A. (1989). Document design from 1980 to 1989: Challenges that remain. *Technical Communication Quarterly, 36,* 316–333.

Schriver, K. A. (1997). *Dynamics in document design.* New York: Wiley.

Schryer, C. F. (1993). Records as genre. *Written Communication, 10*(2), 200–234.

Schryer, C. F. (2000). Walking a fine line: Writing negative letters in an insurance company. *Journal of Business and Technical Communication, 14*(4), 445–497.

Schumacher, G. M., Scott, B. T., Klare, G. R., Cronin, F. C., & Lambert, D. A. (1989). Cognitive processes in journalistic genres: Extending writing models. *Written Communication, 6*(3), 390–407.

Segal, J. Z. (1993). Writing and medicine: Text and context. In R. Spilka (Ed.), *Writing in the workplace: New research perspectives* (pp. 84–97). Carbondale: Southern Illinois University Press.

Sellen, A. J., & Harper, R. H. R. (2002). *The myth of the paperless office.* Cambridge, MA: MIT Press.

Selzer, J. (1993). Intertextuality and the writing process: An overview. In R. Spilka (Ed.), *Writing in the workplace: New research perspectives* (pp. 171–180). Carbondale: Southern Illinois University Press.

Sims, B. R. (1996). Electronic mail in two corporate workplaces. In P. Sullivan & J. Dautermann (Eds.), *Electronic literacies in the workplace: Technologies of writing* (pp. 41–64). Urbana, IL: National Council of Teachers of English.

Smart, G. (1993). Genre as community invention: A central bank's response to its executives' expectations as readers. In R. Spilka (Ed.), *Writing in the workplace: New research perspectives* (pp. 124–140). Carbondale: Southern Illinois University Press.

Smart, G. (2000). Reinventing expertise: Experienced writers in the workplace encounter a new genre. In P. Dias & A. Pare (Eds.), *Transitions: Writing in academic and workplace settings* (pp. 223–252). Cresskill, NJ: Hampton Press.

Spilka, R. (1988). Studying writer–reader interactions in the workplace. *The Technical Writing Teacher, 15,* 208–221.

Spilka, R. (Ed.). (1993). *Writing in the workplace: New research perspectives.* Carbondale: Southern Illinois University Press.

Spooner, M., & Yancey, K. (1996). Postings on a genre of e-mail. *College Composition and Communication, 47*(2), 252–278.

Spyridakis, J. H. (1989a). Signal effects: A review of the research—part I. *Journal of Technical Writing and Communication, 19*(3), 227–240.

Spyridakis, J. H. (1989b). Signaling effects: Increased content retention and new answers—part II. *Journal of Technical Writing and Communication, 19*(4), 395–415.

Stratman, J. F., & Duffy, T. M. (1990). Conceptualizing research on written management communication: Looking through a glass onion. *Management Communication Quarterly, 3*(4), 429–451.

Stygall, G. (1991). Texts in oral context: The "transmission" of jury instructions in an Indiana trial. In C. Bazerman & J. Paradis (Eds.), *Textual dynamics of the professions: Historical and contemporary studies of writing in professional communities* (pp. 234–253). Madison: University of Wisconsin Press.

Sullivan, P., & Dautermann, J. (Eds.). (1996). *Electronic literacies in the workplace: Technologies of writing.* Urbana, IL: National Council of Teachers of English.

Swales, J. M. (1990). *Genre analysis: English in academic and research settings.* Cambridge, UK: Cambridge University Press.

Swales, J. M. (1992). *Re-thinking genre: Another look at discourse community effects.* Unpublished paper, Carleton University Conference on Genre.

Tebeaux, E. (1986). Redesigning professional writing courses to meet the communication needs of writers in business and industry. *College Composition and Communication, 36*(4), 419–428.

Tebeaux, E. (1990). Toward an understanding of gender differences in written business communications: A suggested perspective for future research. *Journal of Business and Technical Communication, 4*(1), 25–43.

Wenger, M. J., & Payne, D. G. (1994). Effects of graphical browsers on readers' efficiency in reading hypertext. *Technical Communications, 41*(2), 224–233.

Wiering, D. R., McCallum, M. C., Morgan, J., Yasutake, J. Y., Isoda, H., & Schumacher, R. M. J. (1996). Automating the writing process: Two case studies. In P. Sullivan & J. Dautermann (Eds.), *Electronic literacies in the workplace: Technologies of writing* (pp. 142–153). Urbana, IL: National Council of Teachers of English.

Winsor, D. (1993). Owning corporate texts. *Journal of Business and Technical Communication, 7*(2), 179–195.

Winsor, D. A. (1989). An engineer's writing and the corporate construction of knowledge. *Written Communication, 6*(3), 270–285.

Winsor, D. A. (1996). *Writing like an engineer: A rhetorical education.* Mahwah, NJ: Erlbaum.

Witte, S. P. (1988). *Some contexts for understanding written literacy.* Unpublished paper.

Witte, S. P. (1992). Context, text, intertext: Toward a constructivist semiotic of writing. *Written Communication, 9*(2), 237–308.

Witte, S. P., & Faigley, L. (1983). *Evaluating college writing programs.* Carbondale: Southern Illinois University Press.

Witte, S. P., & Haas, C. (2001). Writing as an embodied practice: The case of engineering standards. *Journal of Business and Technical Communication, 15*(4), 413–457.

Woolever, K. R. (1989). Coming to terms with different standards of excellence for written communication. In C. B. Matalene (Ed.), *Worlds of writing: Teaching and learning in discourse communities of work* (pp. 3–16). New York: Random House.

Yates, J. (1989). *Control through communication: The rise of system in American management.* Baltimore: Johns Hopkins University Press.

Yates, J., & Orlikowski, W. J. (1992). Genres of organizational communication: A structurational approach to studying communication and media. *Academy of Management Review, 17*(2), 299–326.

Yates, J. A., Orlikowski, W. J., & Okamura, K. (1999). Explicit and implicit structuring of genres in electronic communication: Reinforcement and change of social interaction. *Organization Science, 10*(1), 83–103.

Zimmerman, B. B., & Schultz, J. R. (2000). A study of the effectiveness of information design principles applied to clinical research questionnaires. *Technical Communication, 47*(2), 177–194.

CHAPTER 10

Historical Studies of Composition

David R. Russell

WRITING IS a technology used by people in myriad human activities for myriad purposes, from producing the grandest texts of religion, government, and science to the humblest government forms, grocery lists, and graffiti. And its history of uses reaches far beyond the subject of "composition," defined here as the *conscious and explicit development of students' writing in formal education, from preschool through higher education.* Some historical research on writing extends beyond this definition and will be mentioned only in brief in order to set the limits of this review and suggest the work that many historians of composition have used (or ignored).

First is the research on reception and circulation of texts that does not discuss its production. These generally are termed literacy and reading—by far the most predominant foci of historical research on writing. Of the several traditions of research on the history of literacy, the most provocative traces the effects of the introduction of literacy into an oral culture, such as Havelock's (1982, 1986) study of writing as a technology in ancient Greece, Goody's (1968, 1986, 2000) studies of the origins and effects of literacy in the ancient Middle East and Europe, and Ong's (1958, 2002) studies of Renaissance writing and African literacy. These studies of how writing shapes thinking and social organization are supported by cultural-historical research in anthropology, such as Scribner and Cole's (1981) study of literacy among the Vai in West Africa, Street's (1984) study of literacy in rural Iran, and many others (e.g., Besnier, 1995). Closely allied to this tradition are studies of the effects of print (Eisenstein, 1979) and the "history of the book." Literary studies sometimes have treated the composing of literary texts as well (e.g., Plimpton, 1963).

A few historical studies of writing by "nonliterary" people exist (Gere's [1997] history of writing groups; Brandt's [2001] literacy histories), but these do not focus on writing in formal education. The history of handwriting and its instruction (Thornton, 1996) is related to composition in some ways in that the technology of writing influenced pedagogical practices in writing instruction (as computers do today).

More relevant to composition are studies of the history of literacy related to formal schooling. H. J. Graff's (1987, 1991) radical reading of literacy and Myers's (1996) history of literacy in U.S. schools, beginning with signature literacy, provide insights into writing instruction in terms of changing standards of literacy, although the emphasis is on reception, not production. These studies are, in a sense, answers to those who argue, through historical analyses of test scores, that literacy is declining (e.g., Chall, 1996; Coulson, 1996; Stedman, 1996).

Along with the history of literacy, the history of reading instruction also emphasizes reception (Gordon & Gordon, 2003; Kaestle & Damon-Moore, 1991). These accounts sometimes discuss briefly the teaching of writing in formal schooling, but they are not framed as histories of composition per se. Similarly, the history of English as a profession has been the subject of much research in the past 20 years, and I will refer to the major studies and those that treat figures and programs whose importance to composition is discussed in detail.

And then there is the history of rhetoric, discussed in Chapter 7 of this volume. It is hard to separate rhetoric from composition, as composition grew out of rhetoric in the 19th century and in many ways returned to it in the 1960s. Indeed, composition often is referred to as "composition-rhetoric."

I exclude histories of teaching students to write literary criticism, or physics, or any specific field—unless the studies are explicit about the role of writing in that teaching, as with the Writing Across the Curriculum movement. This distinction is particularly fuzzy when considering fields devoted to specialized kinds of writing, such as creative writing and journalism (Adams, 1993). The history of technical communication instruction has a much larger literature and one more directly related to composition, as these courses often have been taught in English departments, as composition has been. There have been histories of writing (or more generally communication) in the workplace and professions (e.g., Yates, 1989), and in the academic disciplines (e.g., Bazerman, 1988, 1999). There is an even larger literature on the history of business and technical writing, notably Longo (2000), and its teaching (Adams, 1993). But research on the teaching of technical and business writing is not considered in this chapter.

Finally, the history of education has treated literacy rather extensively and influenced much research in the history of composition. But there has been little communication between the two endeavors. Indeed, none of the 15 articles on literacy in *History of Education Quarterly*, the leading journal in the field, mentions composition. This omission is regrettable, as the historians of composition can learn much from the archival and social historical methods of educational history and could contribute much to that field's research. Indeed, historical methods in composition, in my view, rely too much on published sources and not enough on archival materials, with some important exceptions, which I note below.

I'll first discuss elementary and secondary education and proceed through higher education, taking each in roughly chronological order. I have not discussed a number of short articles (five pages or fewer) that do not include developed historical research but do point to a "then and now" connection of some current practice or problem with the past, although these may offer interesting brief insights.

ELEMENTARY AND SECONDARY EDUCATION

There is far less historical research on composition in elementary and secondary schools than in higher education because composition in elementary and secondary schools has been subordinate to reading (particularly literature) and has remained largely so, while in higher education, composition courses have been separate and, during the past 3 decades, have become professionalized. As that happened, composition looked to define itself by studying its history. Indeed, much of the historical research on elementary and secondary composition was motivated by a desire to understand the origins of pedagogical practices in higher education. Although there is a very large body of historical research on reading in elementary and secondary education (and very little on reading in higher education), it treats writing and composition mostly incidentally.

Research journals devoted to elementary and secondary English did not publish much historical work on composition (see Chapter 1 of this volume) until recently. Indeed, the major research journal, *Research in the Teaching of English*, published only three historical studies from its founding in 1967 until 1994. Nevertheless, the research on K–12 composition is important, because a great many of the practices and theories that are central to composition (at any level) had their origins in the schools. And, of course, the vast majority of composition instruction (as well as literature and language instruction) takes place in K–12.

The relative paucity of research on the history of writing in elementary and secondary schools perhaps can be explained also in part by the towering presence of Applebee's (1974) definitive (and only) comprehensive history, a magisterial study that functioned in the way, say, Boring's (1929) history of psychology did, both as a reference work and a definition of the field. Applebee's book was researched rigorously from an impressive range of archival resources, which was necessary as there was very little historical research to build on. Yet it is written in a very readable style, with immense confidence. Although Applebee would go on in his career to study writing, his history gives relatively little attention to composition and writing in comparison to literature and reading—not surprisingly, as the teaching of K–12 English did not either. Indeed, the book has only 10 index entries for composition and none for writing, as compared with dozens each for literature and reading (even drama gets 10). Nevertheless, there has been some excellent historical work on K–12 composition since 1984.

The 19th Century: From Handwriting to Composition

Before about 1830, "writing" at all but the highest levels of formal education was defined as penmanship, or transcription (Monaghan, 2003). This conception persisted well into the 20th century (Thornton, 1996). The origins of what today is called composition occurred in elementary and middle school, for students about ages 6 to 16 (which in part may explain its low status). The teaching of composition, as distinct from handwriting, began with a series of educational reforms in schooling during the 1830s. Woods (1985a) sketched out that history, and his formulations have been refined by others since. As Woods shows, the teaching of handwriting occurred in what aptly were termed grammar schools that emphasized rote drill in the rules of Latinate grammar and spelling, as well as vocabulary and proper handwriting. Writing generally was confined to copying or imitation of adults' texts. But in the 1830s American reformers such as Bronson Alcott, under the influence of European romantic educational reformers—Froebel, Herbart, and, mainly, Pestalozzi—began to introduce "self-active" methods, which came to include students writing about objects in their environment, experiences, and so forth. Woods (1985a) shows how composition (and the culture as a whole) inherited central myths about grammar: its power to discipline the mind, preserve culture from decay, and acculturate new generations.

Schultz (1999) greatly developed Woods's (1985a, 1985b, 1985c) research to produce, as she claims, "our profession's first history of school-based writing instruction" (p. 4), although it covers only the 19th century. Schultz's history begins with the introduction of composition in the 1830s as part of the "Great Awakening" in education, a widespread—if halting—move toward universal primary education, motivated by a Jacksonian democratizing politics and a slightly more secular—although always moralizing—approach to religion in public life. With it came a new and romantic concept of the child as a developing and active learner, rather than a container for content or miniature and defective adult. While pointing out that the old drilling continued to be the dominant pedagogy, Schultz focuses on books that were less popular but advocated "reform pedagogy."

In the new "object teaching," as it was called, students wrote about lived experience, not just abstractions, in an attempt to prepare students for "life," not just college. For example, Frost (1839) introduced topics on how haymaking supports other trades, "drawing from real objects in order to apply the art (of composition) to useful purposes" to "insure success in business" (p. 54). Textbooks, says Schultz (1999), reproduced cultural and class values such as manual labor and a "well-ordered home" (p. 156).

Reformers argued against beginning with rules and in favor of learning to write by writing, not strictly following models but using models in more complex ways. Students began to develop their own subject matter and even write journals. As textbooks gradually moved toward the concrete and practical in writing, students got regular practice in composition, not just memorization or dictation of adult texts. Textbooks began to incorporate visuals (using the new wood engraving technology) as part of the pedagogy, for composition prompts. Indeed, Schultz (1999) concludes, "The school climate was more encouraging of innovation than the university setting" (p. 151).

Schultz (1999) forces a rethinking of Connors's view of the 19th century as dependent on static abstractions—she finds "How I Spent My Summer Vacation" prompts much earlier than Connors does. But it's difficult to know, then as now, how widespread such innovations were, because Schultz, like other historians of the 19th century, relies very heavily on textbooks for her account, although she does bring in some other materials such as school newspapers, prize essays, letters, and memoirs. Because archival material is so important for getting at the actual practices and consequences of classroom instruction, as well as the institutional and social environments, of classroom practices, it would be good to have more of the patient archival digging (particularly using methods of social historians) that allows historians to construct "solid, ethical histories based on fragmentary evidence," as Eldred and Mortensen (2002, p. 41) point out. And it would be important as well to have richer theories of the connections between school practices and wider ideological contexts.

One area that has received a good deal of treatment is the place of women in 19th-century composition—more treatment, indeed, than composition in general has received. Historians have put classroom practices into the context of women's lives, as in Gere's (1994) study of writing workshops and her book-length study of literacy practices (and learning) in women's clubs (see also Greer, 2003). Eldred and Mortensen's study of "composing women of the early U.S.," drawn from descriptions of schools in novels, provides little on composition. Rouse (1995) uses colonization theory to account for women's struggles at eastern and southeastern girls' schools, against patriarchal ideals of "republican motherhood" and "true womanhood," and girls' resistance, in their writing. She argues that the girls constructed identities out of their experience rather than the biological determinism enforced in the schools. This kind of ideological analysis based on sound archival research is, I would suggest, precisely what is necessary for K–12 history research.

African Americans' role in composition has not been researched systematically, but Jacqueline Jones Royster (2000) has studied the opportunities for, obstacles to, and uses of literacy for African American women from colonization to the present. Given such scope, Royster is able to devote little attention to composition per se. In the few mentions she gives to specific instructional practices for writing, Royster opens up a rich area for historians of composition interested in the specific practices of communication instruction and acquisition in schools attended by African Americans, from the Sabbath schools and missionary schools of the 18th and 19th centuries to the "elocution and oratorical training [that] were common interests practiced among African American women during this era, in support of their obvious desires to develop public speaking abilities" (p. 158). Composition needs more of Royster's rigorous archival research, but focused on the teaching and learning of writing by people of color. Such archival work is especially difficult given the paucity—for reasons that should be obvious—of the kinds of documents composition histories have mainly relied on, textbooks and articles.

The remaining research on 19th-century K–12 education includes a number of brief "then and now" articles that discuss the precedents of some teaching or curricular practice, particularly ones that I believe should be more prominent today. Among these one might note Aulbach's (1994) reminder of the importance of the Committee of 10 in 1893 and Rodd (1983) on precedents for the use of models in composition instruction. The practices of elementary and secondary education are crucial to understanding composition's origins, as well as its influence on college composition, as Connors (1997) makes clear in his history of college composition and the history of education in general. It is important to have more of that history available.

The 20th Century: Mass Education

Twentieth-century composition in elementary and secondary schools has received even less attention by historians than that of the 19th century. In the period this review covers, there were no book-length studies and few major articles. The majority of work came in the form of what I have called "then and now" articles (usually published in the periodic special issues of *English Journal* devoted to history) that look at some contemporary practice in light of some historical moment from the past. There has been little attempt to deepen or rethink Applebee's (1974) categories.

Nevertheless, some work treating major figures provides useful insights: Monseau's (1986) study of Dora V. Smith's pioneering work in the 1930s and 1940s; Thomas's (2000) appreciation of Lou La Brant, president of the NCTE in 1954 and advocate of an open curriculum and child-centered teaching; and Thompson's (2000) study of Sylvia Ashton-Warner, an Australian educator of the Maori who anticipated the whole language movement in the 1940s and 1950s. And some of the then and now studies are equally engaging, such as Shadiow's (1984) collection of comments from teachers from the late 19th and early 20th centuries on teaching practices or Waber's (1987) article on finance, curriculum, and teacher recruitment, both of which illustrate *plus ca change, plus c'est la meme chose* in K–12 composition teaching. More substantial are Donelson's (2000) presentation of quotes to illustrate that there was no "golden age" of composition instruction (*pace* conservative critics of the 1990s) or Nelms's (2000) historical reflections on the inability of composition to be more than a "handmaid" of the "master," literary criticism, with all that implies about "the inequity those gender-laden terms imply" (p. 51). More rigorous in method is Donsky's (1984) study of trends in elementary school textbooks, from 1900 to 1959, which shows the ebb and flow of interest in teaching practices such as oral language, grammar, modeling, and prewriting. And Strain (1993) provides a fascinating "herme-neutic" history of the ways the English used composition in the early 1960s both to secure federal funding and to continue composition's marginal status.

English/composition teaching as a profession. There also is, unfortunately, little work on the role of composition in the growth of elementary and secondary English teaching as a profession. Haugh (1996) provides a brief retrospective of the origins and development of *English Education*, the journal of teacher education founded in 1969. And Durst (1992) analyzes the NCTE Promising Research Award dissertations from 1970 to 1989, finding the emphasis overwhelmingly on empirical work on students, although a range of methodologies and theories were borrowed from other disciplines to enrich English studies. Fowler and Fowler (1984) briefly discuss the history of the unfortunate split between composition and speech communication, which occurred just after the formation of the NCTE in 1911, but had roots in the 19th-century elo-cution movement and lamentable consequences for later attempts to integrate communication teaching and learning. This crucial historical break in disciplines, which separated speaking from writing, deserves much more study.

Women. The role of women in 20th-century K–12 education began to be researched in the period of this review, most notably Gerlach, Monseau, and the NCTE Committee on Women in the Profession's (1991) collection. This appreciation of 10 pioneering women in English education begins with the first woman NCTE president, Rewey Belle Inglis (1928) and ends with Ruth G. Strickland, David H. Russell award winner in 1965. Although these essays are often more hagiographical than critical or analytic, they mark the outlines of women's contributions to K–12 English. It is revealing to read them through the lens of composition (more space is devoted to literature instruction). These teachers and educational leaders did a range of work that might well have been groundbreaking if the profession had taken their innovations into widespread practice: Rewey Belle Inglis on viewing the classroom as laboratory for exploration; Dora V. Smith on the "thought method" of teaching grammar, formal grammar instruction as an impediment to learning, analysis of error as individual and caused (a precursor of Shaughnessy, 1977), composition as means of socialization by broadening student interests, and the systematic use of visuals; Harriett Sheridan on analysis of film and teaching the writing process; Ruth G. Strickland on the use of functional rather than formal grammar, concern with process over product, and teaching composition in the whole curriculum; and Ruth Mary Weeks and Luealla B. Cook on research on talk and other spontaneous language use. Almost all were disciples of Evelyn and John Dewey—progressives, not least in their concern for students disadvantaged ethnically, economically, or geographically. The line of work opened by Gerlach and colleagues (but not much pursued since) would yield important insights into the past and the present.

People of color. A good deal of work on the literacy practices of people of color in formal schooling has been done in the history of elementary and secondary education over the past 2 decades, notably Willis (2002) on literacy at Calhoun Colored School from 1892 to 1945, Goodburn (1999) on the Genoa Industrial Indian School, and Lockard (1996) on Navajo literacy in the 1930s and 1940s, in which a Navajo elementary teacher weaves together archival materials (BIA and school) with anecdotes of her father's and her own experiences in both school and church. All discuss writing instruction, although none is framed explicitly as an historical study of composition and none published in a composition journal. Despite the recent interest in ethnic minorities within composition studies, there has been very little work in the history of composition in this crucial area, with the exception of Royster (2000), which treats 20th-century K–12 schooling in vignettes, such as the women's campaign against efforts in the 1910s to "deny African American children access to literature after the sixth grade, a policy supported by the industrial education movement" (p. 216), which led to the founding of the first African American public high school in Atlanta.

Whole language. The whole language movement—important politically as well as pedagogically—deserves thorough historical treatment, but there exist only brief accounts. One of the whole language movement's founders (Goodman, 1989) traces the intellectual roots of the movement, in learning theory (John Dewey, Jean Piaget, L. S. Vygotsky), in reading theory (Louise Rosenblatt, Frank Smith, Ken Goodman, Sylvia Ashton-Warner, and the individualized—anti-basal—reading instruction movement), in composition theory (Alvina Burrows, Donald Graves, James Britton, and the National Writing Project), and in experiments with integrated curriculum beginning with Kilpatrick in the 1920s. She then tells her personal history of the movement's beginnings in the mid- to late 1970s among groups of teachers in the United States and Canada. Daniels, Zemelman, and Bizar (1999) summarize 60 years of research that, they argue, supports holistic, literature-based approaches to writing.

Writing across the curriculum. Attempts to improve writing (and improve learning through writing) in secondary school content areas were chronicled by Russell, from the earliest days of the NCTE and its first president's advocacy of "cooperation" (1986) and the Dewey-inspired correlated curriculum movement of the 1930s to the work of the Bay Area (later National) Writing Project (1991, 2002b).

Assessment. Trachsel (1992) has written the only comprehensive history of the crucially important subject of assessment—focused on the college entrance examinations, not classroom or programmatic assessment practices (other areas ripe for historians). Her book covers the changes in the College Entrance Examination Board (and its successor, the Educational Testing Service), from its origins in the Committee of 10 in the 1890s, through the first exam in 1901 (mainly memory of set books), to the Scholastic Aptitude Test in place in 1990—exclusively multiple choice (and that has since changed again). She sees this history as a battle between competing definitions of literacy associated with geographical, professional, and philosophical interests: the formal, which is associated with schools, "achievement," the eastern United States, literature, form/grammar (a legacy of the Committee of 10); and the functional, which is associated with learning for life (not school), "aptitude," the midwestern and western United States, composition, content, and the legacy of F. N. Scott and other Deweyan reformers.

The formal generally won out, as the notion of "aptitude" became formalized and achievement-oriented, redefined according to the professionalized English (read, literary criticism), which used testing by the literary and formal definitions to mark out its professional place. There was some erosion of eastern college dominance (e.g., the 1920s test included a writing section on nonliterary composition but the reading section remained all literary). Thus, the test was part of the literature/composition split, with literature remaining a discipline and composition reduced to content-free "skills."

But as tests became "objective," literature itself lost control to psychometricans. "Literacy" as officially defined and enforced (the use of tests skyrocketed in the 1950s and beyond) became separated from pedagogy, and from either literature or composition—hence so many "How to Pass the SAT" books. Trachsel's conclusion: Tests are good at predicting academic success but not promoting it. They are essentially conservative, reproducing the status quo. And both literature and composition should work together to regain control over the definition and testing of writing and reading. Trachsel's (1992) analysis is partial and open to much revision, and I hope other historical analyses of assessment will follow.

Disabilities. I have been able to find only two historical studies of writing instruction for students with disabilities (neither framed as composition research), but they provide a starting point for important work yet to be done. Katims (2000) gives a five-page review of historical studies on literacy instruction for people with intellectual disabilities between 1800 and 2000. He divides them into skills-based instruction and "integrated and contextualized" instruction, the former mainly devoted to decoding without writing, the latter offering much more writing instruction, often integrated with reading and speaking. Sawyer (1991) reviews the history of the whole language approach with reference to students with learning disabilities.

Composition in Other Elementary/Secondary Educational Systems

The following review of histories of composition in other educational systems is admittedly partial, owing to the very different ways formal writing instruction is conceived in various systems—and to my own lack of knowledge of the languages and educational systems of the vast majority of nations. Nevertheless, I mention several useful historical works.

Britton (1984) collected descriptions of English teaching in the United Kingdom and Commonwealth nations, each of which contains a section on history, including writing instruction. Tchudi (1986) collected brief histories of English teaching in Australia, New Zealand, Canada, England, and the United States. Green's (1992) collection of articles on the history of education in the United Kingdom and Commonwealth provides more historical detail, particularly Hoskin on the central role of writing and alphabetization in the history of education, Willinsky on the teaching of literacy before the advent of formal elementary education, Christie on the decline of rhetoric and the "corruption" of grammar, and Burgess on the effects of diversity on literacy in the postwar period. Pandian (1997) provides a history of literacy efforts in Malaysia since it gained independence in 1957.

Anglophone Canada has received particular attention from historians. Doige (2001) looks at literacy instruction among First Nations in the Maritime provinces before European contact, suggesting lessons for contemporary educators. Johnson (1987b) summarizes 19th-century Anglophone Canadian grammar and composition teaching and explains its persistence in the 20th century despite reform movements. Luke (1988) provides a complex analysis of the ideology of postwar Anglophone Canadian elementary education by tracing the ideology of textbooks in relation to classroom practice and wider debates over literacy, class, and nationalism.

Herrlitz (1984) surveys language teaching in nine western European educational systems, with a section for each system devoted to history, including writing instruction. The history of writing instruction has not (as far as I can tell) received specific treatment in francophone nations, but Chervel's (1998) history of French schooling devotes a good deal of attention to writing, particularly the history of the genres required on the secondary school exit (and university admissions) exam, the *baccalauréat*, and the pedagogical practices that prepare students to write the exams (cf. Jey, 1998).

COMPOSITION IN U.S. HIGHER EDUCATION

The historical research done from 1984 to 2003 on 19th- and 20th-century writing instruction in higher education is primarily a search for origins by an emerging profession, composition studies. The history is seen through the lens of debates over what the profession should be and what form its central activity, the teaching of first-year college composition courses, should take.

General Histories

There is no standard work at this point that covers the entire history of composition. Connors (1997) comes closest with his collection of essays that he previously published along with material on the 20th century. He covers gender influences, textbooks, grammar and correctness, issues of disciplinary identity and workload, discourse taxonomies, the emphasis on static abstractions, and the role of invention in relation to assignments. He proceeds from a rationalist and pragmatic epistemology, deliberately not a "a work of criticism" (p. 22) but a series of stories, "traditional" history—although the stories always take into account the social and educational contexts. Spear (1997) too provides a brief but helpful overview of composition's history and activity, written to explain the field to those not in it.

Nineteenth-Century Origins

The 19th-century origins of composition in higher education were studied first by Kitzhaber (1953/1990), whose work forms the starting point of most of the studies in the early 1980s. And there was some excellent work on composition before 1984 (see Scott & Castner, 1983). The most balanced and thoughtful short account of the origins of college composition is Brereton's (1995) introduction to his important collection of historical documents from 1875 to 1925.

Berlin (1984) wrote the first published book-length study of writing instruction in 19th-century American colleges. In the first two-thirds of the book, Berlin—always a classifier—draws two of his three "rhetorics" (approaches to writing instruction) from Kitzhaber: classical rhetoric and what Berlin terms "eighteenth century rhetoric"—the psychologized rhetoric drawing heavily on the Scottish Enlightenment. He adds a third, romantic rhetoric, "growing out of the transcendental movement and in most ways uniquely American in its development" (p. 4). Berlin's emphasis is on the theoretical and philosophical (mainly epistemological) roots and assumptions of these rhetorics (he relies on textbooks and accounts rather than archival materials), as he traces the decline of the classical tradition and the growth of the "eighteenth century rhetoric" to become the dominant approach to writing instruction through American imitators of Hugh Blair, George Campbell, Richard Whatley, and others. Berlin clearly prefers what he identifies as an Emersonian, "democratic," romantic rhetoric. He acknowledges it had little effect on either 19th-century or later practice, although he speculates on a connection through Dewey to 20th-century progressive education.

Berlin (1984) looks at the origin of composition at Harvard and locates it philosophically in a "scientistic" approach—positivism. He then praises Fred Newton Scott of Michigan (along with Gertrude Buck and Joseph Denney) in describing a democratic and rhetorical alternative that, he laments, also disappeared under the pressure of scientistic approaches. Woods (1985b) surveys the central psychological theories that informed 19th-century writing instruction: mental discipline, Scottish Commonsense Philosophy, Bain's associationism, and James's functionalist pragmatism.

Johnson's (1987a, 1987b) rethinking of 19th-century rhetorical theory reads the period not in terms of a decline in classical rhetoric or oratorical tradition or in terms of a practical (pedagogical) lens that traces the roots of current problems. Instead she tries to see 19th-century rhetorical theory in 19th-century terms, as a useful synthesis of 18th-century thought that broadened interest from the oral to include the written and that valued the resulting "new rhetoric" in terms of its contribution to liberal education and moral/social betterment. She concludes that this attempt to provide "habits of eloquence" (p. xx) made a significant contribution to 19th-century culture and thought and thus deserves to be studied and valued in its context, not as a scapegoat for late-20th-century projects to revive classical rhetoric and reform pedagogy.

From rhetoric to composition. The issue of origins was debated endlessly from 1984 to 2003 in terms of what Young (1978) termed "current-traditional rhetoric," borrowing Fogarty's (1959) term. Current-traditional rhetoric emphasizes writing in modes (exposition, definition, narration, argument—EDNA); division into words, sentences, and paragraphs; mechanical correctness; the reading of professional models; and other things, depending on the historian. It does not emphasize communication, invention (in the classical tradition), or the process of writing. The current-traditional oxymoron suggested that this paradox was composition's tradition of pedagogy and that the tradition was still very much with us. The highly flexible term provided a useful category, a paradigm, for the emerging profession to position itself against, in order to define new—professionalized—paradigms. And it provided an umbrella term that motivated much historical research on the origins of practices and, more broadly, the theories that lay behind them.

Decline of classical rhetoric.

Decline of classical rhetoric. As composition became professionalized, it looked to a time before the long winter of current-traditional rhetoric and rediscovered classical rhetoric (long studied in speech departments). Corbett (1965) remade classical rhetoric into a composition pedagogy and positioned it as a historically more legitimate alternative to current-traditional rhetoric—one that was beholden to neither modern literary criticism nor modern educational theory and research, the two main alternatives then available to English department composition teachers. Indeed, some of the historical articles of the late 1970s and early 1980s read like jeremiads on the evils of the present age and a call to return to the ancient ways (see, for example, Murphy, 1982). But the historical research gained a less polemical edge quickly, drawing on the work of Halloran and others, to become a major contribution to the field of rhetoric.

An excellent introduction to the issues is Wright and Halloran (2001). They see the 19th century (as do most historians) in terms of a shift from an oral to a written discourse, and from Latin (and to a lesser extent Greek) education to a vernacular curriculum. In the 18th and well into the 19th century, at the highest levels of education, writing was considered primarily as a means of preparing to speak. And it was termed Rhetoric, a distant but strong legacy of ancient rhetoric. Today it often is termed "oratorical culture" (see Clark & Halloran, 1993). Composition ordinarily meant composition in Latin and Greek, when that term was used in higher education (then usually called "colleges"). And students wrote as a means of preparing to speak publicly, providing a rich environment for integrated language learning and practice. The oratorical culture endured in the form of extracurricular student literary societies that provided lively discussions of contemporary learning and issues as well as the opportunity to practice speaking and writing. (Note that until the mid-19th century, many students attended "colleges" at age 16 or even earlier. It's important to understand that the levels of education taken for granted today in the United States evolved slowly.)

The shift from what Wright and Halloran (2001) call "scripted orality to silent prose" (p. 222) has been viewed as an inevitable consequence of social changes, such as technology, American individualism (especially the rise of a middle class with educational aspirations), and professionalism (G. Graff, 1987). Crowley (1990) argues that it lost power mainly through theoretical innovations in philosophy, logic, and psychology. Johnson (1991) sees the shift not as a decline but as a creative synthesis in the face of social and educational exigencies, which lost its creative edge in the late 19th and early 20th centuries. In any case, the emphasis on writing led to a belletristic emphasis on "polite literature," imported mainly from Scotland through such highly influential textbooks as Blair's *Lectures on Rhetoric and Belles Letters*, a trend that led eventually to the dominance of literary criticism over rhetorical education and practice, as Horner (1993) and Miller (1997) have explicated in terms of the split between reading and writing and its consequences for the professionalization of composition (see below).

Connors (1986b, 19876b, 1997) argues that the belletristic influence led to personal writing assignments in higher education (see Schultz's [1999] disagreement above) and a move from objective, "centripetal" writing assignments concerned with issues in the world toward individual, subjective, "centrifugal" tasks. Liu and Young (1998) analyze several problems in reviving rhetoric as a modern academic discipline, locating current-traditional rhetoric in terms of the institutional histories of speech communication and composition studies.

Modes and invention. Perhaps no other current-traditional practice was more confining than the modes of discourse (EDNA) for a profession wishing to teach writing as communication instead of as traditional rules. Connors's (1981) article explaining the modes' long influence in terms of 19th-century social conditions spawned several articles. D'Angelo (1984) investigated further the ways early 19th-century lists of types of discourse (which proliferated in the age of mass printing and literacy) evolved (or to some, devolved) into textbook formulas, which varied in complex ways, according to various theories (particularly Alexander Bain's psychology) and became more or less stabilized as a textbook tradition around 1900. Crowley (1984b) challenged Connors's social explanations by delving further into the *desiccated theory* of 19th-century rhetoric (from Kitzhaber, 1953/1990) that ignored audience and reduced authors' aims to textual features (cf. Adams, 1984). Connors (1997) provides the most complete treatment of discourse taxonomies, especially the modes, including his work on the evolution of scientific discourse in composition under the mode of exposition.

The work on modes spawned a deeper consideration of the decline of the classical canon of invention. How do students (and writers in general) find things to say? The fullest theoretical treatment of this issue is Crowley (1990). Although chiefly a work on rhetorical theory, it digs deeply into the roots of current-traditional composition teaching. She argues that the 18th-century British rhetoricians (George Campbell, Richard Whatley, Joseph Priestly, Adam Smith) did not, as Howell (1971; Howell & Ramus, 1956) and Kitzhaber (1953/1990) had argued and others generally accepted, create a modern, psychological rhetorical theory that was desiccated in the 19th century. Rather, the very problems of current-traditional rhetoric lay in the 18th-century mentalist assumption that there are general principles, true of all people, that allow writers to take fully formed ideas introspectively from memory and transfer them to the page (and know their audiences because they know themselves). This assumption leads, in Crowley's view, to ignoring the communal social processes—especially the role of audience—that were central to classical rhetoric and the differences among people that motivate and necessitate communication. It also leads to an emphasis on textual forms, locating authority in texts rather than in authors and communities, teaching by general principles ("intellectual prescriptions"), a lack of attention to ethos (including ethics) and pathos, the banal five-paragraph theme, and generally prose that "establishes no voice, selects no audience, takes no stand, makes no commitment" (p. 149). In summary, Johnson's (1991) appraisal suggests the usefulness and importance of the 19th-century theoretical synthesis for that century; Crowley shows the unfortunate consequences of the theory's uncritical appropriation and codification in the 20th.

Correctness. The historians' project to understand—and reform—current-traditional rhetoric had no more important task than resisting the pervasive focus on mechanical correctness in composition. Historians all pointed to the extraordinary sameness of complaints about student errors and the lack of any good evidence that students are indeed making more of them than in the past. Connors traces the origin and development of composition's (and the nation's) obsession with correctness, locating it in a cultural and class-based "linguistic anxiety" that developed in the 1840s, as well as the pedagogical constraints of mass education, where the decline of rhetoric and growth of emphasis on the written and the practical, in both secondary and higher education, left poorly trained and overworked teachers "bereft of a discipline" scrambling for handbook answers to this social "problem." Predictably, he looks to the newly emerging discipline of composition to restore the imbalance between rhetoric and correctness. Similarly, Connors (1986a) explains the reduction of grammar instruction and theory from the central and elaborated tradition of classical rhetorical education in the liberal arts (chiefly Latin grammar) to a means of correcting errors and "the strange amalgam of buzzwords, legends, handbook nostrums, half-understood transformational concepts, and decayed eighteenth-century prescription that most of us know today" (p. 22). Boyd (1993) extends Connors's cultural analysis by arguing that the obsession with correctness became a pedagogical ritual for dealing with the modern cultural anxiety, "transporting the novice writer to a new cultural space free of destabilizing elements" (p. 451).

The Beginning of FYC: Harvard and Beyond

The outlines of the origin of first-year composition courses (FYC) were sketched out by Kitzhaber (1953/1990), with important quantitative archival work on programs by Wozniack (1978) (efficiently summarized by Brereton, 1995). Instituted at Harvard by President Eliot in 1872, the course was a first step in moving away from the emphasis on classical languages and toward an elective, fully specialized curriculum (English A soon became the *only* required course). It grew out of an admissions test that was an attempt—very successful—to exert control over secondary school curricula. And, despite a number of other extant approaches, it set the model for the modern U.S. university, which was just emerging after the Civil War (Stewart, 1992; see Wright & Halloran, 2001, for a dissenting view).

Various historians have emphasized Harvard's influence. Berlin (1987) points to the growth of scientific specialization in the preparation of a new middle class of professionals through the teaching of a "narrowly scientific and rational discourse" (p. 30). Connors (1997) emphasizes a turn away from the oral and social toward individualistic self-expression of the written word, with style instruction reduced to static abstractions and a focus on sentences and paragraphs. Jolliffe (1989), who surveyed student themes and forensics from 1865 to 1900 in the Harvard archives, found not a scientistic turn, as Berlin theorized, but rather a moralizing tendency, in line with the Arnoldian ideology of belletristic idealism (in the tradition of Blair) that linked art and morality. And he found (in Wendell's pedagogy) many noncurrent-traditional features (*pace* Kitzhaber, 1953/1990). Crowley (1984a, 1986, 1998) pushes the argument further, interpreting English A as, in Foucault's term, "a political technology of individuals," designed not to teach argumentation or rhetorical communication but rather to make "the bourgeois subject docile" by emphasizing error (Crowley, 1998, pp. 77–78). Miller (1991) locates the origin of FYC in broad cultural terms, as part of nationalistic, colonizing, and political projects of 19th-century American ideologies, and takes to task historians who look for "neoclassical continuity" in their accounts while ignoring, in her view, the changes in technology and literacy practices since the ancients. Russell (1991, 2002b) also draws on the Harvard archives to argue that English A was originally part of a "forensic system" that required writing of upper classmen in the disciplines in a cross-curricular effort to improve it. Simmons (1995a) profiles a chief player at Harvard, Wendell, and also describes the alternative to the Harvard composition that the women of its sister institution, Radcliff, chose (Simmons, 1995b).

Belles-lettres: Origins of English Departments and the Literature/Composition Split

Before the professionalization of composition in the late 1970s, there was very little written on the history of English departments at all, much less in relation to composition, although Parker (1967) and Ohmann and Douglas (1976) are important exceptions. But in the period of this review, such studies exploded, largely as a way of understanding—and resisting—the dominance of literary study in English departments, where the vast majority of composition courses were and are taught. This search not only for origins but for independence—or at least respect—has spawned such a large literature that it is impossible to do justice, in this review, to even the major arguments. So I simply will mention some essentials and some essential texts. The appreciation and criticism of belles-lettres (originally "beautiful writing" in any genre) began to be taught in the late 18th century, especially under the influence of Scottish rhetoricians (notably Blair), "as both an education in intellectual and moral taste and as a means by which practical rhetorical skills could be acquired" (Johnson, 1991, p. 225). Courses in English literature began in the 1830s in a curriculum dominated by Latin. But with the rise of the new, departmentalized university after the Civil War and the decline of Latin, departments of English (by various titles) emerged. And they quickly began to privilege literary study over rhetorical study or, as it came to be called, composition, and the two became separated in the departments' curricula, with composition eventually reduced to FYC. Miller provides excellent background in his study of rhetoric and belles-lettres in the British cultural provinces. Stewart (1985) chronicled the decline in papers about composition at the MLA between 1880 and 1902, as the primary professional organization for English gradually became concerned almost exclusively with literary subjects and disbanded its pedagogical and phonetics (speech) sections.

Berlin (1987) interpreted this history as a continuation of the ancient dialectic between rhetoric and poetic. In his reading (which owes much to Ohmann & Douglas, 1976), the fledgling English departments originally took a scientific approach to both (teaching literature as historical and philological facts) but developed beyond that epistemology to see literature as morally improving "spiritual beauties" (p. xiv). Literary critics left the texts that current-traditional rhetoric read and wrote in a theoretical backwater and derided them as "embodiments of the fallen realms of science and commerce and politics" in an attempt to mark off literature as privileged and gain status—while nevertheless teaching composition as a mark of utility (p. 28). Berlin posited three rhetoric-poetic strands: the meritocratic-scientific, the liberal-cultural, and the social-democratic.

Miller (1991) reads the origins of the literature/composition relation not so much in economic terms but in postmodern (and often Bakhtinian) terms, as the creation of a carvinalesque "low" in the "wholly symbiotic system" of English (p. 53), to legitimize literary studies as the "high" and to give them a secure place in the modern university and thus "assure the maintenance of bourgeois reason" and its power relationships (p. 54; cf. Clifford, 1987).

Crowley argues that it was FYC that made the creation of English as a discipline possible by breaking the hold of Latin and providing a secure curricular base from which to teach literature (which, she emphasizes, was central in FYC classrooms from very early on, as part of developing—and weeding—students based on moral ideals rather than rhetorical action). It was not, as Berlin (1987) argues, separate, although it was certainly not equal. Russell (1992) sees the literature/composition relation in institutional terms, as part of the process of disciplinary "purification" in which composition played a mediating role between literary (disciplinary) purity and the messy institutional politics of higher education. Harkin (1992) engagingly retells the many (conflicting) retellings of the story of Francis Child (1825–1896), hero of literary critics because he professionalized literary study, and villain of composition scholars because he refused to teach English A—and in doing both, she argues, changed the nature of academic labor.

Women. In the period of this review, coinciding with the explosion of feminist scholarship worldwide, there is a wealth of historical studies of women and composition. Perhaps because the role of women in composition was ignored, this work is based on archival research more than other historical work in composition, and is much the better for it. Hobbs (1995) surveys the "cultures and practices" of U.S. women's literacy from colonial times to 1900, an important phase as women often learned to write outside formal schooling in a wide array of practices, and in cultures not official or even recognized by the patriarchal structures. Of particular interest is her discussion of "formal higher education and advanced literacy" (p. 12), which suggests the great variety and innovation in institutions for women, and, she argues, the lack of change in institutional practices with the rise of co-education beginning in the 1870s. Connors's (1997) overview of women's education differs on this point, as he argues that women's entrance into the academy was associated with a decline of agonistic argument and an increase in personal assignments. (For another overview, see Wright & Halloran, 2001).

Particularly important archival work was done by Campbell (1996, 1997), who examined in a series of studies the relationships of women to male authority, specifically their male teachers at Radcliff, Mount Holyoke, and elsewhere. In her studies of a Radcliff student's relationship with her tutor Barrett Wendell, one of the founders of composition at Harvard, Campbell shows the relations between service learning and composition, the dominance of male rhetorical structures, and the subtle forms of resistance among women at Mount Holyoke. Campbell develops a nuanced reading of the social and psychological contradictions women faced and, very often, overcame, although at a price. Weidner's (1995) reading of the diary of one of the first women at co-educational Butler University (c. 1860) is also noteworthy, as is Ricks's (1995) reading of the ways composition instruction both helped and hindered women at Mount Holyoke, Vassar, and Radcliff at the turn of the 20th century. Harmon (1995) tells the contrasting story of a co-educational public university, Illinois State Normal, where there was a more egalitarian ethic by which writing and speaking instruction were distributed across the curriculum and extracurriculum. Mastrangelo uses archival research as well to tell some of the women's histories not included in Berlin's (1984) 19th-century history.

People of color. Although several studies have been published on writing by people of color in the 19th century, there is little on formal writing instruction for or by people of color in 19th-century colleges. Again, the little that has been published focuses on the writing of women of color, such as Logan's (1999) history of how five African American women learned to write in literacy clubs or with personal mentors. Royster and Williams (1999) argue that the experience of African American women in college composition classes in 19th-century colleges was typical of other students, but she gives fascinating detail in her case studies of the extracurricular debating and literary societies that African American women founded or struggled their way into at Oberlin College and Atlanta University. Mihesuah's (1995) brief account of writing in the Cherokee Female Seminary, founded in the Oklahoma Territory as the first nonsectarian institution of higher learning west of the Mississippi in 1851, is one of the few studies that specifically looks at composition. There is a great deal of room for work in this area, particularly by historians willing to do serious archival digging.

The 20th Century: Mass Higher Education

Berlin (1987) published the first history of college composition during the 20th century, drawing primarily on articles published in the professional literature and previous historical studies (especially the work of Stewart, 1985). His interest was in classifying approaches to composition teaching, which he calls rhetorics: first into objective, subjective, and transactional, then into four major "schools": current-traditional rhetoric, the rhetoric of liberal culture, transactional rhetoric for a democracy (his favorite), and the ideas approach. He traces these approaches through the pre–World War I efficiency movement, the interwar progressive education movement, the post–World War II communications movement, the revival of rhetoric in composition during the 1960s and early 1970s, and the early professionalization of composition (to 1975). Although his categories were and are roundly contested, the book remains the most-cited treatment of the 20th century.

FYC history, 1900–professionalization in the 1970s. A good deal of historical research and debate on 20th-century composition has centered on the status of FYC and its teachers, particularly in relation to literary study, but also in relation to other disciplines and the university at large. As with debates over the 19th-century literature/composition split, this history often has been overtly polemical, a way of debating the future of the new profession. Tuman (1986) sees the origins of contemporary composition in the early 20th century in NCTE founder James F. Hosic's advocacy of composition as constructing a personal response to experience, in contrast to the teaching of literature as composition. Connors (1996, 1997) sees the low status of composition largely as an effect of the newly imported German ideal of scholarship in philology and literary history. He argues that this ideal devalued rhetoric, reduced composition to remedial status, and lowered (and "feminized") composition to the status of an ordeal or an apprenticeship. Crowley (1998) sees 20th-century composition's low status as the effect of its teaching not communication but a "humanistic subjectivity," with composition relegated to an adjunct supporting literary studies. Miller (1991) extends her interpretation of composition history as discontinuous and carnivalesque to the 20th century by analyzing English offerings in 75 catalogs from

15 institutions between 1920 and 1960. She found a surprisingly large variety of writing courses early in the period, but these gradually were replaced by literature courses. She then examines the growth of the composition "industry" and the formation of what she sees as a self-sacrificial identity in composition teachers that has perpetuated the myth that FYC must be central to composition studies.

Given these controversies over FYC, historical attempts to abolish composition courses as a requirement were hotly debated by historians. Russell (1988) collected and discussed the major historical statements on the abolition of composition, which he sees as an attempt by advocates of liberal culture to purify English of its utilitarian uses. These statements (and a few others) then were re-interpreted to support or oppose the "new" abolitionists of the 1990s, either pro-abolition (e.g., Connors, 1996; Crowley, 1990; Goggin, 1995) or anti-abolition (e.g., Brooks, 2002a; Roemer, Schultz, & Durst, 1999).

The founding of an organization for college composition in 1949, the Conference on College Composition and Communication (CCCC), evoked several founding narratives, particularly to explain the origin of what became, some 2 decades later, a professional organization. Bartholomae (1989) argues that the founding was an assertion of identity against literature as well as a response to the huge numbers of military veterans flooding higher education. Heyda (1999) argues that composition in fact threw its lot with literature in the 1950s rather than continuing a budding collaboration with speech programs to build an identity beyond literature. Others have examined the persistent lack of interest in the fourth C, oral communication, since the early 1950s. George and Trimbur (1999) trace the decline of oral—and visual—communication, as it pushed composition toward textual readings rather than toward a study of the circulation of culture in many interrelated communicative modes.

Composition teachers. The portraits of teachers collected by Brereton (1985) is a very large cut above the then and now study. These rich portraits of eight figures, from Barrett Wendell through Mina Shaughnessy, show composition in something like its full dimensions, although piecemeal, illuminating the social as well as the personal contexts. More recent histories—autobiographical reminiscences, really—are contained in Roen, Brown, and Enos (1999). Bizzaro (1999) presents personal histories of major figures in composition who wrote dissertations in literature, and Taylor and Holberg (1999) trace the history of graduate students' involvement in composition—both analyses of the complex and conflicted status of graduate students in English department composition programs.

Textbooks. Textbooks have exerted a particularly strong influence on composition, as so many of its teachers had no formal training in the teaching of writing and relied on them. Thus, textbooks have been a powerful means of keeping current-traditional rhetoric traditional. Connors (1986b) traces the history of U.S. textbooks since the 1820s and finds many elements of current textbooks remarkably similar to those of the 19th century. U.S. teachers borrowed from Scottish and English books, such as Blair and Campbell, but introduced drills to aid untrained teachers. Connors shows how textbooks responded to a variety of social and pedagogical influences, such as the reform of higher education after the Civil War, the German influence, and, mainly, the move from the oral to the written. These changes, in his view, took a rich theory and impoverished it, introducing largely untheorized concepts of the modes, paragraph structure, and grammatical correctness. Textbooks, he argues, largely became frozen until the revival of rhetoric in the professionalization of composition beginning in the 1960s. Hawhee (1999) extends Connors's work with her Foucauldian analysis of the history of the most popular 20th-century textbook, the *Harbrace College Handbook*, which constructs student subjectivity as "lacking"—dull and docile.

Grammar and paragraphing. Connors (1986a, 1997) reviews the whole history of grammar and paragraph rhetoric, including the 20th century. Rose (1999) explains the history of sentence-combining exercises, which originated in the 1890s, and D'Angelo (1986) traces the history of the topic sentence, which became engrained in current-traditional rhetoric through F. N. Scott and J. V. Denney in the early 20th century, despite the lack of topic sentences in nonschool writing.

Technology. The role of computers in composition was given a book-length historical treatment by Hawisher, LeBlanc, Moran, and Selfe (1996). They discuss pedagogical developments since this technology was introduced in FYC in 1979, including the World Wide Web, and they tell the story of computers and the writing conference and journal, which the authors played a major role in creating. Unfortunately, there has been little work since to bring greater critical purchase on this increasingly powerful and widespread technology for teaching writing (cf. Baron, 1998).

Collaboration and peer review. Collaboration and peer review, common practices in composition from the 1980s, have received historical treatment from Gaillet (1994), who examined the work of Scottish educator George Jardine. He elaborated a democratic education based on collaboration and peer review in the late 18th and early 19th centuries. Holt (1993, 1994) traces current practices to the Deweyan progressive philosophy of the 1920s and its elaboration, in very different ways, in the 1930s and 1950s.

Assessment. Apart from Trachsel's (1992) book-length study of entrance exams (discussed earlier), there has been little on assessment history. White chronicles the development of holistic writing instruction (or *holisticism*, in his coinage). Yancey (1999) interprets the history of assessment as successive waves, from assessment as objective testing (1950s–1970s) to assessment as a rhetorical act (late 1990s). Anderson (1994) looks at the tradition of impromptu writing for assessment, from the 1920s through the 1950s. There is much room for further work on this crucial aspect of composition practice to extend the work of Trachsel to classroom and program practices.

Writing centers. Although there is no comprehensive history of writing centers, there has been significant historical work, much of it conveniently gathered in collections (Barnett & Blumner, 2001; Murphy & Law, 1995). Carino (1995) summarizes the few previous historical accounts from the 1980s and early 1990s as locating writing centers' origins in the open admissions movement of the 1970s and casting pre-open admissions centers in negative contrast to a purportedly more enlightened age. He then lays out an alternative reading of that history, starting with the turn of the twentieth century "laboratory method" of teaching. He finds in the past many of the methods and attitudes present in contemporary centers. Carino (1996) elaborates his earlier argument by constructing a poststructuralist model of writing centers' history from 1968 to 1983. He argues that open admissions initiatives did not give rise to contemporary centers or make a crucial contribution to the debate on remediation, points he supports with a case study of the Purdue University lab in 1975. Boquet (1999) supports Carino's interpretation with additional historical detail, particularly on the post-World War II, pre-open admissions era, although she draws a distinction between writing centers as pedagogical method and as institutional sites. Kinkead (1996) gives a personal history of the first decade of the National Writing Centers Association. Lerner's (1998) history of writing center technology from drill pads to computers puts teaching technology in amusing context.

Basic writing. The most influential article in the movement or subfield of composition known as *basic writing* (formerly remedial writing) is Rose's (1985) study of how writing came to be thought of as an elementary skill rather than as a developing accomplishment, a discipline. Early 20th-century behaviorist notions of writing as a basic skill, combined with a medical model of remediation, led to what he terms the *myth of transience*: that students who have not mastered literacy at a particular level are "illiterate" and can be remediated through some quick method (not yet found). The myth assumes that writing instruction at "higher" levels thus can be phased out. This myth, he argues, has led to a history of excluding students from higher education who do not already have particular literacies, rather than teaching them what they need to enter new educational and social practices.

Rose (1985) was interpreted as describing the "dark ages" of remediation, in contrast to the enlightened age following the birth of basic writing in the open admissions movement of the late 1960s and early 1970s, and especially in the work of Mina P. Shaughnessy of CUNY (although see Carino, 1995, for a reassessment). The many historical articles and chapters on the history of basic writing are fundamentally—and usually explicitly—debates about Shaughnessy's work and legacy.

Two of these are the closest the field has to a full-fledged history of the basic writing movement. The first chapters of Mutnick (1996) give a richly detailed and admiring description of Shaughnessy's work and the environment at CUNY during the period, as well as a less detailed account of the pre-open admissions era of basic writing (see Maher, 1997, for a biography of Shaughnessy). Horner (1996; see also Horner & Lu, 1999) gives an appreciative but highly critical re-reading of basic writing history, using CUNY archival documents from the period to argue that Shaughnessy and others did little to resist the marginalization of students and teachers, particularly in material terms, despite protest movements going on at the time. A range of other articles debate this founding moment and interpretations of it. These are summarized by Gray-Rosendale (1999) in her spirited defense of Shaughnessy. See also Lu's (1992) critique of Shaughnessy for overlooking the political, Shor's (2001) economic analysis of basic writing history in defense of his proposal for mainstreaming, Lewiecki-Wilson and Sommers's (1999) oral histories of open admissions teachers, and Connors's (1987a) history of basic writing textbooks.

Program histories. In the 1990s historians began to question the narrative of current-traditional rhetoric as the dark ages of composition. They examined program archives and interviewed teachers and students to "reclaim lost generations." Varnum's (1992a, 1992b) history of Theodore Baird's revolutionary program at Amherst from the late 1930s through the 1960s shows how students wrote often and from experience, sharing their drafts and creating a climate of intellectual rigor out of their own imaginative resources released through progressive pedagogy. Varnum connects the program history to social changes in America. Kates (2001) provides similar curricular detail drawn from archives in her book on four composition programs serving middle-class women, African Americans, and workers (spanning the years 1885–1937) that had a specifically activist agenda of engaging civic issues and community service through focusing on language and identity. Gold (2003) and Bradway-Hesse (1998) also provide insight through archival research into, respectively, innovative composition at Texas Woman's University from 1901 to 1939 and midwestern literary societies, especially a "university for the 'farmer and the poor.'" Worth mention are Winterowd's (1998) personal and polemical history of the Rhetoric-Linguistics-Literature Program he started in 1972 in the Department of English at the University of Southern California and Guinn's (1998) appreciation of it (and analysis of its "virtual demise" with Winterowd's retirement in 1997).

Writing across the curriculum. The history of attempts to improve students' writing (and learning through writing) outside composition courses, across the curriculum in the disciplines, is told by Russell (1991, 2002). His book begins with the 19th-century liberal (oratorical) curriculum, where writing supported speaking across the curriculum and extracurriculum, to the split between content and expression that occurred with the birth of college composition courses at Harvard and the resulting "myth of transience." Twentieth-century developments covered include the growth of the German-influenced ideal of research and the "research paper" tradition, the emphasis on utilitarian writing for professional education, and a range of attempts to reform general education originating in the 1930s, such as the cooperation movement to integrate education through writing, the Great Books movement, progressive education's "correlated curriculum," and the project method. Post-World War II efforts to deal with the expansion of higher education include the communications movement, the rise of multiple choice testing, and the growth of business and technical writing. He ends with a history of the writing across the curriculum movement (WAC) from its beginnings in faculty workshops in 1970 to a national education reform movement by the turn of the 21st century. Quinn overviews the history of reading and writing as modes of learning in the 20th century, emphasizing highlights in attempts to integrate reading and writing for learning in higher education. Thaiss (1997) provides a personal history of an important WAC program at George Mason University. Ambron (1991) reflects on the history of WAC and its importance for community colleges. For WAC in historically Black colleges, see Zaluda (1998), discussed later.

Women in composition. There has been somewhat less work on women in composition in higher education from 1900 to professionalization in the 1970s, than on women of the 19th century, despite the fact that there were many important women theorists as well as countless women teachers and researchers in the period during which college composition was "feminized." Campbell's (1996) collection of the writings of Gertrude Buck deserves special mention. Buck was an early-20th-century pioneer, along with Fred Newton Scott, of what Berlin calls "transactional" democratic rhetoric, an early alternative to current-traditional rhetoric. Campbell's introduction makes a case for Buck as a feminist rhetorical theorist. Similarly, Bordelon (2002) describes the work of Mary Yost at Vassar in the early 20th century, who developed a pedagogy based on social engagement and argument. Bordelon challenges Connors's (1997) claim that the "feminization" of composition moved it toward more interior emphasis through personal assignments.

Ritchie and Boardman (1999) provide an excellent overview of the many feminist narratives of composition written since the beginnings of professionalization in the 1960s, narratives aimed at including women, at making intuitive connections, and at relating feminist disruptions. In keeping with feminist and postmodern historiographical practice, these are for the most part personal testimonies and histories (dating from the efforts of Emig and others in the 1970s to valorize and nurture women's work in composition, as well as protect women from discrimination and abuse in the workplace). They are aimed at consciousness raising and rattling as they read the theory and practice of composition in light of possible futures. Miller (1991) explains the marginalization of composition not only in relation to literature but also by its place in a patriarchal symbolic order (by analogy, the "sad woman in the basement" in Freud's analysis of the 19th-century bourgeoisie domestic). Enos (1996) provides personal histories of women in composition, in light of survey data, but no systematic history. Hill (1990) uses the midwife metaphor to read several of composition's male "expressivist" founders as gendered in terms of "birthing" an experiential self and an emphasis on nurturing—an emphasis that, she argues, later was compartmentalized as theory and devalued. Schell combines personal narratives of nontenure track women with institutional and labor history to track the ideologies that co-opt feminism to perpetuate exploitive practices. Gere (1994, 1997) provides an important history of extracurricular writing groups in relation to composition pedagogy, particularly groups for women. And Adams (2001) tells the stories of famous literary women and their experience of composition courses.

People of color. There is unfortunately no book-length history of people of color in composition during the 20th century, and very few articles, despite the fact that historians such as Royster have found many African Americans and other people of color who have contributed to the field. Royster and Williams (1999) have begun what they call "the work of recovery" of teachers of color that suggests "a history of scholarship and a tradition of professional engagement" that began in the 19th century (see also Royster, 2000) and is—*pace* much discourse in the field—not about basic writing but about basic fairness. Gilyard (1999) provides the central outlines of such a history in his overview of African American contributions to composition studies. He begins with context: the famous DuBois/Washington debates over the future of Negro higher education in the early 20th century and, most important, a sketch of the College Language Association (CLA), established in 1937 as the Association of Teachers of English in Negro Colleges, and in the late 1960s the CCCC Black Caucus (cf. Davis, 1994). Gilyard goes on to mention some of the many pedagogical and political reforms accomplished by CLA and CCCC Black Caucus members and allies, especially the landmark *Students' Right to Their Own Language* of 1974. Gilyard calls for "impassioned archival research" (p. 626) on people of color in composition, and although there is still relatively little such work (and a great need as this history is excluded from "standard" histories), there is some fine work that provides excellent models.

Zaluda (1998) traces the history of writing assignments in four disciplines (philosophy, English, history, and sociology) at Howard University, a historically Black institution. He sensitively analyzes them, finding contradictions arising out of the ideological contestation present in the Harlem Renaissance. Similarly, Kates (1997, 2001) analyzes the ideological dimensions of Hallie Quinn Brown, professor of elocution at Wilberforce University from 1893 to 1923, whose "implicitly politicized" (2001, p. 55) pedagogy honored African American cultural identity and developed new features of elocutionary theory. Rose uses citation tracing to show how the profession has iterated Shaughnessy's (1977) concept of a logic of error rather than Smitherman's (1977) description of the grammar of African American English, because of the profession's focus on deficit and error rather than the grammar, rhetoric, history, and politics of African American English. There is room and need for much more such careful archival and statistical work, sensitive to ideology as it is played out in institutional contexts.

Professionalism in U.S. Composition

Although the CCCC was founded in 1949, composition became professionalized only in the 1970s, with its own theories, research agendas, graduate programs, and refereed publications. I hesitate to venture a review of the recent histories of a highly and overtly political era, written by historians in the midst of making that history. But debates over the recent history of the field have been important in its emergence, and I will emphasize work that fronts history as its object (a discussion of the past) rather than reflections on its history in, say, the epideictic of chairs' addresses (e.g., Faigley, 1997; Hairston, 1985), the deliberative rhetoric of "the future of the profession" discussions (Schilb & Pickering, 1989), or personal reflections on personal history (Reynolds, 1990)—realizing that there is no satisfactory way to draw this distinction. (A useful collection on the history of professionalization is Rosner, Boehm, & Journet, 1999.)

North's (1987) early and brief discussion of the origin of professionalization locates it in 1963, with an NCTE committee report on "the state of knowledge in composition." The professionalization of composition also might be said to have begun with the "revival of rhetoric" in English departments in the 1960s (it had been revived 50 years earlier in speech departments)—a story told, only briefly, by Mulderig (1999). Whatever the moment, there was clearly a movement toward re-examining current-traditional rhetoric and pedagogy. Young and Goggin's (1992) study of *College English* and *CCC* articles published between 1950 and 1965 showed a "radical decline" of articles that took up "current-traditional" rhetoric. They argue that "in this period, the questions that were the focus of interest in current-traditional rhetoric (e.g., questions having to do with normative features of finished discourse) ceased to be as vital, interesting, and urgent as questions having to do by and large with the activity of thinking and communicating in actual rhetorical situations" (p. 23). Goggin (2000) develops these insights into a full study of composition journals since World War II.

Histories of professionalization have, understandably, fronted the interests of their authors in current debates. Bizzell (1992) reads the history as a movement from emphasis on personal style (1960s and 1970s) to cognitive writing processes (1970s and early 1980s) to analysis of social and cultural contexts, especially discourse communities. Faigley (1992) gives a postmodern political analysis of professionalism as a response to a series of political battles with the right, beginning in the 1960s and proceeding through the back-to-the-basics literacy "crisis" of the 1970s and the culture wars of the 1980s. He reads the many arguments about the process movement as being fundamentally about whether literacy should be, in the tradition of Dewey, about offering students the means to greater (democratic) control of their lives (cf. Faigley, 1999). Nystrand, Greene, and Wiemelt (1993) locate professionalization not in the political debates within composition, English departments, or the wider cultural discourse on literacy, but rather in intellectual history: the shift in conceptions of language and meaning within several fields that profoundly influenced composition (especially literary criticism and linguistics), from formalism in the 1950s to structuralism/constructivism in the 1970s to social processes ("the rhetorical turn") in the 1980s, to the dialogism of Bakhtin—and the authors. Nystrand (2002) is continuing this line of research with work on the Cambridge (MA) "psycholinguistic revolution" of the 1960s, from which James Moffett, Emig, Frank Smith, and other pioneers emerged.

Movements in composition's early years of professionalization have received a good deal of attention. Tobin (1994) discusses the early years of the process movement—the heady first move toward a theory-based pedagogy—and the stereotype of those years that developed. For a range of criticisms of the process movement based on historical readings, see Pullman (1999), Couture (1999), and Schreiner (1997). Crowley (1998) extends the analysis of process pedagogy's beginnings in a range of important and largely unrecognized contexts: class size, the emergence of theory, student unrest, and student subjectivities.

Harris (1997) traces five key terms since the Dartmouth Seminar of 1966—growth, voice, process, error, and community—to locate movements such as expressivism, cognitive process, and discourse community in historical and political contexts—both before and after they became reduced to counters in theoretical/pedagogical battles. He shows the links between, say, expressivist and process approaches in terms of valuing students' "own writing." Zebroski (1999) traces the ways expressivism (and, later, cognitive psychology) came to be constructed, historically, as a "menace." He sees this construction as a way of distancing the new profession from its old ally, English education, using counts of textbook advertisements in *CCC* from 1969 to 1990, to evidence his claim.

Almost all of the historians of professionalization take politics into account. But particularly worth noting is Ohmann's (1999) reflection on his classic 1977 study. He tries to account for the way composition, unlike most other professions, overtly embraced the political during the process of professionalization. Murphy's (1993) critique of what he calls the "essentialist allegiance to the idea of 'progress'" (p. 345) in composition studies is also worth noting. But a history of composition's debt to the progressive movement in education has yet to be written.

Composition in Other Higher Education Systems

Composition courses in higher education are a relatively new phenomenon in countries other than the United States, so there is little history to tell. In the 2 decades covered by this review, there have been a few attempts to introduce such courses in Canada, Belgium, Denmark, and other countries, and this effort in places has sparked some interest in the history of the teaching practices designed to improve students' writing.

The most significant work has been in Canada, where composition courses (in part influenced by the United States) have been increasingly common. Johnson (1987a) has told the story of Anglophone Canadian efforts in the 19th century (referred to above) in the context of North American efforts more broadly. Hubert (1994) devotes a good deal of attention to composition in his history of English studies in 19th-century Anglophone Canada. Brooks (2002b) describes the 20th-century history of first-year university English instruction in Anglophone Canada in the context of changing conceptions of literacy and nationalism, as well as providing a fascinating case study (1998) of one institution, the University of Manitoba, and important work comparing U.S. and Canadian practices historically (1997). As composition becomes more common in higher education systems of other countries, we can look forward to their histories and comparative work to illuminate historical differences.

HISTORIOGRAPHY

The very large effort to write the history of composition was accompanied by a lively discussion of historiography, usually framed in terms of the historiography of rhetoric rather than of composition (Crowley, 1984a; Schilb, 1986; Vitanza, 1986), although the distinction (as in the field of "composition/rhetoric") was blurred. *Pre/ Text* devoted a special 1987 issue (*8*, 1–2) to the historiography of rhetoric, emphasizing new approaches, and *Rhetoric Review* published an "octalog" among eight historians on the politics of historiography (Murphy et al., 1988). Historians of rhetoric and composition found congenial the postmodern critical theory and, often, the feminist historical approaches that rebellious historians brought to the discipline of academic history during the 1980s (e.g., Bizzell, 2000; Jarratt, 1986, 1990). They saw these new approaches to history as more politically explicit and engaged than traditional historiography, with its attempt to be objective and tell a conventional story. Some historians, notably Connors, continued to write more traditional narrative history and defended the practice. But historians generally eschewed traditional approaches, including quantitative social history, in favor of postmodern ones, and attacked the idea that objective—even more and less objective—history could be written.

Berlin (1986, 1990), advocated a dialectical, neo-Marxist historiography, fronting the political commitments of the historian. Miller (1991) called for a composition historiography separate from rhetorical historiography and argued for (and wrote) history as discontinuous and carnivalesque, emphasizing ruptures, accidental associations, and juxtapositions. Strain (1993) proposed and exemplified a hermeneutic model of historiography.

Most historians did relatively little archival work, focusing on textual readings of published materials instead (methods more familiar in literary study in the period in which most composition historians were trained). There were a number of complaints about the lack of archival work. Miller (1994) calls for institutional histories based on archival work in local programs rather than broad categorizations (as part of his attack on G. Graff's [1987] leaving composition out of his history of English studies). Nelms (1992) advocates oral evidence in composition historiography as an antidote to binary oppositions built on readings of published work rather than primary or archival sources. Varnum (1992a) argues against using the "terministic screen" of current-traditional rhetoric to read composition history as it can lead to ignoring valuable work of earlier generations, available primarily through archival work.

There were a few attempts to provide systematic help for those learning to do historical research. Connors (1984) and North (1987) published brief "how to's" in the 1980s. And there is a chapter in one of the popular composition research methods textbooks on historiography (Connors, 1992), although it devotes only half a page to archival research.

CONCLUSION

My main conclusion is obvious: There was a great deal of excellent historical research published from 1984 to 2003—by far more than in any other profession I know of. And that is something composition studies can be proud of and find useful in understanding itself, representing itself to others, and negotiating its future. My second conclusion is that historical research can be better and more useful. I have two suggestions. First, the profession would profit from more archival research, even from the methods of quantitative social history. The paucity of archival work is certainly not due to the lack of archives; almost every university and many school districts have one, as do professional organizations. And since 1989 there has been an archive devoted to composition at the University of Rhode Island (for papers) and the University of New Hampshire (for textbooks). Where archival work has been necessary— as with the contributions of women and people of color—the results have been impressive. Composition exists within institutions, first of all. So to understand composition one must look deeply into institutional histories, preserved most fully in archives and the memories of teachers and students. Moreover, composition is also a social phenomenon with wide reach, and the methods of social history may be of great help. The lack of archival work is understandable, as composition scholars are not trained in the profession of academic history (although several have formal training in the history of rhetoric). But I look forward to the new generation of historians of composition pushing further into archives, perhaps even sitting in on courses in historical methods of research.

Second, in reviewing this historical literature I often was struck by how little explicit debate there is among authors, as suggested by the few times historians cite one another's work to show where they agree, disagree, add, modify, and so on. Although historians cannot, in my opinion, attain a "God's-eye-view" objectivity, there can be a socially constructed objectivity—an engagement with others' work borne of respect for one another and our mutual enterprise—that lifts scholarship out of solipsism. Where composition historians have focused on particular problems, searched for and debated evidence, there has been remarkable progress in understanding.

Finally, with the turn of a new century, it is time for senior historians to undertake the important work of synthesis, to create work accessible to beginners in the field and stakeholders beyond it. Sadly, many of our finest historians, equipped to undertake that work, passed away in the 1990s (see my note below). But there are many to take up the work and a new generation of historians to further the work.

AUTHOR'S NOTE

This chapter is dedicated to the memory of Jim Berlin, Bob Connors, Wally Douglas, and Don Stewart.

REFERENCES

Adams, K. H. (1993). *A history of professional writing instruction in American colleges: Years of acceptance, growth, and doubt*. Dallas: Southern Methodist University Press.

Adams, K. H. (2001). *A group of their own: College writing courses and American women writers, 1880–1940*. Albany: State University of New York Press.

Adams, K. S. (1984). Forms of discourse: What their originators intended. *Teaching English in the Two-Year College, 11*(2), 17–22.

Ambron, J. (1991). History of WAC and its role in community colleges. *New Directions for Community Colleges, 19*(1), 3–8.

Anderson, L. (1994). Time and writing: Institutional forces and the shape of writing pedagogy. *Writing Instructor, 14*(1), 25–37.

Applebee, A. N. (1974). *Tradition and reform in the teaching of English: A history*. Urbana, IL.: National Council of Teachers of English.

Aulbach, C. (1994). The committee of ten: Ghosts who still haunt us. *English Journal, 83*(3), 16–17.

Barnett, R. W., & Blumner, J. S. (Eds.). (2001). *Writing center theory and practice*. New York: Longman.

Baron, N. S. (1998). Writing in the age of email: The impact of ideology versus technology. *Visible Language, 32*(1), 35–53.

Bartholomae, D. (1989). Freshman English, composition, and CCCC. *College Composition and Communication, 40*(1), 38–50.

Bazerman, C. (1988). *Shaping written knowledge: The genre and activity of the experimental article in science*. Madison: University of Wisconsin Press.

Bazerman, C. (1999). *The languages of Edison's light*. Cambridge, MA: MIT Press.

Berlin, J. A. (1984). *Writing instruction in nineteenth-century American colleges*. Carbondale: Southern Illinois University Press.

Berlin, J. A. (1986). Revisionary rhetorical history: A dialectical perspective. *PrefText, 8*(1–2), 47–61.

Berlin, J. A. (1987). *Rhetoric and reality: Writing instruction in American colleges, 1900–1985*. Carbondale: Southern Illinois University Press.

Berlin, J. A. (1990). Postmodernism, politics, and histories of rhetoric. *PrefText, 11*(3–4), 169–187.

Besnier, N. (1995). *Literacy, emotion, and authority: Reading and writing on a Polynesian atoll*. Cambridge, UK: Cambridge University Press.

Bizzaro, P. (1999). What I learned in grad school, or literacy training and the theorizing of composition. *College Composition and Communication, 50*(4), 722–742.

Bizzell, P. (1992). *Academic discourse and critical consciousness*. Pittsburgh, PA: University of Pittsburgh Press.

Bizzell, P. (2000). Feminist methods of research in the history of rhetoric: What difference do they make? *Rhetoric Society Quarterly, 30*, 5–17.

Boquet, E. H. (1999). "Our little secret": A history of writing centers, pre- to post-open admissions. *College Composition and Communication, 50*(2), 463–482.

Bordelon, S. (2002). *Challenging nineteenth-century feminization narratives: Mary Yost of Vassar College*. Retrieved May 28, 2005, from www.unm.edu/~cwshrc/peitho6_1.htm

Boring, E. G. (1929). *A history of experimental psychology*. New York: Century.

Boyd, R. (1993). Mechanical correctness and ritual in the late nineteenth-century composition classroom. *Rhetoric Review, 11*(2), 436–455.

Bradway-Hesse, B. (1998). Bright access: Midwestern literary societies, with a particular look at a university for the "farmer and the poor." *Rhetoric Review, 17*(1), 50–73.

Brandt, D. (2001). *Literacy in American lives*. Cambridge, UK: Cambridge University Press.

Brereton, J. C. (1985). *Traditions of inquiry*. New York: Oxford University Press.

Brereton, J. C. (1995). *The origins of composition studies in the American college, 1875–1925: A documentary history*. Pittsburgh, PA: University of Pittsburgh Press.

Britton, J. (Ed.). (1984). *English teaching: An international exchange*. London: Heinemann.

Brooks, K. (1997). Liberal education on the great plains: American experiments, Canadian flirtations, 1930–1950. *Great Plains Quarterly, 17*, 103–118.

Brooks, K. (1998). Writing instruction or textual studies? Professionalism and the junior curriculum at the University of Manitoba, 1909–1935. *Textual Studies in Canada, 10/11*, 157–176.

Brooks, K. (2002a). Composition's abolitionist debate: A tool for change. *Composition Studies, 30*(2), 27–42.

Brooks, K. (2002b). National culture and the first-year English curriculum: An historical study of composition in Canadian universities. *American Review of Canadian Studies, 34*, 673–694.

Campbell, J. (1996). Freshman (sic) English: A 1901 Wellesley College "girl" negotiates authority. *Rhetoric Review, 15*(1), 110–127.

Campbell, J. (1997). "A real vexation": Student writing in Mount Holyoke's culture of service, 1837–1865. *College English, 59*(7), 767–788.

Carino, P. (1995). Early writing centers: Toward a history. *Writing Center Journal, 15*(2), 103–115.

Carino, P. (1996). Open admissions and the construction of writing center history: A tale of three models. *Writing Center Journal, 17*(1), 30–49.

Chall, J. S. (1996). American reading achievement: Should we worry? *Research in the Teaching of English, 30*(3), 303–310.

Chervel, A. (1998). *La Culture scholaire, une approche historique.* Paris: Belin.

Clark, G., & Halloran, S. M. (1993). *Oratorical culture in nineteenth-century America: Transformations in the theory and practice of rhetoric.* Carbondale: Southern Illinois University Press.

Clifford, J. (1987). Ideology into discourse: A historical perspective. *Journal of Advanced Composition, 7*(1–2), 121–130.

Connors, R. J. (1981). Current-traditional rhetoric: Thirty years of writing with a purpose. *Rhetoric Society Quarterly, 11*(4), 208–221.

Connors, R. J. (1984). Historical inquiry in composition studies. *Writing Instructor, 3*(4), 157–167.

Connors, R. J. (1986a). Grammar in American college composition: An historical overview. In D. A. McQuade (Ed.), *The territory of language: Linguistics, stylistics, and the teaching of composition* (pp. 3–22). Carbondale: Southern Illinois University Press.

Connors, R. J. (1986b). Textbooks and the evolution of the discipline. *College Composition and Communication, 37*(2), 178–194.

Connors, R. J. (1987a). Basic writing textbooks: History and current avatars. In T. Enos (Ed.), *A sourcebook for basic writing teachers* (pp. 259–274). New York: Random House.

Connors, R. J. (1987b). Personal writing assignments. *College Composition and Communication, 38*(2), 166–183.

Connors, R. J. (1992). Dreams and play: Historical method and methodology. G. Kirsh & P. A. Sullivan (Eds.), *Methods and methodology in composition research* (pp. 15–36). Carbondale: Southern Illinois University Press.

Connors, R. J. (1996). The abolition debate in composition: A short history. In L. Z. Bloom, D. A. Daiker, & E. M. White (Eds.), *Composition in the twenty-first century* (pp. 47–63). Carbondale: Southern Illinois University Press.

Connors, R. J. (1997). *Composition-rhetoric: Backgrounds, theory, and pedagogy.* Pittsburgh, PA: University of Pittsburgh Press.

Corbett, E. P. J. (1965). *Classical rhetoric for the modern student.* New York: Oxford University Press.

Coulson, A. J. (1996). Schooling and literacy over time: The rising cost of stagnation and decline. *Research in the Teaching of English, 30*(3), 311–327.

Couture, B. (1999). Modeling and emulating: Rethinking agency in the writing process. In T. Kent (Ed.), *Post-process theory: Beyond the writing-process paradigm* (pp. 30–48). Carbondale: Southern Illinois University Press.

Crowley, S. (1984a). Neo-romanticism and the history of rhetoric. *Pre/Text, 5*(1), 19–37.

Crowley, S. (1984b). Response to Robert J. Connors, "The rise and fall of the modes of discourse." *College Composition and Communication, 35*(1), 88–91.

Crowley, S. (1986). The perilous life and times of freshman English. *Freshman English News, 14*(3), 11–16.

Crowley, S. (1990). *The methodical memory: Invention in current-traditional rhetoric.* Carbondale: Southern Illinois University Press.

Crowley, S. (1998). *Composition in the university: Historical and polemical essays.* Pittsburgh, PA: University of Pittsburgh Press.

D'Angelo, F. (1984). Nineteenth-century forms/modes of discourse: A critical inquiry. *College Composition and Communication, 35*(1), 31–42.

D'Angelo, F. (1986). The topic sentence revisited. *College Composition and Communication, 37*(4), 431–441.

Daniels, H., Zemelman, S., & Bizar, M. (1999). Whole language works: Sixty years of research. *Educational Leadership, 57*(2), 32–37.

Davis, M. W. (1994). *History of the Black Caucus of the National Council of Teachers of English.* Urbana, IL: NCTE/CCCC Black Caucus.

Doige, L. A. C. (2001). Literacy in aboriginal education: An historical perspective. *Canadian Journal of Native Education, 25*(2), 117–128.

Donelson, K. (2000). Oh, those golden teaching days of yore. *English Journal, 89*(3), 45–48.

Donsky, B. von Bracht. (1984). Trends in elementary writing instruction, 1900–1959. *Language Arts, 61*(8), 795–803.

Durst, R. K. (1992). Promising research: An historical analysis of award-winning inquiry, 1970–1989. *Research in the Teaching of English, 26*(1), 41–70.

Eisenstein, E. L. (1979). *The printing press as an agent of change: Communications and cultural transformations in early-modern Europe.* Cambridge, UK: Cambridge University Press.

Eldred, J. C., & Mortensen, P. (2002). *Imagining rhetoric: Composing women of the early United States.* Pittsburgh, PA: University of Pittsburgh Press.

Enos, T. (1996). *Gender roles and faculty lives in rhetoric and composition.* Carbondale: Southern Illinois University Press.

Faigley, L. (1992). *Fragments of rationality: Postmodernity and the subject of composition.* Pittsburgh, PA: University of Pittsburgh Press.

Faigley, L. (1997). Literacy after the revolution. *College Composition and Communication, 48*(1), 30–43.

Faigley, L. (1999). Veterans' stories on the porch. In M. Rosner, B. Boehm, & D. Journet (Eds.), *History, reflection, and narrative: The professionalization of composition, 1963–1983* (pp. 23–37). Stamford, CT: Ablex.

Fogarty, D. (1959). *Roots for a new rhetoric.* New York: Russell & Russell.

Fowler, D. H., & Fowler, L. J. (1984). Literacy studies and communication skills: Separation or reconciliation. *English Journal, 73*(3), 43–48.

Frost, J. (1839). *Easy exercises in composition.* Philadelphia: W. Marshall.

Gaillet, L. L. (1994). An historical perspective on collaborative learning. *Journal of Advanced Composition, 14*(1), 93–110.

George, D., & Trimbur, J. (1999). The "communication battle," or whatever happened to the 4th c? *College Composition and Communication, 50*(4), 682–698.

Gere, A. R. (1994). Kitchen tables and rented rooms: The extracurriculum of composition. *College Composition and Communication, 45*(1), 75–92.

Gere, A. R. (1997). *Intimate practices: Literacy and cultural work in U.S. Women's Clubs, 1880–1920.* Urbana: University of Illinois Press.

Gerlach, J. M., Monseau, V. R., & NCTE Committee on Women in the Profession. (1991). *Miss-

ing chapters: Ten pioneering women in NCTE and English education.* Urbana, IL: National Council of Teachers of English.

Gilyard, K. (1999). African American contributions to composition studies. *College Composition and Communication, 50*(4), 626–644.

Goggin, M. D. (1995). The disciplinary instability of composition. In J. Petraglia (Ed.), *Reconceiving writing: Rethinking writing instruction* (pp. 27–48). Mahwah, NJ: Erlbaum.

Goggin, M. D. (2000). *Authoring a discipline: Scholarly journals and the post-World War II emergence of rhetoric and composition.* Mahwah, NJ: Erlbaum.

Gold, D. (2003). Beyond the classroom walls: Student writing at Texas Woman's University, 1901–1939. *Rhetoric Review, 22*, 264–281.

Goodburn, A. (1999). Literacy practices at the Genoa Industrial Indian School. *Great Plains Quarterly, 19*(1), 35–52.

Goodman, Y. M. (1989). Roots of the whole-language movement. *Elementary School Journal, 90*(2), 113–127.

Goody, J. (Ed.). (1968). *Literacy in traditional societies.* Cambridge, UK: Cambridge University Press.

Goody, J. (1986). *The logic of writing and the organization of society.* Cambridge, UK: Cambridge University Press.

Goody, J. (2000). *The power of the written tradition.* Washington, DC: Smithsonian Institution Press.

Gordon, E. E., & Gordon, E. H. (2003). *Literacy in America: Historic journey and contemporary solutions.* Westport, CT: Praeger.

Graff, G. (1987). *Professing literature: An institutional history.* Chicago: University of Chicago Press.

Graff, H. J. (1987). *The labyrinths of literacy: Reflections on literacy past and present.* London: Falmer Press.

Graff, H. J. (1991). *The literacy myth: Cultural integration and social structure in the nineteenth century.* New Brunswick, NJ: Transaction.

Gray-Rosendale, L. (1999). Investigating our discursive history: JBW and the construction of the "basic writer's" identity. *Journal of Basic Writing, 18*(2), 108–135.

Green, B. (Ed.). (1992). *The insistence of the letter: Literacy studies and curriculum theorizing.* London: Falmer.

Greer, J. E. (Ed.). (2003). *Girls and literacy in America: Historical perspectives to the present.* Santa Barbara, CA: ABC Clio.

Guinn, D. M. (1998). The rhetoric-linguistics-literature program. *JAC: A Journal of Composition Theory, 18*(3), 489–501.

Hairston, M. (1985). Breaking our bonds and reaffirming our connections. *College Composition and Communication, 36*(3), 272–282.

Harkin, P. (1992). Child's ballads: Narrating histories of composition and literary studies. In D. R. Shumway & C. Dionne (Eds.), *Disciplining English: Alternative histories, critical perspectives* (pp. 19–38). Albany: State University of New York Press.

Harmon, S. D. (1995). "The voice, pen and influence of our women are abroad in the land": Women and the Illinois State Normal University, 1857–1899. In C. Hobbs (Ed.), *Nineteenth-century women learn to write* (pp. 84–102). Charlottesville: University Press of Virginia.

Harris, J. (1997). *A teaching subject: Composition since 1966.* Upper Saddle River, NJ: Prentice-Hall.

Haugh, O. M. (1996). "English education" and its antecedents. *English Education, 28*(3), 174–180.

Havelock, E. A. (1982). *The literate revolution in Greece and its cultural consequences.* Princeton, NJ: Princeton University Press.

Havelock, E. A. (1986). *The muse learns to write: Reflections on orality and literacy from antiquity to the present.* New Haven: Yale University Press.

Hawhee, D. (1999). Composition history and the "Harbrace College handbook." *College Composition and Communication, 50*(3), 504–523.

Hawisher, G., LeBlanc, P., Moran, C., & Selfe, C. (1996). *Computers and the teaching of writing in American higher education, 1979–1994: A history.* Norwood, NJ: Ablex.

Herrlitz, W. et al. (1984). *Mother tongue education in Europe: A survey of standard language teaching in nine European countries.* Enschelde, Netherlands: SLO.

Heyda, J. (1999). Fighting over freshman English: CCCC's early years and the turf wars of the 1950s. *College Composition and Communication, 50*(4), 663–681.

Hill, C. E. (1990). *Writing from the margins: Power and pedagogy for teachers of composition.* New York: Oxford University Press.

Hobbs, C. (Ed.). (1995). *Nineteenth century women learn to write.* Charlottesville: University Press of Virginia.

Holt, M. (1993). Knowledge, social relations, and authority in collaborative practices of the 1930s and the 1950s. *College Composition and Communication, 44*(4), 538–555.

Holt, M. (1994). Dewey and the "cult of efficiency":

Competing ideologies in collaborative pedagogies of the 1920s. *Journal of Advanced Composition, 14*(1), 73–92.

Horner, B. (1996). Discoursing basic writing. *College Composition and Communication, 47*(2), 199–222.

Horner, B., & Lu, M.-Z. (1999). *Representing the "other": Basic writers and the teaching of basic writing.* Urbana, IL: National Council of Teachers of English.

Horner, W. B. (1993). *Nineteenth-century Scottish rhetoric: The American connection.* Carbondale: Southern Illinois University Press.

Howell, W. S. (1971). *Eighteenth-century British logic and rhetoric.* Princeton, NJ: Princeton University Press.

Howell, W. S., & Ramus, P. (1956). *Logic and rhetoric in England, 1500–1700.* Princeton, NJ: Princeton University Press.

Hubert, H. A. (1994). *Harmonious perfection: The development of English studies in nineteenth-century Anglo-Canadian colleges.* East Lansing: Michigan State University Press.

Jarratt, S. C. (1986). Toward a sophistic historiography. *Pre/Text, 8*(1–2), 9–26.

Jarratt, S. C. (1990). Speaking to the past: Feminist historiography in rhetoric. *Pre/Text, 11*(3–4), 189–209.

Jey, M. (1998). *Littérature au lycée: Invention d'une discipline.* Metz: Université de Metz-Klincksieck.

Johnson, N. (1987a). English composition, rhetoric, and English studies at nineteenth-century Canadian colleges and universities. *English Quarterly, 20*(4), 296–304.

Johnson, N. (1987b). The study of English composition in Canadian schools: 1800–1900. *English Quarterly, 20*(3), 205–217.

Johnson, N. (1991). *Nineteenth-century rhetoric in North America.* Carbondale: Southern Illinois University Press.

Jolliffe, D. A. (1989). The moral subject in college composition: A conceptual framework and the case of Harvard, 1865–1900. *College English, 51*(2), 163–173.

Kaestle, C. F., & Damon-Moore, H. (1991). *Literacy in the United States: Readers and reading since 1880.* New Haven: Yale University Press.

Kates, S. (1997). The embodied rhetoric of Hallie Quinn Brown. *College English, 59*(1), 59–71.

Kates, S. (2001). *Activist rhetorics and American higher education, 1885–1937.* Carbondale: Southern Illinois University Press.

Katims, D. S. (2000). Literacy instruction for people with mental retardation: Historical highlights and contemporary analysis. *Education and Training in Mental Retardation and Developmental Disabilities, 35*(1), 3–15.

Kinkead, J. (1996). The national writing centers association as mooring: A personal history of the first decade. *Writing Center Journal, 16*(2), 131–143.

Kitzhaber, A. R. (1990). *Rhetoric in American colleges, 1850–1900.* Dallas: Southern Methodist University Press. (Original work published 1953)

Lerner, N. (1998). Drill pads, teaching machines, and programmed texts: Origins of instructional technology in writing centers. In E. H. Hobson (Ed.), *Wiring the writing center* (pp. 119–136). Logan: Utah State University Press.

Lewiecki-Wilson, C., & Sommers, J. (1999). Professing at the fault lines: Composition at open admissions institutions. *College Composition and Communication, 50*(3), 438–462.

Liu, Y., & Young, R. E. (1998). Disciplinary assumptions and institutional imperatives: Structural tensions in the pedagogy of rhetoric. *JAC: A Journal of Composition Theory, 18*(3), 475–487.

Lockard, L. (1996). New paper words: Historical images of Navajo literacy. *Journal of Navajo Education, 13*(2), 40–48.

Logan, S. W. (1999). *"We are coming": The persuasive discourse of nineteenth-century black women.* Carbondale: Southern Illinois University Press.

Longo, B. (2000). *Spurious coin: A history of science, management, and technical writing.* Albany: State University of New York Press.

Lu, M.-Z. (1992). Conflict and struggle: The enemies or preconditions of basic writing? *College English, 54*(8), 887–913.

Luke, A. (1988). *Literacy, textbooks, and ideology: Postwar literacy instruction and the mythology of Dick and Jane.* London: Falmer Press.

Maher, J. (1997). *Mina P. Shaughnessy: Her life and work.* Urbana, IL: National Council of Teachers of English.

Mastrangelo, L. S. (1999). Learning from the past: Rhetoric, composition, and debate at Mount Holyoke College. *Rhetoric Review, 18*(1), 46–64.

Mihesuah, D. (1995). "Let us strive earnestly to value education aright": Cherokee female seminarians as leaders of a changing culture. In C. Hobbs (Ed.), *Nineteenth-century women learn to write* (pp. 103–119). Charlottesville: University Press of Virginia.

Miller, R. E. (1994). Composing English studies: Towards a social history of the discipline. *College Composition and Communication, 45*(2), 164–179.

Miller, S. (1991). *Textual carnivals: The politics of composition.* Carbondale: Southern Illinois University Press.

Miller, T. P. (1997). *The formation of college English: Rhetoric and belles lettres in the British cultural provinces.* Pittsburgh, Pa.: University of Pittsburgh Press.

Monaghan, J. (2003). The uses of literacy by girls in colonial America. In J. E. Greer (Ed.), *Girls and literacy in America: Historical perspectives to the present* (pp. 53–80). Santa Barbara, CA: ABC Clio.

Monseau, V. (1986). Dora V. Smith: An English educator for the future. *English Journal, 75*(5), 38–41.

Mulderig, G. P. (1999). Is there still a place for rhetorical history in composition studies? In M. Rosner, B. Boehm, & D. Journet (Eds.), *History, reflection, and narrative: The professionalization of composition, 1963–1983* (pp. 163–165). Stamford, CT: Ablex.

Murphy, C., & Law, J. (Eds.). (1995). *Landmark essays on writing centers.* Davis, CA: Hermagoras Press.

Murphy, J. J. (1982). *The rhetorical tradition and modern writing.* New York: Modern Language Association.

Murphy, J. J., Berlin, J., Connors, R. J., Crowley, S., Enos, R. L., Vitanza, V. J., et al. (1988). Octolog: The politics of historiography. *Rhetoric Review, 7*(1), 5–49.

Murphy, M. (1993). After progressivism: Modern composition, institutional service, and cultural studies. *Journal of Advanced Composition, 13*(2), 345–364.

Mutnick, D. (1996). *Writing in an alien world: Basic writing and the struggle for equality in higher education.* Portsmouth, NH: Boynton/Cook.

Myers, M. (1996). *Changing our minds: Negotiating English and literacy.* Urbana, IL: National Council of Teachers of English.

Nelms, B. (2000). Reconstructing English: From the 1890s to the 1990s and beyond. *English Journal, 89*(3), 49–59.

Nelms, G. (1992). The case for oral evidence in composition historiography. *Written Communication, 9*(3), 356–384.

North, S. M. (1987). *The making of knowledge in composition: Portrait of an emerging field.* Upper Montclair, NJ: Boynton/Cook.

Nystrand, M. (2002). Cultural supports for empirical research on writing. In P. Coppock (Ed.), *The semiotics of writing: Transdisciplinary perspectives on the technology of writing* (pp. 115–135). Turnhout, Belgium: Brepols.

Nystrand, M., Greene, S., & Wiemelt, J. (1993).

Where did composition studies come from? An intellectual history. *Written Communication, 10*(3), 267–333.

Ohmann, R. M. (1999). Professionalizing politics. In M. Rosner, B. Boehm, & D. Journet (Eds.), *History, reflection, and narrative: The professionalization of composition, 1963–1983* (pp. 227–234). Stamford, CT: Ablex.

Ohmann, R. M., & Douglas, W. (1976). *English in America: A radical view of the profession.* New York: Oxford University Press.

Ong, W. J. (1958). *Ramus, method, and the decay of dialogue; from the art of discourse to the art of reason.* Cambridge, MA: Harvard University Press.

Ong, W. J. (2002). *Orality and literacy: The technologizing of the word.* London: Routledge.

Pandian, A. (1997). Literacy in postcolonial Malaysia. *Journal of Adolescent & Adult Literacy, 40*(5), 402–404.

Parker, W. R. (1967). Where do English departments come from? *College English, 2*(5), 339–351.

Plimpton, G. (1963). *Writers at work: The Paris review interviews, second series.* New York: Viking Press.

Pullman, G. (1999). Stepping yet again into the same current. In T. Kent (Ed.), *Post-process theory: Beyond the writing-process paradigm* (pp. 16–29). Carbondale: Southern Illinois University Press.

Quinn, K. B. (1995). Teaching reading and writing as modes of learning in college: A glance at the past; a view to the future. *Reading Research and Instruction, 34*(4), 295–314.

Reynolds, M. (1990). Twenty-five years of two-year college English. *Teaching English in the Two-Year College, 17*(4), 230–235.

Ricks, V. (1995). "In an atmosphere of peril": College women and their writing. In C. Hobbs (Ed.), *Nineteenth-century women learn to write* (pp. 59–83). Charlottesville: University Press of Virginia.

Ritchie, J., & Boardman, K. (1999). Feminism in composition: Inclusion, metonymy, and disruption. *College Composition and Communication, 50*(4), 585–606.

Rodd, T., Jr. (1983). Before the flood: Composition teaching in America 1637–1900. *English Journal, 72*(2), 62–69.

Roemer, M., Schultz, L. M., & Durst, R. K. (1999). Reframing the great debate on first-year writing. *College Composition and Communication, 50*(3), 377–392.

Roen, D., Brown, S., & Enos, T. (Eds.). (1999). *Living rhetoric and composition: Stories of the discipline.* Mahwah, NJ: Erlbaum.

Rose, M. (1985). The language of exclusion: Writing instruction at the university. *College English, 47*(4), 341–359.

Rose, S. K. (1999). Two disciplinary narratives for nonstandard English in the classroom: Citation histories of Shaughnessy's *Errors and Expectations* and Smitherman's *Talkin' and Testifyin'* in rhetoric and composition studies. In M. Rosner, B. Boehm, & D. Journet (Eds.), *History, reflection, and narrative: The professionalization of composition, 1963–1983* (pp. 187–203). Stamford, CT: Ablex.

Rosner, M., Boehm, B., & Journet, D. (Eds.). (1999). *History, reflection, and narrative: The professionalization of composition, 1963–1983.* Stamford, CT: Ablex.

Rouse, P. J. (1995). Cultural models of womanhood and female education: Practices of colonization and resistance. In C. Hobbs (Ed.), *Nineteenth-century women learn to write* (pp. 230–247). Charlottesville: University Press of Virginia.

Royster, J. J. (2000). *Traces of a stream: Literacy and social change among African American women.* Pittsburgh: University of Pittsburgh Press.

Royster, J. J., & Williams, J. C. (1999). History in the spaces left: African American presence and narratives of composition studies. *College Composition and Communication, 50*(4), 563–584.

Russell, D. R. (1986). Writing across the curriculum in 1913: James Fleming Hosic on "co-operation." *English Journal, 75*(5), 34–37.

Russell, D. R. (1988). Romantics on rhetoric: Liberal culture and the abolition of composition courses. *Rhetoric Review, 6,* 132–148.

Russell, D. R. (1991). *Writing in the academic disciplines, 1870–1990: A curricular history.* Carbondale: Southern Illinois University Press.

Russell, D. R. (1992). Institutionalizing English: Rhetoric on the boundaries. In D. R. Shumway & C. Dionne (Eds.), *Disciplining English: Alternative histories, critical perspectives* (pp. 39–58). Albany: State University of New York Press.

Russell, D. R. (2002). *Writing in the academic disciplines: A curricular history* (2nd ed.). Carbondale: Southern Illinois University Press.

Sawyer, D. J. (1991). Whole language in context: Insights into the current great debate. *Topics in Language Disorders, 11*(3), 1–13.

Schell, E. (1998). *Gypsy academics and mother-teachers: Gender, contingent labor, and writing instruction.* Portsmouth, NH: Boynton/Cook.

Schilb, J. (1986). The history of rhetoric and the rhetoric of history. *Pre/Text, 7*(1–2), 11–34.

Schilb, J., & Pickering, C. T. (1989). Composition and poststructuralism: A tale of two conferences.

College Composition and Communication, 40(4), 422–443.

Schreiner, S. (1997). A portrait of the student as a young writer: Re-evaluating Emig and the process movement. *College Composition and Communication, 48*(1), 86–104.

Schultz, L. M. (1999). *The young composers: Composition's beginnings in nineteenth-century schools.* Carbondale: Southern Illinois University Press.

Scott, P., & Castner, B. (1983). Reference sources for composition research: A practical survey. *College English, 45*(8), 756–768.

Scribner, S., & Cole, M. (1981). *The psychology of literacy.* Cambridge, UK: Cambridge University Press.

Shadiow, L. (1984). A twist of the kaleidoscope: The voices of teachers. *English Journal, 73*(3), 38–42.

Shaughnessy, M. P. (1977). *Errors and expectations: A guide for the teacher of basic writing.* New York: Oxford University Press.

Shor, I. (2001). Errors and economics: Inequality breeds remediation. In G. McNenny (Ed.), *Mainstreaming basic writers* (pp. 29–54). Mahwah, NJ: Erlbaum.

Simmons, S. C. (1995a). Constructing writers: Barrett Wendell's pedagogy at Harvard. *College Composition and Communication, 46,* 327–352.

Simmons, S. C. (1995b). Radcliffe responses to Harvard rhetoric: "An absurdly stiff way of thinking". In C. Hobbs (Ed.), *Nineteenth-century women learn to write* (pp. 264–292). Charlottesville: University Press of Virginia.

Smitherman, G. (1977). *Talkin and testifyin: The language of black America.* Boston: Houghton Mifflin.

Spear, K. (1997). Controversy and consensus in freshman writing: An overview of the field. *Review of Higher Education, 20*(3), 319–344.

Stedman, L. C. (1996). An assessment of literacy trends, past and present. *Research in the Teaching of English, 30*(3), 283–302.

Stewart, D. C. (1985). The status of composition and rhetoric in American colleges, 1880–1902: An MLA perspective. *College English, 47*(7), 734–746.

Stewart, D. C. (1992). Harvard's influence on English studies: Perceptions from three universities in the early twentieth century. *College Composition and Communication, 43*(4), 455–471.

Strain, M. M. (1993). Toward a hermeneutic model of composition history: Robert Carlsen's "The state of the profession 1961–1962." *Journal of Advanced Composition, 13*(1), 217–240.

Street, B. V. (1984). *Literacy in theory and practice.* Cambridge, UK: Cambridge University Press.

Taylor, M., & Holberg, J. L. (1999). "Tales of neglect and sadism": Disciplinarity and the figuring of the graduate student in composition. *College Composition and Communication, 50*(4), 607–625.

Tchudi, S. N. (Ed.). (1986). *English teachers at work: Ideas and strategies from five countries.* Newark, NJ: International Federation for the Teaching of English.

Thaiss, C. (1997). Reliving the history of WAC—every day. *Composition Chronicle, 10*(1), 11–12.

Thomas, P. L. (2000). Blueprints or houses? Lou Labrant and the writing debate. *English Journal, 89*(3), 85–89.

Thompson, N. S. (2000). Sylvia Ashton-Warner: Reclaiming personal meaning in literacy teaching. *English Journal, 89*(3), 90–96.

Thornton, T. P. (1996). *Handwriting in America: A cultural history.* New Haven: Yale University Press.

Tobin, L. (1994). How the writing process movement was born—and other conversation narratives. In L. Tobin & T. Newkirk (Eds.), *Taking stock: The writing process movement in the '90s* (pp. 1–14). Portsmouth, NH: Boynton Cook.

Trachsel, M. (1992). *Institutionalizing literacy: The historical role of college entrance examinations in English.* Carbondale: Southern Illinois University Press.

Tuman, M. (1986). From Astor Place to Kenyon Road: The NCTE and the origins of English studies. *College English, 48*(4), 339–349.

Varnum, R. (1992a). The history of composition: Reclaiming our lost generations. *Journal of Advanced Composition, 12*(1), 39–55.

Varnum, R. (1992b). Reclaiming our history: Theodore Baird and English 1–2 at Amherst College, 1938–1966. *Writing on the Edge, 4*(1), 31–39.

Vitanza, V. J. (1986). "Notes" towards historiographies of rhetorics; or, the rhetorics of the histories of rhetorics: Traditional, revisionary, and sub/versive. *Pre/Text, 8*(1–2), 63–125.

Waber, E. H. (1987). Our past: Tradition and stereotypes. *English Journal, 76*(5), 28–32.

Weidner, H. Z. (1995). Silks, congress gaiters, and rhetoric: A Butler University graduate of 1860 tells her story. In C. Hobbs (Ed.), *Nineteenth-century women learn to write* (pp. 248–263). Charlottesville: University Press of Virginia.

White, E. M. (1984). Holisticism. *College Composition and Communication, 35*(4), 400–409.

Willis, A. I. (2002). Literacy at Calhoun Colored School, 1892–1945. *Reading Research Quarterly, 37*(1), 8–44.

Winterowd, W. R. (1998). *The English department: A personal and institutional history.* Carbondale: Southern Illinois University Press.

Woods, W. F. (1985a). The cultural tradition of nineteenth-century "traditional" grammar teaching. *Rhetoric Society Quarterly, 15*(1–2), 3–12.

Woods, W. F. (1985b). Nineteenth century psychology and the teaching of writing. *College Composition and Communication, 36*(1), 20–41.

Woods, W. F. (1985c). The reform tradition in nineteenth-century composition teaching. *Written Communication, 2*(4), 377–390.

Wozniack, J. M. (1978). *English composition in eastern colleges, 1850–1940.* Washington, DC: University Press of America.

Wright, A. A., & Halloran, S. M. (2001). From rhetoric to composition: The teaching of writing in America to 1900. In J. J. Murphy (Ed.), *A short history of writing instruction: From ancient Greece to modern America* (pp. 213–246). Mahwah, NJ: Hermagoras Press.

Yancey, K. B. (1999). Looking back as we look forward: Historicizing writing assessment. *College Composition and Communication, 50*(3), 483–503.

Yates, J. (1989). *Control through communication: The rise of system in American management.* Baltimore: Johns Hopkins University Press.

Young, R. E. (1978). Paradigms and problems: Needed research in rhetorical invention. In C. R. Cooper & L. Odell (Eds.), *Research on composing: Points of departure* (pp. 29–47). Urbana, IL: National Council of Teachers of English.

Young, R. E., & Goggin, M. D. (1992). Some issues in dating the birth of the new rhetoric in departments of English: A contribution to a developing historiography. In T. Enos & S. C. Brown (Eds.), *Defining the new rhetorics* (pp. 22–43). Thousand Oaks, CA: Sage.

Zaluda, S. (1998). Lost voices of the Harlem renaissance: Writing assigned at Howard University, 1919–31. *College Composition and Communication, 50*(2), 232–257.

Zebroski, J. T. (1999). The expressivist menace. In M. Rosner, B. Boehm, & D. Journet (Eds.), *History, reflection, and narrative: The professionalization of composition, 1963–1983* (pp. 99–113). Stamford, CT: Ablex.

About the Editor
and the Contributors

Peter Smagorinsky is Professor of English Education in the Department of Language and Literacy Education at The University of Georgia. His work takes a Vygotskian perspective on literacy education, including teachers' conceptions of literacy instruction, students' multimedia composing across the curriculum, and the discourse of character education. His research has been recognized by AERA's Raymond B. Cattell Early Career Award for Programmatic Research and Steve Cahir Award for Research in Writing, and NCTE's Janet Emig Award and Edwin M. Hopkins *English Journal* Award.

JoBeth Allen conducts collaborative action research with teachers who are exploring issues of educational equity and social justice in relation to literacy teaching and learning. This work has been published in *Reading Research Quarterly*, the *Journal of Literacy Research*, *Language Arts*, *The Reading Teacher*, and *Reading and Writing Quarterly*, among others; her books are published by Heinemann and Teachers College Press. She teaches at the University of Georgia in the Department of Language and Literacy Education, where she co-directs the Red Clay Writing Project and the Partnership for Community Learning Centers.

Stuart Barbier is an associate professor at Delta College and a Ph.D. candidate at Michigan State University, where he is specializing in issues related to composing and identity. He has published in *Teaching English in the Two-Year College*, *National Association for Developmental Education Selected Conference Papers*, and *TESOL Journal*. He teaches literature, freshman composition, creative nonfiction, and developmental writing.

Anne Beaufort is an associate professor of writing and rhetoric at Stony Brook University. She is the author of *Writing in the Real World: Making the Transition from School to Work*. Her work in the corporate world for 10 years as writer and editor fueled that project and has led to continued pursuit of the perplexing issue of why college graduates have trouble with workplace writing demands. Her most recent research, a portion of which was published in *Research in the Teaching of English*, chronicles one student's writing development across 4 years of college and 2 years beyond in his first professional job.

Marilyn Chapman is a professor in the Department of Language and Literacy Education at the University of British Columbia, where she teaches courses in written composition, reading, early literacy, and early childhood education. She is the author of *Weaving Webs of Meaning: Writing in the Elementary School*. Her research examines sociocognitive and sociocultural dimensions of young children's literacy learning, with a focus on genre development.

Alister Cumming is a professor and head of the Modern Language Centre at the Ontario Institute for Studies in Education of the University of Toronto. His research and teaching focus on writing, assessment, and policies in second-language education, particularly in respect to English as a Second/Foreign Language but also other languages and situations internationally.

Ellen Cushman is an associate professor at Michigan State University and is currently researching Western Cherokee language and identity as these unfold at the intersections of new media, critical pedagogy, and community literacies. She recently has published shockwave essays in *Computers and Composition*, *Online*, and *Kairos* and chapters in edited collections. She teaches community literacy-based multimedia writing and English education courses, as well as graduate courses for the Critical Studies in Language and Pedagogy, and Rhetoric and Writing Programs.

Russel K. Durst is Professor of English at the University of Cincinnati. He has served as President of the National Conference on Research in Language and Literacy, Chair of the NCTE Standing Committee on Research, and editorial board member for the journals *College Composition and Communication*, *Language and Learning Across the Disciplines*, and *Writing Program Administration*. His essays on composition have appeared in numerous journals and edited collections. His books include *You Are Here: Readings on Higher Education for College Writers*, *Collision Course: Conflict, Negotiation, and Learning in College Composition*, and (co-edited with George Newell) *Exploring Texts: The Role of Discussion and Writing in the Teaching and Learning of Literature*.

Bob Fecho collaboratively conducts research with high school teachers that explores sociocultural issues of literacy among adolescents. He also continues to inquire collaboratively into his own praxis concerning critical inquiry classrooms in teacher education. Currently an associate professor at the University of Georgia in the Department of Language and Literacy Education, he also co-directs the Red Clay Writing Project.

George Hillocks, Jr., is Professor Emeritus of the University of Chicago, having served over 30 years in the Departments of Education and English Language and Literature. He is the author of several books and has won the NCTE David H. Russell Award for Distinguished Research in the Teaching of English (1997 for *Teaching Writing as Reflective Practice*) and the 2004 NCTE Distinguished Service Award.

Hellen Inyega is a doctoral student in the Department of Language and Literacy at the University of Georgia.

Ilona Leki is Professor of English and Director of ESL at the University of Tennessee, author of books and articles related to second-language writing in English, and co-editor of the *Journal of Second Language Writing*. Her research interests include academic literacy development among bilingual students and the literacy experiences of English learners.

Catherine Mazak is Assistant Professor of English at the University of Puerto Rico at Mayagüez. She specializes in colonial language policy, second-language literacy practices, and ESL teacher training. Her current work examines English literacy practices in Puerto Rico. She is a co-author (with Lawrence Zwier and Lynn-Stafford Yilmaz) of *The Michigan Guide to English for Academic Success and Better TOEFL® Scores.*

Claudia Mazaros is a graduate and research assistant in the Reading Program of the Department of Language and Literacy at the University of Georgia. Formerly a high school teacher in Utah, she is presently instructing pre-service teachers. Her research interests focus on adolescent literacy, content-area teacher identities, sociocultural perspectives, and practitioner research. She has presented her work at meetings of the Utah Association of Teacher Educators, Utah Council of the International Reading Association, Northern Rocky Mountain Education Research Association, and National Council of Teachers of English.

Susan McDowall received her Ph.D. from Washington State University in December 2004, with a dissertation titled "Toward a Sophistic Rhetoric of Basic Writing." Her scholarly interests include basic writing and ESL pedagogy. She looks forward to pursuing a career theorizing the intersections of pedagogy, critical theory, classical rhetoric, and politics. She is the mother of two.

Robert Petrone is pursuing his Ph.D. in English Education at Michigan State University and currently is conducting a multiyear ethnographic study that examines the intersections among adolescent critical literacies, new media textual practices, and social action. He recently has published articles in state and national practitioner journals, including the *English Journal*, and he teaches English methods courses for the Teacher Education Department at MSU.

David R. Russell is Professor of English at Iowa State University, where he teaches in the Ph.D. program in Rhetoric and Professional Communication. His book *Writing in the Academic Disciplines: A Curricular History* examines the history of American writing instruction outside composition courses. He has published many articles on writing across the curriculum, drawing on activity theory and genre theory, and co-edited (with David Foster) *Writing and Learning in Cross-National Perspective: Transitions from Secondary to Higher Education.*

Tony Silva is Professor of ESL in the Department of English at Purdue University, where he directs the ESL Writing Program and teaches undergraduate and graduate courses for ESL students and ESL teachers. With Ilona Leki, he founded and edits the *Journal of Second Language Writing*; with Paul Kei Matsuda, he founded and hosts the Symposium on Second Language Writing and edited *On Second Language Writing, Landmark Essays in ESL Writing*, and *Second Language Writing Research: Perspectives on the Process of Knowledge Construction*; and with Colleen Brice and Melinda Reichelt, he compiled the *Annotated Bibliography of Scholarship on Second Language Writing.*

C. Jan Swearingen is Professor of English at Texas A & M University, where she teaches courses in approaches to literacy studies, and the history and theory of rhetoric. She is a past president (1998–2000) of the Rhetoric Society of America. Her book, *Rhetoric and Irony: Western Literacy and Western Lies*, shared the *Journal of Advanced Composition* W. Ross Winterowd Award for best book in composition theory published in 1991. She writes and speaks widely on rhetoric, composition, and their close ties to one another in the past and present.

Victor Villanueva is the Edward R. Meyer Distinguished Professor of Liberal Arts, a former chair of the Conference on College Composition and Communication, and winner of the National Council of Teachers of English Russell Award for Distinguished Research and Scholarship in English, the Conference on English Education Meade Award for Scholarship in English Education, Rhetorician of the Year (1999), and other awards. He has published over 30 articles and several books, and has delivered over 80 public lectures on matters concerning racism and literacy.

Index